THE MOTORCYCLE YEARBOOK
2005

ISBN 2-84707-091-5
Also available in french **ISBN 2-84707-103-2**, and in spanish **ISBN 84-95709-08-2**

© NOVEMBRE 2005, CHRONOSPORTS S.A - Jordils Park, Chemin des Jordils 40, CH-1025 St-Sulpice, Switzerland.
Tél: +41 (0) 21 694 24 44 - Fax: +41 (0) 21 694 24 46 - E-mail. info@chronosports.com - www.chronosports.com

CONCEPTION   Patricia Soler

PAGE LAYOUT   Loraine Lequint

PRINTED BY IMPRIMERIE CLERC - 18206 St-Amand Montrond, France.

BOUND BY LES RELIURES BRUN - 45331 Malesherbes Cedex, France.

All rights reserved. Reproduction, even partial, is forbidden in all countries, in any form and for whatever purpose without written, permission from the publisher.

THE MOTORCYLCE YEARBOOK
2005

PHOTOS Stan Perec Lukasz Swiderek
THANKS TO Nello Zoppe (Nikon France) for his valued collaboration and to Jaime Olivares, who have provided some of the photos in this book.
TEXTS Jean-Claude Schertenleib

CONTENTS

007	**EDITORIAL: TO MAURICE BÜLA**	
008	**CHINA AND TURKEY: DISCOVERIES**	
012	**TEAMS MOTOGP**	
026	**TEAMS 250**	
042	**TEAMS 125**	
058	**CHAMPIONS**	
060	VALENTINO ROSSI, CHAMPION MOTOGP	
064	DANIEL PEDROSA, CHAMPION 250	
068	THOMAS LÜTHI, CHAMPION 125	
072	**THE 17 GP REVIEW**	
072	GP SPAIN	
078	GP PORTUGAL	
084	GP CHINA	
090	GP FRANCE	
096	GP ITALY	
102	GP CATALUNYA	
108	GP THE NETHERLANDS	
114	GP UNITED STATES	
118	GP GREAT BRITAIN	
124	GP GERMANY	
130	GP CZECH REPUBLIC	
136	GP JAPAN	
142	GP MALAYSIA	
148	GP QATAR	
154	GP AUSTRALIA	
160	GP TURKEY	
166	GP VALENCIA	
172	**STATISTICS**	
172	MOTOGP STATISTICS	
174	250 STATISTICS	
176	125 STATISTICS	
178	**RESULTS OF OTHER CHAMPIONSHIPS**	

CALENDAR 2006

26th March	GP Spain	Jerez de la Frontera
8th April	GP Qatar	Doha
30th April	GP Turkey	Istanbul
14th May	GP China	Shanghai
21st May	GP France	Le Mans
4th June	GP Italy	Mugello
18th June	GP Catalunya	Catalunya
24th June	GP Netherlands	Assen
2nd July	GP Great Bretain	Donington
16th July	GP Germany	Sachsenring
23rd July	GP USA (*)	Laguna Seca
20th August	GP Czech Republic	Brno
10th Sept.	GP Malaysia	Sepang
17th Sept.	GP Australia	Phillip Island
24th Sept.,	GP Japan	Motegi
22nd October	GP Portugal	Estoril
29th October	GP Valencia	Cheste

(*): Only MotoGP.

* Photographer Maurice "Momo" Büla was born on 10th January 1934, and died on 21st September 2005. His photos have gone round the world, his archives were unique. He was rightly regarded as the living memory of the road racing World Championships. He was the first to spend hours researching, collating, checking GP results since 1949, producing compendiums from them that have become indispensable. Thanks to the meticulous work of this racing enthusiast, who had been a mechanic in the garage of sidecarist Florian Camathias (Maurice had been one of his passengers), who had himself taken part in numerous international races and a few GPs (his name appears on the winners' list for the Ulster 250 cc GP in 1956 - 6th, riding an NSU), racing enthusiasts today can delve into the very roots of competitive motorcycling. Besides "Continental Circus 1949-2000", from the publisher Éditions Chronosports, in particular, Maurice Büla was also behind the launch of "The GP Moto Year", back in 1997.

EDITORIAL

2005, THE YEAR OF TEARS

" 6th November 2005, just before noon. In the overheated paddock of the Ricardo Tormo circuit, at Cheste, near Valencia, I was trying to make my way through the crowd. Just like every year, the place was like a busy shopping street a few days before Christmas. People were jostling one another, chatting, admiring, taking photos of each other.
I head for Stand 38, where in a few moments the new World 125 cc Champion should be arriving - Thomas Lüthi, 19, Swiss. Our country has been waiting twenty years for this moment. Twenty years during which we have laughed together, Momo.*
I raise my eyes heavenwards, I cry. Emotions are running too high, the tension has been too intense. I raise my eyes, and I say to you: "It's OK, Momo, the lad is Champion…"
Do you remember, old chap, the way we cried for joy together, the day of his first victory, at Le Mans? Do you remember, old chap, how you trembled for him during that crazy last lap in the Dutch GP at Assen? Do you remember, old chap, his second victory, in Brno? The illness, terrible, insidious, was already in you; you knew that you hadn't got long to live, but you didn't want to miss that televised event for anything in the world.
Do you remember, my dear Momo, the last time we saw each other? I was about to set off for three weeks in Japan. I realized then we'd never see each other again down here on earth. That day, we looked at each other, our eyes moist. When you were helped to bed after we'd enjoyed a good meal together, I wanted to ask you if you were afraid, a few days, a few weeks away from your final journey. But my throat was all knotted up, no sound came out, I just kissed you, and you clasped your hand in mine with all the strength you had left.
Ten days later, I was in Malaysia, and Gaby called me: you had left us, Momo, serenely, your face pressed into the arms of the one who loves you and whom you love. I cried all over again, because you didn't wait for me, although often, so often, we had travelled together. Four days later, the "lad" won. And I know that, from up there, you won't have missed a moment of that race. Nor of the KTM coup in Qatar, of Tom's renewed success in Australia, of the first Turkish GP in history, and of this final. Here, yesterday.
The lad is Champion, Momo, and yesterday evening, I didn't feel like going to celebrate the event without you. Rest well, old chap, you've given so much to the Grand Prix… "

JEAN-CLAUDE SCHERTENLEIB

The modernism of Shanghai and the classicism of Istanbul: two new looks for the motorcycle GP

CHINA AND TURKEY
DISCOVER THE GP

TWO NEW CIRCUITS WITH ONE COMMON POINT: THE GERMAN ARCHITECT, HERMANN TIELKE, WHO WAS ALSO RESPONSIBLE FOR THE SEPANG CIRCUIT, DESIGNED BOTH OF THE TRACKS, AND THE MODERN BUILDINGS THAT SURROUND THEM.

CHINA AND TURKEY DISCOVERIES

After Qatar the year before, two new countries joined the already long list of nations who have hosted, since 1949, at least one stage of the road racing world championships, the Grand Prix. China and Turkey, the two countries registered as numbers 28 and 29 in the history book, have nothing in common. Except, now, an ultra-modern circuit, conceived and designed by the same German engineer, Hermann Tielke.

"Although, in China, the creators of the circuit were obviously only thinking of Formula 1, the Istanbul track has a few stretches which are very inspired by motorcycling, which are particularly difficult", explains the 125 cc world champion, the Swiss rider Thomas Lüthi.

The Turkish course, on the eastern side of Istanbul, has been unanimously praised by riders, be the in the 125cc category, like Lüthi, or the MotoGP, like Valentino Rossi. It has to be said that it is an absolute rule, going back to the dawn of time (or of racing: see the famous old Nürburgring, or the corkscrews of Laguna Seca, known across the world), that circuits with varying levels have always been riders' favourites. And this is the case in Istanbul, with its first plunging left, an astonishing long climb, then another descent which takes us, a little further on, into a quadruple left, which has given a lot of problems to some riders.

And if the track is superb, the surroundings aren't bad either. The main buildings which top the main stand draw on the Eastern style and, even if this year the

On the Shanghai market stall, Mao's little red book rubs shoulders with Tintin; on the eve of the qualifiers, the paddock was treated to a display of classical dance (top). Bottom, sunrise over the district of Istanbul where the most modern race circuit in the world has been built.

10 MOTORCYCLE YEARBOOK 2005

CHINA AND TURKEY DISCOVERIES

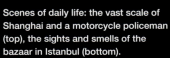
Scenes of daily life: the vast scale of Shanghai and a motorcycle policeman (top), the sights and smells of the bazaar in Istanbul (bottom).

Turkish GP was classed as an "overseas GP", meaning no trailer-workshops and no hospitality, we already can't wait for 2006 and for this paddock, which this year was too empty, to come to life.

On the subject of the giant scale, Hermann Tielke and his employees didn't hesitate when they designed the Shanghai circuit: "The paddock even looked too big for the Formula 1, so imagine what it'll be like for the motorcycling", noted a follower of the autosport at the start of the season.

It gives an impression of everything being too small-scale in this environment on such a huge scale. Giant stands, but empty (the authorities had intentionally limited the number of tickets sold, because of fear of the unknown!), a giant paddock which became the main square of a medium-sized town: it was the place where everyone met up before, during and after the qualifiers. As for the track, it is interesting in terms of its design - especially with the descending spiral which follows the long (and wide...) starting straight - but somewhat less

so for the enjoyment of the spectators, and the riders, since it is definitely too big.

The key point remains, however: by opening the doors of the Chinese and Turkish markets, the promoters of the world championship are pursuing the globalisation of their product, since nowadays motorcycle racing must be considered as such!

MOTORCYCLE YEARBOOK 2005   11

TEAMS | MOTO GP

SEVEN HONDAS, FOUR YAMAHAS, THE SAME AGAIN OF DUCATIS, TWO SUZUKIS, TWO KAWASAKIS AND TWO BRAVE "PRIVATE" ENTRANTS, THE BLATA RIDERS: THE STAGE IS SET FOR 2005.

YAMAHA DIGEST MOTO GP

The M1 2005 was completely redesigned: the general architecture may have been the same, but the frame and the engine were both completely new. The bulk of the work was on the rear part (redesigned suspension and swing arm), while the engine and the fuel tank were moved to perfect the balance: "More power, and more stability were the points we had to improve" Rossi explained, a few days from the start of the season.
In this jubilee year¬ - Yamaha is celebrating its 50th anniversary - the brand with the three tuning forks lined up four more riders. The American Colin Edwards joined the outgoing champion, Valentino Rossi, in the Gauloises colours (a superb design, with more white in the blue livery), while the Tech 3 team M1s were in Fortuna colours (two Spanish riders were established in the team, Ruben Xaus and the rookie, Toni Elias).

FORTUNA YAMAHA

Tech 3, 635 chemin du Niel, 83230 Bormes-les-Mimosas (France).
www.fortunaracing.com

ORGANISATION CHART
Team manager: Hervé Poncharal.
Coordinator: Gérard Valle.
Crew chiefs: Guy Coulon (Ruben Xaus) et Antonio Jimenez (Toni Elias).

11 RUBEN XAUS   **24** TONI ELIAS

RIDERS
Ruben Xaus
Date of birth: 10th February 1978.
Place of birth: Sant Cugat del Vallés (Spain).
First race: 1992.
First GP: Great Britain, 1995 (250cc).
- Winner of 80cc Supermotard Championship of Catalunya (1993).

Antonio «Toni» Elias
Date of birth: 26th March 1983.
Place of birth: Manresa (Spain).
First race: 1997.
First GP: Spain, 1999 (125cc).
Number of GP victories: 9 (2/125; 7/250).
- First GP victory: Netherlands, 2001 (125cc).

GAULOISES YAMAHA

Yamaha Factory Racing, Via A. Tinelli 67/69, Gerno di Lesmo, 20050 Milan (Italy).
www.yamahamotogp.com

ORGANISATION CHART
Managing Director: Lin Jarvis.
Team manager: Davide Brivio.
Coordinator: Marc Canela.
Crew chiefs: Daniele Romagnoli (Colin Edwards) and Jeremy Burgess (Valentino Rossi).

5 COLIN EDWARDS   **46** VALENTINO ROSSI

RIDERS
Colin Edwards
Date of birth: 27th February 1974.
Place of birth: Conroe (Texas/United States).
First race: 1990.
First GP: Japan, 2003 (MotoGP).
- United States 250cc Champion (1992).
- World Superbike Champion (2000 and 2002).

Valentino Rossi
Date of birth: 16th February 1979.
Place of birth: Urbino (Italy).
First race: 1992.
First GP: Malaysia, 1996 (125cc).
Number of GP victories: 79 (12/125cc; 14/250cc; 13/500cc; 40 MotoGP).
First GP victory: Czech Republic, 1996 (125cc).
- Go-kart regional champion (1990).
- Italian Minibike Endurance Champion (1992).
- Italian 125cc Sport Production Champion (1994).
- 125cc Italian Champion (1995).
- 125cc World Champion (1997).
- 250cc World Champion (1999).
- 500cc World Champion (2001).
- MotoGP World Champion (2002, 2003, 2004, 2005).

MOTO GP YAMAHA DIGEST

FORTUNA YAMAHA

GAULOISES YAMAHA

MOTORCYLCE YEARBOOK 2005

HONDA DIGEST MOTO GP

Massimiliano Biaggi finally got the ride he had long dreamt of, joining the official Repsol team, and insisting on taking his top guru, Erv Kanemoto, with him. There were seven RC211V bikes on the grid, and the best two were, on paper, Biaggi's and Sete Gibernau's (still with Fausto Gresini). As the races progressed, HRC adapted its policy to the circumstances, and, from mid-season, it was Nicky Hayden and Marco Melandri who had priority for the new ones.
Special efforts were made to eliminate the infamous "chattering" (vibration of the front wheel), which held the brand's riders back so much in recent seasons. Still dominated by the Rossi-Yamaha pairing, Honda brought a totally new machine from Japan, which was tested the day before the Czech GP, but the prototype was unreliable and was not brought in, as initially thought, by the end of the season.

REPSOL HONDA TEAM

Honda Racing Corporation, European Office, Industrial Noord V, Wijngaardveld, 1, 9300 Aalst (Belgium). www.repsolhondateam.com

ORGANISATION CHART
Team manager: Makoto Tanaka.
Technical director: Erv Kanemoto.
Sport manager: Carlo Fiorani.
Chiefs mechanics: Hideki Iwano (Massimiliano Biaggi) et Pete Benson (Nicky Hayden).

3 MASSIMILIANO BIAGGI
69 NICKY HAYDEN

RIDERS
Massimiliano Biaggi
Date of birth: 26th June 1971.
Place of birth: Rome (Italy).
First race: 1989.
First GP: Europe, 1991 (250cc).
Number of GP victories: 42 (29/250cc; 8/500cc; 5/MotoGP).
First GP victory: South Africa, 1992 (250cc).
- Italian 125cc Sport Production Champion, 1990 (Aprilia).
- 250cc European Champion, 1991 (Aprilia).
- 250cc World Champion, 1994 (Aprilia).
- 250cc World Champion, 1995 (Aprilia).
- 250cc World Champion, 1996 (Aprilia).
- 250cc World Champion, 1997 (Honda).

Nicky Hayden
Date of birth: 30th July 1981.
Place of birth: Owensboro/Kentucky (United States).
First race: 1986.
First GP: Japan, 2003 (MotoGP).
Number of GP victories: 1 (MotoGP).
First GP victory: United States, 2005 (MotoGP).
- Winner of United States 600 Supersport Championship (1999).
- Winner of United States Superbike Championship, 2002 (Honda).

MOVISTAR HONDA MOTOGP

Via Fra'Domenico Paganelli 8, 48018 Faenza (Italy).
www.gresiniracing.com

ORGANISATION CHART
Team manager: Fausto Gresini.
Crew Chiefs: Juan Martinez (Sete Gibernau) et Fabrizio Cecchini (Marco Melandri).

15 SETE GIBERNAU
33 MARCO MELANDRI

RIDERS
Sete Gibernau
Date of birth: 15th December 1972.
Place of birth: Barcelona (Spain).
First race: 1990.
First GP: Spain, 1992 (250cc).
Number of GP victories: 9 (1/500cc; 8/MotoGP).
First GP victory: Valencia, 2001 (500cc).
- Winner of Spanish and Catalan 125cc Junior Championship, 1991 (Cagiva).

Marco Melandri
Date of birth: 7th August 1982.
Place of birth: Ravenna (Italy).
First race: 1989.
First GP: Czech Republic, 1997 (125cc).
Number of GP victories: 19 (7/125cc; 10/250cc; 2/MotoGP).
First GP victory: Netherlands, 1998 (125cc).
- Italian Minibike Junior A Champion, 1992.
- Italian Minibike Junior B Champion, 1994.
- Italian 125cc Champion and Honda Italy trophy winner, 1997 (Honda).
- 250cc World Champion, 2002 (Aprilia).

MOTO GP HONDA DIGEST

REPSOL HONDA TEAM

MOVISTAR HONDA MOTOGP

MOTORCYLE YEARBOOK 2005

HONDA DIGEST MOTO GP

CAMEL HONDA MOTOGP

Poligono Industrial Sta. Rita, C/Acustica 16, 08755 Castellbisbal, Barcelona (Spain).
www.camelhonda.com

ORGANISATION CHART
<u>Team manager:</u> Sito Pons.
<u>Coordinator:</u> Félix Rodriguez.
<u>Crew Chiefs:</u> Ramon Forcada (Alexandre Barros) and Santi Mulero (Troy Bayliss).

4 ALEXANDRE BARROS   **12** TROY BAYLISS

RIDERS
<u>Alexandre Barros</u>
Date of birth: 18th October 1970.
Place of birth: São Paulo (Brazil).
First race: 1978.
First GP: Spain, 1986 (80cc).
Number of GP victories: 7 (4/500cc; 3/MotoGP).
First GP victory: FIM, 1993 (500cc).
- Brazilian Moped Champion, 1978 (Mobilette).
- Brazilian Moped Champion, 1979 (Mobilette).
- Brazilian Moped Champion, 1980 (Mobilette).
- Brazilian 50cc Champion, 1981 (Minarelli).
- Brazilian 250cc Champion, 1985 (Yamaha).

<u>Troy Bayliss</u>
Date of birth: 30th March 1969.
Place of birth: Taree (New South Wales/Australia).
First race: 1979.
First GP: Australia, 1997 (250cc).
- Winner of British Superbike Championship, 1999 (Ducati).
- World Superbike Champion, 2001 (Ducati).

KONICA MINOLTA HONDA

Place de Moulins, Le Continental B, 98000 Monaco (Principality of Monaco).
www.konicaminoltahonda.com

ORGANISATION CHART
<u>Team manager:</u> Gianluca Montiron.
<u>Technical director:</u> Giulio Bernardelle.
<u>Chief mechanic:</u> Hirano Yutaka (Makoto Tamada).

6 MAKOTO TAMADA

RIDER
<u>Makoto Tamada</u>
Date of birth: 4th November 1976.
Place of birth: Ehime (Japan).
First race: 1993.
First GP: Japan, 1998 (250cc).
Number of GP victories: 2 (MotoGP).
First GP victory: Rio, 2004 (MotoGP).
- Japanese 250cc Production Regional Champion, 1994 (Honda).

MOTO GP HONDA DIGEST

CAMEL HONDA MOTOGP

KONICA MINOLTA HONDA

MOTORCYCLE YEARBOOK 2005 **19**

DUCATI DIGEST MOTO GP

There was plenty going on in Borgo Panigale. Firstly, as anticipated since the launch of the Desmosedici project, the Italian brand outfitted a second team. The team, directed by Luis D'Antin, put Roberto Rolfo on a 2004 Desmo "GP4" with Dunlop tyres. The official team was this year made up of Loris Capirossi and Carlos Checa and, in a dramatic move, "the Reds" entered the Bridgestone bosom. Compared with 2004, the Italian engineers did not start from scratch; the GP5 was in fact an evolution of the GP4 from the end of the previous season. The swing arm was stiffer, but lighter, and the exhausts had been modified. But the big news, as mentioned above, was the name of the new supplier of tyres. The progress in performance was directly related to the progress of the tyres, with Ducati looking very much at ease in Brno after the break.

DUCATI MARLBORO TEAM

Via Cavalieri Ducati 3, 40132 Bologne (Italy).
www.ducati.com

ORGANISATION CHART
Managing Director de Ducati Corse: Claudio Domenicali.
Team manager: Livio Suppo.
Technical Director: Corrado Cecchinelli.
Crew Chiefs: Bruno Leoni (Carlos Checa) and Massimo Bracconi (Loris Capirossi).

RIDERS
Carlos Checa
Date of birth: 15th October 1972.
Place of birth: Sant Fruitos de Bages (Spain).
First race: 1989.
First GP: Europe, 1993 (125cc).
Number of GP victories: 2 (500cc).
First GP victory: Catalunya, 1996 (500cc).
- 80cc Spanish Champion (1991).

Loris Capirossi
Date of birth: 4th April 1973.
Place of birth: Castel San Pietro (Italy).
First race: 1987.
First GP: Japan, 1990 (125cc).
Number of GP victories: 25 (8/125cc; 12/250cc; 2/500cc; 3/MotoGP).
First GP victory: Great Britain, 1990 (125cc).
- 125cc World Champion (1990).
- 125cc World Champion (1991).
- 250cc World Champion (1998).

| **7** CARLOS CHECA | **65** LORIS CAPIROSSI |

D'ANTIN MOTOGP

Poligono Industrial Gitesa, c/Ramon y Cajal 25, 28814 Daganzo de Arriba, Madrid (Spain).
www.dantinmotogp.com

ORGANISATION CHART
Owner: Luis D'Antin.
Chief mechanic: André Laugier.
Telemetry engineer: Bernard Martignac.

RIDER
Roberto Rolfo
Date of birth: 23rd March 1980.
Place of birth: Turin (Italy).
First race: 1994.
First GP: Italy, 1996 (250cc).
Number of GP victories: 3 (250cc).
First GP victory: Germany, 2003 (250cc).

44 ROBERTO ROLFO

MOTO GP DUCATI DIGEST

DUCATI MARLBORO TEAM

D'ANTIN MOTOGP

SUZUKI / KAWASAKI DIGEST MOTO GP

SUZUKI MOTOGP

With the legendary Garry Taylor lost to retirement, it was his young compatriot, Paul Denning (38 years old) who took over management of the Suzuki official team. Denning, who brought the brand the British superbike title in 2004, had been a rider himself. In technical terms, the new GSV-R990 gained power, though the development leader, Kunio Arase, was also keen to improve the use made of the power, announced by Suzuki to be more than 240 horsepower (new fuel injection technology allowed an 8% gain in fuel efficiency, with a new 22-litre limit placed on fuel). Extensive work was also carried out on engine braking. The riders went unchanged (Hopkins and Roberts Junior, who was not to last the season), as did the tyres (Bridgestone).

Crescent Suzuki Performance Centre, 23 Black Moor Road, Ebblake Industrial Estate, Verwood, Dorset, BH31 6AX (Great Britain).
www.suzuki-racing.com

ORGANISATION CHART
Team manager: Paul Denning.
Technical Director: Shinichi Sahara.
Crew Chiefs: Tom O'Kane (Kenny Roberts) and Stuart Shenton (John Hopkins).

RIDERS
Kenny Roberts
Date of birth: 25th July 1973.
Place of birth: Mountain View (California/United States).
First race: 1988.
First GP: United States, 1993 (250cc).
Number of GP victories: 8 (500cc).
First GP victory: Malaysia, 1999 (500cc).
- 500cc World Champion (2000).

John Hopkins
Date of birth: 22nd May 1983.
Place of birth: Ramona (California/United States).
First race: 1987.
First GP:†Japan, 2002 (MotoGP).
- Winner of US Aprilia RS250 Challenge (1999).
- Winner of United States 750 Supersport Championship (2000).
- United States Formula Xtreme Champion (2001).

10 KENNY ROBERTS **24** JOHN HOPKINS

KAWASAKI RACING TEAM

Year 3 of Kawasaki's MotoGP operation, still with the Ninja ZX-RR. The codename may have stayed the same, but the green team made a splash over the winter, with the biggest technical transfer of the year: Ichiro Yoda, who was project leader at Yamaha when Olivier Jacque won his 250cc title and subsequently designed the M1, moved to Kawasaki, as did crew chief Fiorenzo Fanali, also ex-Yamaha. The chassis was still produced by the Swiss company Suter Engineering, but at the Japanese GP we learned that the green team had decided to take control there, too, with a view to the future. As for the riders, events -Hofmann's injury during an exhibition ride before the Portugal- GP allowed Olivier Jacque to really cause a sensation in China.

Im Gstaudach 6, 92648 Vohenstrauss (Germany).
www.kawasaki-eckl.com

ORGANISATION CHART
Team manager: Harald Eckl.
Technical Director: Ichiro Yoda.
Crew Chiefs: Fiorenzo Fanali (Shinya Nakano)
and Christophe Bourguignon (Alexander Hofmann).

RIDERS
Shinya Nakano
Date of birth: 10th October 1977.
Place of birth: Chiba Prefecture (Japan).
First race: 1982.
First GP: Japan, 1998 (250cc).
Number of GP victories: 6 (250cc).
First GP victory:†Japan, 1999 (250cc).
- Pocketbike regional champion (1985).
- Japan 250cc Champion (1998).

Alexander Hofmann
Date of birth: 25th May 1980.
Place of birth: Mindelheim (Germany).
First race: 1984.
First GP:†Germany, 1997 (125cc).
- Europe 250cc Champion (1998).
- Germany 250cc Champion (1998).

56 SHINYA NAKANO **66** ALEXANDER HOFMANN

MOTO GP SUZUKI / KAWASAKI DIGEST

SUZUKI MOTOGP

KAWASAKI RACING TEAM

KR-KTM / BLATA DIGEST MOTO GP

KR-KTM DIGEST

It should have been one of the technical events of the year - the arrival of a new manufacturer, KTM, in the MotoGP class - instead it was a long and strange saga, where what Kenny Roberts Senior said about the obligations of the Austrian brand, and the responses from Stefan Pierer, the brand's boss, rarely resembled each other. This was to such an extent that, with no development budget, the divorce was finalised in Brno, and Kenny brought back his old Proton V5, which we saw again for a final time in Valencia. What does the future hold? If all goes well, team Roberts should bring in a KR-Honda next year, for Kenny Junior.

Team Roberts
3, Lombard Way, Banbury, Oxon (Great Britain).
www.protonteamkr.com

ORGANISATION CHART
Owner: Kenny Roberts.
Team manager: Chuck Aksland.

RIDER
Shane Daniel Byrne
Date of birth: 10th December 1976.
Place of birth: Lambeth/London (Great Britain).
First race: 1996.
First GP: South Africa, 2004 (MotoGP).
- British Supersport Clubmans Champion, (1997).
- British Superbike Champion (2003).

67 SHANE BYRNE

BLATA DIGEST

Peter Clifford really is an old devil. The last living specimen of a private team's boss in motorcycle racing's ruling category, he moved his team's head office to the Czech Republic, where he found a technical partner - the pocket-bike specialist, Blata - who designed an original V6 to power the Harris chassis. It was so original that is has never been seen, except as a mock-up (malicious gossip would insinuate that the operation was only launched to get money from the EU!) As a result, the WCMs were to run for the whole season with their good old in-line fours, an adapted Yamaha engine.

Blata WCM
Prazska 9, 67801 Blansko (Czech Republic).
www.blata-wcm.com

ORGANISATION CHART
Owner: Bob MacLean.
Team manager: Peter Clifford.
Technical director: François Charlot.
Crew Chiefs: Paul Trevathan (James Ellison) and Gérard Roussel (Franco Battaini).

RIDERS
Franco Battaini
Date of birth: 22nd July 1972.
Place of birth: Brescia (Italy).
First race: 1992.
First GP: Italy, 1996 (250cc).
Italian Suzuki 250 trophy winner (1994).

James Ellison
Date of birth: 19th September 1980.
Place of birth: Kendal (Lancaster/Great Britain).
First race: 1995.
First GP: Czech Republic, 2004 (MotoGP).
- European Superstock Champion (2001).

27 FRANCO BATTAIN   **77** JAMES ELLISON

MOTO GP KR-KTM / BLATA DIGEST

KR-KTM DIGEST

BLATA

TEAMS | 250 CC

REJUVENATION OF THE TROOPS, WITH MANY RIDERS WHO SHONE IN 125CC LAST YEAR BEING PROMOTED, LIKE WORLD CHAMPION ANDREA DOVIZIOSO, AND ALSO JORGE LORENZO AND HECTÓR BARBERA.

HONDA DIGEST 250cc

Three teams with official machines: that makes six riders out to launch an attack on what has long been the gold standard in the category, the Aprilia RSW. The outgoing world champion, Daniel Pedrosa, was defending his title, under the guidance of Alberto Puig (with Hiroshi Aoyama at his side). The world's largest motorcycle manufacturer showed its ambition: at Pedrosa's side were three young riders, promoted from the 125cc class: the champion Andrea Dovizioso (in Team Scot, with Takahashi as fellow team member) and the extremely ambitious Spaniards, Jorge Lorenzo (who, we would quickly realise, has absolutely no inhibitions) and Hector Barberá.

TELEFONICA MOVISTAR HONDA

c/del Puy 16, Escalera A, 2 floor, Andorra La Vella (Andorra).
www.movistarhonda.com

ORGANISATION CHART
Team manager: Alberto Puig.
Coordinator: Jaume Colom.
Chief mecahnics: Mike Leitner (Daniel Pedrosa) and Gilles Bigot (Hiroshi Aoyama).

1 DANIEL PEDROSA
73 HIROSHI AOYAMA

RIDERS
Daniel Pedrosa
Date of birth: 29th September 1985.
Place of birth: Castellar del Vallés (Spain).
First race: 1993.
First GP: Japan, 2001 (125cc).
Number of GP victories: 23 (8/125cc; 15/250cc).
First GP victory: Netherlands, 2002 (125cc).
- Spanish Minibike Champion (1998).
- 125cc World Champion (2003).
- 250cc World Champion (2004).
- 250cc World Champion (2005).

Hiroshi Aoyama
Date of birth: 25th October 1981.
Place of birth: Chiba (Japan).
First race: 1999.
First GP: Pacific, 2000 (250cc).
Number of GP victories: 1 (250cc).
First GP victory: Japan, 2005 (250cc).

FORTUNA HONDA

c/Bronce 28, Pol. Ind. Can Guixeras, 08915 Badalona (Spain).
www.motorsport48.com

ORGANISATION CHART
Team manager: Dani Amatriàn.
Coordinator: Jordi Perez.
Chiefs mechanics: Guido Cechinni (Jorge Lorenzo) and Massimo Capanna (Hector Barberá).

48 JORGE LORENZO
80 HECTOR BARBERÁ

RIDERS
Jorge Lorenzo
Date of birth: 4th May 1987.
Place of birth: Palma de Mallorca (Spain).
First race: 1990.
First GP: Spain, 2002 (125cc).
Number of GP victories: 4 (125cc).
First GP victory: Rio, 2003 (125cc).

Hector Barberá
Date of birth: 2nd November 1986.
Place of birth: Dos Aguas (Valencia/Spain).
First race: 1995.
First GP: Japan, 2002 (125cc).
Number of GP victories: 6 (125cc).
First GP victory: Great Britain, 2003 (125cc).

TEAM SCOT

Via Brodolini 55/2, 61025 Montelabbate, Pesaro (Italy).
www.racingworldteam.com

ORGANISATION CHART
President: Giancarlo Cecchini.
Team manager: Cirano Mularoni.
Chiefs mechanics: Gary Reynders (Andrea Dovizioso) and Trevor Morris (Yuki Takahashi).

34 ANDREA DOVIZIOSO
55 YUKI TAKAHASHI

RIDERS
Andrea Dovizioso
Date of birth: 23rd March 1986.
Place of birth: Forlimpopoli (Italy).
First race: 1994.
First GP: Italy, 2001 (125cc).
Number of GP victories: 5 (125cc).
First GP victory: South Africa, 2004 (125cc).
- Italian Pocketbike Junior B Champion (1997).
- Italian Pocketbike Junior B Champion (1998).
- Winner of Italy Aprilia Under-16 Challenge (2000).
- European 125cc Champion (2001).
- 125cc World Champion (2004).

Yuki Takahashi
Date of birth: 12th July 1984.
Place of birth: Saitama (Japan).
First race: 2000.
First GP: Pacific, 2001 (125cc).

250cc HONDA DIGEST

TELEFONICA MOVISTAR HONDA

FORTUNA HONDA

TEAM SCOT

HONDA DIGEST 250cc

WÜRTH HONDA BQR

Mestre Nicolau, 6 Nave 3, Pol. Ind. Sud, 08440 Cardedeu (Barcelone, Spain).
www.hondabqr.com

ORGANISATION CHART
President: Raoul Romero.
Team manager: Kino Contreras.
Chief mechanic: Fausto Martinez (Alex Debon and Radomil Rous).

RIDERS
Alex Debon
Date of birth: 1st March 1976.
Place of birth: Vall d'Uixo (Spain).
First race: 1992.
First GP: Madrid, 1998 (250cc).
- 250cc Spanish Champion (2001).

Radomil Rous
Date of birth: 21st May 1978.
Place of birth: Trebic (Czech Republic).
First race: 1994.
First GP: Czech Republic, 1997 (250cc).

ALEX DEBON

RADOMIL ROUS

MOLENAAR RACING

Panoven 20, 3401 RA Ijsselstein (Netherlands).
www.molenaarracing.com

ORGANISATION CHART
Owner: Arie Molenaar.
Team manager: Martin Van Genderen.
Technical director: Hans Spaan (Jakub Smrz).

RIDER
Jakub Smrz
Date of birth: 7th April 1983.
Place of birth: Jilovice (Czech Republic).
First race: 1995.
First GP: Czech Republic, 1998 (125cc).
- Czech Republic 125cc Champion (1998).
- Czech Republic 125cc Champion (1999).

JAKUB SMRZ

KIEFER-BOS-CASTROL

Zur Rothheck 12, 55743 Idar-Oberstein (Germany).
www.kiefer-mot.de

ORGANISATION CHART
President: Jochen Kiefer.
Team manager: Stefan Kiefer.
Chief mechanic: Jürgen Lingg (Dirk Heidolf).

RIDER
Dirk Heidolf
Date of birth: 14th September 1976.
Place of birth: Hohenstein-Ernsthal (Germany).
First race: 1994.
First GP: Germany, 1997 (125cc).

DIRK HEIDOLF

250cc HONDA DIGEST

WÜRTH HONDA BQR

MOLENAAR RACING

KIEFER-BOS-CASTROL

APRILIA DIGEST 250cc

The brand from Noale, which has entered the bosom of the Piaggio group, remained faithful to its policy of recent years, offering official RSW machines to Team MS, to Lucio Cecchinello's Team Carrera and to Team Repsol-Aspar, managed by Jorge Martinez; making, on paper, six "factory" riders. Among them, the promising young Italian rider, Simone Corsi, transferred from Honda (and the 125cc class), who was to have serious problems adapting, throughout the season. There were also some very good RS machines, like the one ridden by Sylvain Guintoli in the Equipe GP de France, which was to prove the best private team of the championship. It should also be noted that Aprilia was undertaking its first post-Jan Witteveen season, with the legendary Noale race bike creator taking a step back from the racetrack.

MS APRILIA ITALIA CORSE

Via Consiglio dei Sessenta 153, 47891 Dogana (San Marino).
www.racingaprilia.com

ORGANISATION CHART
Team manager: Francesco Guidotti.
Crew Chiefs: Giovanni Sandi (Alex De Angelis) and Rossano Brazzi (Simone Corsi).

5 ALEX DE ANGELIS
24 SIMONE CORSI

RIDERS
Alex De Angelis
Date of birth: 26th February 1984.
Place of birth: Rimini (Italy).
First race: 1995.
First GP: Imola, 1999 (125cc).

Simone Corsi
Date of birth: 24th April 1987.
Place of birth: Rome (Italy).
First race: 1994.
First GP: Italy, 2002 (125cc)

CARRERA-LCR

Gildo Pastor Centre, 7 rue du Gabian, 98000 Monaco.
www.carrerasunglasseslcr.com

ORGANISATION CHART
Team manager: Lucio Cecchinello.
Technical director: Pietro Caprara.
Crew Chiefs: Federico Becucci (Roberto Locatelli) and Roberto Guidi (Casey Stoner).

15 ROBERTO LOCATELLI
27 CASEY STONER

RIDERS
Roberto Locatelli
Date of birth: 5th July 1974.
Place of birth: Bergamo (Italy).
First race: 1989.
First GP: Italy, 1994 (125cc).
Number of GP victories: 9 (125cc).
First GP victory: France, 1999 (125cc).
- Italian 125cc Sport Production Champion (1993).
- 125cc World Champion (2000)

Casey Stoner
Date of birth: 16th October 1985.
Place of birth: Kurri-Kurri (Gold Coast/Australia).
First race: 1989.
First GP: Great Britain, 2001 (125cc)
Number of GP victories: 6 (2/125cc; 4/250cc).
First GP victory: Valencia, 2003 (125cc).
- Winner of Australian Aprilia RS125 Challenge (2000).

REPSOL ASPAR

Poligono Industrial No2, Avenida de los Deportes, Travesia, 46600 Alzira (Spain).
www.teamaspar.com

ORGANISATION CHART
Team manager: Jorge Martinez.
Technical director: Paolo Cordioli.
Crew Chiefs: Emanuele Martinelli (Randy De Puniet) and Francesco Tamburini (Sebastián Porto).

7 RANDY DE PUNIET
19 SEBASTIÁN PORTO

RIDERS
Randy De Puniet
Date of birth: 14th February 1981.
Place of birth: Andrésy (France).
First race: 1987.
First GP: France, 1998 (125cc).
Number of GP victories: 5 (250).
First GP victory: Catalunya, 2003 (250cc).
- Winner of Typhoon Cup, France (1995).
- Winner of 125cc Promosport Cup (1997).
- Winner of Cagiva Mito Cup, France (1997).
- French 250cc Champion (1998).

Sebastián Porto
Date of birth: 12th September 1978.
Place of birth: Rafaela-Santa Fe (Argentina).
First race: 1988.
First GP: Argentina, 1994 (125cc)
Number of GP victories: 7 (250cc).
First GP victory: Rio, 2002 (250cc).
- Argentina Minibike Champion (1988).
- Argentina 250cc Champion (1994).
- Europe 250cc Open Champion (1996).

250cc APRILIA DIGEST

MS APRILIA ITALIA CORSE

CARRERA-LCR

REPSOL ASPAR

APRILIA DIGEST 250cc

EQUIPE GP DE FRANCE SCRAB

Avenue des Sports, 32110 Nogaro (France).
www.scrab-competition.com

ORGANISATION CHART
Team manager: Jean-Claude Besse.
Technical director: Didier Langouët.
Chiefs mechanics: Franck Gallou (Gregory Leblanc) and Yannis Maigret (Sylvain Guintoli).

RIDERS
Gregory Leblanc
Date of birth: 30th June 1985.
Place of birth: Nesles-la-Montagne (France).
First race: 2000.
First GP: France, 2002 (125cc).

Sylvain Guintoli
Date of birth: 24th June 1982.
Place of birth: Montélimar (France).
First race: 1995.
First GP: France, 2000 (250cc).

38 GREGORY LEBLANC **50** SYLVAIN GUINTOLI

CAMPETELLA RACING

Via De Gasperi 74, 62010 Montecassiano (Italy).
www.campetella.it

ORGANISATION CHART
Team manager: Carlo Campetella.
Technical director: Eros Braconi.
Crew Chiefs: Fabio Braconi (Alex Baldolini) and Gianluca Montanari (Taro Sekiguchi).

RIDERS
Alex Baldolini
Date of birth: 24th January 1985.
Place of birth: Cesena (Italy).
First race: 1994.
First GP: Italy, 2000 (125cc).

Taro Sekiguchi
Date of birth: 5th December 1975.
Place of birth: Tokyo (Japan).
First race: 1989.
First GP: Japan, 1999 (250cc).

25 ALEX BALDOLINI  **44** TARO SEKIGUCHI

NOCABLE.IT RACE

43, route d'Arlon, 8009 Strassen (Luxembourg).
www.worldwiderace.net

ORGANISATION CHART
Team manager: Fiorenzo Caponera.
Crew Chief: Aligi Deganello

RIDER
Steve Jenkner
Date of birth: 31st May 1976.
Place of birth: Hoenstein-Ernstthal (Germany).
First race: 1989.
First GP: Germany, 1996 (125cc).
Number of GP victories: 1 (125cc).
First GP victory: Netherlands, 2003 (125cc).
- Germany Minibike Champion (1993).

17 STEVE JENKNER

250cc APRILIA DIGEST

EQUIPE GP DE FRANCE SCRAB

CAMPETELLA RACING

NOCABLE.IT RACE

APRILIA DIGEST 250cc

MATTEONI RACING

Via Bandi 5, 47814 Bellaria Igea Marina (Italy).
www.matteoniracing.net

ORGANISATION CHART
Team manager: Massimo Matteoni.
Executive team manager: Pietro Gallonetto.
Chief mechanic: Claudio Macciotta (Mirko Giansanti).

RIDER
Mirko Giansanti
Date of birth: 14th September 1976.
Place of birth: Terni (Italy).
First race: 1991.
First GP: Italy, 1996 (125cc).

32 MIRKO GIANSANTI

APRILIA GERMANY

P.O. Box 23, 7205 Zizers (Suisse).
www.250apriliagermany.com

ORGANISATION CHART
Team manager: Dieter Stappert.
Technical director: Eros Braconi.
Crew Chiefs: Stefan Kirsch (Martin Cardeñas) and Stefan Kurfiss (Chaz Davies).

RIDERS
Martin Cardeñas
Date of birth: 28th January 1982.
Place of birth: Medellin (Colombia).
First race: 1991.
First GP: Spain, 2005 (250cc).

Chaz Davies
Date of birth: 10th February 1987,
Place of birth: Knighton (Great Britain).
First race: 1995.
First GP: Japan, 2002 (125cc).
- British Minibike Champion (1996).
- British Minibike Champion (1997).
- British Minibike Champion (1998).

36 MARTIN CARDEÑAS **57** CHAZ DAVIES

ABRUZZO RACING

Via del Consorzio 10, 60015 Falconara, Ancona (Italy).
www.synracing.com

ORGANISATION CHART
Team manager: Giordano Cerigioni.
Crew Chief: Andrea Orlandi (Andrea Ballerini).

RIDER
Andrea Ballerini
Date of birth: 2nd July 1973.
Place of birth: Florence (Italy).
First race: 1992.
First GP: Australia, 1995 (125cc).
Number of GP victories: 1 (125cc).
First GP victory: Australia, 2003 (125cc).

8 ANDREA BALLERINI

250cc APRILIA DIGEST

MATTEONI RACING

APRILIA GERMANY

ABRUZZO RACING

KTM DIGEST / FANTIC DIGEST 250cc

KTM

In just three years, the Austrian brand has made its RRF125 a machine to compete for the title. This year, KTM launched an attack on the category above, with an RRF250 whose race debut was to be endlessly put off, until the British GP, halfway through the season. And there, bingo: the bike made its appearance and, in the rain, Antony West climbed onto the second step of the podium! What followed was a different story: this beautiful machine certainly also picked up points in the dry (coming tenth in Germany), but tensions escalated between Harald Bartol and the rider, the Australian Anthony West, to such an extent that, on the eve of the Qatar GP, there was a serious scene in the stands, and we were not to see West, or KTM again until the end of the season. One to watch in 2006...

Stallhofnerstrasse 3, 5230 Mattighofen (Austria).
www.ktm.at

ORGANISATION CHART
President: Stefan Pierer.
Team manager: Harald Bartol.
Crew Chief: Mario Galeotti (Anthony West).

RIDER
Anthony West
Date of birth: 17th July 1981.
Place of birth: Mayborough (Australia).
First race: 1997.
First GP: Australia, 1998 (125cc).
Number of GP victories: 1 (250cc).
First GP victory: Netherlands, 2003 (250cc).
- 125cc Australia Champion (1998).
- 250cc Production Australia Champion (1998).

14 ANTHONY WEST

FANTIC

A specialist in small-engine motorcycles, this Italian brand was founded in 1968, by Mario Agrati and Henry Keppel, originally from Holland, who managed sales of Garelli machines in export markets. Fantic was hugely successful in trial and endurance biking until the end of the nineties. In 2003, two industrialists from the Treviso region, Federico Fregnan and Massimo Bianchi, took control of the brand and revitalised it. The sensation came at the end of 2004, when Federico Fregnan launched his "Grand Prix" operation. The company the project was entrusted to was that of Franco Moro - a technician who had worked with Loris Capirossi, Max Biaggi, Valentino Rossi and Alex De Angelis - and the task was quickly carried out: the Fantic Motor R 250 was already there for the IRTA tests at the Circuit de Catalunya. Nonetheless, just before the Turkey GP, the decision was taken not to continue the venture.

Via Cesare della Chiesa. 41100 Modena (Italy).
www.fanticmotor.it

ORGANISATION CHART
President Federico Fregnan.
Engine engineer: Franco Moro.
Chassis engineer: Franco Cevolini.
Chief mechanic: Massimo Biagini.

PILOTES
Gabriele Ferro
Date of birth: 17th August 1988.
Place of birth: Biella (Italy).
First race: 1998.
First GP: Spain, 2005 (250cc).
- Italian Minibike Champion (2003).

Arnaud Vincent
Date of birth: 30th November 1974.
Place of birth: Laxou (France).
First race: 1993.
First GP: France, 1996 (125cc)
Number of GP victories: 7 (125cc).
First GP victory: Catalunya, 1999 (125cc).

20 GABRIELE FERRO **21** ARNAUD VINCENT

250cc KTM DIGEST / FANTIC DIGEST

KTM

FANTIC

YAMAHA DIGEST 250cc

The German Team Kurz mainly made an impression this year because of the constant changing of its riders (who we guess were paying them). The Yamaha TZ250s were not really developed by the factory, and it was Horst and Jörg Seel's "Seel Company" who attempted, over the winter, to improve the performance of these machines, which often came right up against the qualification limit.

TEAM KURZ

Geiselroter Heidle 1, 73494 Rosenberg (Germany).
www.yamaha-kurz.de

ORGANISATION CHART
President: Hermann Kurz
Technical directors: Horst & Jörg Seel.
Chief mechanic: Thomas Eatmann

RIDERS
Nicolas Cajback
Date of birth: 9th June 1986.
Place of birth: Stockholm (Sweden).
First race: 2003.
First GP: Great Britain, 2005 (250cc).

Erwan Nigon
Date of birth: 27th September 1983.
Place of birth: Riom (France).
First race: 1997.
First GP: France, 2000 (125cc).

23 NICOLAS CAJBACK
63 ERWAN NIGON

250cc YAMAHA DIGEST

TEAM KURZ

TEAMS 125 cc

PHOTO OF AN EXTENDED, AND INCREASINGLY YOUTHFUL FAMILY: THE CATEGORY IS NOW CLOSED TO RIDERS OVER 28 YEARS OLD.

HONDA DIGEST 125cc

Since Daniel Pedrosa's title, two years ago, Honda has not really had what could be called a "factory" bike; there are instead different levels of equipment. On paper, it was Fabrizio Lai (Scot) and Alvaro Bautista (Seedorf) who had the best status (engine + chassis). The previous year, this had caused problems for the Swiss rider, Thomas Lüthi, so he received an engine kit. However, Team Elit worked all season with a standard chassis: in decisive races, HRC's support was hence to be ever more important..

ELIT GRAND PRIX

Jeremiasova 18/1283, 15500 Prague 5, Stodulky (Czech Republic).
www.paddock.cz

ORGANISATION CHART
Team manager: Daniel M. Epp.
Technical director: Franz Josef "Sepp" Schlögl.
Coordinator: Igor Strauss.
Mechanics: Stefan Fuhrer et Stefan Haseneder (Thomas Lüthi).

RIDER
Thomas Lüthi
Date of birth: 6th September 1986.
Place of birth: Linden (Switzerland).
First race: 1997.
First GP: Germany, 2002 (125cc).
Number of GP victories: 4 (125cc).
First GP victory: France, 2005 (125cc).
- Swiss Pocketbike Junior A Champion (1999).
- Swiss Pocketbike Junior B Champion (2000).
- 125cc World Champion (2005).

12 THOMAS LÜTHI

KOPRON RACING WORLD

Via Quattro Giugno 39, Serravalle (San Marino).
www.racingworldteam.com

ORGANISATION CHART
Owner: Gino Borsoi.
Executive team manager: Stefano Bedon.
Chiefs mechanics: Roberto Dalla Nora (Fabrizio Lai)
and Tiziano Altabella (Mike Di Meglio).

RIDERS
Fabrizio Lai
Date of birth: 14th December 1978.
Place of birth: Rho (Italy).
First race: 1994.
First GP: Valencia, 2001 (125cc).
- Europe Minibike Champion (1996).
- Europe Minibike Champion (1997).
- Winner of Honda Italy Trophy (1999).
- 125cc Italian Champion (2002).

Mike Di Meglio
Date of birth: 17th February 1988.
Place of birth: Toulouse (France).
First race: 2001.
First GP: Japan, 2003 (125cc).
Number of GP victories: 1 (125cc).
First GP victory: Turkey, 2005 (125cc).

32 FABRIZIO LAI   **63 MIKE DI MEGLIO**

AJO MOTORSPORT

Hämeentie 20, 37800 Toijala (Finlande).
www.ajo.fi

ORGANISATION CHART
Team manager: Aki Ajo.
Chiefs mechanics: Hannu Möttönen (Alexis Masbou)
and Tadashi Ohshima (Tomoyoshi Koyama).

RIDERS
Alexis Masbou
Date of birth: 2nd June 1987.
Place of birth: Nîmes (France).
First race: 2001.
First GP: France, 2003 (125cc).

Tomoyoshi Koyama
Date of birth: 19th March 1983.
Place of birth: Kanagawa (Japan).
First race: 1999.
First GP: Pacific, 2000 (125cc).
- Japan 125cc Champion (2000).

7 ALEXIS MASBOU   **71 TOMOYOSHI KOYAMA**

125cc HONDA DIGEST

ELIT GRAND PRIX

KOPRON RACING WORLD

AJO MOTORSPORT

HONDA DIGEST 125cc

SEEDORF RC3

Poligono Industrial Norte, c/Charco del Aliso DL9, Nave 48m N-1, km 36, 28750 San Agustin de Guadalix (Madrid/Spain).
www.seedorfrc3.com

ORGANISATION CHART
Team manager: Susana López Pichot.
Chiefs mechanics: Tommaso Raponi (Álvaro Bautista) and Antonio Haba (Aleix Espargaro).

19 ÁLVARO BAUTISTA
41 ALEIX ESPARGARO

RIDERS
Alvaro Bautista
Date of birth: 21st November 1984.
Place of birth: Tavera de la Reina (Spain).
First race: 1995.
First GP: Spain, 2002 (125cc).
- 125cc Spanish Champion (2003).

Aleix Espargaro
Date of birth: 31st July 1989.
Place of birth: Barcelona (Spain).
First race: 2001.
First GP: Valencia, 2004 (125cc).

TEAM ANGAIA RACING

Corso Peschiera 336/a, Torino (Italy).
www.angaiaracing.com

ORGANISATION CHART
Team manager: Paolo Tajana.
Chiefs mechanics: Simone Falconi (Toshihisa Kuzuhara) and Romano Fusaro (Federico Sandi).

9 TOSHIHISA KUZUHARA
10 FEDERICO SANDI

RIDERS
Toshihisa Kuzuhara
Date of birth: 23rd May 1980.
Place of birth: Tokushima (Japan).
First race: 1998.
First GP: Pacific, 2001 (125cc).

Federico Sandi
Date of birth: 12th August 1989.
Place of birth: Voghera (Italy).
First race: 1998.
First GP: Spain, 2005 (125cc).

KIEFER-BOS

Zur Rothheck 12, 55743 Idar-Oberstein (Germany).
www.kiefer-mot.de

ORGANISATION CHART
Team manager: Stefan Kiefer.
Chief mechanic: Markus Egloff.

11 SANDRO CORTESE

RIDER
Sandro Cortese
Date of birth: 6th January 1990.
Place of birth: Ochsenhausen (Germany).
First race: 1997.
First GP: Spain, 2005 (125cc).
- European Pocketbike Junior A Champion (1999).
- Germany Minibike Champion (2002).

MOLENAAR RACING

Panoven 20, 3401 RA Ijsselstein (Netherlands).
www.molenaarracing.com

ORGANISATION CHART
Team manager: Arie Molenaar.
Chief mechanic: Robbert Van Dorrestein.

16 RAYMOND SCHOUTEN

RIDER
Raymond Schouten
Date of birth: 15th March 1985.
Place of birth: Waardhuizen (Netherlands).
First race: 1999.
First GP: Netherlands, 2002 (125cc).

125cc HONDA DIGEST

SEEDORF RC3

TEAM ANGAIA RACING

KIEFER-BOS

MOLENAAR RACING

APRILIA DIGEST 125cc

One had the impression we were witnessing a year of transition for the Piaggio group, which has now taken control of Aprilia. There were hence three different brands (Aprilia, Derbi, Gilera) in this category. Aprilia's best equipment went to Mattia Pasini (wearing the colours of the Italian footballer, Francesco Totti), Marco Simoncelli and Jorge Martinez's team (Hectór Faubel and Sergio Gadea).

TOTTI TOP SPORT

Rosellon 219, 08008 Barcelone (Spain).
www.team3c-racing.com

ORGANISATION CHART
Team manager: Valerio Sbarra.
Technical director: Christian Lundberg.
Chiefs mechanics: Fernando Fabiani (Manuel Hernandez) and Roger Marcaccini (Mattia Pasini).

RIDERS
Manuel A. Hernandez
Date of birth: 24th August 1984.
Place of birth: Cartagena (Spain).
First race: 2000.
First GP: Valencia, 2003 (125cc).

Mattia Pasini
Date of birth: 13th August 1985.
Place of birth: Rimini (Italy).
First race: 1994.
First GP: South Africa, 2004 (125cc).
Number of GP victories: 2 (125cc).
First GP victory: China, 2005 (125cc).

43 MANUEL HERNANDEZ | **75** MATTIA PASINI

NOCABLE.IT

48, route d'Arlon, 8009 Strassen (Luxembourg).
www.worldwiderace.net

ORGANISATION CHART
Team manager: Fiorenzo Caponera.
Chiefs mechanics: Aligi Deganello (Joan Olivé) and Alessandro Tognelli (Marco Simoncelli).

RIDERS
Joan Olivé
Date of birth: 22nd November 1984.
Place of birth: Tarragona (Spain).
First race: 1992.
First GP: Japan, 2001 (125cc).
- Winner of the Spanish Joven Cup (1999).
- 125cc Spanish Champion (2000).

Marco Simoncelli
Date of birth: 20th January 1987.
Place of birth: Cattolica (Italy).
First race: 1996.
First GP: Czech Republic, 2002 (125cc).
Number of GP victories: 2 (125cc).
First GP victory: Spain, 2004 (125cc).
- Italian Minibike Champion (1999).
- Italian Minibike Champion (2000).
- European 125cc Champion (2002).

6 JOAN OLIVÉ | **58** MARCO SIMONCELLI

MASTER ASPAR

Poligono Industrial No 2, Avenida de los Deportes, Travesia, s/n, 46600 Alzira (Valencia/Spain).
www.teamaspar.com

ORGANISATION CHART
Team manager: Jorge Martinez.
Technical director: Kike Peris.
Chiefs mechanics: Enrique Quijal (Sergio Gadea) and Sergio Bonaldo (Hectór Faubel).

RIDERS
Sergio Gadea
Date of birth: 30th December 1984.
Place of birth: Puzol (Spain).
First race: 2001.
First GP: Spain, 2003 (125cc).

Hectór Faubel
Date of birth: 10th August 1983.
Place of birth: Lliria (Italy).
First race: 1993.
First GP: Spain, 2000 (125cc).
- 250cc Spanish Champion (2002).

33 SERGIO GADEA | **55** HECTÓR FAUBEL

125cc APRILIA DIGEST

TOTTI TOP SPORT

NOCABLE.IT

MASTER ASPAR

APRILIA DIGEST 125cc

SKILLED I.S.P.A.

Via Cavou 33, 46043 Castiglione delle Stiviere (Mantova/Italy).
www.fontanaracing.com

ORGANISATION CHART
Team manager: Italo Fontana.
Mechanic: Roberto Materassi (Lorenzo Zanetti).

RIDER
Lorenzo Zanetti
Date of birth: 10th August 1987.
Place of birth: Lumezzane (Italy).
First race: 1996.
First GP: Italy, 2004 (125cc).

8 LORENZO ZANETTI

ABRUZZO RACING

Via del Consorzio 10, 60015 Falconara (Italy).
www.synracing.com

ORGANISATION CHART
Team manager: Giordano Cerigioni.
Chief mechanic: Andrea Orlandi.

RIDER
Andrea Iannone
Date of birth: 9th August 1989.
Place of birth: Vasto (Italy).
First race: 2004.
First GP: Spain, 2005 (125cc).

29 ANDREA IANNONE

RACING TEAM TOTH

Foti ùt, 055 Hrsz, 2120 Dunakeszi (Hungary).
www.tothimi.com

ORGANISATION CHART
Team manager: Balasz Nagy.
Technical director: Roberto Baglioni.
Chiefs mechanics: Andrea Castellari (Vincent Braillard) and Stefano Cozzini (Imre Toth).

RIDERS
Vincent Braillard
Date of birth: 29th April 1985.
Place of birth: Montet (Switzerland).
First race: 1997.
First GP: France, 2002 (125cc).
- Swiss Pocketbike Champion (1999).

Imre Toth
Date of birth: 6th September 1985.
Place of birth: Budapest (Hungary).
First race: 2000.
First GP: Japan, 2002 (125cc).

26 VINCENT BRAILLARD **45** IMRE TOTH

125cc APRILIA DIGEST

SKILLED I.S.P.A.

ABRUZZO RACING

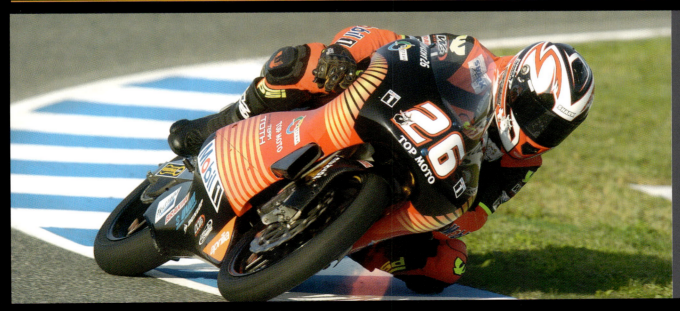

RACING TEAM TOTH

APRILIA DIGEST 125cc

MATTEONI RACING

Via Bandi 5, 47814 Bellaria Igea Marina (Italy).
www.matteoniracing.net

ORGANISATION CHART
Team manager: Massimo Matteoni.
Technical director: Pietro Gallonetto
Chief mechanic: Sanzio Raffaeli

RIDER
Raffaele De Rosa
Date of birth: 25th March 1987.
Place of birth: Naples (Italy)
First race: 2003.
First GP: Spain, 2005 (125cc).

35 RAFFAELE DE ROSA

MVA-ASPAR

Poligono Industrial No 2, Avenida de los Deportes, Travesia, s/n, 46600 Alzira (Valencia(Spain).
www.teamaspar.com

ORGANISATION CHART
Team manager: Jorge Martinez
Chief mechanics: Enrique Quijal (Jordi Carchano) and Julian Miralles Senior (Julian Miralles Junior).

RIDERS
Jordi Carchano
Date of birth: 2nd July 1984.
Place of birth: Sant Quirze del Vallès (Spain).
First race: 2001.
First GP: Catalunya, 2003 (125cc).

Julian Miralles Junior
Date of birth: 16th November 1988.
Place of birth: Alberique (Spain).
First race: 1999.
First GP: Spain, 2004 (125cc).

28 JORDI CARCHANO   **84** JULIAN MIRALLES JUNIOR

CARDION AB BLAUER USA

Via Villagrande 228, 61024 Mombaroccio, Pesaro (Italy).
www.wtr-team.com

ORGANISATION CHART
Team manager: Giorgio Semprucci.
Technical director: Loris Castellucci.
Chief mechanics: Romano Ciatti (Dario Giuseppetti) and Marco Grana (Karel Abraham).

RIDERS
Dario Giuseppetti
Date of birth: 1st March 1985.
Place of birth: Berlin (Germany).
First race: 2000.
First GP: Germany, 2002 (125cc).
- Winner of ADAC Pro Junior Cup (2001).
- Germany 125cc Champion (2003).

Karel Abraham
Date of birth: 2nd January 1990.
Place of birth: Brno (Czech Republic).
First race: 2001.
First GP: Spain, 2005 (125cc).

25 DARIO GIUSEPPETTI   **44** KAREL ABRAHAM

125cc APRILIA DIGEST

MATTEONI RACING

MVA-ASPAR

CARDION AB BLAUER USA

DERBI / GILERA DIGEST 125cc

After having lost Harald Bartol a few years earlier - he left with the success we know, to KTM -, the Spanish, which had worked in 2004 with Olivier Liégeois, a Belgian, was now under the technical leadership of Luigi Dall'Igna, the engineer who had designed the MotoGP Aprilia. However, since the absorption of Aprilia by the Piaggio group came late in the winter, the 2005 vintage 125cc Derbi and Gilera was still very close to the one of the previous year. The revolution, in the group, is expected this winter, looking to 2006. Note, however, the return to 125cc of Manuel Poggiali, once world champion, in Gilera's colours.

CAJA MADRID DERBI

c/La Barca 5-7, 08107 Martorelles (Spain).
www.derbiracing.com

ORGANISATION CHART
Team manager: Giampiero Sacchi.
Sport Manager: Luca Boscoscuro.
Technical director: Luigi Dall'Igna.
Chief mechanics: Alfio Tosi (Nicolas Terol) and Antonio Alfosea (Pablo Nieto).

RIDERS
Nicolas Terol
Date of birth: 27th September 1988.
Place of birth: Alcoy (Spain).
First race: 2000.
First GP: Valencia, 2004 (125cc).

Pablo Nieto
Date of birth: 4th June 1980.
Place of birth: Madrid (Spain).
First race: 1995.
First GP: Catalunya, 1998 (125cc).
Number of GP victories: 1 (125cc).
First GP victory: Portugal, 2003 (125cc).

18 NICOLAS TEROL   **22** PABLO NIETO

METIS RACING GILERA

Corso Sempione 43, 20145 Milano (Italy).
www.gilera.com

ORGANISATION CHART
Team manager: Giampiero Sacchi.
Sport Manager: Luca Boscoscuro.
Technical director: Luigi Dall'Igna.
Chief mechanics: Andrea Serrentino (Lukas Pesek) and Giuseppe Torcolacci (Manuel Poggiali).

RIDERS
Lukas Pesek
Date of birth: 22nd November 1985.
Place of birth: Prague (Czech Republic).
First race: 2002.
First GP: Czech Republic, 2002 (125cc).

Manuel Poggiali
Date of birth: 14th February 1983.
Place of birth: Chiesa Nuova (San Marino).
First race: 1994.
First GP: Imola, 1998 (125cc).
Number of GP victories: 12 (7/125cc; 5/250cc).
First GP victory: France, 2001 (125cc).
- Italian Minibike Champion (1997).
- 125cc Italian Champion (1998).
- Winner of 125cc Honda Italy Trophy (1998).
- 125cc World Champion (2001).
- 250cc World Champion (2003).

52 LUKAS PESEK   **54** MANUEL POGGIALI

125cc DERBI / GILERA DIGEST

CAJA MADRID DERBI

METIS RACING GILERA

KTM / MALAGUTI DIGEST 125cc

RED BULL KTM GP

The big favourite for the world title, and the only factory truly represented directly in the category (now brought together in the Piaggio group, Derbi, Gilera and Aprilia are going through a transition year). KTM, after having learned, and after having tasted the joys of the podium, presented an impressive armada, with three top-rank riders: Mika Kallio, Gabor Talmacsi and Julian Simón. The RRF125, the result of the work done by the Austrian engineer, Harald Bartol, would quickly confirm itself as the machine to beat, starting right from the pre-season tests. Alas (for the Austrians…), too much good can sometimes be a bad thing, and too many errors, by Kallio, but also in the psychology of the team management, would allow an outsider to give a pounding to what should have been a hegemony.

Stallhofnerstrasse 3, 5230 Mattighofen (Austria).
www.ktm.at

ORGANIGRAMME
President: Stefan Pierer.
Team manager: Harald Bartol.
Chief mechanics: Mario Galeotti, Warren Willing and Xavier Palacin together take charge of Gabor Talmacsi, Mika Kallio and Julian Simón.

14 GABOR TALMACSI | **36** MIKA KALLIO | **60** JULIAN SIMÓN

RIDERS
Gabor Talmacsi
Date of birth: 28th May 1981.
Place of birth: Budapest (Hungary).
First race: 1995.
First GP: Czech Republic, 1997 (125cc).
Number of GP victories: 3 (125cc).
First GP victory: Italy, 2005 (125cc).
- Hungary 125cc Champion (1999).

Mika Kallio
Date of birth: 8th November 1982.
Place of birth: Valkeakoski (Finland).
First race: 1997.
First GP: Germany, 2001 (125cc).
Number of GP victories: 4 (125cc).
First GP victory: Portugal, 2005 (125cc).

Julian Simón
Date of birth: 3rd April 1987.
Place of birth: Villacañas (Spain).
First race: 1994.
First GP: Spain, 2002 (125cc).
Number of GP victories: 1 (125cc).
First GP victory: Great Britain, 2005 (125cc).

MALAGUTI DIGEST

The Italian brand was involved in the GP for the third year running, with two new riders (Michele Pirro, and the German rider, Sascha Hommel, neither of whom would finish the season). Nicola Casadei was still the jack-of-all-trades, though the technical part was now entrusted to Olivier Liégeois, from Belgium, who we wouldn't see often in the field, but who worked further upstream in the process (for the last two GPs of the season, he would present to us the new jewel he had unearthed, the young French rider, Jules Cluzel).

Malaguti Reparto Corse
Via Emilia 498, 40068 San Lazzaro du Savena, Bologne (Italie).
www.malaguti.com

ORGANISATION CHART
President: Alberto Strazzari.
Team manager: Nicola Casadei.
Technical director: Olivier Liégeois.
Crew Chief: Pierluigi Aldrovandi.
Chief mechanicss: Davide Goretti (Michele Pirro) and Manfred Wittenborn (Sascha Hommel).

15 MICHELE PIRRO | **31** SASCHA HOMMEL

RIDERS
Michele Pirro
Date of birth: 5th July 1986.
Place of birth: San Giovanni Rotondo (Italy).
First race: 2000.
First GP: Italy, 2003 (125cc).

Sascha Hommel
Date of birth: 27th February 1990.
Place of birth: Reichenbach (Germany).
First race: 2000.
First GP: Spain, 2005 (125cc).
Number of GP victories:
First GP victory:
- Germany Minibike Champion (2001).

125cc KTM / MALAGUTI DIGEST

RED BULL KTM GP

MALAGUTI DIGEST

THE CHAMPIONS

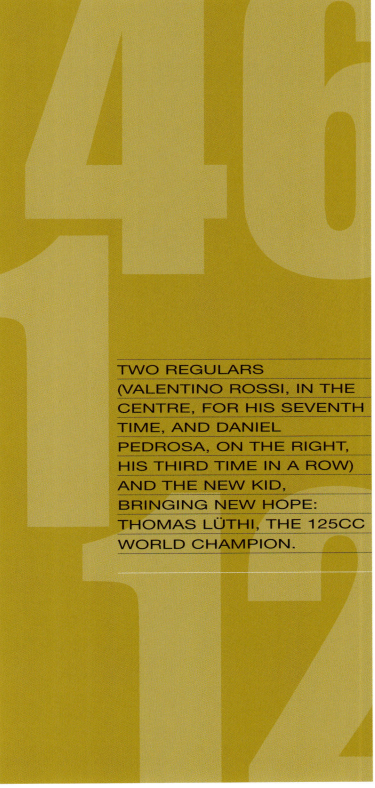

TWO REGULARS (VALENTINO ROSSI, IN THE CENTRE, FOR HIS SEVENTH TIME, AND DANIEL PEDROSA, ON THE RIGHT, HIS THIRD TIME IN A ROW) AND THE NEW KID, BRINGING NEW HOPE: THOMAS LÜTHI, THE 125CC WORLD CHAMPION.

Rossimania in all its splendour at the Italy GP.

46 VALENTINO:
ROSSI OR "ROSSA"?

A seventh title was always on the cards. Rossi did everything he had to do from the first corner of the first GP onwards in order to kill off any ambitions Sete Gibernau may have had. Gibernau was the only man to have given Rossi any cause for concern over the previous two seasons. Eleven wins and just one mistake - crashing at the Japanese GP - in twenty-seven races! We could have seen that coming, such is the man's superhuman hold over an aging competition. But will some real competition has come his way next year from the new boys, in the form of Marco Melandri and Nicky Hayden? Let's hope so. But that can't change history. No, if it's still Valentino Rossi this and Valentino Rossi that he even terrifies the introspective world of Formula 1! He underwent a first test ("to see how things were"), a second ("to get a better understanding of something"), a third ("to answer some questions we had"), so that the now seven-times world motorcycling champion has increased his claim to the title of 'most celebrated sports personality' in Italy. But someone who likes to have so much fun also has to hide himself away to some extent in order to lead a normal life. And so we have Valentino Rossi, or will it soon be Valentino "Rossa" if he becomes emblazoned in the red colours of the Scuderia Ferrari F1?

VALENTINO ROSSI CHAMPION MOTOGP

ROSSI ON...

... MENTAL STRENGTH
"This is an ingrained part of your personality - you can't learn it from a textbook. Anyone who is mentally strong can keep a calm head when things aren't going their way. They will never lose self-confidence and will always have faith in the work of their team".

... MOTIVATION
"All high-level sportsmen run the risk of losing their motivation. Looking back, I can say that the strongest point in my career was my win at Welkom in 2004. Should I have retired from racing at that point? I thought about it. Maybe I would have done if I had been a bit older: I had just won my first race on a new bike - thank you and goodbye! Oh, that would have been good. But anyway, I carried on. I said to myself: even if I don't have a race as good as that again, I might still get the same amount of enjoyment from what I do".

... HIS FAULTS
"There are so many! I should be more organised. And I'm never punctual. But I'm trying - I'm working on it".

... RELIGION
"I'm a catholic, and I'm very religious. But I think faith is a very personal thing for people. So I'd rather not talk about that too much".

... HIS STATUS AS A STAR
"I can't remember the last time I met someone who didn't recognise me, in Italy at least. In fact, I don't think that's ever happened to me. I'm not sure I like being thought of as a kind of big brother to everybody. It's kind of nice at the start, but it weighs you down after a while. People watch your every move - you can't go out for a walk without people talking about it. Everyone wants to know what you're doing, where you're going, who you're with".

... MONEY
"Money is very important. Better to have it than not. Anyone who says otherwise aren't thinking about it properly. But the freedoms that I have lost can't be bought with the folding stuff... For example: if you have money, you can buy huge mansion and fill it with all kinds of wonderful stuff. And therein lies the rub: what does all that matter if you can't go out to share an ice-cream with your mates in town? For the time being, I'm lucky to live in London, because I don't come across many Italians, so I can do more or less as I please. But if a group of schoolchildren sees me, all that goes out of the window - no more anonymity!

... WHAT HE HAS LOST THROUGH BECOMING A CELEBRITY
"I miss things you wouldn't image. I can't stop and get out of my car at a motorway service station. A few years ago, I was just starting out and I stopped off on the motorway and chanced upon Roccia, one of the bodyguards for the singer Vasco Rossi. "What are you doing here? Where is Vasco?", I asked him. "He has to stay in the car. He can't get out or he'll never get away", he said. At the time, I thought he must have been exaggerating. But now I know better".

... WHY HE HAS THE SUN AND THE MOON PAINTED ON HIS HELMET
"The sun and the moon - that's the world - my two main character traits. There's Valentino the man - signified by the sun, and Rossi the moon - the rider. The moon represents my marketing and press conference obligations. Above all, it represents the need to always give the same answers to the same questions. That's something that could turn me into the Jack Nicholson character in "The Shining". But the flip side is the sun - when I talk to my team, my mechanics. It represents my real life around the circuits. In reality, their roles are reversed: the daytime is represented by the moon and at night my sun shines, because I can't do what I want during the day".

... WOMEN
"Women always have various suns and various moons. A woman can be represented by the moon when she decides to play the fool. And what's worse, she does it by choice. And that goes for all women - even my mother. A woman's sun can be so many things - such a huge power. A nice, intelligent girl can turn your world on its head".

... THE MYTHICAL SIDE OF HIS STORY - THE HERO STRAIGHT OUT OF THE PAGES OF A BOOK
"I think I'm the product of Graziano (Valentino always calls his father by his first name). I mean I'm here to take up where he left off and to finish the job. Graziano was a champion. He did amazing things, but he never won the title. He never had the satisfaction of saying he was the best. He did make some mistakes, but he was also unlucky and prevented himself from winning. But I follow a different path. I have been able to keep some of Graziano's character traits. He loved life and always went into a race with a smile. And I think that's why people wish me well and enjoy watching me".

.... TEARS
"As far as I'm concerned, crying is a natural reflex. I don't cry when I win, and I don't cry when everything goes wrong. You might not believe me, but I sob like a baby at films. The last time it happened to me was at the cinema. I was watching "Gladiator" and I had to leave the building because I was too ashamed. I was walking down the street with tears running down my face. Thankfully, there weren't many people around. But there were enough to see me and laugh".

It's Rossi who laughed, Rossi who won, and Rossi who set the tone: the Italian was unstoppable once again this season

VISITING CARD	TITLES		
Surname: Rossi.	1990	Karting regional champion.	1997 125cc World Champion (Aprilia).
First name: Valentino.	1991	Fifth place in the Junior Italian Karting Championship, first win on a Minibike.	1998 2nd place 250cc World Championship (Aprilia).
Date of birth: 16th February 1979.			1999 250cc World Champion (Aprilia).
Place of birth: Urbino/Pesaro (Italy).	1992	Italian Minibike Endurance Champion.	2000 2nd in the 500cc World Championship (Honda.).
Marital status: single (Valentino currently lives with his partner, Arianna Matteuzzi).	1993	12th place in the 125cc Italian Sport Production Championship (Cagiva).	2001 500cc World Champion (Honda).
First race: 1992.	1994	125cc Italian Sport Prod. Champion (Cagiva).	2002 MotoGP World Champion (Honda).
First GP: Malaysia, 1996 (125).	1995	3rd in the European 125cc Championship, 11th in the 125cc Spanish Open Championship, 125cc Italian Champion (Aprilia).	2003 MotoGP World Champion (Honda).
Number of GP victories: 79 (12/125; 14/250; 13/500; 40/MotoGP).			2004 MotoGP World Champion (Yamaha).
First GP victory: République tchèque, 1996 (125).	1996	9th in the 125cc World Championship, 10th 125cc European Open Championship (Aprilia).	2005 MotoGP World Champion (Yamaha).

CHAMPION MOTOGP VALENTINO ROSSI

Daniel Pedrosa and his winning number 1: the young Spaniard followed to the letter the advice of his mentor, Alberto Puig.

1 PEDROSA:
THE ROBOT HAS A HEART!

While not being entirely unlike him, Pedrosa is very different from Valentino Rossi. Just turned twenty, he already has more trophies under his belt than Valentino Rossi: three consecutive world titles - one at 125cc and two at 250cc. Quite simply, Daniel Pedrosa is a phenomenon. It's surprising, because the boy is almost like a robot, as created by his mentor, the former rider Alberto Puig. He is often labelled as an introvert, but that's just a way of being. Some people even unkindly label him as autistic. Dani just laughs that off. He knows he will never have the appeal of a Rossi, but along with many people, he believes he can become a pivotal figure over the coming years. He doesn't smile a great deal. He keeps his emotions under control. The exception that proves the rule would be after his 2005 title won at Phillip Island, when the emotions broke through. He told the world what only those very close to him knew: he had been riding with a fractured shoulder for the past two races - a painful reminder of one of his crashes in Motegi! And suddenly, we found out that the robot had a heart. We found out that after years of the flamboyant Rossi, the years of Daniel Pedrosa's "perfection" were upon us. He had eight wins under his belt this year, and he said goodbye to the 250cc category in Valencia with style: a pole position, a victory and a lap record. A new challenge awaits him in 2006: the top rider's position on the Repsol team's Honda RC211V. Pedrosa is ready to take on this challenge, but he's not going to change...

DANIEL PEDROSA CHAMPION 250cc

PEDROSA ON...

... THE MEDIA
"Before a crucial race, it hasn't been very nice to hear and to read what people have bee saying about me, but I haven't let it bother me. Stoner thought that the pressure had got to me. He thought I wasn't as strong as I seemed to be. Well, he was wrong. I've listened to a lot of rubbish over the past few months. I've even heard some really nasty comments made about me. Even worse, some sections of the media have told stories about me over the past year without the slightest substance to them, but I just kept on winning. I'm the champion, and now it's my turn to talk".

... HIS FIRST REACTIONS AFTER HIS DECISIVE WIN IN AUSTRALIA
"I told myself: my God, I've won the race. I couldn't believe it. The Phillip Island circuit is the toughest in the championship, in my opinion. I crossed the finish line and immediately thought: that's it, mate! You've got the title! And then I started crying tears of joy".

... THE PRESSURE:
"After my accidents in Motegi, the situation got quite difficult. The pressure was immense. I tried to just live with it, but I fell again in Malaysia. In Qatar, I immediately realised that I wasn't in a position to go for a win and I lost some important points. And then we got to Phillips Island. Like I said before, that circuit is so complex, and I had a lot of unhappy memories from that place".

... THE WIN ITSELF
"Winning the title on a track I didn't like up until that point was a really strange feeling. I don't know if I'd go so far as to say that I love Phillips Island now, but I can tell you that something has changed in my feelings for the place".

... WHAT THIS SECOND CONSECUTIVE 250CC TITLE MEANS TO HIM
"I knew at the start of the season that I had just as much to lose as to win by trying to defend the number one spot. The riders were saying all sorts of things at the beginning of the year. But everything was crystal clear to us: the only rival we were worried about was Sebastián Porto. I knew he was the only one who could cause me any real problems. He ran into a few problems as the year wore on, and I managed to build up a good lead...until Japan, when he went past me, as you know. Then I dropped a lot of points, and he shouldn't have let his guard down. Having said that, I had things pretty clear in my mind. I knew that everything that is said during the winter qualifiers - all the theories that people put together - rarely turn into fact".

... HIS FUTURE WITH MOTOGP
"To be perfectly honest, I don't know what lies in store in the future. I had to save all my concentration into not making any mistakes at crucial times - I don't really have the energy to think about the future at the moment".

... HIS THOUGHTS ON THE 2005 SEASON
"This year's championship was more competitive than the one before it. You really had to fight to get on to that podium. But this was also the season that saw a fair few riders fail to deliver on their promise".

... HIS TWENTIETH BIRTHDAY CELEBRATIONS IN QATAR
"Celebrations? "What was there to celebrate about? I didn't come here to party. If I do mark the occasion, I'll do it in private. People reading this might think I've gone mad, but I see a huge difference between 19 and 20. Basically because you change...the first figure! I feel old all of a sudden!"

... HIS RECORDS, BEING SO YOUNG
"People often think that I don't realise all that has happened up to now. But that's wrong. Having said that, I'm not interested in breaking records. Maybe that's what Rossi is interested in, but not me. What matters is taking each race as it comes - each year as it comes."

... ALL THE COMPARISONS MADE BETWEEN HIM AND ROSSI
Rossi is Rossi. He is unique. And as for me...well, I'm me, aren't I!"

... HIS PRECOCIOUS TALENT
"I sometimes marvel at what other people achieve and at other sportsmen's achievements: My God! Look at what that guy has done! And he's only 19!' And suddenly, I remember that I'm the same age. But when I'm on my bike, I just forget all about it. I don't mean that I think I'm different, or more mature, but I'm always much more impressed with what other young sportsmen are doing than by what happens in my own life".

The moment where Daniel Pedrosa broke down: in his lap of honour at Phillip Island, he stopped to take his world champion T-shirt, and cried...

VISITING CARD
Surname: Pedrosa.
First name: Daniel "Dani".
Date of birth: 29th September 1985.
Place of birth: Castellar del Vallés (Spain).
Marital status: single.
First race: 1993.
First GP: Japan, 2001 (125).
Number of GP victories: 23 (8/125; 15/250).
First GP victory: Netherlands, 2002 (125).

TITLES
- **1996** 2nd place in the Spanish Minibike Championship.
- **1997** 3rd place in the Spanish Minibike Championship.
- **1998** Spanish Minibike Champion.
- **1999** 8th place in the Honda Spanish Youth Cup
- **2000** 4th place in the 125cc Spanish Championship (Honda).
- **2001** 8th place in the 125cc World Championship (Honda
- **2002** 3rd place in the 125cc World Championship (Honda).
- **2003** 125cc World Champion (Honda).
- **2004** 250cc World Champion (Honda).
- **2005** 250cc World Champion (Honda).

CHAMPION 250cc DANIEL PEDROSA

A Swiss world champion: the country, where public track races are prohibited, had been waiting 20 years for this

12 LÜTHI:
"THE" SURPRISE

It's a fine story: a rider from a private team, coming out of a very difficult season - 25th in the 2004 World Championship - who right from the pre-season trials asserts himself as one of the principal opponents of the KTM armada; at only 19, Swiss rider Thomas Lüthi has become World 125 cc Champion. In his performance, one discerns a nice cock-a-snook at the growing tendency over the last few years for team managers to fight over young riders with salary promises that some of them don't manage to keep. None of that in the 2005 champion's entourage: this was Thomas Lüthi's third year of "apprenticeship", with a fixed salary of just 2,000 SF per month (1,400), plus performance-related bonuses - laughable, in comparison with the competition. In all this title year, he will have earned around 100,000 SF, or 60,000. Alongside him, two mechanics, an experienced engineer - the German Sepp Schlögl, himself a former World Champion several times, along with compatriots Dieter Braun and Anton Mang - and a support team that's 100% behind him: a psychological coach who has transformed him, forging an amazing psyche for his protégé, and a driving instructor who has helped him get to grips with the various traps encountered throughout the season. Riding for Honda ever since his first GPs in 2002, Lüthi is a reserved lad, but with a rare degree of will-power. He is the one has committed the least errors (a single zero, a technical problem in Jerez), and again he is the one who has managed to combine panache (his wins in France and Australia), courage (winning in Malaysia just one week after an accident in Japan that could have spelt the end of his season, or worse) and intelligence (his race of patience in the deciding GP, the last of the season, in Valencia).

THOMAS LÜTHI CHAMPION 125 cc

LÜTHI AND...

... HIS STATUS AS A LOW-INCOME RIDER
"That's never been the slightest problem for me. Maybe one day I'll earn lots of money, but for the moment that's not something I worry about. If Rossi goes fast, it's not because he earns millions: he earns millions because he goes fast. That's quite different!"

... HIS CALM, PARTICULARLY IN THE DECIDING RACE
"Apparently, in Valencia, even my mum could hardly recognize me, it's a laugh. All weekend, I had the impression of being the calmest of everyone around me. There's a big difference inside my head compared to last year. I've always done everything in order to succeed… even when things weren't going too well. But here, it's different; the work with my psychological coach, Marlies Bernhard, has helped me a great deal."

... HIS SECRECY, ABOUT THE PSYCHOLOGICAL WORK HE'S DONE
"The secret aspect, that's just part of… the treatment. Quite frankly, sometimes just 10 minutes' contact a day is enough to do your soul a lot of good."

... HIS PROGRESS… IN ENGLISH:
At first, people around me laughed at my way of learning the language. It's quite simple: for three years, I've always recorded the after-race press conferences, and I started by learning whole phrases at a time. Since then, I've broadened my vocabulary."

... HIS (COPIOUS) TRIALS PROGRAMME
"Three days' trials in Jerez de la Frontera, two in Valencia, two days' work in Calafat, the IRTA trials - all this was essential stuff. When the championship started, I was ready, and even though I retired in the first GP, ever since Jerez I knew that I was in with a chance this year."

... MANAGING POST-2004, VERY DIFFICULT
"What about 2004? What happened in 2004? For me, there's a big empty space in my mind, I've wiped everything out, as if that season never existed. Try as I might, I haven't been able to find anything positive about last season; so, I remembered the good times in 2003 (a first podium, in Catalunya). And I soon realized that the difficult time I had last year had strengthened me; if I could manage to pick myself up after that, I was convinced that nothing worse could happen to me."

... HIS DECIDIGN RACE, IN VALENCIA
"I tried to start out on my own, but right from the first bend, I realized that wouldn't be possible. So, I had to fall back on Plan B. I was sure Kallio was going to win, so all that remained was to make sure of that crucial place amongst the first thirteen, and I was being kept constantly informed about my position in the pack and the nature of the group behind me. Something odd happened this weekend. I knew that I was facing the most important race of my career, but I was less nervous than in Istanbul, two weeks earlier. I slept like a log, as usual."

... THE PUBLIC HYSTERIA THAT'S ENGULFED SWITZERLAND
"Our country has been waiting 20 years for this. I'm rather a reserved person, but I must say I'm not unhappy when I see that a whole country has all of a sudden taken an interest in motorcycle sport, and that TV audience ratings have exploded. I think it's good for the future of our sport… especially in a country where races on 'public' circuits are prohibited."

... HIS FUTURE
"I don't want to take any short-cuts. In 2006, I shall still be in 125. Then, if all goes well, I'll move into 250 for two seasons. After that, we'll know if I have the capacity to one day ride in MotoGP."

... HIS LUKCY NUMBER 12
"I've had good and not-so-good luck with this number. But now I think I'm going to be unfaithful: riding for a year with the 1, it's great, isn't it? But then I see that the "1" didn't bring Pedrosa bad luck this year. So…"

... THE HIGHPOINT OF HIS SEASON
"Of course there was my first GP win at Le Mans, a magical moment. But I think the turning-point of the championship was in Malaysia. One week before, there'd been a serious accident in Japan, I hurt everywhere, and they wondered if I'd be able to take my place in Sepang… and I went and won! At Motegi, as soon as I came to in the ambulance taking me to the infirmary, I said to the amazed first-aiders: 'Hurry up, I've got an important race next week'; now at that precise moment, I still didn't know if both my feet weren't broken! But for me, everything was clear: I wanted to ride in Malaysia. After that, everyone worked towards that single goal - and it paid off."

... WHAT HE WANTS MOST, FIVE HOURS AFTER HIS TITLE
"To get back to my hotel and sleep for a few hours. Ever since the end of the race, I've done nothing but give interviews, and now I'm wiped out. But don't worry, I'll have enough strength left to celebrate this evening."

Some of the keys of Thomas Lüthi's success: absolute concentration, perfect harmony with his technical team (above, Stefan Fuhrer pushes his rider towards a new achievement) and immense psychological preparation work with Marlies Bernhard (also above).

VISITING CARD	TITLES		
Surname: Lüthi.	**1997**	3rd in the Swiss Pocketbike Championship.	**2003** 15th in the World 125 cc Championship, 14th in the Spanish 125 cc Championship (Honda)
First name: Thomas, "Tom".	**1998**	2nd in the Swiss Pocketbike Championship.	**2004** 25th in the World 125 cc Championship (Honda)
Date of birth: 6th September 1986.	**1999**	Swiss Pocketbike Champion	**2005** World 125 cc Champion (Honda)
Place of birth: Linden (Switzerland).	**2000**	Swiss Minibike Champion.	
Martial status: bachelor.	**2001**	6th in the ADAC Junior 125 cc Cup (Aprilia)	
First race 1997.	**2002**	27th in the World 125 cc Championship, 20th in the European 125 cc Championship, 10th in the Spanish 125 cc Championship, 3rd in the German 125 cc Championship (Honda)	
First GP: Allemagne, 2002 (125).			
Number of GP wins: 4 (125).			
First GP win: France, 2005 (125).			

CHAMPION 125 cc THOMAS LÜTHI

The action that would cause a lot of ink to be spilled: Rossi works his way into a mousehole

01

15th April 2005
SPAIN JEREZ DE LA FRONTERA

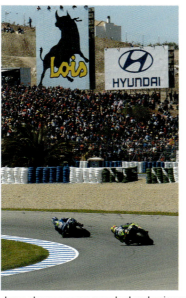

Jerez always means a packed and noisy crowd; and, for the Spanish riders (here Gadea) the risk of pushing it too hard...

THE DOCTOR'S SHOCK
TREATMENT

MUSCLING IN ON SETE GIBERNAU, AND TAKING HIM BY SURPRISE, IN THE LAST CURVE OF THE FIRST GP OF THE SEASON, VALENTINO ROSSI WANTED TO SHOW FROM THE OUTSET THAT HE INTENDED TO REMAIN LEADER OF THE PACK.

MOTORCYCLE YEARBOOK 2005 73

01 MOTO GP SPAIN

THE RACE

VALENTINO ROSSI ONLY NEEDED ONE RACE - THE FIRST - TO FURTHER ESTABLISH HIS NUMBER 1 POSITION.

Throughout the off-season test sessions, Valentino Rossi had the opportunity to assess the progress made by Honda, with HRC wanting to take back, at all costs, that which it considers it alone has the right to: the title in the top category. Rossi also understood that Sete Gibernau would again this year be the most dangerous of his opponents, since, despite his status as rider in a satellite team, the Spaniard had obtained some serious technical guarantees over the winter.

"Il Dottore" therefore had to deal out a first round of treatment: preferably shock treatment, of the kind that still stays in the mind even after a few weeks' recovery... Valentino therefore started his week-end in Andalusia discreetly (for him…), leaving it to Gibernau to dictate the rhythm: a better time on Friday morning, a better time Friday afternoon, a better time Saturday morning, most tipsters fell into the trap, putting the Spaniard in top position on their cards.

This, though, was without counting on the master's first lesson, given on Saturday during the hitherto unique qualifying session. A perfect lap with his first set of qualification tyres, an even better lap in the last seconds of the decisive session: in front of the home crowd of his "enemy", Rossi had made the first few precious points.

The race was to be in the same vein, with the two best riders of the moment forgetting all about their peers, for a final altercation, elbow to elbow - the phrase has never been so apt -, which was to rumble on in the days following this first GP of the season. This was because, more than the five points' difference ¬- 25 for Rossi, 20 for Gibernau - this medicine had its effect on the psyche.

One one side, Gibernau played the poor little duckling, hit by the big bad wolf, Valentino Rossi. So we got Tweety Sete, with a hurt shoulder, for which he had treatment all week… while Rossi relaxed, enjoyed and laughed. Were we going to have to write off the Spaniard from just the second GP of the season? Would he come back to get his revenge? While on one side of the fence they handled the situation in a way that was, to say the least, unusual, on the other we only heard them refer to an action that was "maybe rough, but fair", the racing community judged and asked themselves questions. Even the president of the F.I.M., the international federation, Francesco Zerbi, the lawyer from Rome, became involved with his e-mail to the two concerned in the "incident"…

The championship had barely begun, and already all the ingredients were in place to write a story in seventeen acts; a story which looked set to be full of drama. Dramatic for the public, of course, and for the ever-growing number of people watching on television, but even more so for those within this strange racing family, where Italians and Spaniards have been in the majority for a number of years, and where they make and remake the news through their powerful media.

The pack has just passed under the futuristic building that overhangs the Jerez de la Frontera circuit

Sete Gibernau grimaces, holding his wrist, Rossi triumphs and Melandri already establishes himself as one of the revelations of the season

SPAIN MOTO GP 01

The Fortuna Yamaha design pays homage to Miró.

QUALIFYINGS

A new format for the category, with the two sessions on the Friday and the one on the Saturday just being used to prepare for the race, and with the starting grid being decided in just one session. Even though Gibernau was the quickest on the track in the first three appearances, it was Rossi who had best understood the new deal, playing with two sets of qualifying tyres, and managing a perfect lap in the final seconds of the session. The outcome: 0.496 seconds lead over Gibernau! It was a heavy blow, but it was even worse for Biaggi, who came 16th, laying the blame on a "Da Vinci Code"-type conspiracy. A warning for Rossi in the warm-up: the world champion fell, and his heir apparent came out as the fastest.

START

Rossi took the corner ahead of Gibernau and Hayden, but Sete quickly took control of the race, with Hayden in his wake. At the end of the first lap, Gibernau was 0.209 seconds ahead of the American, and 0.741 seconds in front of the outgoing champion.

LAP 3

Four riders battled it out up front: Gibernau, Hayden, Rossi and Melandri, spread over more than a second. Nakano was by himself, in fifth place. Shane Byrne (Proton-KTM) dropped out.

LAP 5

Rossi passed Hayden to take second, making the best lap time, and coming within 0.288 seconds of Gibernau..

LAP 8

Gibernau steps up the pace. The result: 0.948 seconds lead on Rossi, who was being constantly attacked by Hayden.

MID-RACE (13 LAPS)

Roberts had just dropped out, Gibernau and Rossi were still elbow-to-elbow (0.281 seconds). Hayden (1.246 seconds from the leader) had been shaken off, Melandri was in fourth, and Nakano saw Barros coming up on him.

LAP 16

Barros took Nakano by surprise.

LAP 21

Hayden crashed.

LAP 25

Rossi places his attack at the braking point in the hairpin. The outcome: 0.048 seconds lead at the line.

FINISH (27 LAPS)

Ahead 0.3 seconds entering the final lap, Rossi commits his first mistake, Gibernau works his way in, Rossi counters once, Sete a second time, the two men arriven at the final hairpin: the champion is on the inside, the two make contact, and Sete is sent into the sand trap. "Vale" Rossi had once again managed the impossible.

FROM THE VERY FIRST RACE, ROSSI MANAGED THE IMPOSSIBLE, WHILE BIAGGI (ALREADY) CRIED CONSPIRACY...

A STRONG LINE-UP

The new face of the 2005 pack is well-known, with its sensational transfers (Edwards with Yamaha, Melandri with Honda, Checa with Ducati) and a significant technical change, with Ducati going over to Bridgestone. There was just one Proton KTM on the track (Shane Byrne's) and the Blata WCM team was still using its machines from last year, with the 6-cylinder engine developed in the Czech Republic not yet completed.

Sunset over the paddock in Andalusia, the evening before events restart.

GP SPAIN | 10th April 2005 | Jerez | 4.423 m

STARTING GRID

1	46	V. Rossi	Yamaha	1'39.419
2	15	S. Gibernau	Honda	1'39.915
3	33	M. Melandri	Honda	1'40.179
4	69	N. Hayden	Honda	1'40.465
5	56	S. Nakano	Kawasaki	1'40.542
6	65	L. Capirossi	Ducati	1'40.648
7	6	M. Tamada	Honda	1'40.707
8	4	A. Barros	Honda	1'40.720
9	12	T. Bayliss	Honda	1'40.774
10	66	A. Hofmann	Kawasaki	1'40.812
11	21	J. Hopkins	Suzuki	1'40.825
12	7	C. Checa	Ducati	1'40.948
13	24	T. Elias	Yamaha	1'41.029
14	10	K. Roberts	Suzuki	1'41.058
15	5	C. Edwards	Yamaha	1'41.176
16	3	M. Biaggi	Honda	1'41.233
17	11	R. Xaus	Yamaha	1'42.286
18	44	R. Rolfo	Ducati	1'43.523
19	27	F. Battaini	Blata	1'44.576
20	67	S. Byrne	Proton KR	1'44.728
21	77	J. Ellison	Blata	1'44.833

RACE: 27 laps = 119.421 km

1	Valentino Rossi	45'43.156 (156.722 km/h)
2	Sete Gibernau	+ 8"631
3	Marco Melandri	+ 18"460
4	Alex Barros	+ 26"938
5	Shinya Nakano	+ 27"659
6	Troy Bayliss	+ 28"509
7	Max Biaggi	+ 30"618
8	Makoto Tamada	+ 36"887
9	Colin Edwards	+ 37"608
10	Carlos Checa	+ 39"678
11	Alex Hofmann	+ 42"283
12	Toni Elias	+ 55"457
13	Loris Capirossi	+ 1'02.372
14	John Hopkins	+ 1'19.346
15	Roberto Rolfo	+ 1'33.607
16	James Ellison	+ 1 lap
17	Franco Battaini	+ 1 lap
18	Ruben Xaus	+ 3 laps

Fastest lap
Rossi, in 1'40.596 (158.284 km/h). New record.
Previous: Rossi, in 1'42.788 (154.909 km/h/2003).

Outright fastest lap
Rossi, in 1'39.419 (160.158 km/h/2005).

CHAMPIONSHIP

1	V. Rossi	25 (1 win)
2	S. Gibernau	20
3	M. Melandri	16
4	A. Barros	13
5	S. Nakano	11
6	T. Bayliss	10
7	M. Biaggi	9
8	M. Tamada	8
9	C. Edwards	7
10	C. Checa	6

01 250cc SPAIN

WORLD CHAMPION DANIEL PEDROSA DOMINATED THE WEEK-END.

A STRONG LINE-UP
Honda strengthened its presence considerably with two other "official" teams alongside the world champion team (Pedrosa still partnered by the Japanese rider, Hiroshi Aoyama). The two Spaniards, Hector Barbera and Jorge Lorenzo, who came from the 125cc category, were in Fortuna colours, while the reigning 125cc world champion, Andrea Dovizioso, teamed up with the Japanese rider, Yuki Takahashi, in Team Scot. While the KTM 250s were not yet ready, Arnaud Vincent and Gabriele Ferro's two Fantics got their first outing for the IRTA tests in Barcelona, and were present in Jerez. There was already one injury: the Japanese rider Taro Sekiguchi fell heavily during the Jerez tests, and was replaced by the Frenchman Hugo Marchand.

QUALIFYINGS
The world champion, Daniel Pedrosa, didn't leave it to anyone else to dictate the rhythm. He was the quickest on both the Friday and the Saturday (despite the wind, which was increasingly violent) and put his Honda number 1 ahead of four Aprilia machines (in order, those of Sebastian Porto, Casey Stoner, Randy De Puniet and Alex De Angelis).

START
Superb reflexes from Pedrosa, ahead of Porto and Aoyama. The world champion and the Argentinean finished the first lap neck and neck (0.094 seconds between them).

Pedrosa and his shadow, on the big screen: the Spaniard was flawless. His fellow team member Aoyama (left) and the Australian Casey Stoner (27) both crashed.

Aoyama was in third, but already 0.6 seconds behind, followed by Barbera, De Angelis and De Puniet.

LAP 2
Colombian rider Martin Cardeñas crashed.

LAP 3
Randy De Puniet passed Aoyama, and in doing so, notched up the best lap time.

LAP 5
Pedrosa still in front, now with a lead of 0.514 seconds over Porto. De Puniet was still the fastest rider on the track, and was hot on the tail of his fellow team member, Porto.

LAP 9
Aoyama crashed, after coming into contact with Barbera. Pedrosa increased his lead, which by now was 1.5 seconds.

LAP 12
Crash by Randy de Puniet, who until then had been unable to get past Porto.

MID-RACE (13 LAPS)
Pedrosa continued his fun: he now had 2.079 seconds lead over Porto. Casey Stoner found himself on the virtual podium, though nearly 7 seconds behind the Argentinean.

LAP 14
Stoner crashed..

LAP 15
More and more sand blown onto the track: German rider Steve Jenkner crashed.

FINISH (26 LAPS)
Pedrosa was still evolving on his cloud: he stamped his authority on the Jerez circuit, which until then had not been good to him. The category, despite the influx of new blood, wasn't saved yet: De Angelis, in third place, finished the race almost 30 seconds behind the winner. No comment…

GP SPAIN | 10th April 2005 | Jerez | 4.423 m

STARTING GRID

1	1	D. Pedrosa	Honda	1'42.868
2	19	S. Porto	Aprilia	1'43.195
3	27	C. Stoner	Aprilia	1'43.212
4	7	R. De Puniet	Aprilia	1'43.444
5	5	A. De Angelis	Aprilia	1'43.744
6	73	H. Aoyama	Honda	1'43.813
7	80	H. Barbera	Honda	1'44.038
8	15	R. Locatelli	Aprilia	1'44.330
9	48	J. Lorenzo	Honda	1'44.345
10	34	A. Dovizioso	Honda	1'44.426
11	55	Y. Takahashi	Honda	1'44.462
12	24	S. Corsi	Aprilia	1'44.706
13	17	S. Jenkner	Aprilia	1'44.764
14	6	A. Debon	Honda	1'45.267
15	96	J. Smrz	Honda	1'45.364
16	50	S. Guintoli	Aprilia	1'45.374
17	41	A. Molina	Aprilia	1'45.648
18	25	A. Baldolini	Aprilia	1'45.734
19	57	C. Davies	Aprilia	1'45.988
20	64	R. Rous	Honda	1'46.007
21	32	M. Giansanti	Aprilia	1'46.090
22	28	D. Heidolf	Honda	1'46.256
23	8	A. Ballerini	Aprilia	1'46.881
24	36	M. Cardeñas	Aprilia	1'47.103
25	38	G. Leblanc	Aprilia	1'47.183
26	9	H. Marchand	Aprilia	1'47.515
27	12	G. Rizmayer	Yamaha	1'48.003
28	21	A. Vincent	Fantic	1'48.262
Not qualified:				
	42	Y. Polzer	Aprilia	1'50.389
	16	F. Aschenbrenner	Yamaha	1'50.409
	20	G. Ferro	Fantic	1'58.033

RACE: 26 laps = 114.998 km

1	Daniel Pedrosa		45'36.679 (151.275 km/h)
2	Sebastian Porto		+ 2"136
3	Alex De Angelis		+ 29"682
4	Andrea Dovizioso		+ 36"539
5	Hector Barbera		+ 37"499
6	Jorge Lorenzo		+ 37"728
7	Roberto Locatelli		+ 45"038
8	Alex Debon		+ 56"339
9	Simone Corsi		+ 1'02.844
10	Mirko Giansanti		+ 1'10.708
11	Chaz Davies		+ 1'20.790
12	Radomil Rous		+ 1'20.950
13	Alex Baldolini		+ 1 lap
14	Andrea Ballerini		+ 1 lap
15	Gregory Leblanc		+ 1 lap
16	Gabor Rizmayer		+ 1 lap

Fastest lap
De Puniet, in 1'44.459 (152.431 km/h).
Record: Kato, in 1'44.444 (152.452 km/h/2001).

Outright fastest lap
Pedrosa, in 1'42.868 (154.788 km/h/2005).

CHAMPIONSHIP

1	D. Pedrosa	25 (1 win)
2	S. Porto	20
3	A. De Angelis	16
4	A. Dovizioso	13
5	H. Barbera	11
6	J. Lorenzo	10
7	R. Locatelli	9
8	A. Debon	8
9	S. Corsi	7
10	M. Giansanti	6

SPAIN 125cc 01

THE SANDSTORM GETS THE BETTER OF THOMAS LÜTHI'S NEW AMBITIONS.

A STRONG LINE-UP
The category has had a real injection of fresh blood - the upper age limit of 28 years has pushed riders like Locatelli, Giansanti, Jenkner and other up to the 250cc category. It has also been marked by the arrival of many new riders, since some of last year's best (from the world champion, Andrea Dovizioso, to Barbera, Lorenzo and Corsi) have been promoted into the higher category. Making his return, on the other hand, is Manuel Poggiali: world champion in the category in 2001, and a GP winner in 250cc in 2003, he had problems in 2004. Overall average age: 19 years and 21 weeks.

QUALIFYINGS
They dominated all the winter qualifiers, and showed themselves in the first official clash: Simoncelli (winner here even last year), Pasini and the Swiss rider, Thomas Lüthi, stood out from the first day. On the Saturday, the gusts of wind determined the 125cc qualifiers, and only Lai (Honda official team) managed to improve on his time of the previous day (falls by Simoncelli and Pasini had no effect). A great performance by Raffaele De Rosa, Massimo Matteoni's discovery, coming in eighth.

START
Talmacsi, Pasini et Kallio réussissent le meilleur départ. Chutes de Bautista et de Pirro. Simoncelli n'est que septième. Au premier passage sur la ligne, Pasini compte 211 millièmes d'avance sur Talmacsi, que suit Kallio et Lüthi.

LAP 3
Lüthi took control of the race, ahead of Lai, taking advantage of a mistake by Pasini.

LAP 4
Lüthi had a lead of 0.946 seconds, beating the lap record.

LAP 6
Still Lüthi. Kallio narrowed the time to 0.3 seconds, taking Simoncelli with him.

LAP 7
There were now five riders within just 0.903 seconds of each other: Lüthi, Kallio, Simoncelli, Lai and Nieto.

LAP 8
Kallio in front.

LAP 10
Passing Braillard, Kallio pushed Lüthi to the outside of the track; Nieto took advantage, taking the lead ahead of Kallio, Lai and Simoncelli.

MID-RACE (12 LAPS)
And then there were seven. Marco Simoncelli had a lead of 0.003 seconds, ahead of Lai, Kallio, Lüthi, Talmacsi, Nieto and Pasini, who rounded off the leading pack 0.750 seconds behind the race leader.

LAP 13
Lüthi back in front, with Simoncelli close on his heels.

LAP 15
Simoncelli in front by 0.199 seconds. Lai was 2 seconds behind, in third place.

LAP 16
Lüthi dropped out with piston problems.

LAP 21
Pablo Nieto crashed, but remounted and continued the race.

FINISH (23 LAPS)
A win for Simoncelli, as last year. Mika Kallio had the last word over Lai. Pasini came in fourth, more than 8 seconds down.

The wind gets up, and sand whips across the track. Pablo Nieto (left) crashes out, while Lüthi, having led the pack at the start of the race, is forced to drop out.

GP SPAIN | 10th April 2005 | Jerez | 4.423 m

STARTING GRID

1	58	M. Simoncelli	Aprilia	1'46.996
2	75	M. Pasini	Aprilia	1'47.397
3	12	T. Lüthi	Honda	1'47.747
4	32	F. Lai	Honda	1'47.873
5	36	M. Kallio	KTM	1'47.934
6	14	G. Talmacsi	KTM	1'48.286
7	55	H. Faubel	Aprilia	1'48.611
8	35	R. De Rosa	Aprilia	1'48.632
9	8	L. Zanetti	Aprilia	1'48.764
10	71	T. Koyama	Honda	1'48.810
11	54	M. Poggiali	Gilera	1'48.898
12	52	L. Pesek	Derbi	1'49.088
13	22	P. Nieto	Derbi	1'49.155
14	60	J. Simón	KTM	1'49.174
15	43	M. Hernandez	Aprilia	1'49.386
16	63	M. Di Meglio	Honda	1'49.473
17	28	J. Carchano	Aprilia	1'49.592
18	33	S. Gadea	Aprilia	1'49.666
19	45	I. Toth	Aprilia	1'49.719
20	19	A. Bautista	Honda	1'49.767
21	11	S. Cortese	Honda	1'49.991
22	41	A. Espargaro	Honda	1'50.039
23	9	T. Kuzuhara	Honda	1'50.219
24	6	J. Olivé	Aprilia	1'50.255
25	10	F. Sandi	Honda	1'50.443
26	18	N. Terol	Derbi	1'50.452
27	26	V. Braillard	Aprilia	1'50.524
28	7	A. Masbou	Honda	1'50.586
29	29	A. Iannone	Aprilia	1'50.619
30	84	J. Miralles	Aprilia	1'50.660
31	25	D. Giuseppetti	Aprilia	1'50.676
32	86	M. Tuñez	Aprilia	1'50.945
33	47	A. Rodriguez	Honda	1'51.212
34	15	M. Pirro	Malaguti	1'51.283
35	16	R. Schouten	Honda	1'51.970
36	44	K. Abraham	Aprilia	1'52.223
37	31	S. Hommel	Malaguti	1'52.284
38	49	D. Saez	Aprilia	1'52.456
39	48	D. Bonache	Honda	1'53.136

Not qualified:
| | 87 | P. Vostarek | Honda | 1'54.847 |

RACE: 23 laps = 101.729 km

1	Marco Simoncelli	42'27.960 (143.732 km/h)
2	Mika Kallio	+ 1"418
3	Fabrizio Lai	+ 1"510
4	Mattia Pasini	+ 8"282
5	Gabor Talmacsi	+ 8"930
6	Manuel Poggiali	+ 13"651
7	Hector Faubel	+ 14"590
8	Joan Olivé	+ 17"164
9	Julian Simón	+ 17"262
10	Manuel Hernandez	+ 31"147
11	Mike Di Meglio	+ 34"737
12	Pablo Nieto	+ 34"801
13	Jordi Carchano	+ 37"146
14	Aleix Espargaro	+ 49"591
15	Nicolas Terol	+ 51"629
16	Imre Toth	+ 54"608
17	Mateo Tuñez	+ 54"747
18	Federico Sandi	+ 54"960
19	Julian Miralles	+ 55"527
20	Sandro Cortese	+ 1'10.864
21	Andrea Iannone	+ 1'22.697
22	Karel Abraham	+ 1'26.626
23	Raymond Schouten	+ 1'38.103
24	Sascha Hommel	+ 1'47.461
25	Vincent Braillard	+ 1 lap

Fastest lap
Nieto, in 1'49.176 (145.845 km/h).
Record: Perugini, in 1'47.766 (147.753 km/h/2003).

Outright fastest lap
Pedrosa, in 1'46.938 (148.897 km/h/2003).

CHAMPIONSHIP

1	M. Simoncelli	25 (1 win)
2	M. Kallio	20
3	F. Lai	16
4	M. Pasini	13
5	G. Talmacsi	11
6	M. Poggiali	10
7	H. Faubel	9
8	J. Olivé	8
9	J. Simón	7
10	M. Hernandez	6

Gibernau, the only one in the front of the pack on slicks when the rain began making the track wet, slides out.

02

17th April 2005
PORTUGAL ESTORIL

Everyone has a good-luck charm. The Swiss rider Thomas Lüthi (125cc) found his: a magnum of champagne!

SETE, THE "FLAG TO FLAG"...
AND BARROS

NO LUCK FOR SETE GIBERNAU: MUCH AGAINST HIS WILL, HE PLAYED THE PILOT FISH FOR HIS COMPETITORS, WHEN THE RAIN CAME ON. VICTORY FOR THE EXPERIENCED BARROS

MOTOR YEARBOOK 2005 79

02 MOTO GP PORTUGAL

THE RACE

AFTER SETE GIBERNAU'S FALL, ALEXANDRE BARROS IS A REMINDER THAT CAUTION IS SOMETIMES THE BEST POLICY.

A champagne shower for Barros, who was making his 243rd GP start that day.

A proud gesture by the winner, Alexandre Barros.

Once friends, Rossi and Gibernau became enemies. A new rule applied under the changeable Estoril sky, which they had to take in: the first application of the "flag to flag" rule in history, where a MotoGP race is not stopped because of weather conditions, but the riders have the opportunity to entering their pit area to change motorcycle. In these difficult acrobatics we found the most experienced GP rider: the Brazilian, Alexandre Barros.

This second act in the season was full of twists and turns: incidents (good and bad), secret meetings, statements... All this was because, one week earlier, Gibernau and Rossi had squabbled in the last turn of the Spanish GP, and because the Estiril GP, earlier in the season than previous years, was again one with changeable conditions: gusting winds, black clouds and scattered showers.

Gibernau to start with. The Spaniard, whose soul had taken a harder hit than his body in the altercation in the last bend at Jerez, had decided to take his revenge. A low-profile and late arrival at Estirol ¬- Sete refused the confrontation with Rossi at the traditional pre-GP press conference - Gibernau hurt himself again in a crash on the Saturday. This wouldn't have stopped him dictating the rhythm at the start of the race... until his crash: "In the whole weekend, the only mistake I made was to lead from the start. When it started to rain, I just had to trust the marshals' flags: wherever there was a flag I slowed down and where there wasn't one I sped up. They must have been laughing behind me: I was opening the way, and I was doing all the work, until I fell. I actually noticed that, after I dropped out, the rhythm of the race dropped by almost 3 seconds per lap - as if by chance..."

Failure for Gibernau, then. And if you say "failure" for Sete, you naturally think "bingo" for Rossi. And possibly for an outsider. In these unusual conditions, this man was the experienced Alexandre Barros, who was on the 243rd GP start of his career that day, and he quickly realised that caution is sometimes the best policy: "Sometimes the rain was heavier. Sete continued at his pace, but me, I kept my passion under control" said the Brazilian.

It's true that he found an ally of the moment for the occasion: sure of his second place, and above all sure of receiving 20 precious points more than Gibernau in the championship, Rossi quickly understood that he was getting a great deal: "You know, racing with slicks in the rain isn't great", he joked, smiling broadly. At the same moment, looking gloomy, Gibernau was leaving the circuit, to go and recharge his batteries in his Swiss apartment, and to forget these first two GPs that had been so difficult for him.

PORTUGAL MOTO GP

WHEN THE RAIN TRIGGERED TEARS OF RAGE FROM SETE GIBERNAU… ROSSI, FOR HIS PART, WAS ALREADY LAUGHING.

A STRONG LINE-UP
Terrible bad luck for the German rider, Alexander Hofmann, who crashed his bike during a promotional procession organised on the Wednesday before the GP outside the casino in Estoril, resulting in a scaphoid fracture for the Kawasaki rider.

QUALIFYINGS
Barros remembered that he had Portuguese roots… and that this weekend should have been the Rio GP: the Brazilian was the key man in the qualifiers, and took his first pole in a long time. Gibernau, who had crashed on the Saturday morning, suffered again from his famous shoulder… GP of the season; Sete made the second best time, ahead of the surprising Checa, whose Bridgestone tyres (Tamada in pole, last year) have always behaved well at Estoril. Rossi came fourth, while Tamada fractured his right wrist.

START
A few drops of rain were falling while the riders set up on the grid. Gibernau made an excellent start, widening the gap immediately. Behind, Rossi, Biaggi and Barros were doing each other no favours. The end of the first lap saw Sete with a 1.746 second lead over Biaggi, who would soon be surprised by Barros.

LAP 4
Rossi found a way past Biaggi. Gibernau was still ahead of Barros, and Rossi was a second behind the Brazilian.

LAP 7
Barros was the quickest on the track, and had come within 1.396 seconds of Gibernau. Rossi was still in third place.

LAP 9
The white flag goes up, and any rider who wanted to could now enter the pit area. Barros had narrowed the gap to less than one second.

MID-RACE (14 LAPS)
Gibernau still led, 1.338 seconds ahead of Barros. Behind the front pair there was already a large gap: Rossi, third, was over 9 seconds behind Barros, but was still holding off Biaggi.

LAP 17
The gap had narrowed to 1.212 seconds, and Gibernau fell. A little further on, Hopkins did the same. Barros was now alone up front, with a 8.644 second lead over Rossi. It began to rain more heavily in places.

LAP 20
Bayliss crashed.

LAP 24
Edwards crashed, and Rossi swerved. Riders are racing as if on eggshells..

FINISH (28 LAPS)
Barros plays with the nerves of his supporters, and with his own even more, putting his rear wheel over the white line in the last lap: the Brazilian miraculously controlled the skid to collect his victory.

CHAMPIONSHIP
A big success for Rossi, who notched up 20 points more than his main contender for the title, Sete Gibernau. The champion was up to 45 points, compared with 38 for Barros and 29 for the excellent Melandri.

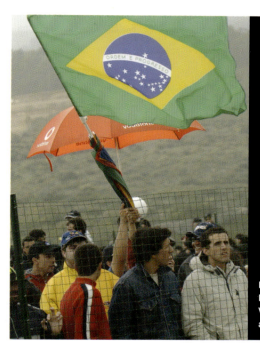

Brazilian flag under the cloudy Estoril sky. Barros' win suits Valentino Rossi, a perfectionist as ever.

GP PORTUGAL | 17th April 2005 | Estoril | 4.182 m

STARTING GRID				
1	4	A. Barros	Honda	1'37.202
2	15	S. Gibernau	Honda	1'37.329
3	7	C. Checa	Ducati	1'37.456
4	46	V. Rossi	Yamaha	1'37.643
5	33	M. Melandri	Honda	1'37.835
6	65	L. Capirossi	Ducati	1'38.000
7	5	C. Edwards	Yamaha	1'38.003
8	3	M. Biaggi	Honda	1'38.009
9	69	N. Hayden	Honda	1'38.123
10	56	S. Nakano	Kawasaki	1'38.283
11	21	J. Hopkins	Suzuki	1'38.412
12	11	R. Xaus	Yamaha	1'38.949
13	12	T. Bayliss	Honda	1'39.033
14	10	K. Roberts	Suzuki	1'39.628
15	24	T. Elias	Yamaha	1'39.836
16	44	R. Rolfo	Ducati	1'41.327
17	77	J. Ellison	Blata	1'41.699
18	67	S. Byrne	Proton KR	1'41.705
19	27	F. Battaini	Blata	1'41.728
20	6	M. Tamada	Honda	1'41.930 (*)

(*): M. Tamada (Jap, Honda), having fallen on Saturday afternoon, is forced to pull out (right wrist fracture).

RACE: 28 laps = 117.096 km		
1	Alex Barros	47'14.053 (148.743 km/h)
2	Valentino Rossi	+ 2"771
3	Max Biaggi	+ 6"071
4	Marco Melandri	+ 29"546
5	Carlos Checa	+ 29"774
6	Colin Edwards	+ 44"216
7	Nicky Hayden	+ 57"121
8	Shinya Nakano	+ 59"847
9	Loris Capirossi	+ 1'07.718
10	Ruben Xaus	+ 1'22.431
11	Troy Bayliss	+ 1'33.529
12	Kenny Roberts	+ 1'34.051
13	Roberto Rolfo	+ 1'35.956
14	Toni Elias	+ 1'36.492
15	James Ellison	+ 2 laps
16	Shane Byrne	+ 4 laps

Fastest lap
Barros, in 1'38.480 (152.875 km/h).
Record: Rossi, in 1'38.423 (152.964 km/h/2004).

Outright fastest lap
Barros, en 1'37.202 (154.885 km/h/2005).

CHAMPIONSHIP		
1	V. Rossi	45 (1 win)
2	A. Barros	38 (1 win)
3	M. Melandri	29
4	M. Biaggi	25
5	S. Gibernau	20
6	S. Nakano	19
7	C. Checa	17
8	C. Edwards	17
9	T. Bayliss	15
10	L. Capirossi	10

02 250cc PORTUGAL

TWO "BEGINNERS" (STONER AND DOVIZIOSO) IN THE FIRST TWO PLACES.

A STRONG LINE-UP
No changes from the Spain GP. Though injured in the Jerez qualifiers, French rider Hugo Marchand still replaced Japanese rider Taro Sekiguchi in team Campetella.

QUALIFYINGS
For Steve Jenkner the GP was already over on the Friday, when the German rider was the victim of a crash in which he fractured his right 5th metacarpal. On the track, Randy de Puniet also had a scare on Friday morning, and would have a second scare during the warm-up on Sunday when it was still damp. The evening before, he came off on top against his fellow team member, Sebastian Porto. Dani Pedrosa was third, ahead of the reigning 125cc world champion, Andrea Dovizioso.

START
Porto and De Puniet went through the turn in the lead, ahead of Pedrosa and Hiroshi Aoyama, who would be surprised by De Angelis. At the end of the first lap, Porto already had a lead of 2.157 seconds over his first heir apparent, Dovizioso.

LAP 2
Pedrosa sensed the danger and snatched second place, but he was already 4.227 behind Porto.

LAP 6
Porto was still alone up front, having put 3.636 seconds between him and the group chasing him, made up of Pedrosa, Dovizioso, Stoner and De Angelis.

LAP 9
Locatelli crashed out.

Casey Stoner breaks away, Randy De Puniet's not unhappy with third, and it's finally Dani Pedrosa (in the lead, bottom photo) who's duped.

LAP 11
The hunters have caught up with their prey, with Pedrosa now just half a second behind Porto.

LAP 12
Pedrosa has gone in front, with Dovizioso and Stoner close on his heels. Leblanc crashed.

MID-RACE (13 LAPS)
Two groups of three have been formed: Pedrosa, Dovizioso and Stoner are within a hair's breadth of each other: 0.126 seconds. De Puniet is fourth, 1.6 seconds behind

LAP 15
Dovizioso only needed one GP and a half to take the 250 cc in hand: he went 0.246 seconds in front. De Puniet is back.

LAP 19
De Puniet did brilliantly to put 0.287 seconds between him and Dovizioso, who was still in position.

LAP 20
Chaz Davies crashed.

LAP 23
Stoner, after a superb attack on De Puniet - which Dovizioso took advantage of to take the lead for a moment - is the new leader.

FINISH (26 LAPS)
Stoner, De Puniet and Dovizioso are within 0.270 seconds of each other entering the final lap. The Frenchman goes past at the end of the straight, then Stoner takes the lead a little further on, Dovizioso passes Randy at the chicane, but has to settle for second. In first and second place were two rookies… and Pedrosa got mad with Casey Stoner during the lap of honour.

CHAMPIONNAT
The winner at Jerez, Pedrosa kept his lead, but Dovizioso, the reigning 125cc champion, was just 5 lengths behind. Porto and De Angelis were 11 points adrift, and Stoner, 13.11 points de retard, Stoner 13.

GP PORTUGAL | 17th April 2005 | Estoril | 4.182 m

STARTING GRID

1	7	R. De Puniet	Aprilia	1'41.104
2	19	S. Porto	Aprilia	1'41.152
3	1	D. Pedrosa	Honda	1'41.285
4	34	A. Dovizioso	Honda	1'41.462
5	80	H. Barbera	Honda	1'41.597
6	5	A. De Angelis	Aprilia	1'41.700
7	73	H. Aoyama	Honda	1'41.790
8	48	J. Lorenzo	Honda	1'42.049
9	15	R. Locatelli	Aprilia	1'42.116
10	24	S. Corsi	Aprilia	1'42.206
11	55	Y. Takahashi	Honda	1'42.250
12	27	C. Stoner	Aprilia	1'42.269
13	50	S. Guintoli	Aprilia	1'42.395
14	96	J. Smrz	Honda	1'42.815
15	57	C. Davies	Aprilia	1'43.151
16	6	A. Debon	Honda	1'43.232
17	32	M. Giansanti	Aprilia	1'43.254
18	25	A. Baldolini	Aprilia	1'43.472
19	64	R. Rous	Honda	1'43.768
20	41	A. Molina	Aprilia	1'43.895
21	28	D. Heidolf	Honda	1'43.916
22	9	H. Marchand	Aprilia	1'43.946
23	38	G. Leblanc	Aprilia	1'44.205
24	8	A. Ballerini	Aprilia	1'44.639
25	12	G. Rizmayer	Yamaha	1'45.049
26	36	M. Cardeñas	Aprilia	1'45.505
27	42	Y. Polzer	Aprilia	1'48.109
28	21	A. Vincent	Fantic	1'48.129

Not qualified:
	16	F. Aschenbrenner	Yamaha	1'49.318
	20	G. Ferro	Fantic	1'55.959
	17	S. Jenkner	Aprilia	---

RACE: 26 laps = 108.732 km

1	Casey Stoner	45'36.009 (143.067 km/h)
2	Andrea Dovizioso	+ 0"404
3	Randy De Puniet	+ 0"431
4	Daniel Pedrosa	+ 2"009
5	Alex De Angelis	+ 2"204
6	Hiroshi Aoyama	+ 18"855
7	Yuki Takahashi	+ 17"914
8	Sylvain Guintoli	+ 23"810
9	Sebastian Porto	+ 26"407
10	Jorge Lorenzo	+ 45"921
11	Hector Barbera	+ 51"533
12	Jakub Smrz	+ 56"920
13	Alex Debon	+ 1'04.103
14	Mirko Giansanti	+ 1'09.512
15	Martin Cardeñas	+ 1'18.508
16	Dirk Heidolf	+ 1'23.940
17	Simone Corsi	+ 1'26.950
18	Andrea Ballerini	+ 1'27.179
19	Radomil Rous	+ 1'27.332
20	Gabor Rizmayer	+ 1 lap
21	Yves Polzer	+ 2 laps

Fastest lap
De Angelis, in 1'43.484 (145.483 km/h).
Record: Elias, in 1'41.595 (148.188 km/h/2004).

Outright fastest lap
De Puniet, en 1'41.104 (148.908 km/h/2005).

CHAMPIONSHIP

1	D. Pedrosa	38 (1 win)
2	A. Dovizioso	33
3	S. Porto	27
4	A. De Angelis	27
5	C. Stoner	25 (1 win)
6	R. De Puniet	16
7	H. Barbera	16
8	J. Lorenzo	16
9	A. Debon	11
10	H. Aoyama	10

PORTUGAL 125cc 02

MIKA KALLIO GETS HIS FIRST WIN, BY 8 THOUSANDTHS OF A SECOND.

A STRONG LINE-UP
All the team riders were present, plus two guests: the Czech rider Vostarek (as at Jerez) and the Portuguese rider Ferreira, whose Honda was a patchwork of parts from different years. His desire wasn't enough to overcome this technical handicap, and Ferreira was to fail the qualifying time by 2.5 seconds (Hommel, with the second Malaguti, was also outside the 107%... but by a tenth of a second!)

ESSAIS
We had seen an impressive Simoncelli at Jerez; at Estoril we discovered Mika Kallio (the three KTMs were in the top nine in the rankings), where he took his first pole, ahead of Thomas Lüthi, still in great form. Simoncelli came in third, and the Spanish rider Faubel completed the first row.

START
Kallio, Talmacsi (in the second row) and Lüthi were the quickest off the mark. There were only 0.087 seconds between the three men on the first time across the line

LAP 2
Pesek crashed. Kallio led, ahead of Talmacsi, Lüthi and Lai.

LAP 3
Talmacsi crashed, and Lüthi ran into him while he was on the ground, coming off the track, but came back to finish the lap in 11th place. Kallio was half a second ahead of Faubel and Simón.

LAP 4
A better lap for Lüthi, already in ninth..

LAP 5
Always quicker: Lüthi made sixth.

LAP 7
Kallio was still in front, with 0.269 seconds between him and Faubel. Lüthi had come up to fourth.

LAP 9
Lüthi was third, having got a new best lap time

MID-RACE (12 LAPS)
Kallio and Faubel were neck and neck (0.194 seconds between them). Lüthi in third, but still 3.950 seconds behind, with Lai in his slipstream. A mighty battle for fifth between Poggiali, Di Meglio, Simón, Pasini and Koyama.

LAP 17
The status quo held, though Lai had caught right up with Lüthi.

LAP 18
Kallio lets Faubel past to observe him.

LAP 19
Faubel still led, but the pace had dropped somewhat (Lüthi had made 4 tenths of a second on the two frontrunners).

LAP 22
Kallio took back the lead,

FINISH (23 LAPS)
Crouched tight inside his fairing, in the slipstream of Mika Kallio's KTM, Faubel missed out on his first victory by just 0.008 seconds, giving Kallio the first GP victory for a Finn in 30 years! Lüthi, in third, was the other hero of the day.

CHAMPIONSHIP
45 points out of a possible 50, the taciturn Mika Kallio made a perfect start to the championship. This year, consistency would once again prove all-important in this category, this being the consecutive 40th GP without the same winner ever triumphing twice in a row.

A high voltage final lap between Kallio (36) and Faubel. Lüthi, in third, slipped behind in the third lap, when Talmacsi crashed in front of him.

GP PORTUGAL | 17th April 2005 | Estoril | 4.182 m

STARTING GRID

1	36	M. Kallio	KTM	1'45.279
2	12	T. Lüthi	Honda	1'45.393
3	58	M. Simoncelli	Aprilia	1'45.622
4	55	H. Faubel	Aprilia	1'46.059
5	52	L. Pesek	Derbi	1'46.060
6	14	G. Talmacsi	KTM	1'46.205
7	75	M. Pasini	Aprilia	1'46.369
8	32	F. Lai	Honda	1'46.440
9	60	J. Simón	KTM	1'46.503
10	54	M. Poggiali	Gilera	1'46.517
11	19	A. Bautista	Honda	1'46.566
12	63	M. Di Meglio	Honda	1'46.752
13	43	M. Hernandez	Aprilia	1'47.132
14	22	P. Nieto	Derbi	1'47.252
15	9	T. Kuzuhara	Honda	1'47.428
16	71	T. Koyama	Honda	1'47.442
17	41	A. Espargaro	Honda	1'47.583
18	6	J. Olivé	Aprilia	1'47.597
19	11	S. Cortese	Honda	1'47.639
20	7	A. Masbou	Honda	1'47.705
21	45	I. Toth	Aprilia	1'47.749
22	15	M. Pirro	Malaguti	1'48.127
23	33	S. Gadea	Aprilia	1'48.157
24	21	J. Carchano	Aprilia	1'48.364
25	18	N. Terol	Derbi	1'48.437
26	10	F. Sandi	Honda	1'48.493
27	84	J. Miralles	Aprilia	1'48.535
28	29	A. Iannone	Aprilia	1'48.583
29	35	R. De Rosa	Aprilia	1'48.584
30	26	V. Braillard	Aprilia	1'48.680
31	8	L. Zanetti	Aprilia	1'48.789
32	25	D. Giuseppetti	Aprilia	1'48.896
33	16	R. Schouten	Honda	1'48.986
34	47	A. Rodriguez	Honda	1'49.196
35	44	K. Abraham	Aprilia	1'50.349
36	87	P. Vostarek	Honda	1'51.138
Not qualified:				
31	S. Hommel		Malaguti	1'52.785
50	C. Ferreira		Honda	1'55.286

RACE: 23 laps = 96.186 km

1	Mika Kallio	41'19.431 (139.656 km/h)
2	Hector Faubel	+ 0"008
3	Thomas Lüthi	+ 2"898
4	Fabrizio Lai	+ 2"940
5	Manuel Poggiali	+ 11"276
6	Tomoyoshi Koyama	+ 13"543
7	Alvaro Bautista	+ 13"547
8	Mattia Pasini	+ 14"493
9	Julian Simón	+ 14"710
10	Marco Simoncelli	+ 15"194
11	Mike Di Meglio	+ 15"208
12	Pablo Nieto	+ 36"518
13	Alexis Masbou	+ 36"858
14	Toshihisa Kuzuhara	+ 36"917
15	Manuel Hernandez	+ 37"025
16	Aleix Espargaro	+ 37"073
17	Jordi Carchano	+ 54"909
18	Joan Olivé	+ 56"816
19	Michele Pirro	+ 59"761
20	Sergio Gadea	+ 1'01.246
21	Angel Rodriguez	+ 1'01.344
22	Imre Toth	+ 1'04.776
23	Nicolas Terol	+ 1'10.415
24	Raffaele De Rosa	+ 1'10.515
25	Sandro Cortese	+ 1'10.677
26	Andrea Iannone	+ 1'11.309
27	Federico Sandi	+ 1'11.362
28	Julian Miralles	+ 1'13.203
29	Dario Giuseppetti	+ 1'14.968
30	Raymond Schouten	+ 1'18.257
31	Vincent Braillard	+ 1'18.879
32	Patrik Vostarek	+ 1 lap

Fastest lap
Faubel, in 1'46.654 (141.159 km/h).
Record: Barbera, in 1'45.573 (142.604 km/h/2004).

Outright fastest lap
Kallio, in 1'45.279 (143.002 km/h/2005).

CHAMPIONSHIP

1	M. Kallio	45 (1 win)
2	M. Simoncelli	31 (1 win)
3	H. Faubel	29
4	F. Lai	29
5	M. Pasini	21
6	M. Poggiali	21
7	T. Lüthi	20
8	J. Simón	14
9	G. Talmacsi	11
10	T. Koyama	10

Futuristic decor and someone surprising chasing behind Valentino Rossi: OJ, Olivier Jacque.

03

1st May 2005

CHINA SHANGHAI

Chinese winks...

JACQUE, THE MYSTERIOUS
"MISTER O"

VALENTINO ROSSI HAD A SURPRISE WHEN HE SPOTTED AN "O" ON HIS PIT BOARD. "O" AS IN... OLIVIER JACQUE, A SURPRISE GUEST ON THE FIRST PODIUM IN SHANGHAI.

MOTO GP CHINA

THE RACE

OLIVIER JACQUE: HE HAD BECOME A RALLY DRIVER, BUT FOUND HIMSELF THREATENING THE KING OF MOTOGP, VALENTINO ROSSI.

"All of a sudden, I noticed that my pit board said my lead was being measured in relation to some Mr. O. I had no idea what it was about. I told myself, 'OK - they're talking about one of the Chinese guys….Riiight, I get it'. We didn't have the name "Jacque" on our signs, it must have been him…". The winner, Valentino Rossi, couldn't stop laughing. He turned to Olivier Jacque, who was ecstatic to be dining at the table of honour. "What worries me is that I read somewhere that you were treating the Chinese GP like a training session for France. Now if that's true - if that's how you train - I really do have something to worry about…".

Jacque? This was the best story to come out of the past two weeks. A motoring fairy tale - a script that film critics would find just too surreal. And yet…

Having taken early retirement from GP motor racing fifteen months previously, "OJ" passed his time cultivating different hobbies. A car enthusiast, he has a few real gems in his private collection, such as a modern Ferrari and an immaculately restored 4 CV. This year, he is also taking part in the French Rally Championship, in Group N, for Renault-Sport.

Two weeks before this, the first Chinese GP in history, he was in Lyon for the first stage of his new Championship. There, he received a phone call from Kawasaki. "We're hoping you could come down to Estoril to enter the qualifying for the GP the day after tomorrow." Two days later, Alexander Hofmann - one of the two riders of the team managed by the German

Kisses for a good performance. Top, Valentino Rossi found himself an ally of the moment. Bottom, Kawasaki celebrate..

Harald Eckl - fractured his wrist during a promotional ride…in front of the Estoril casino. Out of action for a year, nobody thought this would be the jackpot for Jacque.

Jacque accepted the invitation, but wasn't expecting any miracles. And now it's almost seven months since he got back in the saddle of a motorbike. The day he got that phone call, he led his category in the first speed trials, before seriously damaging his Renault Clio. The day after, he was flying out to the Portuguese GP. And the day after that, he found himself back in the saddle of a Kawasaki. Only two weeks later, he came second in a GP. Having put the fear of God into Rossi: "It's even better than winning my 250 cc world title. It's magical", he said, during an interview. "On Thursday, when I was invited to take part in a press conference before the GP, I was a bit annoyed at where I found myself. I felt like a fish on a bicycle, but now I've taken to it again like a duck to water".

Did the thought of victory cross his mind during the race? "Of course! I suddenly saw a blue shape coming up ahead of me. I didn't think I had passed Valentino yet. I really thought it must have been first place right there", he continued, laughing.

Rossi had just found a new ally of circumstance - a big hitter to take up all the points between him and his rivals.

"OJ" making an attack. His eye is as keen as ever; talent doesn't disappear that easily.

CHINA MOTO GP 03

Valentino Rossi triumphs, Massimiliano Biaggi satisfies himself with following the action (from a distance). Or, when the emperor increasingly questions himself

ROSSI WINS AGAIN, JACQUE SURPRISES, AND GIBERNAU CONTINUES HIS DESCENT INTO HELL.

A STRONG LINE-UP
Two surprises: the former 250 cc champion, Olivier Jacque, arrived in Estoril the day after the Portuguese GP to team up with Alex Hofmann and Kawasaki. "OJ" replaced the German for the Shanghai and France GPs. Business as usual for the Dutchman Jurgen Van Den Goorbergh, who regained his position on the RC211V following Tamada's injury. The Proton-KTM team was not present.

QUALIFYINGS
Some people like Estoril (Gibernau) while others don't like it ("this circuit - it's like an empty shell. It's pretty from the outside, but there's no substance", said Rossi). The main issue was the changeable weather during qualifying, with the front row seeing an all-Movistar line-up. Giberneau came in faster than Melandri in Fausto Gresini's team.

START
Hopkins surprised everybody, including Gibernau, who got off to the best start. Barros and Elias both had a false start, and so had to go through the pit lane. At the end of the first lap, Kenny Roberts led the race ahead of Rossi (0.682 secs between them), Elias, Hopkins, Gibernau and Melandri..

LAP 2
Nakano retired. Roberts, Rossi and Elias were still leading. Olivier Jacque was doing incredibly well - already up into ninth place.

LAP 5
Roberts failed to brake because of technical problems and Rossi took the lead. Bayliss crashed…then Checa, who slid down the pit lane on his back.

LAP 6
Elias stopped for his time penalty, and Hopkins went off into the sand trap. "OJ" stood in fourth position.

LAP 8
Best lap for Jacque. Barros did his "drive through".

LAP 9
OJ was sensational: a new record - the man who came in at such short notice was in third place.

MID-COURSE (11 LAPS)
Rossi was still in command of the race. But it was all happening behind him, as we witnessed a fight for second place between Gibernau (who didn't dare make a mistake following his failure to score any points in Estoril) and Jacque - a man who took early retirement 15 months previously.

LAP 15
Jacque surprised Gibernau, taking second 6.128s behind Rossi.

LAP 17
Melandri overtook Biaggi for fourth place.

LAP 18
Jacque narrowed the time to 4.379s behind Rossi.

LAP 19
A new lap record for OJ. Gap between the leaders: 3.297s.

LAP 20
Rossi had to up his pace. OJ was only 3.205s behind him.

FINISH (22 LAPS)
Rossi held him off, but Jacque was the true hero of the day. Melandri took advantage to get past Gibernau on the last lap, and Sete got off his bike immediately after the finish line (poor choice of tyres).

CHAMPIONSHIP
Rossi was firmly in the driving seat, already having a 25 point lead (a full race) over his closest rival, now Melandri. Barros was in third place.

GP CHINA | 1st May 2005 | Shanghai | 5.281 m

STARTING GRID

1	15	S. Gibernau	Honda	1'59.710
2	33	M. Melandri	Honda	1'59.873
3	65	L. Capirossi	Ducati	2'00.480
4	21	J. Hopkins	Suzuki	2'00.666
5	69	N. Hayden	Honda	2'00.747
6	46	V. Rossi	Yamaha	2'00.821
7	7	C. Checa	Ducati	2'00.902
8	24	T. Elias	Yamaha	2'01.081
9	10	K. Roberts	Suzuki	2'01.085
10	56	S. Nakano	Kawasaki	2'01.098
11	4	A. Barros	Honda	2'01.117
12	12	T. Bayliss	Honda	2'01.328
13	5	C. Edwards	Yamaha	2'01.401
14	3	M. Biaggi	Honda	2'01.502
15	19	O. Jacque	Kawasaki	2'02.072
16	11	R. Xaus	Yamaha	2'02.869
17	44	R. Rolfo	Ducati	2'03.886
18	72	T. Ukawa	Moriwaki	2'04.223
19	16	J. Van Den Goorbergh	Honda	2'04.594
20	27	F. Battaini	Blata	2'05.468
21	77	J. Ellison	Blata	2'06.496

RACE: 22 laps = 116.182 km

1	Valentino Rossi	50'02.463 (139.304 km/h)
2	Olivier Jacque	+ 1"700
3	Marco Melandri	+ 16"574
4	Sete Gibernau	+ 18"906
5	Max Biaggi	+ 19"551
6	Jurgen Van Den Goorbergh	+ 21"622
7	John Hopkins	+ 25"883
8	Colin Edwards	+ 31"033
9	Nicky Hayden	+ 39"299
10	Ruben Xaus	+ 40"991
11	Alex Barros	+ 44"014
12	Loris Capirossi	+ 44"401
13	James Ellison	+ 53"449
14	Toni Elias	+ 1'05.853
15	Tohru Ukawa	+ 1'09.480
16	Roberto Rolfo	+ 1'15.293

Fastest lap
Barros, in 2'13.716 (142.178 km/h).
New record (new circuit).

Outright fastest lap
Gibernau, in 1'59.710 (158.813 km/h/2005).

CHAMPIONSHIP

1	V. Rossi	70 (2 wins)
2	M. Melandri	45
3	A. Barros	43 (1 win)
4	M. Biaggi	36
5	S. Gibernau	33
6	C. Edwards	25
7	O. Jacque	20
8	S. Nakano	19
7	C. Checa	17
10	N. Hayden	16

03 250cc CHINA

SECOND WIN IN A ROW FOR STONER. DOVIZIOSO TAKES THE LEAD IN THE CHAMPIONSHIP.

A STRONG LINE-UP

Hugo Marchand carried on riding the Aprilia of the Campetella team (replacing Taro Sekiguchi). Five Chinese riders had wildcards. The Fantic team decided not to make the trip in order to carry on work developing its bikes. The Swede Frederik Watz climbed on the second Yamaha for the Kurz team.

QUALIFYINGS

There were some concerns for the Aprilia Aspar team (De Puniet and Porto), while Honda were having a ball (Pedrosa, Dovizioso, Lorenzo, Aoyama and Barbera in the top six): only Stoner denied Honda overall supremacy with good results on his Aprilia. Hugo Marchand was forced out of this race, after having injured his foot in a crash during Friday's session

START

Having eased off during the 125 cc race, the rain started up again. Superb reflexes from Pedrosa and Davizioso, who moved into the lead ahead of De Puniet, Aoyama, Locatelli and Stoner, who secured first place after a dream first lap.

LAP 3

The Stoner - Dovizioso duo opened up a gap - already over three seconds ahead of the chasing group led by Pedrosa.

LAP 4

De Puniet managed to leapfrog Pedrosa, but the Frenchman was already six seconds behind the leader.

LAP 7

And it was still Stoner and Dovizioso making up the lead. They seemed to be driving at a whole different level. As it stood, that gave them a lead of more than fourteen seconds over the third place man, De Puniet, who couldn't break away from De Angelis, Aoyama, Pedrosa, Barbera and Porto.

MID-RACE (10 LAPS)

Only 0.305 secs separated Stoner and Dovizioso. They were still the fastest men on the track. Behind them, another duo had formed to fight for third place. De Puniet and De Angelis (17 seconds behind the leader).

LAP 13

Aoyama passed De Angelis, and would soon see off De Puniet to hold third position

LAP 18

De Puniet raised his hand and slowed down, with a split piston.

AP

It started raining heavily again, and there were just 0.308 secs between the two top men attacking the last lap.

FINISH (21 LAPS)

With a flawless performance, Casey Stoner didn't disappoint his boss, Lucio Cecchinello. He took his second win in a row, once again placing him above Dovizioso. Pedrosa had visibility problems, and "only" came in sixth.

CHAMPIONSHIP

With only three races down, the reigning 125 cc champion, Andrea Dovizioso took the lead in the overall classification. He had three points over his rival Stoner and five more than the previous champion, Dani Pedrosa, who was made to understand that the competition from Honda was to be intense this year.

Stoner turns, Dovizioso isn't far behind: the newcomers are in great form. On the starting grid, the outgoing 125cc champion didn't guess that he would thereby take the lead in the championship.

GP CHINA | 1st May 2005 | Shanghai | 5.281 m

STARTING GRID

1	27	C. Stoner	Aprilia	2'06.196
2	1	D. Pedrosa	Honda	2'06.214
3	34	A. Dovizioso	Honda	2'06.473
4	48	J. Lorenzo	Honda	2'06.544
5	73	H. Aoyama	Honda	2'06.615
6	80	H. Barbera	Honda	2'07.437
7	7	R. De Puniet	Aprilia	2'07.653
8	19	S. Porto	Aprilia	2'07.665
9	24	S. Corsi	Aprilia	2'07.709
10	55	Y. Takahashi	Honda	2'07.889
11	5	A. De Angelis	Aprilia	2'08.018
12	15	R. Locatelli	Aprilia	2'08.567
13	57	C. Davies	Aprilia	2'08.840
14	6	A. Debon	Honda	2'08.886
15	50	S. Guintoli	Aprilia	2'09.016
16	25	A. Baldolini	Aprilia	2'09.057
17	8	A. Ballerini	Aprilia	2'09.166
18	28	D. Heidolf	Honda	2'09.212
19	96	J. Smrz	Honda	2'09.420
20	64	R. Rous	Honda	2'09.579
21	32	M. Giansanti	Aprilia	2'09.673
22	12	G. Rizmayer	Yamaha	2'11.900
23	38	G. Leblanc	Aprilia	2'12.237
24	17	S. Jenkner	Aprilia	2'12.743
25	18	F. Watz	Yamaha	2'13.260
26	58	S. Huang	Yamaha	2'13.307
27	36	M. Cardeñas	Aprilia	2'13.422
28	62	Z. He	Yamaha	2'14.434
Not qualified:				
	60	Z. Wang	Aprilia	2'18.458
	9	H. Marchand	Aprilia	2'19.113
	61	Z. Li	Aprilia	2'19.312
	59	Z. Huang	Honda	2'24.652

RACE: 21 laps = 110.901 km

1	Casey Stoner	48'07.205 (138.280 km/h)
2	Andrea Dovizioso	+ 0"249
3	Hiroshi Aoyama	+ 21"434
4	Alex De Angelis	+ 28"589
5	Sebastian Porto	+ 31"879
6	Daniel Pedrosa	+ 40"520
7	Hector Barbera	+ 46"332
8	Simone Corsi	+ 1'01.615
9	Jorge Lorenzo	+ 1'04.261
10	Yuki Takahashi	+ 1'05.823
11	Alex Debon	+ 1'08.145
12	Sylvain Guintoli	+ 1'09.653
13	Alex Baldolini	+ 2'01.116
14	Jakub Smrz	+ 2'01.367
15	Dirk Heidolf	+ 2'01.893
16	Roberto Locatelli	+ 2'05.297
17	Frederik Watz	+ 2'07.361
18	Randy De Puniet	+ 2'13.455
19	Gabor Rizmayer	+ 2'26.199
20	Zi Xian He	+ 1 lap
21	Shi Zhao Huang	+ 1 lap

Fastest lap
Dovizioso, in 2'15.608 (140.195 km/h).
New record (new circuit).

Outright fastest lap
Stoner, in 2'06.196 (150.651 km/h/2005).

CHAMPIONSHIP

1	A. Dovizioso	53
2	C. Stoner	50 (2 victoires)
3	D. Pedrosa	48 (1 victoire)
4	A. De Angelis	40
5	S. Porto	38
6	H. Aoyama	26
7	H. Barbera	25
8	J. Lorenzo	23
9	R. De Puniet	16
10	A. Debon	16

CHINA 125cc 03

Lai, Pasini and Talmacsi on the podium, the same riders in a different order on the track: the race was hot. Opposite: Mike Di Meglio, the French hopeful.

PASINI-LAI: AN ITALIAN DUEL UNDER THE RAIN IN SHANGHAI.

A STRONG LINE-UP
There was only one absentee: the Italian Lorenzo Zanetti (injured in the Portuguese GP). Three local riders were trying their luck: Wai On Cheung, Ho Wan Chow and You Rao Zhou. They rose through the ranks to emerge from the Chinese Championship, where young riders learn their trade on the saddle of an 80 cc machine.

QUALIFYINGS
Some initial trends emerged from the winter qualifiers - trends which were to become a reality during the first two GPs: the KTM riders (Mika Kallio, Gabor Talmacsi and Simón) all started in the top five of the grid, and the two Italians, Simoncelli and Lai, and the Swiss rider, Lüthi, turned out to be the lynchpins for the opening races of the season. They were in a very good position following the free practices on Friday morning on this new circuit..

START
The rain poured down and a fog settled over the circuit. The starter's pistol was delayed for half an hour. The track was waterlogged, but it stopped raining in time for the race to start. Lai stormed forward from the second row, in front of Kallio, Lüthi and Talmacsi. At the end of the first lap, the Italian had a 1.662 second lead over Talmacsi. Simon, Pasini, Kallio, Lüthi and Koyama followed, with Simoncelli in eighth place.

LAP 2
Pasini was the fastest man on the track, reclaiming second position.

LAP 3
Pasini took the lead ahead of Lai, Talmacsi and Simon. Behind them, a gap opened up. Koyama, Lüthi and Kallio - the world leader - followed.

LAP 5
Koyama made the fastest lap, becoming the fifth member of the leading group of riders.

LAP 6
It was Lüthi's turn to get the fastest lap, remaining in sixth place, but still 4.826 seconds off the leader.

LAP 8
Still Pasini in front of Lai, Talmasci and Koyama. Lüthi was in fifth place, with Simoncelli in his slipstream.

MID-RACE (10 LAPS)
Lai took over the lead. But his slender lead made him just 0.443 secs ahead of Pasini. Talmasci was third, at 0.765 secs, Koyama fourth at 2.707 secs and Lüthi fifth place at 3.732 secs. Simoncelli was next behind the Swiss rider.

LAP 15
Lüthi finally spotted an opening to get past Koyama, and in doing so got the fastest lap and found himself a shade over six seconds behind the leader.

FINISH (19 LAPS)
There were only 0.410 secs separating Lai and Pasini as they started their last lap. Talmacsi gave up the chase. But the two Italians wouldn't give up an inch in the last lap - almost touching over the last few metres: only 0.065 secs separated the two as they crossed the line.

CHAMPIONSHIP
Kallio played it safe (finishing 11th in the race) and remained at the top of the Championship. His opponents bunched closer behind him: Lai had 1 point, Pasini had 4 and Simoncelli had 9.

GP CHINA | 1st May 2005 | Shanghai | 5.281 m

STARTING GRID

#	No.	Rider	Bike	Time
1	36	M. Kallio	KTM	2'13.535
2	58	M. Simoncelli	Aprilia	2'13.631
3	14	G. Talmacsi	KTM	2'14.293
4	12	T. Lüthi	Honda	2'14.341
5	60	J. Simón	KTM	2'14.530
6	32	F. Lai	Honda	2'14.773
7	52	L. Pesek	Derbi	2'14.954
8	71	T. Koyama	Honda	2'15.085
9	9	T. Kuzuhara	Honda	2'15.130
10	55	H. Faubel	Aprilia	2'15.489
11	15	M. Pirro	Malaguti	2'15.607
12	63	M. Di Meglio	Honda	2'15.627
13	19	A. Bautista	Honda	2'15.995
14	22	P. Nieto	Derbi	2'16.179
15	75	M. Pasini	Aprilia	2'16.259
16	41	A. Espargaro	Honda	2'16.316
17	54	M. Poggiali	Gilera	2'16.376
18	11	S. Cortese	Honda	2'16.408
19	7	A. Masbou	Honda	2'16.433
20	43	M. Hernandez	Aprilia	2'16.450
21	29	A. Iannone	Aprilia	2'16.734
22	33	S. Gadea	Aprilia	2'17.079
23	84	J. Miralles	Aprilia	2'17.357
24	47	A. Rodriguez	Honda	2'17.424
25	45	I. Toth	Aprilia	2'17.575
26	35	R. De Rosa	Aprilia	2'17.650
27	6	J. Olivé	Aprilia	2'17.654
28	25	D. Giuseppetti	Aprilia	2'18.000
29	44	K. Abraham	Aprilia	2'18.156
30	18	N. Terol	Derbi	2'18.260
31	26	V. Braillard	Aprilia	2'18.006
32	16	R. Schouten	Honda	2'18.356
33	28	J. Carchano	Aprilia	2'18.767
34	10	F. Sandi	Honda	2'18.826
35	31	S. Hommel	Malaguti	2'18.851
36	38	W. Cheung	Honda	2'21.609
37	39	H. Chow	Honda	2'22.649
Non qualifié au temps				
	85	Y. Zhou	Honda	2'43.981

RACE: 19 laps = 100.339 km

#	Rider	Time/Gap
1	Mattia Pasini	46'30.273 (129.457 km/h)
2	Fabrizio Lai	+ 0"065
3	Gabor Talmacsi	+ 4"953
4	Thomas Lüthi	+ 8"785
5	Tomoyoshi Koyama	+ 10"707
6	Marco Simoncelli	+ 11"959
7	Aleix Espargaro	+ 25"951
8	Pablo Nieto	+ 27"152
9	Lukas Pesek	+ 28"154
10	Julian Simón	+ 28"707
11	Mika Kallio	+ 32"488
12	Manuel Poggiali	+ 44"317
13	Michele Pirro	+ 58"618
14	Joan Olivé	+ 59"376
15	Hector Faubel	+ 59"879
16	Toshihisa Kuzuhara	+ 1'00.836
17	Alvaro Bautista	+ 1'05.476
18	Andrea Iannone	+ 1'06.354
19	Raymond Schouten	+ 1'13.199
20	Mike Di Meglio	+ 1'14.696
21	Alexis Masbou	+ 1'42.293
22	Jordi Carchano	+ 1'46.227
23	Julian Miralles	+ 1'48.723
24	Wai On Cheung	+ 1'52.912
25	Federico Sandi	+ 2'06.791
26	Nicolas Terol	+ 2'21.419
27	Karel Abraham	+ 2'21.591
28	Raffaele De Rosa	+ 2'24.441
29	Sergio Gadea	+ 1 lap
30	Imre Toth	+ 2 laps
31	Ho Wan Chow	+ 4 laps

Fastest lap
Lai, in 2'23.967 (132.055 km/h).
New record (new circuit).

Outright fastest lap
Kallio, in 2'13.535 (142.371 km/h/2005).

CHAMPIONSHIP

#	Rider	Points
1	M. Kallio	50 (1 win)
2	F. Lai	49
3	M. Pasini	46 (1 win)
4	M. Simoncelli	41 (1 win)
5	H. Faubel	30
6	T. Lüthi	29
7	G. Talmacsi	27
8	M. Poggiali	25
9	T. Koyama	21
10	J. Simón	20

This time, the duel took place between the two big guns of the last two seasons. The winner was the same as ever: Valentino Rossi.

04
15th May 2005
FRANCE LE MANS

A colourful marshal, and passionate Brazilian supporters: the Bugatti circuit in Le Mans is more successful each year.

PARIS DESERVES
KIND WORDS…

BEFORE BEATING GIBERNAU ON THE TRACK, VALENTINO ROSSI LIT THE FIRE, WALKING ALONG THE SEINE. HE SAID A LOT ABOUT FORMULA 1…

04 MOTO GP FRANCE

THE RACE

ON THE SEINE: A TOURIST LIKE ANY OTHER? NO, IT'S VALENTINO ROSSI, WHO WAS TO WHIP UP A STORM IN THE MEDIA.

Rossi in civvies, and Rossi in action: wherever the champion goes, the competition just have to prepare themselves. "Vale" is the best communicator in this day and age.

Claude Michy, the French GP promoter - the man who saved this classic contest after the closure of the Castellet circuit - is a man of many surprises. Everybody has an opinion about him. As is always the case with such people, there are those who support them wholeheartedly and there are also those who make fun of him - those who are jealous of his success, who envy him. But this was the man who saved the French GP. Better still, he adds to the show every year, offering spectators - his customers - a programme of activities ranging from technical exhibitions to rock concerts. That's great: not only do fans get a little extra something, but they also stay at the Le Mans circuit, living there and spending money there. A perfect demonstration of modern economics.

Spring 2005 was highly anticipated by fans everywhere. Claude Michy dreamed of organising a Paris event based around Rossi in order to promote "his" French GP in the capital. The crown prince of motorcycling agreed to this plan and set aside an afternoon to explore the charms of the city of light from the upper deck of a tour boat. This was a great promotional exercise which was to be echoed around the world two days later, with Valentino Rossi of course taking the opportunity to launch something new on the media - something a deep red and with four wheels: the Ferrari F1.

What did he actually say? Nobody really knows. The most appropriate statement came from the king of motorcycling himself, who furthered his claim to the world championship after masterfully winning the 2005 French GP. He let it be known that he would be open to all offers in 2006, after the end of a new twelve-month contract. Even Formula 1…

A wild storm whipped up over the GP couldn't have had a more dramatic effect. Everyone benefited from this door that has been left ajar, scaling up the secret conditions of future contracts ("everything is set technically and financially for next year - the only sticking points are the number of test days, because Valentino wants to set aside the maximum amount of time after 2006 to be able to work behind the wheel of a Ferrari."). Some people have even gone as far as confirming that the king of the motorcycle has seriously looked at the possibility of taking on a mixed job in the near future - one Sunday on two wheels, the next on four!

This should have been a simple promotional event, but was instead to become the hottest media topic of the two weeks. Things reached such a fever pitch that on the evening of his 71st GP victory (not a bad statistic, out of 144 starts!), the man who was to receive an honorary doctorate in documentation at the University of Urbino a few days later was compelled to calm things down. "I think some people misunderstood what I said the other day. In fact, what I decided this weekend is perfectly simple: I intend to ride my bike for the next ten years. So you'll have to put up with me for some time yet".

And so the king of motorcycling left with a smile on his face, more than ever fitting into his role as ringmaster.

FRANCE MOTO GP | 04

How to cause a Ducati sandwich, in three images: Carlos Checa goes down at the chicane, Roberto Rolfo is unable to avoid him. The Italian from the D'Antin team would continue the race.

ROSSI WINS AGAIN, BUT THIS TIME, GIBERNAU FOUGHT UNTIL THE END...

A STRONG LINE-UP
The French fans cheer as Jacque still rides in place of Hofmann for Kawasaki. Tamada tried his luck on the Friday morning to see if he had fully recovered from his wrist operation, but he had to withdraw. Van den Goorbergh rode the Konica-Minolta RC211V. The Proton-KTM team returned to the competition.

QUALIFYINGS
Rain on Friday? Rossi was the fastest man on the track. Dry conditions on Saturday? Rossi again. The Honda riders weren't too happy, especially Biaggi - who complained of communications problems. We saw confirmation of Melandri's new-found confidence, taking third place on the grid.

START
A great start from Edwards, moving ahead of Hayden and Capirossi. Checa and Rolfo went out in the chicane. Hopkins made a start after the other riders. Byrne didn't finish the first lap. The former double world champion was 0.314 secs ahead of Hayden over the line after the first lap. Rossi was "only" sixth.

LAP 3
Edwards was still ahead, 0.536 secs ahead of his compatriot, who followed Capirossi. Rossi had already moved up into fourth place by this time..

LAP 6
Rossi passed Capirossi - already in a podium position.

LAP 9
Rossi surprised Hayden. Edwards was still in front, and Gibernau passed Melandri to take fifth place.

LAP 12
0.334 secs separated the two Yamaha riders, with Edwards staying in front. Gibernau was the fastest man on the track at this point, and would soon overtake Capirossi.

LAP 13
Barros crashed

MID-RACE (14 LAP)
Edwards was still in control of the situation. His lead over his world champion team-mate had increased to 0.459 secs. Hayden was third, 1.659 secs off the leader, and Gibernau was fourth, 1.415 secs off the podium spots. Capirossi broke away from the pack.

LAP 16
Gibernau put on a great display, breaking lap records - he was in third place, 1.491 secs behind Rossi.

LAP 18
Rossi made another attack on Edwards' position, after being spurred on by seeing Gibernau coming up behind him. The Texan put on a burst of speed and Rossi's attempt to overtake failed. Sete took advantage of the situation to go past and claim second place.

LAP 19
The 3 men kept hard on each others' heels, only 0.459 seconds between them.

LAP 25
Edwards could not match the pace of the Rossi-Gibernau pairing. And so began a new battle for the top spot. Behind them, Melandri overtook Biaggi to take 4th place

FINISH (28 LAPS)
0.154 secs separated the two men fighting it out over the last lap, but Gibernau couldn't make the necessary headway. Rossi took his rival's hand and the two of them rode side by side to do a lap of honour.

CHAMPIONSHIP
Rossi strengthened his position. His lead over Melandri had extended to 37 lengths. Gibernau climbed to third position, but was already 42 points off Rossi's lead.

A good day for Davide Brivio, the boss of the Yamaha team: Rossi and Edwards on the podium.

GP FRANCE | 15th May 2005 | Le Mans | 4.180 m

#	No	STARTING GRID		Time
1	46	V. Rossi	Yamaha	1'33.226
2	5	C. Edwards	Yamaha	1'33.449
3	33	M. Melandri	Honda	1'33.465
4	15	S. Gibernau	Honda	1'33.467
5	69	N. Hayden	Honda	1'33.514
6	56	S. Nakano	Kawasaki	1'33.536
7	21	J. Hopkins	Suzuki	1'33.594
8	3	M. Biaggi	Honda	1'33.699
9	7	C. Checa	Ducati	1'33.727
10	65	L. Capirossi	Ducati	1'33.773
11	4	A. Barros	Honda	1'33.876
12	24	T. Elias	Yamaha	1'33.991
13	19	O. Jacque	Kawasaki	1'34.403
14	10	K. Roberts	Suzuki	1'35.068
15	12	T. Bayliss	Honda	1'35.231
16	11	R. Xaus	Yamaha	1'35.772
17	67	S. Byrne	Proton KR	1'36.249
18	44	R. Rolfo	Ducati	1'36.319
19	16	J. Van Den Goorbergh	Honda	1'36.595
20	77	J. Ellison	Blata	1'37.265
21	27	F. Battaini	Blata	1'37.341

#	RACE: 28 laps = 117.040 km	Time
1	Valentino Rossi	44'12.223 (158.864 km/h)
2	Sete Gibernau	+ 0''382
3	Colin Edwards	+ 5''711
4	Marco Melandri	+ 7''276
5	Max Biaggi	+ 7''703
6	Nicky Hayden	+ 21''770
7	Loris Capirossi	+ 24''664
8	Shinya Nakano	+ 35''940
9	Toni Elias	+ 38''062
10	Troy Bayliss	+ 52''607
11	Olivier Jacque	+ 53''302
12	Ruben Xaus	+ 1'00.342
13	Kenny Roberts	+ 1'00.514
14	Jurgen Van Den Goorbergh	+ 1'17.993
15	Roberto Rolfo	+ 1'32.233
16	John Hopkins	+ 1 lap
17	Franco Battaini	+ 1 lap

Fastest lap
Rossi, in 1'33.678 (160.635 km/h). New record.
Previous: Biaggi, in 1'34.088 (159.935 km/h/2004).

Outright fastest lap
Rossi, in 1'33.226 (161.414 km/h/2005).

#	CHAMPIONSHIP	
1	V. Rossi	95 (3 wins)
2	M. Melandri	58
3	S. Gibernau	53
4	M. Biaggi	47
5	A. Barros	43 (1 win)
6	C. Edwards	41
7	S. Nakano	27
8	N. Hayden	26
9	O. Jacque	25
10	L. Capirossi	23

04 250cc FRANCE

RANDY DE PUNIET HAD A SUPERB RACE, IN FRONT OF HIS FANS. PEDROSA EMERGED VICTORIOUS.

A STRONG LINE-UP
Fantic came back to join this race (the Italian team had done three days of testing in Italy during the break from competition it had through not entering the Chinese GP). Hugo Marchand was still riding instead of Taro Sekiguchi, with Campetella, and the KTM rider Anthony West (who was to give the new Austrian machine its first run the day after the GP) rode the Aprilia of the German team - a position normally held by the Colombian Martin Cardeñas.

QUALIFYINGS
A storm hit on Friday afternoon, and only eighteen riders took to their bikes (with the best time going to Anthony West, ahead of Arnaud Vincent). Things returned to normal on the Saturday, and the outgoing champion, Dani Pedrosa, made the best show, ahead of Casey Stoner, Jorge Lorenzo and Sebastian Porto. Sylvain Guintoli did particularly well, claiming eighth place on his independent Aprilia. The Fantics failed to qualify.

START
Andrea Dovizioso, the world leader, made a perfect start and finished the first lap in the lead ahead of Pedrosa, Stoner, De Puniet and Porto. Behind them, things were not going well for the German camp. Steve Jenkner was the victim of a highside and crashed, taking his compatriot, Dirk Heidolf, along with him!

LAP 8
Dovizioso couldn't get away. Stoner was right on his wheel, De Puniet was in third place in front of his team-mate Sebastian Porto. Alex de Angelis suffered a spectacular crash.

LAP 10
The crowd saw a change of leader: Casey Stoner finally found an opening. He led a compact, disciplined pack behind him made up of Randy de Puniet, Jorge Lorenzo, Dovizioso, Porto and Daniel Pedrosa. Hector Barbera broke away from the pack.

MID-RACE (13 LAPS)
The crowd were going crazy. Randy De Puniet led his home GP.

LAP 14
Porto retired from the race.

LAP 19
Pedrosa, who had been quiet up until that point, took over the lead.

LAP 22
The world champion upped the pace, gaining a 0.7 second lead.

LAP 24
Randy de Puniet went onto all cylinders. He caught up to the number one man and was soon to take over the lead.

FINISH (26 LAPS)
It was a great fight for the finish. De Puniet gave it his all on the last lap, but couldn't beat Pedrosa, who went on to win the GP. Dovizioso was in third place.

CHAMPIONSHIP
Pedrosa went ahead of Dovizioso (73 points to 69). Stoner was still in reach of the top (63), but behind him, the biggest losers of the weekend, De Angelis and Porto fell by the wayside more than 20 lengths off the podium

The pack on the first time through the chicane: Pedrosa ahead of Dovizioso, Casey Stoner (thoughtful, in his pit area) and Randy De Puniet - who would celebrate his excellent second place with great dignity.

GP FRANCE | 15th May 2005 | Le Mans | 4.180 m

STARTING GRID

1	1	D. Pedrosa	Honda	1'37.391
2	27	C. Stoner	Aprilia	1'37.880
3	48	J. Lorenzo	Honda	1'37.882
4	19	S. Porto	Aprilia	1'38.123
5	34	A. Dovizioso	Honda	1'38.448
6	7	R. De Puniet	Aprilia	1'38.554
7	5	A. De Angelis	Aprilia	1'38.588
8	50	S. Guintoli	Aprilia	1'38.641
9	80	H. Barbera	Honda	1'38.707
10	73	H. Aoyama	Honda	1'38.729
11	57	C. Davies	Aprilia	1'39.447
12	96	J. Smrz	Honda	1'39.516
13	55	Y. Takahashi	Honda	1'39.528
14	8	A. Ballerini	Aprilia	1'39.540
15	6	A. Debon	Honda	1'39.599
16	15	R. Locatelli	Aprilia	1'39.737
17	24	S. Corsi	Aprilia	1'39.855
18	32	M. Giansanti	Aprilia	1'40.239
19	25	A. Baldolini	Aprilia	1'40.355
20	17	S. Jenkner	Aprilia	1'40.495
21	63	E. Nigon	Aprilia	1'40.857
22	38	G. Leblanc	Aprilia	1'41.420
23	28	D. Heidolf	Honda	1'41.444
24	64	R. Rous	Honda	1'41.464
25	14	A. West	Aprilia	1'42.339
26	12	G. Rizmayer	Yamaha	1'42.540
27	9	H. Marchand	Aprilia	1'42.700 (*)
28	18	F. Watz	Yamaha	1'43.061
Not qualified:				
	21	A. Vincent	Fantic	1'44.587
	65	S. Aubry	Honda	1'46.103
	20	G. Ferro	Fantic	1'46.430
	47	M. Scaccia	Yamaha	1'47.251
	61	Z. Li	Aprilia	21'31.231

(*): Having fallen on Saturday, H. Marchand (F, Aprilia) pulls out (dislocation of the fifth metacarpus of the right hand)

RACE: 24 laps = 100.320 km

1	Daniel Pedrosa	42'55.152 (151.932 km/h)
2	Randy De Puniet	+ 0''251
3	Andrea Dovizioso	+ 1''554
4	Casey Stoner	+ 4''230
5	Jorge Lorenzo	+ 6''027
6	Hiroshi Aoyama	+ 23''969
7	Hector Barbera	+ 30''667
8	Alex Debon	+ 32''039
9	Sylvain Guintoli	+ 32''452
10	Yuki Takahashi	+ 37''772
11	Simone Corsi	+ 49''285
12	Chaz Davies	+ 49''509
13	Alex Baldolini	+ 49''530
14	Roberto Locatelli	+ 49''771
15	Andrea Ballerini	+ 49''895
16	Jakub Smrz	+ 1'02.122
17	Mirko Giansanti	+ 1'02.612
18	Anthony West	+ 1'17.358
19	Gregory Leblanc	+ 1'17.502
20	Erwan Nigon	+ 1'18.382
21	Radomil Rous	+ 1'22.698
22.	Gabor Rizmayer	+ 1 lap

Fastest lap
De Puniet, in 1'37.594 (154.189 km/h). New record.
Previous: Pedrosa, in 1'38.202 (153.235 km/h/2004).

Outright fastest lap
Pedrosa, in 1'37.123 (154.937 km/h/2004).

CHAMPIONSHIP

1	D. Pedrosa	73 (2 wins)
2	A. Dovizioso	69
3	C. Stoner	63 (2 wins)
4	A. De Angelis	40
5	S. Porto	38
6	R. De Puniet	36
7	H. Aoyama	36
8	J. Lorenzo	34
9	H. Barbera	34
10	A. Debon	24

FRANCE 125cc 04

DEMONSTRATION BY THE SWISS RIDER, THOMAS LÜTHI, WHO WON HIS FIRST GP.

In eight laps, Lüthi left everyone behind. Behind him, there was an impressive battle between Kallio, Gadea, Di Meglio and Simoncelli (some nice acrobatics, opposite). 15th May 2005 was to be the day the Swiss rider claimed his first GP victory.

A STRONG LINE-UP
This race marked the return of Lorenzo Zanetti, but the German rider Sascha Hommel was to play no part in it, having suffered a shoulder injury during the warm-up for the Chinese GP. He was to be replaced by the Italian Giole Pellino with the Malaguti team. Five young French riders entered with wildcards.

QUALIFYINGS
The weather proved changeable over the course of the weekend, but the 125 cc riders were lucky enough to have dry conditions for both qualifying sessions. Mattia Pasini, the winner at Shanghai, was the first victim of the French circuit: he suffered a double fracture to the left wrist. The Japanese rider, Kuzuhara, injured his collarbone on the Saturday. Thomas Lüthi won his first pole position. This was something Swiss fans had been waiting for almost 16 years (Stefan Dörflinger, 80 cc Czech GP on 27th August 1989).

START
Talmasci and Lüthi got off to the fastest start from the front row. Lai and French team-mate Mike di Meglio, boosted by riding in his home GP, went into the fight from the outset. Lüthi was in front of Talmasci after the first lap, with an almost 0.3 second lead..

LAP 2
Lai briefly took the lead. What spectators didn't yet know was that this was the only point of the race where the number 12 (Thomas Lüthi) did not appear at the head of the pack.

LAP 8
Lüthi started to hit good form. He got the best three lap times in a row and had over four seconds lead over the chasing group (Kallio, Di Meglio, Talmasci and Lai), all of whom were fighting for their places. Faubel retired from the race.

LAP 9
Alvaro Bautista crashed.

MID-RACE (12 LAPS)
Lüthi's lead extended to 6.250s. Behind him, Kallio, Di Meglio and Talmasci saw Marco Simoncelli climb places to join their group. Lai's place was no longer so safe, with Gadea hot on his heels.

LAP 18
The lead rider was now 8.078 seconds ahead of his closest rival. Lai retired from the race

FINISH (24 TOURS)
At 12.02pm on Sunday 15th May 2005, a Swiss rider won a GP for the first time in 16 years (Jacques Cornu, Belgian GP 250cc, 2nd July 1989). Lüthi rode a perfect race. The fight for second place was the most interesting for the spectators, with Gadea having the last word after some very forceful riding (KTM's claims that he passed a yellow flag were dismissed - Gadea then swept past his rivals).

CHAMPIONSHIP
Kallio (66 points) kept his lead, but the man who gained most out of the day was, of course, Lüthi, who was now in second place (54) in spite of his initial 0 (mechanical failure in Jeréz).

GP FRANCE | 15th May 2005 | Le Mans | 4.180 m

STARTING GRID

1	12	T. Lüthi	Honda	1'43.405
2	36	M. Kallio	KTM	1'43.688
3	55	H. Faubel	Aprilia	1'43.939
4	14	G. Talmacsi	KTM	1'43.940
5	58	M. Simoncelli	Aprilia	1'44.005
6	52	L. Pesek	Derbi	1'44.088
7	32	F. Lai	Honda	1'44.201
8	60	J. Simón	KTM	1'44.325
9	63	M. Di Meglio	Honda	1'44.468
10	33	S. Gadea	Aprilia	1'44.610
11	7	A. Masbou	Honda	1'44.694
12	22	P. Nieto	Derbi	1'44.770
13	6	J. Olivé	Aprilia	1'44.791
14	71	T. Koyama	Honda	1'44.820
15	54	M. Poggiali	Gilera	1'45.000
16	75	M. Pasini	Aprilia	1'45.001 (*)
17	43	M. Hernandez	Aprilia	1'45.014
18	19	A. Bautista	Honda	1'45.019
19	45	I. Toth	Aprilia	1'45.120
20	11	S. Cortese	Honda	1'45.147
21	9	T. Kuzuhara	Honda	1'45.157 (**)
22	47	A. Rodriguez	Honda	1'45.157
23	8	L. Zanetti	Aprilia	1'45.521
24	84	J. Miralles	Aprilia	1'45.629
25	41	A. Espargaro	Honda	1'45.651
26	89	J. Cluzel	Honda	1'45.838
27	25	D. Giuseppetti	Aprilia	1'45.906
28	26	V. Braillard	Aprilia	1'45.916
29	28	J. Carchano	Aprilia	1'46.068
30	10	F. Sandi	Honda	1'46.084
31	35	R. De Rosa	Aprilia	1'46.215
32	74	M. Gines	Honda	1'46.291
33	88	M. Lussiana	Honda	1'46.415
34	18	N. Terol	Derbi	1'46.460
35	29	A. Iannone	Aprilia	1'46.470
36	15	M. Pirro	Malaguti	1'46.616
37	16	R. Schouten	Honda	1'46.649
38	44	K. Abraham	Aprilia	1'47.154
39	73	Y. Deschamps	Honda	1'47.358
40	42	G. Pellino	Malaguti	1'47.781
41	90	A. Michel	Honda	1'48.485

(*): Having fallen on Friday, M. Pasini (I, Aprilia) pulls out (double fracture left wrist).
(**): Having fallen on Saturday, T. Kuzuhara (J, Honda) is forced to pull out with a broken right collarbone.

RACE: 24 laps = 100.320 km

1	Thomas Lüthi	41'52.772 (143.726 km/h)
2	Sergio Gadea	+ 3''080
3	Mika Kallio	+ 3''263
4	Mike Di Meglio	+ 4''237
5	Marco Simoncelli	+ 4''311
6	Gabor Talmacsi	+ 4''882
7	Pablo Nieto	+ 25''823
8	Julian Simón	+ 26''349
9	Imre Toth	+ 31''661
10	Manuel Poggiali	+ 32''853
11	Lorenzo Zanetti	+ 33''270
12	Aleix Espargaro	+ 40''620
13	Dario Giuseppetti	+ 43''477
14	Manuel Hernandez	+ 45''390
15	Sandro Cortese	+ 53''924
16	Julian Miralles	+ 56''940
17	Gioele Pellino	+ 1'01.388
18	Mathieu Lussiana	+ 1'07.555
19	Federico Sandi	+ 1'07.750
20	Raffaele De Rosa	+ 1'08.159
21	Karel Abraham	+ 1'09.907
22	Nicolas Terol	+ 1'11.161
23	Andrea Iannone	+ 1'16.897
24	Raymond Schouten	+ 1'17.642
31	Ho Wan Chow	+ 4 laps

Fastest lap
Kallio, in 1'43.373 (145.569 km/h).
Record: Dovizioso, in 1'42.651 (146.593/2004).
Outright fastest lap
Barbera, in 1'42.536 (146.758 km/h/2004).

CHAMPIONSHIP

1	M. Kallio	66 (1 win)
2	T. Lüthi	54 (1 win)
3	M. Simoncelli	52 (1 win)
4	F. Lai	49
5	M. Pasini	46 (1 win)
6	G. Talmacsi	37
7	M. Poggiali	31
8	H. Faubel	30
9	J. Simón	28
10	P. Nieto	25

Beautiful verdant Tuscan scenery. It's the first lap of the Italian GP and Loris Capirossi has taken things in hand. Valentino Rossi, though, is not far behind.

05

5th June 2005

ITALY MUGELLO

Mugello, always a hot GP: in the true sense of the word, as well as the figurative...

THE MAN'S GOT BRAINS!

GRANTED AN HONORARY DOCTORATE IN COMMUNICATIONS A FEW DAYS BEFORE THIS MAGICAL ITALIAN GP, VALENTINO ROSSI ALSO REMINDED US ON THE TRACK THAT HE WAS ABSOLUTE MASTER OF THE RACE.

MOTO GP ITALY

THE RACE

A DOCTOR ON THE TRACK, AND A DOCTOR OFF IT: VALENTINO ROSSI VICTORIOUS ONCE AGAIN!

The whole thing started as a joke, told a few years earlier by Valentino Rossi. "I was just taking a look in the Tavullia area telephone directory. It's pretty much full of people called Rossi. And the surprising thing is that almost half of these people sharing my name are doctors. What did they do to deserve that? I'm starting to think I should be a doctor, too!"

We all know what happened next. The nickname of "dottore" started to be given to the champion. He pretended to be a doctor, giving his bike a full bill of health after a check-up with every win. And then we saw the shock treatment he gave to his opponents - consenting patients who couldn't escape what this impostor of a doctor had in store for them. Too late: his own good health was assured!

The seasons passed by and a great many races were won. And no two wins were the same. But Valentino Rossi continued to lay on the charm, to make people talk abut him, to annoy his rivals and to satisfy his partners.

And so he had taken on the fictitious title of "Dottore". An idea was born to involve the historic University of Urbino - the closest city to Tavullia. The 31st May 2005 saw Valentino Rossi be awarded an honorary doctorate in communications sciences from that venerable institution. Most people laughed at this new turn of events in the paddock. But this "marketing" gimmick was met with mixed feelings in intellectual circles. "It's a shame for students who have worked for years to get their doctorate", some people said. "This is not a great advertisement for the university", complained angry university lecturers.

With the formalities over, the new doctor celebrated as only he knows how. The timing was good, because that same week the Italian GP wound around the Tuscan hills of Mugello. The doctor gave another masterful showing. Right from the qualifying sessions, and through onto the race. Afterwards, he made a doctor's hat out of the chequered flag.

He went on to finish his celebrations with the crowd. He examined his "patients" on the track. He made time to carry on the party for the impatient fans crowded around his podium. Earlier in the day, Sete Gibernau crashed out in the sixth lap. His sister and his girlfriend, the supermodel Esther Cañadas, had to leave Mugello. It was a dreadful time for them. They were ferried to the hospital by helicopter. In contrast to the racetrack, there they found some peace and quiet. There, the championship runner-up of the past two years searched for the answer to a simple question - an answer he had been looking for since the last bend of the first GP of the season in Jeréz: why?

Valentino Rossi knew the answer to that. Of course he did - he's a doctor! The problem for his rivals is that not everyone gets the best prescriptions from "il dottore".

He has perfectly tamed his Yamaha M1 - with surgical precision, naturally!

Master Rossi, perched on his podium, and in his hands he held: a magnum…

ITALY MOTO GP 05

ROSSI AT THE HEAD OF A GREEN WHITE AND RED QUARTET: MOTORCYCLING DOES WELL IN ITALY.

A STRONG LINE-UP
Bad luck for Toni Elias, who suffered an injury the day after the French GP (radius and scaphoid bones in the left wrist, fracture of the left leg). Carlos Checa's brother, David, came in to replace him.

QUALIFYING
Three races in four weeks. This was an important period. Would this be the last chance for Gibernau? "No", said the Spaniard, who dominated the free qualifying sessions. But once again, he was taken by surprise by Rossi in the last round of qualifiers. Max Biaggi would start the race from the front row.

START
Capirossi, Gibernau, Checa, Rossi, Biaggi and Melandri: the race started off at a high standard. Even moreso when Rossi quickly passed Checa, then Gibernau, then Capirossi… He eventually completed the first lap with a 0.307 second lead over Sete!

LAP 2
Melandri was in second place, 0.417 secs off the leader.

LAP 4
Biaggi found a chink in Gibernau's armour. He moved into third, but was already 1.916 seconds off the leader.

LAP 6
Gibernau crashed. He didn't appear to have been concentrating at all during the race. Biaggi was in second place, 2.076s behind Rossi.

LAP 9
Biaggi accelerated to get right behind Rossi (0.158 secs). Melandri wasn't far behind. Capirossi was in fourth place. And so the top four spots were all occupied by Italians.

LAP 11
Madness broke out. Melandri was in front and Capirossi tried to make a come-back.

HALF-WAY POINT (LAP 12)
Was the natural order re-established? Rossi was once again in the lead, with 0.225 secs ahead of Biaggi. Melandri was in third place, 0.011 secs behind Max. Capirossi closed the gap to 1.055s off the top three.

LAP 15
Melandri appeared to react to what was going on around him. Rossi and Biaggi were still wheel to wheel (with 0.157 secs separating them). The Melandri-Capirossi duo were now 1.3 seconds behind the leader.

LAP 17
But we see that Rossi can be taken by surprise. Biaggi proved it by taking the lead for the first time during the race.

LAP 19
Biaggi, Rossi, Melandri, Capirossi = four Italians within 0.967 secs.

LAP 21
Rossi once again took the lead. The fight for third place between Melandri and Capirossi was almost as gripping as the fight for the lead.

FINISH (LAP 23)
0.345 secs was Rossi's lead at the end of the last lap. He didn't make even the tiniest mistake. Capirossi earned a place on the podium. The crowd swarmed onto the track - as per usual.

CHAMPIONSHIP
Rossi's lead grows to 49 points - two GPs. Melandri was still in second place, but Biaggi was gaining ground on him. The biggest loser of the day was of course Gibernau, who found himself 67 lengths away from the current…

Another triumph for Valentino Rossi, while the battle prize goes jointly to Marco Melandri (33) and Loris Capirossi (65).

ITALIAN GRAND PRIX | 5th June 2005 | Mugello | 5.245 m

STARTING GRID:

1	46	V. Rossi	Yamaha	1'49.223
2	15	S. Gibernau	Honda	1'49.361
3	3	M. Biaggi	Honda	1'49.458
4	69	N. Hayden	Honda	1'49.546
5	21	J. Hopkins	Suzuki	1'49.556
6	65	L. Capirossi	Ducati	1'49.633
7	33	M. Melandri	Honda	1'49.805
8	7	C. Checa	Ducati	1'49.811
9	56	S. Nakano	Kawasaki	1'49.856
10	6	M. Tamada	Honda	1'49.951
11	10	K. Roberts	Suzuki	1'50.052
12	5	C. Edwards	Yamaha	1'50.176
13	4	A. Barros	Honda	1'50.281
14	66	A. Hofmann	Kawasaki	1'51.056
15	11	R. Xaus	Yamaha	1'51.585
16	94	D. Checa	Yamaha	1'51.610
17	12	T. Bayliss	Honda	1'51.764
18	67	S. Byrne	Proton KR	1'52.117
19	44	R. Rolfo	Ducati	1'53.010
20	77	J. Ellison	Blata	1'54.177
21	27	F. Battaini	Blata	1'54.820

RACE: 23 laps = 120.635 km

1.	Valentino Rossi	42'42.994 (169.444 km/h)
2.	Max Biaggi	+ 0''359
3.	Loris Capirossi	+ 3''874
4.	Marco Melandri	+ 3''979
5.	Carlos Checa	+ 7''898
6.	Nicky Hayden	+ 8''204
7.	Alex Barros	+ 11''572
8.	Makoto Tamada	+ 25''394
9.	Colin Edwards	+ 25''485
10.	Shinya Nakano	+ 36''549
11.	John Hopkins	+ 41''637
12.	Alex Hofmann	+ 43''659
13.	Troy Bayliss	+ 43''916
14.	Ruben Xaus	+ 51''575
15.	Kenny Roberts	+ 1'10.275
16.	Shane Byrne	+ 1'12.582
17.	Roberto Rolfo	+ 1'13.047
18.	Franco Battaini	+ 1 lap
19.	David Checa	+ 1 lap

Fastest lap
Biaggi, in 1'50.117 (171.472 km/h). New record.
Previous record: Gibernau, in 1'51.133 (169.904 km/2004)

Outright fastest lap
Rossi, in 1'49.223 (172.875 km/h/2005).

CHAMPIONSHIP

1	V. Rossi	120 (4 wins)
2	M. Melandri	71
3	M. Biaggi	67
4	S. Gibernau	53
5	A. Barros	52 (1 win)
6	C. Edwards	48
7	L. Capirossi	39
8	N. Hayden	36
9	S. Nakano	33
10	C. Checa	28

05 250cc ITALY

PEDROSA PERFORMED FLAWLESSLY, WHILE THE UNINHIBITED LORENZO PUTS ON A SHOW.

A STRONG LINE-UP
Steve Jenkner, who had tried a comeback in France, withdrew again. His ride on the Aprilia was instead passed on to the Italian, Jarno Ronzoni, who made an occasional appearance in 2004. The Frenchman, Hugo Marchand, stayed on as the replacement for the Japanese rider, Taro Sekiguchi. Two wildcards entered this race - two big names from the European Championship from this category: the Spaniard Molina and the Austrian Yves Polzer

QUALIFYING
Mugello is the Aprilia 250 cc circuit, but the first day of qualifying saw the Honda riders were reading from a different hymnsheet (provisional pole for Stoner, in front of De Angelis and Porto). The grid was reorganised after the Saturday session, and the (generally) good surprise was that Jorge Lorenzo had the last word ahead of Stoner, Dovizioso (a good show from the new boys) and De Puniet. Porto and Barbera crashed, and Pedrosa was "only" seventh. This was not a great problem for him…

START
Pedrosa shot away like a bullet from the second line, and led into the first corner. It only took him a few hundred metres to correct his qualifying performance. The world champion was to lead right to the end of the lap, before giving up his position to De Puniet.

LAP 3
Stoner took control of the race.

LAP 6
De Puniet crashed in fourth place.

LAP 9
Dovizioso had a few problems and dropped back. Only four riders remained in the top 0.559 secs time band: Stoner, De Angelis, Pedrosa and Lorenzo.

HALF-WAY POINT (LAP 10)
Stoner was in control, 0.339 secs ahead of Alex de Angelis. Lorenzo was third, with Pedrosa right on his tail. Dovizioso rode alone just over two seconds behind them.

LAP 12
Smrz and Guintoli crashed whilst fighting for tenth place.

LAP 15
Superb riding by Lorenzo, who held off his brakes as long as possible at the end of the long straight, taking the lead. He finished his lap with a 0.120 lead over De Angelis.

LAP 16
De Angelis got a big shock. Dovizioso still had problems (tyres) and lost places, moving down the field.

LAP 17
Takahashi crashed out.

LAP 19
Pedrosa took the lead.

FINISH (LAP 21)
Pedrosa won 0.526 secs ahead of De Angelis. He didn't make a single mistake, even though he came under heavy pressure throughout the last lap. Lorenzo let leash an attack he had been saving up and took De Angelis by surprise. He managed to hold on to his third place under pressure from Stoner.

CHAMPIONSHIP
This was the first good performance from the outgoing champion, Pedrosa, who came out with a 21 point lead over Dovizioso and a 22 point lead over Stoner.

De Angelis, Pedrosa, Lorenzo: the race started with the bar set high. It ended with a Spanish double, with Lorenzo (above) the heir apparent to the outgoing champion, Daniel Pedrosa.

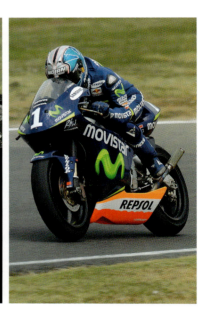

ITALIAN GRAND PRIX | 5th June 2005 | Mugello | 5.245 m

STARTING GRID

1	48	J. Lorenzo	Honda	1'53.494
2	27	C. Stoner	Aprilia	1'53.548
3	34	A. Dovizioso	Honda	1'53.674
4	7	R. De Puniet	Aprilia	1'53.714
5	5	A. De Angelis	Aprilia	1'53.841
6	19	S. Porto	Aprilia	1'53.889
7	1	D. Pedrosa	Honda	1'53.991
8	80	H. Barbera	Honda	1'54.800
9	73	H. Aoyama	Honda	1'54.815
10	8	A. Ballerini	Aprilia	1'54.971
11	96	J. Smrz	Honda	1'55.054
12	24	S. Corsi	Aprilia	1'55.111
13	55	Y. Takahashi	Honda	1'55.205
14	50	S. Guintoli	Aprilia	1'55.378
15	25	A. Baldolini	Aprilia	1'55.676
16	15	R. Locatelli	Aprilia	1'55.794
17	57	C. Davies	Aprilia	1'55.879
18	32	M. Giansanti	Aprilia	1'55.885
19	9	H. Marchand	Aprilia	1'57.032
20	38	G. Leblanc	Aprilia	1'57.213
21	28	D. Heidolf	Honda	1'57.395
22	71	J. Ronzoni	Aprilia	1'57.668
23	64	R. Rous	Honda	1'57.794
24	42	Y. Polzer	Aprilia	1'57.803
25	21	A. Vincent	Fantic	1'57.846
26	6	A. Debon	Honda	1'58.019
27	12	G. Rizmayer	Yamaha	1'58.372
28	41	A. Molina	Aprilia	1'58.399
29	18	F. Watz	Yamaha	1'58.636
30	36	M. Cardeñas	Aprilia	1'59.689
Not qualified:				
	20	G. Ferro	Fantic	2'03.009

RACE: 21 laps = 110.145 km

1. Daniel Pedrosa		40'31.909 (163.049 km/h)
2. Jorge Lorenzo		+ 1''186
3. Alex De Angelis		+ 1''557
4. Casey Stoner		+ 1''590
5. Sebastian Porto		+ 6''106
6. Hector Barbera		+ 8''291
7. Hiroshi Aoyama		+ 11''801
8. Andrea Dovizioso		+ 11''869
9. Simone Corsi		+ 21''975
10. Chaz Davies		+ 42''381
11. Andrea Ballerini		+ 42''499
12. Mirko Giansanti		+ 43''082
13. Radomil Rous		+ 1'06.264
14. Gregory Leblanc		+ 1'16.905
15. Hugo Marchand		+ 1'28.269
16. Alvaro Molina		+ 1'31.411
17. Martin Cardeñas		+ 1'35.652
18. Jarno Ronzoni		+ 1'39.461

Fastest lap
De Angelis, in 1'54.332 (165.150 km/h). New record.
Previous record: Nakano, in 1'54.462 (164.963 km/h/2004).

Outright fastest lap
Lorenzo, in 1'53.457 (166.424 km/h/2004).

CHAMPIONSHIP

1	D. Pedrosa	98 (3 wins)
2	A. Dovizioso	77
2	C. Stoner	76 (2 wins)
4	A. De Angelis	56
5	J. Lorenzo	54
6	S. Porto	49
7	H. Aoyama	45
8	H. Barbera	44
9	R. De Puniet	36
10	S. Corsi	27

ITALY 125cc 05

KALLIO AND FAUBEL FALL IN THE FINAL TURN, TALMACSI AND LÜTHI LAUGH!

A STRONG LINE-UP
Sascha Hommel (Malaguti) couldn't make a come-back, and Gioele Pellino rode a bike which had undergone a number of recent developments. Five Italian riders entered on wildcards, including the leaders of the European Championship (Michele Conti) and the Italian Championship (Lorenzo Baroni).

QUALIFYING
The KTM riders were on form - particularly Mika Kallio, who dominated both the Friday and Saturday sessions. On the last lap of the last day, only the Swiss rider, Thomas Lüthi seemed able to keep up with the Finn over two-thirds of the circuit before making a mistake. He ended up in sixth place.

START
Kallio made the best start from the front line of the grid. Lüthi did very well in second and immediately came up behind the Finn. Talmacsi would soon give the Swiss rider a surprise, though. At the end of the first lap, Kallio had a 0.296 secs lead over Pasini, who was ahead of Lüthi by 0.015 secs, with Lai, Talmacsi and Simoncelli coming up behind them.

LAP 3
Kallio, Simoncelli, Faubel, Lüthi and Talmacsi - all five of them rode within 0.827 secs of each other. A gap had started to form behind them, after which Pasini led the chasing group. The Hungarian rider's KTM was 1.6 seconds behind the leaders.

LAP 6
Lüthi was now in second place behind Kallio, and overtook to gain the lead at the end of the straight

LAP 8
Pesek crashed.

HALF-WAY POINT (LAP 10)
The same five stayed in their respective positions - Kallio, Faubel, Lüthi, Simoncelli and Talmacsi, with 0.848 secs between them. Pasini was in sixth place, trying to fend off Koyama, but was now 3.259 seconds off the leading group.

LAP 12
Simoncelli crashed. 0.105 secs separated Kallio and Faubel. Lüthi momentarily dropped back, but then came back to stick to Faubel's trail.

LAP 15
The pace of the race slowed down. The chess game began, but the leader at this point in the proceedings would not be the eventual winner! (Faubel was in the lead).

LAP 18
Di Meglio crashed

FINISH (LAP 20)
Kallio went on the attack in the last lap, leading Faubel and Lüthi by 0.6 seconds. Kallio knew he made a mistake on the last corner. He accelerated too hard coming out of the turn. He lost control of his rear wheel, and the Finn came to earth with a bump. Faubel couldn't avoid the collision and both men were out of the race (the riders suffered concussion, but there were no serious injuries) and in the sand trap. Talmacsi gained his first win, 0.06 secs ahead of Lüthi

CHAMPIONSHIP
Five races, five different winners: this category rewards regular high scorers, and Lüthi led the championship rankings for the first time. He managed to compensate for his only zero (a mechanical problem in Jeréz).

In the lead until the final turn, Mika Kallio (KTM 36) would crash out. His team-mate Talmacsi goes past Lüthi, the two passing over the line sharing the same joy.

ITALIAN GRAND PRIX | 5th June 2005 | Mugello | 5.245 m

STARTING GRID

1	36	M. Kallio	KTM	1'58.662
2	14	G. Talmacsi	KTM	1'59.152
3	55	H. Faubel	Aprilia	1'59.712
4	75	M. Pasini	Aprilia	1'59.776
5	58	M. Simoncelli	Aprilia	1'59.796
6	12	T. Lüthi	Honda	1'59.947
7	61	M. Conti	Honda	2'00.037
8	60	J. Simón	KTM	2'00.152
9	32	F. Lai	Honda	2'00.178
10	52	L. Pesek	Derbi	2'00.203
11	63	M. Di Meglio	Honda	2'00.387
12	47	A. Rodriguez	Honda	2'00.493
13	6	J. Olivé	Aprilia	2'00.519
14	9	T. Kuzuhara	Honda	2'00.572
15	33	S. Gadea	Aprilia	2'00.599
16	8	L. Zanetti	Aprilia	2'00.623
17	54	M. Poggiali	Gilera	2'00.664
18	15	M. Pirro	Malaguti	2'00.716
19	91	L. Baroni	Aprilia	2'00.718
20	71	T. Koyama	Honda	2'00.931
21	35	R. De Rosa	Aprilia	2'00.964
22	7	A. Masbou	Honda	2'00.982
23	41	A. Espargaro	Honda	2'00.995
24	93	N. Vivarelli	Hondda	2'01.101
25	84	J. Miralles	Aprilia	2'01.168 (*)
26	42	G. Pellino	Malaguti	2'01.170
27	11	S. Cortese	Honda	2'01.275
28	22	P. Nieto	Derbi	2'01.312
29	43	M. Hernandez	Aprilia	2'01.392
30	19	A. Bautista	Honda	2'01.397
31	29	A. Iannone	Aprilia	2'01.445
32	16	R. Schouten	Honda	2'01.571
33	45	I. Toth	Aprilia	2'01.596
34	28	J. Carchano	Aprilia	2'01.680
35	18	N. Terol	Derbi	2'02.065
36	25	D. Giuseppetti	Aprilia	2'02.210
37	44	K. Abraham	Aprilia	2'02.422
38	92	L. Verdini	Aprilia	2'02.887
39	62	S. Grotzki Giorgi	Aprilia	2'03.321
40	10	F. Sandi	Honda	2'03.659
41	26	V. Braillard	Aprilia	2'03.749

(*)Having fallen on Saturday afternoon, J. Miralles (E, Aprilia)is forced to pull out with a broken right shinbone)

RACE: 20 laps = 104.900 km

1.	Gabor Talmacsi	40'12.658 (156.524 km/h)
2.	Thomas Lüthi	+ 0''060
3.	Joan Olivé	+ 14''713
4.	Mattia Pasini	+ 14''725
5.	Tomoyoshi Koyama	+ 15''079
6.	Manuel Poggiali	+ 18''040
7.	Julian Simón	+ 18''200
8.	Fabrizio Lai	+ 18''683
9.	Toshihisa Kuzuhara	+ 20''133
10.	Alexis Masbou	+ 20''311
11.	Michele Conti	+ 28''626
12.	Alvaro Bautista	+ 31''791
13.	Manuel Hernandez	+ 31''817
14.	Lorenzo Zanetti	+ 34''742
15.	Raffaele De Rosa	+ 34''752
16.	Andrea Iannone	+ 45''303
17.	Aleix Espargaro	+ 45''410
18.	Dario Giuseppetti	+ 48''459
19.	Michele Pirro	+ 48''510
20.	Gioele Pellino	+ 48''615
21.	Nicolas Terol	+ 49''412
22.	Pablo Nieto	+ 49''450
23.	Jordi Carchano	+ 53''125
24.	Lorenzo Baroni	+ 1'02.887
25.	Imre Toth	+ 1'05.235
26.	Raymond Schouten	+ 1'05.289
27.	Karel Abraham	+ 1'05.307
28.	Vincent Braillard	+ 1'07.881
29.	Luca Verdini	+ 1'38.237

Fastest lap
Faubel, in 1'59.464 (158.055 km/h).
Record: Borsoi, in 1'58.969 (158.713/2003).
Outright fastest lap
Jenkner, in 1'58.575 (159.240 km/h/2004).

CHAMPIONSHIP

1	T. Lüthi	74 (1 win)
2	M. Kallio	66 (1 win)
3	G. Talmacsi	62 (1 win)
4	M. Pasini	59 (1 win)
5	F. Lai	57
6	M. Simoncelli	52 (1 win)
7	M. Poggiali	41
8	J. Simón	37
9	T. Koyama	32
10	H. Faubel	30

Barcelona supporting Madrid 2012 (in vain, it would be London that would win it!), a record crowd at the Catalunya circuit.

06
12th June 2005
CATALUNYA CATALUNYA

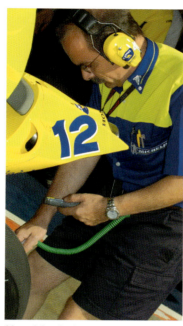

Men of the shadows...

SETE: BRUISES ON HIS SOUL

ON HIS HOME GROUND, IN FRONT OF HIS FANS, THIS CATALUNYA GP COULD ONLY BE SETE GIBERNAU'S. DESPITE THIS, IT ROSSI TRIUMPHED AGAIN. IN THE SPANISH MEDIA, THE CALL WENT UP: WE WANT PEDROSA!

06 MOTO GP CATALUNYA

THE RACE

> GIBERNAU WANTED IT, BUT ONCE AGAIN, HE COULDN'T DO IT.
> IN HIS SPANISH RIVAL'S TERRITORY, ROSSI STRUCK.

Saturday, 11th June 2005, a few minutes past three in the afternoon. Fausto Gresini, the Movistar-Honda chief is all smiles. His two drivers, Sete Gibernau and Marco Melandri just made the best two qualifying session times for the Catalunya GP. Better yet, they opened up a significant gap (0.4 secs) in front of the big rival - Valentino Rossi. Performing in front of his home crowd and surrounded by an increasingly large fan base, Gibernau had a good idea that the time was right for him to strike. He knew - he could feel it - that he could make this weekend his own. For the first time in many long months, he had the opportunity to win against a man who was no longer his friend.

What Sete Gibernau didn't know is that ever since the business at the 2004 Qatar GP (which put an end to the friendship by the two riders who had been dominating the championship), Valentino Rossi had sworn that the dark blue colours of the Movistar team would never finish a race in front of him. And he kept to his word. The emergence of Marco Melandri, a childhood friend of Rossi was not intended to displease His Majesty Valentino the First. Firstly, he was already well aware that Marco was not yet in a position to pose a serious threat to him during the Championship. Also - and above all - he had already guessed that the progress made by the number 2 rider from Fausto Gresini's team could only provoke tension and annoyance in his rival's camp. This would affect the only driver that Rossi still feared: Sete Gibernau.

And there we have it. Sete - having emerged as such a

Thursday's press conference: Rossi talks, Gibernau ignores. Sunday's race: Vale wins, Sete rages.

strength over recent years hadn't changed much, even though he made great demands of himself. Swept up in the media frenzy that accompanies every hero that emerges into the limelight, Gibernau' concentration was being distracted. Or to be more precise, his attention was spread across a great many things, because the man is very good-natured and finds it very difficult to say no. For goodness' sake, he's having a nice life courting the most sought-after supermodel in Spain - Esther Cañadas - and constantly having his favourite little sister cheering him on from the sidelines. But he did have some insidious troubles. This point in the season marked eight consecutive races without a win for Gibernau. He simply couldn't make any headway against Valentino Rossi, who had taken half a season's lead over his rival. But this weekend, he wanted revenge. Sete wanted to win again in front of the crowd, who were all draped in blue. Unfortunately, it wasn't to be. Even the Spanish stands held fewer Sete fans than usual - the ultimate insult - as almost as many Italian tifosi decked in yellow were there as blue Sete fans. And of course, once the Melandri problem had been sorted out, Valentino Rossi would once again turn his attention to Gibernau. Once again, Rossi would win after his usual strategic attack. Valentino would pounce when and where he wanted. In the parade. His move went perfectly So Sete had to suffer the indignity of saying how satisfied he was with second place, because that is the way it is done. He went back to his family - his father, his mother, his sister and the supermodel. Better company for him than the blues…

The Gibernau-Rossi duel, on the track and on the big screen. The Spaniard did his job, but it wasn't enough.

CATALUNYA MOTO GP   06

An all-blue podium… but always the same winner: Valentino Rossi.

ROSSI, GIBERNAU, MELANDRI: MOTOGP HAS BEEN TURNED BLUE THIS SEASON.

A STRONG LINE-UP
The prize for bravery rightfully returned to Toni Elias who had a real desire to start "his" GP, even though he had suffered a serious setback through injury (he crashed the day after the French GP during testing in Le Mans). He tried his luck on the Friday, but left his M! in the hands of David Checa for the rest of the weekend

QUALIFYING
Marco Melandri was unstoppable. On paper at least, the young Italian was the top Honda rider in the championship. The young man went into qualifying with all guns blazing, and emerged 0.053 secs ahead of his more prominent colleague Sete Gibernau. Rossi was the other man on the front row, Biaggi missed out due to a misunderstanding with his technical team when his second set of tyres were being fitted for qualifying.

START
Gibernau, Melandri and Biaggi got off to the best starts. Rossi put in a brilliant lap, ending up just behind Gibernau.

LAP 3
Gibernau nudged Melandri's rear wheel and put him off his stride. His teammate started to scrap for position with Rossi. Barros, Hayden, Biaggi and Tamada were still in the running.

LAP 5
Rossi was late braking at the end of the straight and took the lead. Gibernau knew he didn't want to just let this happen and made sure he stuck close to the world champion, staying in his slipstream.

LAP 6
Tamada crashed. Gibernau took a 0.222 second lead.

LAP 10
Gibernau extended his lead to 0.718 seconds during the course of this lap, consolidating his position.

HALF-WAY POINT (LAP 12)
The pace was still very intense, with the lap record being consistently beaten by a full second. Gibernau was 0.583 secs ahead of Rossi. Hayden was in third place (at 1.733 secs behind the lead), while Melandri was in the fourth spot, still scrapping it out with Barros. Biaggi rode alone in sixth position. Hofman made a pitstop to change a tyre

LAP 14
It was Hopkins' turn to go into the pits for a fresh set of tyres. Rossi closed the gap behind the leader to 0.290 seconds

LAP 17
Melandri went into third place. The gap between Gibernau and Rossi stood at 0.4 seconds. Hopkins goes off the track.

LAP 23
Rossi took the lead at the end of the straight, setting a lap record into the bargain: gaining a 0.271 second lead! Melandri and Barros passed Hayden

FINISH (LAP 25)
0.367 secs stood between the leaders over the last lap. This turned into 1.094 secs when the chequered flag signalled the end of the race. Valentino Rossi really was unbeatable. Melandri had the last word to claim third place

CHAMPIONSHIP
145 points for Rossi, 87 for Melandri - 5 wins and a second place over six races. What more is there to say?

CATALUNYAN GRAND PRIX | 12th June 2005 | Catalunya | 4.727 m

STARTING GRID				
1	15	S. Gibernau	Honda	1'42.337
2	33	M. Melandri	Honda	1'42.390
3	46	V. Rossi	Yamaha	1'42.723
4	3	M. Biaggi	Honda	1'42.756
5	69	N. Hayden	Honda	1'42.847
6	65	L. Capirossi	Ducati	1'42.992
7	5	C. Edwards	Yamaha	1'43.109
8	7	C. Checa	Ducati	1'43.129
9	4	A. Barros	Honda	1'43.159
10	6	M. Tamada	Honda	1'43.207
11	21	J. Hopkins	Suzuki	1'43.291
12	56	S. Nakano	Kawasaki	1'43.607
13	10	K. Roberts	Suzuki	1'43.787
14	66	A. Hofmann	Kawasaki	1'43.864
15	12	T. Bayliss	Honda	1'44.122
16	11	R. Xaus	Yamaha	1'44.193
17	44	R. Rolfo	Ducati	1'44.934
18	94	D. Checa	Yamaha	1'45.310
19	67	S. Byrne	Proton KR	1'45.636
20	77	J. Ellison	Blata	1'46.750
21	27	F. Battaini	Blata	1'47.599

RACE: 25 laps = 118.175 km		
1	Valentino Rossi	43'16.487 (163.848 km/h)
2	Sete Gibernau	+ 1''094
3	Marco Melandri	+ 7''810
4	Alex Barros	+ 8''204
5	Nicky Hayden	+ 8''273
6	Max Biaggi	+ 12''051
7	Colin Edwards	+ 18''762
8	Troy Bayliss	+ 42''631
9	Shinya Nakano	+ 46''638
10	Ruben Xaus	+ 46''692
11	Carlos Checa	+ 1'00.357
12	Loris Capirossi	+ 1'03.864
13	David Checa	+ 1'03.985
14	Roberto Rolfo	+ 1'10.258
15	Kenny Roberts	+ 1'23.731
16	Shane Byrne	+ 1'34.624
17	Alex Hofmann	+ 1 tour
18	James Ellison	+ 1 tour
19	Franco Battaini	+ 1 tour

Fastest lap
Rossi, in 1'43.195 (164.903 km/h). New record.
Previous: Gibernau, in 1'44.641 (162.624 km/h/2004).

Outright fastest lap
Gibernau, in 1'42.337 (166.285 km/h/2005).

CHAMPIONSHIP		
1	V. Rossi	145 (5 wins)
2	M. Melandri	87
3	M. Biaggi	77
4	S. Gibernau	73
5	A. Barros	65 (1 win)
6	C. Edwards	57
7	N. Hayden	47
8	L. Capirossi	43
9	S. Nakano	40
10	C. Checa	33

06 250cc CATALUNYA

A PERFECT RACE BY DANI PEDROSA, THE REAL NUMBER 1 IN SPANISH MOTORCYCLE RACING.

A STRONG LINE-UP
Steve Jenkner made his come-back. Taro Sekiguchi was still absent (and still replaced by Hugo Marchand). Erwan Nigon, rode the Honda of Keifer team usually ridden by the German Dirk Heidolf. No wildcards entered this race (a European Championship race was held at Rijeka on the same weekend).

QUALIFYING
Jorge Lorenzo had absolutely no inhibitions, he said "anyone can catch Pedrosa by surprise in the braking areas - the problem lies in keeping up with him!". His actions on the track matched his words, as he made the best time of the weekend. The world champion made everybody talk on Saturday, producing a Spanish Honda double. There was a terrible crash on Saturday morning for the 125 cc championship-holder, the Italian Andrea Dovizioso, who ended up with very bruised. He withdrew from the second qualifying session, but would take part in the race itself.

START
Randy de Puniet made a perfect start, setting off in the lead ahead of Barbera, Porto and Aoyama. Pedrosa could just make eleventh place at this point, after a bad start. The Frenchman was 0.235 secs ahead of the Spaniard at the end of the first lap.

LAP 2
Porto crashed. De Puniet - Barbera were riding wheel to wheel, with De Angelis in third place, 0.8 secs slower. Pedrosa had already climbed to sixth place by this time.

LAP 3
De Puniet crashed, but rejoined the race. Aoyama went out into the sand trap. Barbera was in the lead, 0.251 secs ahead of De Angelis. Lorenzo and Pedrosa followed.

LAP 4
De Angelis took the lead.

LAP 6
Smrz crashed.

LAP 10
Seven riders were bunched together across 1.341 secs: it has been a long time since that has happened in this category. De Angelis still held off the Spaniards Barbera, Lorenzo and Pedrosa respectively).

LAP 11
Alex de Angelis crashed, after colliding with Lorenzo. Pedrosa was 0.942 ahead of Barbera. Corsi was in third place. De Puniet got into a point-scoring position (15th).

HALF-WAY POINT (LAP 12)
The 105,698 crowd was on its feet: Pedrosa was 1.887 secs ahead of Barbera, who followed Stoner.

LAP 16
Corsi and Barbera went into the straight at high speed. Pedrosa stayed in front and in control.

LAP 18
Barbera suddenly slowed down, as his bike developed problems. De Puniet regained ninth position.

FINISH LAP (23 LAPS)
Dani Pedrosa was definitely the strongest rider. It was just another perfect race for the world champion. Stoner could only look on in admiration. We should also doff our caps to Andrea Dovizioso, who fought on through his pain.

CHAMPIONSHIP
123 points for Pedrosa - 96 for Stoner. That gave the outgoing champion a whole race to spare - even before the halfway mark in the season.

Pedrosa all alone (above): not the case for Yuko Takahashi and Sylvain Guintoli (50), who battled all weekend.

CATALUNYAN GRAND PRIX | 12th June 2005 | Catalunya | 4.727 m

STARTING GRID

1	1	D. Pedrosa	Honda	1'46.238
2	48	J. Lorenzo	Honda	1'46.617
3	19	S. Porto	Aprilia	1'46.706
4	7	R. De Puniet	Aprilia	1'46.825
5	73	H. Aoyama	Honda	1'47.082
6	5	A. De Angelis	Aprilia	1'47.090
7	80	H. Barbera	Honda	1'47.454
8	27	C. Stoner	Aprilia	1'47.486
9	34	A. Dovizioso	Honda	1'47.495
10	24	S. Corsi	Aprilia	1'47.650
11	50	S. Guintoli	Aprilia	1'48.207
12	55	Y. Takahashi	Honda	1'48.217
13	96	J. Smrz	Honda	1'48.661
14	17	S. Jenkner	Aprilia	1'48.961
15	57	C. Davies	Aprilia	1'49.012
16	32	M. Giansanti	Aprilia	1'49.126
17	8	A. Ballerini	Aprilia	1'49.132
18	6	A. Debon	Honda	1'49.150
19	25	A. Baldolini	Aprilia	1'49.178
20	63	E. Nigon	Honda	1'49.185
21	9	H. Marchand	Aprilia	1'49.204
22	15	R. Locatelli	Aprilia	1'49.277
23	38	G. Leblanc	Aprilia	1'49.974
24	21	A. Vincent	Fantic	1'50.135
25	36	M. Cardeñas	Aprilia	1'50.499
26	64	R. Rous	Honda	1'50.618 (*)
27	18	F. Watz	Yamaha	1'50.995
28	12	G. Rizmayer	Yamaha	1'51.966
29	20	G. Ferro	Fantic	1'53.459

(*) Having fallen on Saturday during the free practice, R. Rous (CZ, Honda) is forced to pull out with a broken left wrist.

RACE: 23 laps = 108.721 km

1	Daniel Pedrosa	41'29.428 (157.223 km/h)
2	Casey Stoner	+ 5''637
3	Andrea Dovizioso	+ 10''597
4	Hiroshi Aoyama	+ 17''638
5	Simone Corsi	+ 19''499
6	Randy De Puniet	+ 33''235
7	Yuko Takahashi	+ 37''408
8	Sylvain Guintoli	+ 37''530
9	Mirko Giansanti	+ 42''814
10	Alex Baldolini	+ 43''611
11	Alex Debon	+ 43''891
12	Roberto Locatelli	+ 45''800
13	Erwan Nigon	+ 58''190
14	Hugo Marchand	+ 1'04.356
15	Gregory Leblanc	+ 1'04.399
16	Hector Barbera	+ 1'19.129
17	Martin Cardeñas	+ 1'20.909
18	Frederik Watz	+ 1'35.685
19	Steve Jenkner	+ 1 lap
20	Gabor Rizmayer	+ 1 lap
21	Gabriele Ferro	+ 1 lap

Fastest lap
Pedrosa, in 1'47.373 (158.486 km/h).
Record: Pedrosa, in 1'47.302 (158.591 km/h/2004).

Outright fastest lap
Lorenzo, in 1'46.220 (160.207 km/h/2005).

CHAMPIONSHIP

1	D. Pedrosa	123 (4 wins)
2	C. Stoner	96 (2 wins)
3	A. Dovizioso	93
4	H. Aoyama	58
5	A. De Angelis	56
6	J. Lorenzo	54
7	S. Porto	49
8	R. De Puniet	46
9	H. Barbera	44
10	S. Corsi	38

CATALUNYA 125cc 06

Bradl Sr. and son (Helmut and Stefan) discover the GPs. On the podium, Pasini, who everyone forgot about, can be proud of his work.

LIKE LÜTHI IN FRANCE, PASINI HAD A LONELY RUN OUT FRONT IN CATALUNYA.

A STRONG LINE-UP
Hommel still wouldn't make an appearance. He was busy building up his confidence in the European Championship). Another absentee was the unfortunate Julian Miralles, who was seriously injured at Mugello and did not receive all the treatment he needed when he was admitted to hospital in Florence. A number of wildcards entered the race - among them the young Stefan Bradl (the son of Helmut Bradl - one of the driving forces behind the 250 cc competition in the nineties) and Michael Ranseder - an Austrian rider competing in the German and the European Championships (both riders competing in the KTM Junior team).

QUALIFYING
Pasini had made the best time during the IRTA qualifiers this spring. He was the fastest during Friday's session, before Mika Kallio stope the best time on the Saturday (the 4th pole position for the Finn). The ten fastest riders were less than a second apart, and the world leader - the Swiss rider - was at the back of this group.

START
Lüthi arrived to take the lead after starting from the third row, beating Kallio, Lai and Pasini. The rider had a 0.619 second lead over Pasini at the end of the first lap, followed by Kallio, Talmacsi and Lai.

LAP 2
Pablo Nieto crashed. Pasini took the lead ahead of Lüthi and the three official KTMs (Kallio, Simón and Talmasci, respectively).

LAP 3
Braillard crashed

LAP 5
Pasini increased his lead to 0.885 secs over Lüthi, followed by Kallio, Simón and Faubel. Talmacsi was in sixth position, sitting at the back of the leading group.

LAP 9
Pasini was still in front. Kallio was 1.180 secs behind him. Lüthi broke away from the pack, but would shortly lose his third place to Faubel. Simoncelli moved his way up the field into the chasing group, which still included Talmacsi and Simón.

HALF-WAY (LAP 11)
Faubel retired from the race. Pasini was the strongest man on the track. He managed to extend his lead to 2.399 secs over Kallio. Simoncelli was in third place, over three seconds behind the Finn, and was closely followed by Talmacsi. Lüthi and Simón fought over fifth place.

LAP 16
Simoncelli overtook Kallio. And so the race had two Aprilias in the lead. Behind them, Koyama took advantage of problems between Simón and Lüthi to take fifth place.

FINISH (22 LAPS)
Pasini completed a perfect lap, as did Simoncelli -but he had lost too much time at the start of the race- Kallio was in 3rd place.

CHAMPIONSHIP
This was a perfect illustration of the balance of power. The top 5 in the provisional listings were only separated by 12 points. Mattia Pasini took the lead over Lüthi by a single point. Likewise, Lüthi only led Kallio by the same margin. And so we look forward to Assen!

CATALUNYAN GRAND PRIX | 12th June 2005 | Catalunya | 4.727 m

GRILLE DE DÉPART

1	36	M. Kallio	KTM	1'51.451
2	75	M. Pasini	Aprilia	1'51.515
3	58	M. Simoncelli	Aprilia	1'51.562
4	8	L. Zanetti	Aprilia	1'51.949
5	9	T. Kuzuhara	Honda	1'52.005
6	14	G. Talmacsi	KTM	1'52.052
7	55	H. Faubel	Aprilia	1'52.056
8	32	F. Lai	Honda	1'52.223
9	54	M. Poggiali	Gilera	1'52.285
10	12	T. Lüthi	Honda	1'52.407
11	22	P. Nieto	Derbi	1'52.579
12	71	T. Koyama	Honda	1'52.586
13	60	J. Simón	KTM	1'52.598
14	52	L. Pesek	Derbi	1'52.605
15	33	S. Gadea	Aprilia	1'52.805
16	19	A. Bautista	Honda	1'52.918
17	29	A. Iannone	Aprilia	1'52.963
18	63	M. Di Meglio	Honda	1'52.985
19	43	M. Hernandez	Aprilia	1'52.990
20	7	A. Masbou	Honda	1'53.031
21	76	M. Ranseder	KTM	1'53.073
22	25	D. Giuseppetti	Aprilia	1'53.222
23	86	M. Tuñez	Aprilia	1'53.272
24	41	A. Espargaro	Honda	1'53.319
25	35	R. De Rosa	Aprilia	1'53.331
26	16	R. Schouten	Honda	1'53.465
27	6	J. Olivé	Aprilia	1'53.511
28	18	N. Terol	Derbi	1'53.617
29	28	J. Carchano	Aprilia	1'53.629
30	42	G. Pellino	Malaguti	1'53.746
31	11	S. Cortese	Honda	1'53.813
32	47	A. Rodriguez	Honda	1'53.873
33	77	S. Bradl	KTM	1'53.880
34	10	F. Sandi	Honda	1'54.111
35	26	V. Braillard	Aprilia	1'54.256
36	15	M. Pirro	Malaguti	1'54.377
37	51	E. Jerez	Derbi	1'54.546
38	49	D. Saez	Aprilia	1'54.779
39	78	H. Van den Berg	Aprilia	1'54.849
40	45	I. Toth	Aprilia	1'55.022
41	44	K. Abraham	Aprilia	2'02.422

COURSE: 22 tours = 103.994 km

1	Mattia Pasini	41'15.125 (151.256 km/h)
2	Marco Simoncelli	+ 9''034
3	Mika Kallio	+ 12''408
4	Gabor Talmacsi	+ 18''256
5	Tomoyoshi Koyama	+ 18''440
6	Manuel Poggiali	+ 18''544
7	Thomas Lüthi	+ 21''460
8	Julian Simón	+ 21''566
9	Lorenzo Zanetti	+ 29''029
10	Fabrizio Lai	+ 29''471
11	Andrea Iannone	+ 30''483
12	Michael Ranseder	+ 35''214
13	Sergio Gadea	+ 38''639
14	Alvaro Bautista	+ 39''559
15	Aleix Espargaro	+ 44''218
16	Mike Di Meglio	+ 44''228
17	Dario Giuseppetti	+ 50''251
18	Federico Sandi	+ 51''219
19	Mateo Tuñez	+ 51''227
20	Angel Rodriguez	+ 55''449
21	Toshihisa Kuzuhara	+ 55''469
22	Raffaele De Rosa	+ 55''504
23	Sandro Cortese	+ 1'01.121
24	Daniel Saez	+ 1'01.933
25	Raymond Schouten	+ 1'02.622
26	Manuel Hernandez	+ 1'04.894
27	Jordi Carchano	+ 1'10.672
28	Gioele Pellino	+ 1'15.210
29	Hugo Van den Berg	+ 1'47.881

Fastest lap
Kallio, in 1'51.744 (152.287 km/h).
Record: Barbera, in 1'50.903 (153.442/2004).

Outright fastest lap
Pedrosa, in 1'50.178 (154.451 km/h/2003).

CHAMPIONSHIP

1	M. Pasini	84 (2 wins)
2	T. Lüthi	83 (1 win)
3	M. Kallio	82 (1 win)
4	G. Talmacsi	75 (1 win)
5	M. Simoncelli	72 (1 win)
6	F. Lai	63
7	M. Poggiali	51
8	J. Simón	45
9	T. Koyama	43
10	H. Faubel	30

A high-voltage scene in the chicane: Rossi leads, ahead of Capirossi.

07
25th June 2005
THE NETHERLANDS ASSEN

Orange is KTM's colour. It is also the colour of the Netherlands, and of Assen, where each year fans from dozens of different countries gather.

MAX: A BITTER BIRTHDAY

EVERY YEAR AT ASSEN, MASSIMILIANO "MAX" BIAGGI CELEBRATES HIS BIRTHDAY. AFTER THE CAKE, THOUGH, THINGS WENT DOWNHILL: HE WAS SLAPPED WITH TWO SEPARATE FINES.

MOTO GP NETHERLANDS

THE RACE

> MAX BIAGGI LOSES GRIP ON THE TRACK; HIS UNCLE VALERIO LOSES HIS COOL IN THE STANDS.

Biaggi, the chef and Hayden: when everything was still going well...

When Max attacks.
To what end?

The Netherlands GP is special for Massimiliano Biaggi. Set for the last Saturday of June, the *"Dutch TT"* falls within a few days of the Italian quadruple world champion's birthday. Every year, he shares a cake with his close friends, his family – with his father, Piero, in the role of genial comic, the perfect caricature of an Italian man of a certain age – while his Uncle Valerio is his biggest fan, bursting with enthusiasm. So far, so good.
andnd so Max was there, smiling at what he wanted to achieve, reigniting all his hopes. But it wasn't to be. Worse – he was kidding himself. Because Max, who had already performed rather poorly over recent seasons – he was the first victim of the extravagant arrival of Valentino Rossi in the category of champions – knew that he was in the perfect position: the number one status for HRC he had coveted for so long, the support of Erv Kanemoto that he had demanded. It was perfectly positioned, but the results were late in coming. Rossi had been uncatchable since the beginning of the season. A Honda rider was the winner of one race up to that point, but unfortunately for Max, it was *"only"* Alex Barros, who was defending the colours of a related team.
The flair just wasn't there. Frequent good performances? Once again, no. The best Honda rider of the Championship, supplanting the stellar talent of Gibernau, was Marco Melandri. Another Italian, and another direct rival for Max – another boy with absolutely no shyness about him and who was now putting Max in the shade as far as the media and the public were concerned.
Was the Roman Emperor on the verge of definitively stepping down from his throne? But if that's what you think, then you don't know Max. Max would never back down without a fight. But who was to start making mistakes on the track – in Friday afternoon's qualifying session – and who would find themselves at the centre of a scandal at the weekend when, during the qualifying sessions, Uncle Valerio would get out his claws (both literally and figuratively) when meeting Melandri, who dared elbow his way in at the most crucial moments of these qualifications.
And so Massimiliano received a penalty (5000 dollars for *"irresponsible conduct, placing other riders in danger"*, and 1000 more dollars for *"having tried to start on the track before the flag was waved"*). And so Valerio was sent back to the paddock (and was banned from coming on the track for the rest of the year!). And to think Max wanted to run out under glory for his family. Instead he had to defend his family. He gravely stated: *"This is the worst thing that could have happened. First of all, there was the thing with Melandri on the track, and then there was my uncle's hot-headed reaction. He argued a bit too strongly with the Telefonica rider. Then there was the fine from the race management. I'm not going to apologise for my uncle's behaviour. He reacted instinctively. He was only trying to defend me. Valerio is the best, most honest man that you could ever meet"*. Max's world gets more constrictive week by week.

NETHERLANDS MOTO GP 07

Gibernau celebrates his 150th GP, David Checa finds himself in MotoGP.

VALENTINO ROSSI AGAIN, MARCO MELANDRI ALREADY. THE OTHER STARS ARE SUFFERING...

A STRONG LINE-UP:
"Toni understood that there was no point trying to defy the laws of nature. Hofman and Tamada were essential for almost six weeks. There was no reason why he should return within three." Hervé Poncheral, the Fortuna Yamaha team boss, confirmed that Elias would once more be replaced by David Checa.

QUALIFYING:
A fresh demonstration of flair and style came from Rossi. The front row was entirely blue (Gibernau was in second and Melandri in third). Everybody talked about Max Biaggi a lot on the Friday qualifying session. The Roman bungled his first chance in the chicane and made Battaini fall off his bike. He then had to do a qualifying lap before the session finished, provoking the ire of Marco Melandri, who had to go into the sand trap to avoid him. But it wasn't over yet. Two men would exchange strong words...before Max's uncle, Valerio Biaggi, would come and enter the fray.

START:
The skies cleared, allowing some rays of sunshine to break through. Melandri, Gibernau and Nakano all had good starts, in contrast to Rossi, who was only in fifth place at the first time checkpoint. Melandri finished the first lap with a 0.457 second lead over Hayden and a 0.570 second lead over Gibernau. Nakano, Rossi, Capirossi, Edwards, Hofmann and Barros followed.

LAP 3:
Rossi got the fastest lap, who moved up to fourth place, 0.230 secs behind Gibernau. Corollary: The lead group, four-strong (Melandri, Hayden, Gibernau and Rossi) started to break away.

LAP 5:
Edwards got a lap record, moving back into contention.

LAP 6:
Gibernau and Rossi passed Hayden. Edwards was to do the same a lap later.

LAP 6:
Rossi was in second place, 0.310 secs behind Melandri.

HALF-WAY POINT (LAP 10):
The crowd got to their feet – their favourite had gained the lead. Rossi had a 0.519 second lead over Melandri, who was hot on his tail. Gibernau peeled away with Edwards, who would soon pass him to take third place. Hayden was not far behind.

LAP 13:
Rossi increased the pace. Melandri found himself 0.937 secs behind. Hayden overtook Gibernau. Hofman retired from the race.

FINISH (LAP 19):
Rossi held a 0545 second lead coming into the last lap. What more could he want? He just wanted to make history at Assen by making a lap record over the last lap – a record that would stay in place forever, as the Dutch circuit would be completely changed by the time the next year comes around.

CHAMPIONSHIP:
Six out of seven races have been run. In statistics, that makes 170 points for Rossi against 107 for his closest rival – Melandri. Difference: 63 points – or 2 more GPs.

Blue leader: behind a still-unbeaten Valentino Rossi, Marco Melandri would be a constant threat.

DUTCH GP NETHERLAND | 25th june 2005 | Assen | 5.997 m

STARTING GRID

1	46	V. Rossi	Yamaha	1'58.936
2	15	S. Gibernau	Honda	1'59.247
3	33	M. Melandri	Honda	1'59.632
4	56	S. Nakano	Kawasaki	1'59.760
5	69	N. Hayden	Honda	1'59.784
6	5	C. Edwards	Yamaha	2'00.006
7	65	L. Capirossi	Ducati	2'00.136
8	4	A. Barros	Honda	2'00.232
9	3	M. Biaggi	Honda	2'00.281
10	66	A. Hofmann	Kawasaki	2'00.298
11	6	M. Tamada	Honda	2'00.656
12	21	J. Hopkins	Suzuki	2'00.810
13	7	C. Checa	Ducati	2'00.883
14	12	T. Bayliss	Honda	2'01.216
15	10	K. Roberts	Suzuki	2'01.836
16	11	R. Xaus	Yamaha	2'01.854
17	94	D. Checa	Yamaha	2'02.639
18	44	R. Rolfo	Ducati	2'02.704
19	67	S. Byrne	Proton KR	2'03.442
20	77	J. Ellison	Blata	2'03.488
21	27	F. Battaini	Blata	2'06.527

RACE: 19 laps = 113.943 km

1	Valentino Rossi	38'41.808 (176.670 km/h)
2	Marco Melandri	+ 1''583
3	Colin Edwards	+ 7''643
4	Nicky Hayden	+ 10''128
5	Sete Gibernau	+ 14''795
6	Max Biaggi	+ 21''575
7	Alex Barros	+ 22''725
8	Shinya Nakano	+ 26''477
9	Carlos Checa	+ 30''221
10	Loris Capirossi	+ 30''465
11	Troy Bayliss	+ 43''802
12	Ruben Xaus	+ 49''864
13	John Hopkins	+ 50''830
14	Makoto Tamada	+ 53''370
15	David Checa	+ 54''965
16	Kenny Roberts	+ 1'06.939
17	Shane Byrne	+ 1'06.999
18	Roberto Rolfo	+ 1'29.048
20	Franco Battaini	+ 1 tour

Fastest lap:
Rossi, in 2'00.991 (178.436 km/h).
New record (new circuit).

Outright fastest lap:
Rossi, in 1'58.936 (181.519 km/h/2005).

CHAMPIONSHIP

1	V. Rossi	170 (6 wins)
2	M. Melandri	107
3	M. Biaggi	87
4	S. Gibernau	84
5	A. Barros	74 (1 win)
6	C. Edwards	73
7	N. Hayden	60
8	L. Capirossi	49
9	S. Nakano	48
10	C. Checa	40

07 | 250cc NETHERLANDS

Jorge Lorenzo looks unconcerned ahead of Porto, Stoner and Pedrosa (left), De Angelis and Stoner make contact in the chicane, and Porto triumphs: the "Dutch TT" 250cc in three images.

PORTO, THE ARGENTINEAN RIDER, GETS HIS FIRST WIN OF THE SEASON, PEDROSA HOLDS OFF LORENZO.

A STRONG LINE-UP:
Having picked up an injury while qualifying in Catalunya, the Czech Radomil Rous (with a fracture of the left scaphoid) was replaced by the Australian Anthony West in the Wurth Honda BQR team, loaned out by his own team (West was the designated rider of the KTM 250 – the bike everyone was dying to see and which would eventually make an appearance in Donington). The Italian, Michele Danese replaced Taro Sekiguchi (still injured) at the Campetella team. At Yamaha-Kurz, the Bulgarian Todorov replaced the Swede Watz (an ability to shuffle riders around brought in a bit of money for the German team).

QUALIFYING:
Jorge Lorenzo suffered a painful crash in Catalunya (with a fractured collarbone). In this race, he gritted his teeth and was the talk of the town, getting the best time during Friday's session, ahead of Sebastian Porto, Dani Pedrosa and Casey Stoner. Randy De Puniet (9th place) was still experiencing difficulties with the front of his Aprilia (after a crash).

START:
It rained during the night, and the 250 cc riders had a damp warm-up session. The track had dried out by 12.15, however, when the pack set off. Porto was the first man off the grid, but Lorenzo took the lead by overtaking him on the outside. Crossing the line, Lorenzo led ahead of Porto and Stoner. The three men were almost a full second ahead of the second trio of Alex de Angelis, Pedrosa and Dovizioso.

LAP 4:
Steve Jenker crashed. Lorenzo was still in the lead by 0.188 seconds. He was followed by Stoner, Pedrosa and De Angelis. The six leading riders were all racing within the space of a second.

HALF-WAY POINT (LAP 9):
The pace increased at the head of the race. Lorenzo and Porto were wheel to wheel (0.152 secs between them). Pedrosa was in third place, 1.041 away from the Argentinian. Behind them, the chasing group made up of De Angelis, Stoner, Dovizioso and Barbera was over two seconds off the leader. Dovizioso would soon break away.

LAP 11:
Two lap records later, Pedrosa came back within reach of the lead.

LAP 15:
Lorenzo, Porto and Pedrosa: the victory would be decided between the three of them.

LAP 17:
Porto made an excellent manoeuvre to regain the lead in the chicane. He ended the lap in front of Pedrosa and Lorenzo (0.444 seconds between them).

FINISH (LAP 18):
Porto didn't make a single mistake. The Argentinian rode a perfect race and won his first victory of the season.

CHAMPIONSHIP:
Beaten into first place, Pedrosa didn't do too badly out of it, as he slightly increased his general ranking in spite of his main opponents – Stoner and Dovizioso, now at almost 40 points and soon two races.

DUTCH GP NETHERLAND | 25th june 2005 | Assen | 5.997 m

STARTING GRID
1	48	J. Lorenzo	Honda	2'04.562
2	19	S. Porto	Aprilia	2'04.738
3	1	D. Pedrosa	Honda	2'04.901
4	27	C. Stoner	Aprilia	2'05.251
5	5	A. De Angelis	Aprilia	2'05.456
6	73	H. Aoyama	Honda	2'05.702
7	34	A. Dovizioso	Honda	2'05.864
8	80	H. Barbera	Honda	2'06.255
9	7	R. De Puniet	Aprilia	2'06.263
10	24	S. Corsi	Aprilia	2'06.809
11	96	J. Smrz	Honda	2'06.950
12	57	C. Davies	Aprilia	2'07.322
13	55	Y. Takahashi	Honda	2'07.410
14	17	S. Jenkner	Aprilia	2'07.523
15	32	M. Giansanti	Aprilia	2'07.614
16	25	A. Baldolini	Aprilia	2'07.684
17	50	S. Guintoli	Aprilia	2'07.756
18	28	D. Heidolf	Honda	2'07.851
19	8	A. Ballerini	Aprilia	2'07.854
20	15	R. Locatelli	Aprilia	2'07.976
21	6	A. Debon	Honda	2'08.412
22	38	G. Leblanc	Aprilia	2'08.952
23	14	A. West	Honda	2'09.149
24	21	A. Vincent	Fantic	2'09.568
25	36	M. Cardeñas	Aprilia	2'10.218
26	45	M. Danese	Aprilia	2'10.331
27	67	R. Gevers	Aprilia	2'10.627
28	66	H. Smees	Aprilia	2'10.692
29	12	G. Rizmayer	Yamaha	2'11.204

Not qualified:
	68	J. Roelofs	Yamaha	2'13.529
	22	A. Todorov	Yamaha	2'14.354
	20	G. Ferro	Fantic	2'14.600
	69	M. Velthjzen	Honda	2'15.810

RACE: 18 laps = 107.946 km
1	Sebastian Porto	38'02.148 (170.280 km/h)
2	Daniel Pedrosa	+ 0''381
3	Jorge Lorenzo	+ 1''232
4	Hiroshi Aoyama	+ 11''757
5	Alex De Angelis	+ 12''017
6	Casey Stoner	+ 12''026
7	Andrea Dovizioso	+ 12''354
8	Randy De Puniet	+ 13''935
9	Hector Barbera	+ 14''406
10	Simone Corsi	+ 29''294
11	Roberto Locatelli	+ 53''684
12	Sylvain Guintoli	+ 55''365
13	Alex Debon	+ 55''366
14	Chaz Davies	+ 55''627
15	Yuko Takahashi	+ 55''913
16	Jakub Smrz	+ 55''974
17	Andrea Ballerini	+ 58''837
18	Mirko Giansanti	+ 1'12.101
19	Dirk Heidolf	+ 1'12.202
20	Gregory Leblanc	+ 1'25.107
21	Martin Cardeñas	+ 1'25.193
22	Michele Danese	+ 1'32.360
23	Hans Smees	+ 1'41.190
24	Arnaud Vincent	+ 1'54.581
25	Gabor Rizmayer	+ 1'55.648

Fastest lap:
Porto, in 2'05.191 (172.450 km/h).
New record (new circuit).

Outright fastest lap:
Lorenzo, in 2'04.562 (173.320 km/h/2005).

CHAMPIONSHIP
1	D. Pedrosa	143 (4 wins)
2	C. Stoner	106 (2 wins)
3	A. Dovizioso	102
4	S. Porto	74 (1 win)
5	H. Aoyama	71
6	J. Lorenzo	70
7	A. De Angelis	67
8	R. De Puniet	54
9	H. Barbera	51
10	S. Corsi	44

NETHERLANDS 125cc

LÜTHI AND SIMONCELLI TOUCH ON THE FINAL LAP, GABOR TALMACSI TAKES HIS SECOND GP.

A STRONG LINE-UP:
Still no sign of the young German, Sascha Hommel at Malaguti. Pellino was in the saddle in his place. Having picked up an injury in Mugello, Julian Miralles was replaced by Mateo Tuñez, who won the second round of the Spanish Championship in Valencia a few days previously.

QUALIFYING:
Although Pasini got the best time in the first day (0.003 secs ahead of Kallio), the KTM boys restored the status quo on the Friday to get a neat double. Kallio and Talmacsi rode together so as to start from the same row of the grid, with 0.06 seconds between them. Pasini, Simoncelli and Lüthi followed, making the top five riders on the starting grid the same men who won the first six GPs. Hats off to Alexis Masbou, the French hope, displaying great confidence in this changed circuit of Assen (in eighth position).

START:
Talmacsi, Kallio and Poggiali made the best start. Lüthi was very aggressive in the first corners and moved into third place. At the end of the first lap, Kallio led ahead of Lüthi, Simón, Talmacsi and Bautista, who was to take the lead.

LAP 2:
Espargaro and Sandi crashed.

LAP 3:
Lüthi led ahead of the young Frenchman Masbou, Talmacsi, Kallio, Bautista, Simón, Simoncelli and Pasini.

LAP 4:
Lüthi held a 0.153 secs lead over Simoncelli, who would overtake at the end of the straight. The nine leading riders all passed by in 1.368 seconds.

LAP 7:
Kallio and Lüthi overtook Simoncelli. Talmacsi would soon do exactly the same.

HALF-WAY POINT (LAP 8):
It was a Dantesque scene. There were now eight of them all clumped together in 0.967 seconds. Kallio, Talmacsi, Lüthi, Bautista, Pasini, Simoncelli, Masbou and Faubel.

LAP 9:
Lüthi led by 0.223 seconds.

LAP 10:
It was Simoncelli's turn to lead ahead of Kallio, Talmacsi and Lüthi.

LAP 12:
A small gap started to form behind Faubel. And then there were six fighting for places. And what a fight it was!

LAP 14:
Kallio crashed. Simoncelli led ahead of Talmacsi, Lüthi, Faubel and Bautista.

FINISH (LAP 17):
This was the craziest race in recent years. A little over 300 metres from the finish line, Simoncelli left his braking until the last possible moment. Lüthi did not back away and the two bikes hit each other. Simoncelli fell, but Lüthi got his bike back under control from the sand trap. He salvaged some points by finishing in tenth position. Away from all that, Talmacsi got the last laugh, getting his second win – the second of his career.

CHAMPIONSHIP:
100 points went to Talmacsi and Pasini. Lüthi was now in third place in the rankings, but 11 lengths down. Simoncelli and Kallio were the ones who lost most over the course of the weekend.

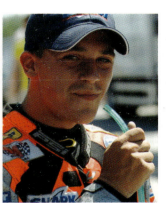

Plenty of battling, particularly between Simoncelli (what attack!), Kallio and Talmacsi, who was to have the last word. Far right, Alexis Masbou, the revelation of the week-end.

DUTCH GP NETHERLAND | 25th june 2005 | Assen | 5.997 m

STARTING GRID

1	36	M. Kallio	KTM	2'11.855
2	14	G. Talmacsi	KTM	2'11.915
3	75	M. Pasini	Aprilia	2'12.300
4	58	M. Simoncelli	Aprilia	2'12.729
5	12	T. Lüthi	Honda	2'12.911
6	33	S. Gadea	Aprilia	2'13.170
7	54	M. Poggiali	Gilera	2'13.217
8	7	A. Masbou	Honda	2'13.357
9	55	H. Faubel	Aprilia	2'13.370
10	60	J. Simón	KTM	2'13.403
11	71	T. Koyama	Honda	2'13.403
12	52	L. Pesek	Derbi	2'13.465
13	63	M. Di Meglio	Honda	2'13.524
14	19	A. Bautista	Honda	2'13.631
15	43	M. Hernandez	Aprilia	2'13.646
16	6	J. Olivé	Aprilia	2'13.973
17	76	M. Ranseder	KTM	2'13.991
18	32	F. Lai	Honda	2'14.272
19	35	R. De Rosa	Aprilia	2'14.363
20	41	A. Espargaro	Honda	2'14.389
21	29	A. Iannone	Aprilia	2'14.433
22	18	N. Terol	Derbi	2'14.463
23	22	P. Nieto	Derbi	2'14.596
24	11	S. Cortese	Honda	2'14.716
25	16	R. Schouten	Honda	2'14.975
26	8	L. Zanetti	Aprilia	2'15.150
27	9	T. Kuzuhara	Honda	2'15.250
28	47	A. Rodriguez	Honda	2'15.370
29	44	K. Abraham	Aprilia	2'15.399
30	45	I. Toth	Aprilia	2'15.457
31	10	F. Sandi	Honda	2'15.666
32	15	M. Pirro	Malaguti	2'15.951
33	25	D. Giuseppetti	Aprilia	2'15.965
34	28	J. Carchano	Aprilia	2'16.146
35	26	V. Braillard	Aprilia	2'16.150
36	42	G. Pellino	Malaguti	2'16.321
37	86	M. Tuñez	Aprilia	2'16.427
38	37	J. Litjens	Honda	2'16.918
39	78	H. Van den Berg	Aprilia	2'17.682
40	79	G. Kok	Honda	2'18.113

Not qualified:
| | 80 | M. Van Kreij | Honda | 2'22.202 |

RACE: 17 laps = 101.949 km

1	Gabor Talmacsi	38'09.487 (160.305 km/h)
2	Hector Faubel	+ 0''657
3	Mattia Pasini	+ 0''801
4	Alvaro Bautista	+ 0''847
5	Alexis Masbou	+ 1''403
6	Julian Simón	+ 3''972
7	Tomoyoshi Koyama	+ 4''259
8	Manuel Poggiali	+ 4''323
9	Sergio Gadea	+ 4''492
10	Thomas Lüthi	+ 13''934
11	Pablo Nieto	+ 18''262
12	Michael Ranseder	+ 20''693
13	Joan Olivé	+ 21''091
14	Mike Di Meglio	+ 21''196
15	Lukas Pesek	+ 21''304
16	Nicolas Terol	+ 21''439
17	Manuel Hernandez	+ 21''574
18	Fabrizio Lai	+ 21''575
19	Lorenzo Zanetti	+ 30''737
20	Marco Simoncelli	+ 37''546
21	Gioele Pellino	+ 37''777
22	Angel Rodriguez	+ 37''843
23	Dario Giuseppetti	+ 40''976
24	Sandro Cortese	+ 41''021
25	Imre Toth	+ 50''079
26	Andrea Iannone	+ 51''815
27	Vincent Braillard	+ 51''862
28	Jordi Carchano	+ 55''996
29	Gert-Jan Kok	+ 1'15.161
30	Joey Litjens	+ 1'43.235
31	Hugo Van den Berg	+ 1'50.080

Fastest lap:
Faubel, in 2'13.536 (161.673 km/h). New record (new circuit).

Outright fastest lap:
Kallio, in 2'11.855 (163.734 km/h/2003).

CHAMPIONSHIP

1	M. Pasini	100 (2 wins)
2	G. Talmacsi	100 (2 wins)
3	T. Lüthi	89 (1 win)
4	M. Kallio	82 (1 win)
5	M. Simoncelli	72 (1 win)
6	F. Lai	63
7	M. Poggiali	59
8	J. Simón	55
9	T. Koyama	52
10	H. Faubel	50

For the brand's fiftieth anniversary, Valentino Rossi and Colin Edwards' Yamaha M1s are decorated in the historic Yamaha US yellow.

08

10th July 2005
UNITED STATES LAGUNA SECA

That's what you call a good line-up of champions (Doohan, Spencer, Lawson and Roberts Senior, surrounding Wayne Rainey)... and someone else (an anonymous marshal).

HAYDEN: : WHAT A FAMILY!

NICKY HAYDEN HAD HIS FIRST GP SUCCESS, TO THE GREAT PLEASURE OF HIS FATHER, EARL: AN AMAZING CHARACTER IN THE PADDOCK.

MOTORCYCLE YEARBOOK 2005 **115**

08 MOTO GP UNITED STATES

THE RACE

A FIRST VICTORY FOR NICKY HAYDEN, THE SECOND OF EARL'S THREE SONS. EARL IS ONE PASSIONATE FAN!

Nicky took Earl, his dad, on the lap of honour (note the Kawasaki US shirt Earl is wearing!) While the hero of the day celebrated his victory on the podium, dad had to deal with his other offspring, Tommy and Roger-Lee

There are certain people who raised a sly, understanding smile when Nicky Hayden started his first Grand Prix at the beginning of 2003, under his favourite number 69. It's not what they were thinking, though… "No, no - it's not that. My father always fell in competitions. He chose this number because it's the only one you can read when the bike is upside-down". That's what the boy from Kentucky said in that distinctive accent of his. Nicky? A very talented man - the US superbike champion 2002 with the looks of an angel (when Honda unveiled their new rider, his then team-mate, Valentino Rossi, couldn't stop himself from giving his own slant on the situation: "What bothers me most about him is that he is so much more handsome than me. All the girls will look at him first!"). He had an almost caricature Yankee look. Basically, the boy has a rosy future. He is a star of the future for Honda, should the Japanese team need a solution to replace Rossi. We all know what happened next. Valentino left, and so the official Repsol team stopped winning. Well - it stopped winning, but the return weekend in the MotoGP class in the United States, Nicky Hayden put in a flawless performance. To the pleasure and immense pride of his father, Earl, who toured all the circuits of the world with his son, played a key role in the development of Nicky's passion for the sport, along with his two brothers, Tommy and Roger-Lee. Earl Hayden? Now there's a character. A used-car salesman, he is mad about motorcycle racing. In the garden of the family home, he built an oval dirt track so that his three sons could learn to skid while racing. They were to become the kings of the dirt-track, before dreaming of becoming kings of the tarmac surface. "I remember very well that the roof of the house was full of holes, but that didn't worry dad: instead of repairing it, he preferred to save his money for the motorbikes. Mom put buckets inside the house to catch the water", explained Nicky on this glorious day for him: Sunday, 10th July 2005. Silence descended. "The worst thing, I gotta tell ya: the fastest member of my family wasn't me. It was Tommy, my older brother. I'll never forget how he used to pass me. But there you are, people go down different paths in their lives. Of the two, I was the only one to get to be a GP racer".

Nicky Hayden said all this during the press conference that follows each GP. He tried to catch his father's eye in the room, but couldn't. But dad had other things to think about. He had to go to a medical centre to get news of Tommy, who injured his hand when racing in the US Championship just before the GP that was so important to the Hayden family. He went to the Laguna Seca grid straight from the infirmary. Roger-Lee, the youngest member of the family was ready to shine in his super sport. And victory would only be snatched from his grasp in the last corner.

UNITED STATES MOTO GP 08

Marco Melandri was the first European to criticise the Californian circuit, and he would also be the first to hurt himself on the exit of the famous "corkscrew".

LAGUNA, THE YANKEE FORTRESS...

A STRONG LINE-UP
Toni Elias made a come-back. The Yamaha officials weren't wearing the Gauloises colours, but rather the traditional yellow and black of the US importer. The Suzukis were decked out in dark blue (Red Bull).

QUALIFYING
Marco Melandri was the first to get angry ("safety here is not on the same par as at Suzuka"). He was also the first man to fall - thrown off while passing through the famous "corkscrew" descent. Rossi started the weekend cautiously. The same could not be said of Nicky Hayden - a character trait that was to dominate the qualifiers (the first session was extended by an hour).

START
Hayden' reflexes didn't fault him. It started in the lead ahead of Troy Bayliss and Rossi, who started quickly from second place. Edwards stayed right on the line and Melandri (his third crash of the weekend!) failed to finish the first lap, after glancing Barros' machine in the tight left which brought the pack onto the straight.

LAP 3
Since the beginning of the weekend, everyone knew Nicky Hayden wouldn't miss an opportunity. the Kentucky kid was ahead of Rossi by 1.762 seconds, forming a first gap ahead of a small group made up of Edwards, Bayliss, Gibernau (who had moved up from thirteenth on the grid), Biaggi, Hopkins and Checa respectively.

LAP 8
Carlos Checa crashed.

LAP 11
Biaggi ovettook Gibernau to take fifth place. Hayden was still the definite leader (with a 2.775 second lead). Edwards came up against his illustrious colleague, Valentino Rossi.

HALF-WAY POINT (LAP 16)
Colin Edwards was magnificent, spectacularly taking Rossi by surprise at the top of the hill. Crossing the line, Hayden had a 2.424 second lead over his Texan compatriot, and a 3.413 second lead over Valentino Rossi. Biaggi was in fourth place.

LAP 18
Edwards pulled out all the stops to try and close the gap: 2.163 secs..

LAP 19
The Texan reduced the gap by a further 0.1 seconds, thereby becoming the fastest man on the track.

LAP 21
Hayden kept things under control and maintained his distance from his closest rival. The race was as good as over.

FINISH (LAP 32)
Rossi came back to threaten Edwards, but didn't take any risks over the last metres. And so it was an American double - the first win for Nicky Hayden: the Kentucky kid had become a giant!

CHAMPIONSHIP
Beaten, Rossi was all smiles on the podium: he had ridden a good race, and was 79 points ahead of his Marco Melandri - his closest rival.

Xaus, a steam-powered Yamaha!

GP UNITED STATES | 10th July | Laguna Seca | 3.610 m

STARTING GRID

1	69	N. Hayden	Honda	1'22.670
2	46	V. Rossi	Yamaha	1'23.024
3	4	A. Barros	Honda	1'23.312
4	12	T. Bayliss	Honda	1'23.358
5	5	C. Edwards	Yamaha	1'23.469
6	21	J. Hopkins	Suzuki	1'23.493
7	3	M. Biaggi	Honda	1'23.596
8	7	C. Checa	Ducati	1'23.597
9	6	M. Tamada	Honda	1'23.750
10	56	S. Nakano	Kawasaki	1'23.799
11	33	M. Melandri	Honda	1'23.905
12	10	K. Roberts	Suzuki	1'24.011
13	15	S. Gibernau	Honda	1'24.145
14	65	L. Capirossi	Ducati	1'24.257
15	66	A. Hofmann	Kawasaki	1'24.480
16	11	R. Xaus	Yamaha	1'24.741
17	24	T. Elias	Yamaha	1'25.462
18	44	R. Rolfo	Ducati	1'25.881
19	67	S. Byrne	Proton KR	1'25.937
20	77	J. Ellison	Blata	1'26.800
21	27	F. Battaini	Blata	1'28.435

RACE: 32 laps = 115.520 km

1	Nicky Hayden	45'15.374 (153.154 km/h)
2	Colin Edwards	+ 1''941
3	Valentino Rossi	+ 2''312
4	Max Biaggi	+ 4''216
5	Sete Gibernau	+ 4''478
6	Troy Bayliss	+ 22''381
7	Makoto Tamada	+ 22''493
8	John Hopkins	+ 23''148
9	Shinya Nakano	+ 23''625
10	Loris Capirossi	+ 26''123
11	Ruben Xaus	+ 43''512
12	Alex Hofmann	+ 50''957
13	Toni Elias	+ 51''343
14	Kenny Roberts	+ 1'13.749
15	Shane Byrne	+ 1'24.256
16	James Ellison	+ 1'24.524
17	Franco Battaini	+ 1 lap

Fastest lap
Edwards, in 1'23.915 (154.871 km/h).
New record (new circuit).

Outright fastest lap
Hayden, in 1'22.670 (157.203 km/h/2005).

CHAMPIONSHIP

1	V. Rossi	186 (6 wins)
2	M. Melandri	107
3	M. Biaggi	100
4	S. Gibernau	95
5	C. Edwards	93
6	N. Hayden	85 (1 win)
7	A. Barros	74 (1 win)
8	L. Capirossi	55
9	S. Nakano	55
10	T. Bayliss	47

Rossi caught up with Alexandre Barros, the most capped of the GP riders. Just another couple of moments and all the Brazilian would be able to do would be shake his head in bitter disappointment.

09

24th July 2005

GREAT BRITAIN DONINGTON

Alex De Angelis on the 250cc grid and Ruben Xaus on the track: odd weather…

WE KNEW ROSSI,
WE DISCOVERED MOÏSE

ON THIS RAINY SUNDAY AT DONINGTON, VALENTINO ROSSI FLEW OVER THE PROCEEDINGS, AN ACROBAT IN PERFECT CONTROL OF HIS TWO-WHEEL OUTBOARD!

MOTO GP GREAT BRITAIN

THE RACE

IN DANTESQUE CONDITIONS, VALENTINO ROSSI GAVE A BREATHTAKING PERFORMANCE. THIS MAN IS A GENIUS...

"I didn't really get the feeling that I was taking part in a motorcycling GP. It was more along the lines of a speedboat race! The motorbike was really flying at some points. It surfed over the track, which was more like a waterbed. Honestly, I think I completed one of the most difficult races of my career today. The cold!", he shivered, laughing, "We were sliding around all over the place! I've never seen anything like it". The others said much the same thing. Valentino Rossi had never experienced a race like it, either. But there was a slight difference: the others hadn't really understood how Rossi had managed to act like Moses during this very British Sunday. How had Valentino managed to keep his wheels firmly on the floor at the beginning of the race, while his opponents were dropping like flies? They kept on falling, as did the rain. How once, ten times, a hundred times, Rossi succeeded in controlling his machine, which simply didn't want to go in the direction its driver wanted to steer it.

And what of Biaggi and his stylish riding? 3.37pm and 3.44pm: two falls in the space of seven minutes! Had he become a fearless acrobat? And out of the eleven riders (in GPs - there are ten more in private testing during this 2005 season)? Hayden? Melandri? The experienced Bayliss? Nope!

The only other rider to wait for was Sete Gibernau. Of course, Sete was the only one to have threatened the dominance of Valentino Rossi over the previous two years, especially in difficult conditions. But he couldn't do it. At 3.42pm, he came off his bike at the second corner, but the rider was unhurt.

Sete was a shadow of the feisty challenger he was twelve months earlier. Valentino was still the most uncontrollable, unbeatable, uncatchable, everything-able man you could ever think of. There aren't enough superlatives to describe this great rider.

Under these conditions, we can scarcely think of any other riders who could work with the rain to succeed in their season (Byrne, Ellison or Battaini): on man alone could win in this weather. Better than Moses. Moses just had to walk...

There were two experienced men flanking him on the podium: Kenny Roberts and Alexandre Barros. Barros was the only one to try and offer up a semblance of a challenge before dipping his head resignedly when, two laps and a few hundred metres later, Valentino had left him in his tracks. He stayed in his position to ride alone through the storm.

The most surprising thing with the champion of champions is that every race - every occasion - he creates new ways of consolidating his domination of the sport. This is crucial for his ride plan - managing the weather and technical mastery. Even moreso psychologically, Valentino Rossi is light years ahead of his rivals, event though he hasn't had a long career. It's a shame for everyone else, but what glory for Rossi!

And to think that not so long ago, riding in the wet was the only aspect of the motorcycling king's sport that had room for improvement.

On the podium, the man who is as popular in Britain as in his native Italy, gets the crowd going.

"It wasn't like riding a bike, it was like riding a boat": the image is proof that Valentino Rossi never lies...

GREAT BRITAIN MOTO GP

Sete Gibernau attempts to right his Honda, in vain. The old rain king has fallen again.

THIS BRITISH GP QUICKLY TURNED INTO A GAME OF SKITTLES… ON WATER.

A STRONG LINE-UP
Nothing to report other than the fact that the line-up was complete, freshly returned from a trip to the United States, leaving the Americans with broad smiles on their faces and happy memories immortalised on people's cameras.

QUALIFYING
"After the Laguna Seca episode, we're getting back to the real world", said Valentino Rossi at the end of the qualifying sessions. The "real world" is his oyster. Valentino won another pole position, once again getting the best time on the circuit and moving ahead of Gibernau and Melandri.

START
Nakano had a few problems at the start, which had to be delayed. And so the race started a little late, and would be shortened by one lap. Gibernau got off to a great start, but Rossi certainly didn't - only making seventh place in the descent. Biaggi crashed. At the end of the first lap, Gibernau was over two seconds ahead of Barros, Melandri and Rossi.

LAP 2
Xaus crashed, followed by Hayden. Barros narrowed the time to 1.476 secs behind Gibernau.

LAP 3
Melandri crashed at the hairpin bend. Bayliss hit him and ended up on the ground. Rossi was now in second place…but not for long, because it was soon to be Gibernau's turn to make a mistake. Rossi then led ahead of Barros and Roberts.

LAP 4
Rossi was flying along, but Barros overtook him and Hopkins was in fourth place. Nakano crashed.

LAP 5
Hopkins was in the lead. Biaggi crashed for the second time. Barros crashed.

LAP 7
Barros took the lead, 1.224 seconds ahead of Rossi and Hopkins

LAP 8
Ellison crashed.

LAP 9
Hopkins crashed. Barros, Roberrts, Rossi and Edwards formed a pack 0.357 seconds between them.

LAP 11
Edwards fell behind and Roberts took the lead.

LAP 12
Rossi went off at the chicane, enabling Edwards to come back into contention. Barros once again took the lead.

HALF-WAY POINT (LAP 15)
Barros, Rossi (who had rejoined the race), Roberts and Edwards were still leading the race, 1.570 seconds between them. A large gap formed behind them, and the next rider was Checa in fifth place, over twelve seconds off the pace of the leaders.

LAP 22
Rossi moved ahead by 0.251 seconds…getting the best lap time in the process. One lap and a best lap time later, the motorcycle master extended his lead to 1.847 seconds.

FINISH (LAP 29)
Once again, he did what he wanted, when he wanted. Rossi is a true artist. The fight for second place put Roberts on the attack against Barros at a good time - only three obstacles away from the finish line.

CHAMPIONSHIP
Rossi was 104 points ahead of Melandri, who was being chased hard by Edwards. If things were left like that, Rossi could have been crowned the world champion at the Malaysian GP - four races early.

A crash party, did we say? Ask Marco Melandri… and Troy Bayliss, who managed to avoid it. Before falling a little further on.

GP GREAT BRITAIN | 24th July 2005 | Donington | 4.023 m

STARTING GRID

1	46	V. Rossi	Yamaha	1'27.897
2	15	S. Gibernau	Honda	1'28.182
3	33	M. Melandri	Honda	1'28.295
4	4	A. Barros	Honda	1'28.394
5	69	N. Hayden	Honda	1'28.415
6	5	C. Edwards	Yamaha	1'28.656
7	12	T. Bayliss	Honda	1'28.720
8	3	M. Biaggi	Honda	1'28.726
9	6	M. Tamada	Honda	1'28.976
10	21	J. Hopkins	Suzuki	1'29.231
11	65	L. Capirossi	Ducati	1'29.731
12	56	S. Nakano	Kawasaki	1'29.742
13	7	C. Checa	Ducati	1'29.816
14	11	R. Xaus	Yamaha	1'29.890
15	66	A. Hofmann	Kawasaki	1'30.151
16	10	K. Roberts	Suzuki	1'30.260
17	24	T. Elias	Yamaha	1'30.342
18	67	S. Byrne	Proton KR	1'31.026
19	44	R. Rolfo	Ducati	1'31.180
20	77	J. Ellison	Blata	1'31.791
21	27	F. Battaini	Blata	1'32.684

RACE: 29 laps = 116.667 km

1	Valentino Rossi	52'58.675 (132.130 km/h)
2	Kenny Roberts	+ 3''169
3	Alex Barros	+ 4''006
4	Colin Edwards	+ 10''291
5	Carlos Checa	+ 13''020
6	Loris Capirossi	+ 23''321
7	Makoto Tamada	+ 37''833
8	Alex Hofmann	+ 44''617
9	Toni Elias	+ 1 lap
10	Roberto Rolfo	+ 1 lap
11	John Hopkins	+ 2 laps

Fastest lap
Rossi, in 1'45.377 (137.437 km/h).
Record: Edwards, in 1'29.973 (160.968 km/h/2004).

Outright fastest lap
Rossi, en 1'27.897 (164.770 km/h/2005).

CHAMPIONSHIP

1	V. Rossi	211 (7 wins)
2	M. Melandri	107
3	C. Edwards	106
4	M. Biaggi	100
4	S. Gibernau	95
5	A. Barros	90 (1 win)
7	N. Hayden	85 (1 win)
8	L. Capirossi	65
9	S. Nakano	55
10	C. Checa	51

09 250cc GREAT BRITAIN

SUPER DE PUNIET, WHO MADE HIS MARK IN THE TORMENT. AND WHAT AN ACHIEVEMENT FOR KTM!

A STRONG LINE-UP
The big event of the weekend was the appearance of the impressive KTM 250 of Anthony West. This was the first GP for the 19 year-old Swde, Niklas Cajback, who joined his compatriot Andreas Martensson with Yamaha-Kurz.

QUALIFYING
Not happy with his performance, Dani Pedrosa fell during the final qualifying session, but that didn't change anything on the starting grid. The world champion made pole position, ahead of his most scathing rival, Jorge Lorenzo. Alex De Angelis and Dovizioso completed the front row.

START
There was nothing that could be done. It was pouring it down with rain. Aoyama secured his first lap in the lead ahead of De Puniet (at 1.008 seconds) and Dovizioso. Takahashi and Debon crashed. West was sixth on the KTM.

LAP 3
Aoyama was still there, ahead of De Puniet by 2.347 seconds. West was in third.

LAP 8
Aoyama was magisterial: he opened up a 4.484 second lead over De Puniet. West was still in third place, s.135 seconds off the Frenchman. Pedrosa was only sixth.

LAP 9
De Angelis crashed. West was less than 0.9 secs off Randy de Puniet.

The raging fist of the winner: Randy De Puniet was perfect, just like the new KTM 250 (first race, first podium). Bottom, the De Puniet-Stoner duel, before the Australian left the track.

LAP 11
West overtook De Puniet, but the Frenchman immediately went onto the counter-attack. Stoner was the fastest man on the track, climbing back to a second off the lead..

HALF-WAY POINT (LAP 13)
Aoyama fell on Redgate corner. West took the lead, 0.569 secs ahead of De Puniet. Stoner was in third, 1.378 secs off the leader, and Pedrosa was fourth ahead of Porto and the excellent Guintoli.

LAP 14
De Puniet took the lead.

LAP 16
De Puniet was scrapping with Stoner, and West got a shock.

LAP 17
Stoner was in the lead, but not for long. He hit the white line and Randy took the lead back into his hands.

LAP 23
The riders went crazy. De Puniet ran off the track in the descent, but was able to rejoin the action. Crossing the line, West led ahead of Stoner and Randy by 0.669 seconds

LAP 24
Stoner led. Davies crashed.

LAP 25
De Puniet went ahead of West once again, this time by 0.366 secs. Stoner went off the course at the end of the straight.

FINISH (LAP 27)
A 0.172 second gap developed over the last lap, with West giving himself a bad scare. De Puniet took his first win of the year. KTM won their first GP podium place.

CHAMPIONSHIP
Pedrosa had a good race, with Stoner only taking three points off him. De Puniet deserved an honourable mention. He gave the crowd a great show in spite of the heaviest rain for a long time.points.

GP GREAT BRITAIN | 24th July 2005 | Donington | 4.023 m

STARTING GRID

1	1	D. Pedrosa	Honda	1'31.834
2	48	J. Lorenzo	Honda	1'31.964
3	5	A. De Angelis	Aprilia	1'32.489
4	34	A. Dovizioso	Honda	1'32.597
5	19	S. Porto	Aprilia	1'32.615
6	7	R. De Puniet	Aprilia	1'32.804
7	80	H. Barbera	Honda	1'32.812
8	73	H. Aoyama	Honda	1'32.826
9	55	Y. Takahashi	Honda	1'32.984
10	27	C. Stoner	Aprilia	1'32.992
11	15	R. Locatelli	Aprilia	1'33.262
12	50	S. Guintoli	Aprilia	1'33.468
13	6	A. Debon	Honda	1'33.488
14	24	S. Corsi	Aprilia	1'33.850
15	14	A. West	KTM	1'33.910
16	57	C. Davies	Aprilia	1'33.972
17	96	J. Smrz	Honda	1'34.118
18	17	S. Jenkner	Aprilia	1'34.306
19	25	A. Baldolini	Aprilia	1'34.424
20	8	A. Ballerini	Aprilia	1'34.706
21	28	D. Heidolf	Honda	1'34.913
22	32	M. Giansanti	Aprilia	1'34.959
23	36	M. Cardeñas	Aprilia	1'35.268
24	38	G. Leblanc	Aprilia	1'35.390
25	64	R. Rous	Honda	1'35.629
26	44	T. Sekiguchi	Aprilia	1'35.976
27	21	A. Vincent	Fantic	1'36.421
28	42	Y. Polzer	Aprilia	1'36.508
29	41	A. Molina	Aprilia	1'36.561
30	26	A. Martensson	Yamaha	1'37.257
31	20	G. Ferro	Fantic	1'38.054
Not qualified:				
	23	N. Cajback	Yamaha	1'38.673

RACE: 27 laps = 108.621 km

1	Randy De Puniet	49'11.337 (132.494 km/h)
2	Anthony West	+ 1''236
3	Casey Stoner	+ 16''740
4	Daniel Pedrosa	+ 47''825
5	Sebastian Porto	+ 1'03.449
6	Simone Corsi	+ 1'32.437
7	Andrea Dovizioso	+ 1'34.560
8	Jorge Lorenzo	+ 1'45.964
9	Sylvain Guintoli	+ 1 tour
10	Andrea Ballerini	+ 1 tour
11	Mirko Giansanti	+ 1 tour
12	Roberto Locatelli	+ 1 tour
13	Alex Baldolini	+ 1 tour
14	Gregory Leblanc	+ 2 tours
15	Radomil Rous	+ 2 tours
16	Jakub Smrz	+ 2 tours
17	Steve Jenkner	+ 2 tours
18	Alvaro Molina	+ 2 tours
19	Gabriele Ferro	+ 4 tours

Fastest lap
West, in 1'47.025 (135.321 km/h).
Record: Pedrosa, in 1'33.217 (155.366 km/h/2004).

Outright fastest lap
Pedrosa, in 1'31.834 (157.706 km/h/2005).

CHAMPIONSHIP

1	D. Pedrosa	156 (4 wins)
2	C. Stoner	122 (2 wins)
3	A. Dovizioso	111
4	S. Porto	85 (1 win)
5	R. De Puniet	79 (1 win)
6	J. Lorenzo	78
7	H. Aoyama	71
8	A. De Angelis	67
9	S. Corsi	54
10	H. Barbera	51

GREAT BRITAIN 125cc 09

THE TURN OF THE SPANIARD JULIAN SIMÓN TO JOIN THE FAMILY OF WINNERS.

A STRONG LINE-UP
The holidays are being managed differently. Some riders did a bit of work (with Lüthi testing at the Sachsenring and in Brno), while others (Simoncelli and Pasini) took care of their physical condition and their image by taking part in a beach soccer tournament with…Diego Armando Maradona..

QUALIFYING
Kallio very much deserved his pole position. He got the best time during both the Friday and the Saturday sessions. Alongside him on the front row were the other strong riders in this championship: Pasini, Simoncelli and Lüthi. Joint leader in the general rankings, Talmacsi was "only" seventh. He flew through the damp warm-up on the Sunday morning.

START
It was drizzling at the start point. Kallio and Lüthi started out in front, with Talmacsi passing the Swiss rider in the descent. Kallio was 0.254 secs ahead of Lüthi at the end of the first lap.

LAP 2
Thomas Lüthi was 0.361 secs ahead of Talmacsi, Kallio and Pasini.

LAP 5
For the second time in the race, Pasini got a fright. In front of him, Lüthi carried on leading ahead of Talmacsi, Kallio, Lai, Di Meglio, Bautista, Simoncelli and Pasini.

LAP 7
Bautista was the fastest man on the track, taking the lead ahead of Kallio and Lüthi. Faubel crashed.

The Frenchman Mike Di Meglio outstrips Julian Simón (in civvies, right): the 125cc season is definitely the one with all the revelations - and some spectacular manoeuvres (Lukas Pesek, above).

LAP 8
Bautista suffered a spectacular crash after it started to rain. Simoncelli also fell. The red flag was waved. The race restarted for nine laps, with an adjusted starting grid according to the positioning at the end of the "first" stage. Bautista, Kallio, Lüthi and Talmacsi made up the front row.

SECOND START
Pasini crashed in the warm-up lap. Talmacsi moved in front of Lüthi and Lai, who would later take the lead. Talmacsi passed in front of Lai, Lüthi, Di Meglio and Simon.

LAP 2
Talmacsi had a 1.239 second lead, but would crash later on

LAP 3
Di Meglio took the lead ahead of Simón, Lüthi went off the track but was able to rejoin in ninth place.

LAP 4
Still Di Meglio out in front - this time ahead of Bautista. Talmacsi crashed for the second time.

LAP 6
Bautista crashed for a second time, and then Espargaro, who was fourth. Di Meglio and Lai were separated by 0.545 seconds. Lüthi moved up to sixth place.

LAP 7
Simón took the lead.

FINISH (LAP 9)
Julian Simón won a first lead ahead of Di Meglio, Lai, Simoncelli, Nieto and Lüthi.

CHAMPIONSHIP
This was the second time the two championship leaders, Pasini and Talmacsi failed to score. Lüthi got one point, and Kallio 9 lengths. The seven top placed riders were separated by 21 units.

GP GREAT BRITAIN | 24th July 2005 | Donington | 4.023 m

STARTING GRID

1	36	M. Kallio	KTM	1'37.295
2	75	M. Pasini	Aprilia	1'37.396
3	58	M. Simoncelli	Aprilia	1'37.407
4	12	T. Lüthi	Honda	1'37.634
5	32	F. Lai	Honda	1'37.660
6	60	J. Simón	KTM	1'37.701
7	14	G. Talmacsi	KTM	1'37.952
8	71	T. Koyama	Honda	1'38.034
9	63	M. Di Meglio	Honda	1'38.060
10	7	A. Masbou	Honda	1'38.238
11	54	M. Poggiali	Gilera	1'38.238
12	19	A. Bautista	Honda	1'38.352
13	55	H. Faubel	Aprilia	1'38.372
14	33	S. Gadea	Aprilia	1'38.551
15	6	J. Olivé	Aprilia	1'38.745
16	43	M. Hernandez	Aprilia	1'38.820
17	22	P. Nieto	Derbi	1'38.866
18	18	N. Terol	Derbi	1'38.978
19	41	A. Espargaro	Honda	1'39.040
20	52	L. Pesek	Derbi	1'39.136
21	35	R. De Rosa	Aprilia	1'39.148
22	29	A. Iannone	Aprilia	1'39.166
23	47	A. Rodriguez	Honda	1'39.261
24	86	M. Tuñez	Aprilia	1'39.265
25	16	R. Schouten	Honda	1'39.417
26	28	J. Carchano	Aprilia	1'39.459
27	8	L. Zanetti	Aprilia	1'39.480
28	11	S. Cortese	Honda	1'39.538
29	25	D. Giuseppetti	Aprilia	1'39.579
30	9	T. Kuzuhara	Honda	1'39.635
31	10	F. Sandi	Honda	1'39.895
32	15	M. Pirro	Malaguti	1'40.110
33	26	V. Braillard	Aprilia	1'40.149
34	45	I. Toth	Aprilia	1'40.293
35	96	K. Coghlan		1'40.301
36	44	K. abraham	Aprilia	1'40.401
37	95	J. Westmorland	Honda	1'40.742
38	42	G. Pellino	Malaguti	1'40.919
39	94	D. Linfoot	Honda	1'40.996
40	57	R. Guiver	Honda	1'41.272
41	56	C. Elkin	Honda	1'41.699

RACE: 9 laps = 36.207 km (*)

1	Julian Simón	17'35.523 (123.488 km/h)
2	Mike Di Meglio	+ 2''406
3	Fabrizio Lai	+ 8''896
4	Marco Simoncelli	+ 9''169
5	Pablo Nieto	+ 13''837
6	Thomas Lüthi	+ 18''323
7	Mika Kallio	+ 23''453
8	Joan Olivé	+ 31''424
9	Dan Linfoot	+ 33''865
10	Toshihisa Kuzuhara	+ 40''094
11	Sergio Gadea	+ 40''345
12	Christian Elkin	+ 40''761
13	Jordi Carchano	+ 42''789
14	Lorenzo Zanetti	+ 42''833
15	Sandro Cortese	+ 43''420
16	Raymond Schouten	+ 43''587
17	Karel abraham	+ 45''101
18	Gioele Pellino	+ 47''077
19	Federico Sandi	+ 48''901
20	Raffaele De Rosa	+ 49''088
21	Nicolas Terol	+ 54''566
22	James Westmoreland	+ 59''769
23	Vincent Braillard	+ 1'00.672
24	Mateo Tuñez	+ 1'02.134
25	Manuel Poggiali	+ 1'26.419
26	Imre Toth	+ 1'28.411

(*): First, the race was red flagged due to the rain.

Fastest lap
Bautista, in 1'38.408 (147.170 km/h).
Record: Bautista, in 1'38.263 (147,388 km/h/2004).

Outright fastest lap
Dovizioso, in 1'37.211 (148.983 km/h/2004).

CHaMPIONSHIP

	M. Pasini	100 (2 wins)
2	G. Talmacsi	100 (2 wins)
3	T. Lüthi	99 (1 win)
4	M. Kallio	91 (1 win)
5	M. Simoncelli	85 (1 win)
6	J. Simón	80 (1 win)
7	F. Lai	79
8	M. Poggiali	59
9	T. Koyama	52
10	H. Faubel	50

A little lesson in excessive attack, by Nicky Hayden: superb!

10

31st July 2005

GERMANY SACHSENRING

German smiles. Alexander Hofmann's would disappear at the first turn...

GIBERNAU,
A MAN IN HELL

ONCE AGAIN, HE THOUGHT HE HAD DONE THE HARDEST, BUT ONCE AGAIN, HE WOULD MAKE A HUGE MISTAKE ENTERING THE FINAL LAP. GIBERNAU IS A DAMAGED MAN.

10 MOTO GP GERMANY

THE RACE

VALENTINO ROSSI, WHO SAYS HE DOES NOT PARTICULARLY LIKE THE SACHSENRING, CHALKS UP ANOTHER WIN.

Rossi contains his joy, Gibernau sulks: an odd atmosphere on the podium. Opposite, Olivier Jacque, now a GP wild card.

Races followed one another at a frantic pace this Summer in Europe. For the ones who have success in them, those who win, it's a fortnightly guarantee of passing some unforgettable moments, during which, helped by adrenalin, the rider is taken onto another plane. Euphoria, when it is controlled, is an important ally. After just such a moment, Valentino Rossi proclaimed that there is nothing finer than the motorcycle GP.

But for a man with problems, a constant succession of races like this can also become so many descents into hell. In this case, the adrenalin is no help at all. You have to try to understand, to persuade yourself it's just a bad patch you're going through, and that bad patches in life are made to be forgotten. Ever since that too well known final bend in the first GP of the season at Jerez de la Frontera, Sete Gibernau, the only rider to have given Rossi anything to worry about over the last two years, has been going through what we call a rough patch. For all he may say that he's doing everything he can, for all he may convince himself that the feared adversary of the last two years has not in just a few months turned into friendly fall-guy, that doesn't change a thing. Did he do everything he ought to have done at the start of the race at Estoril? There he was, all alone out in front, he should have been playing the pilot fish for the rest of the pack, just as the first drops started to fall. Then came the crash… Rain, one of his favourite goings, in China? He was seen to park his bike a few metres after the finish line and show the whole world the tyres that his supplier is supposed to have recommended to him, without his having tried them out…

So did he finally think he was going to be able to take Rossi by surprise at Le Mans? He got overtaken. Just as he would be beaten in Catalunya, in front of "his" public. "His" public? In Spain, the media have had their orders now: "Gibernau is no longer a good seller, we want more of Pedrosa!" Ouch! While he closes in on himself, hides in a cocoon where his family is assuming increasing importance, and seems to be all at sea in a world that's not his own ever since he's been sharing his life with Esther Cañadas, "the" Spanish top model, Sete is getting himself in a right pickle. So there was torrential rain at Donington? Yet again he crashes, while Rossi plays Moses, parting the waters and flying along in a cloud of spray. And now we get to the Sachsenring, for the latest episode of the anticipated duel. Valentino Rossi does not like this "Mickey Mouse" circuit, so on the eve of the qualifyings, Sete Gibernau says exactly the opposite. The race soon turned into the confrontation we've been enjoying so much over the last two years. This time, it's going well, Sete is all set to win. He takes the lead in the last lap, he brakes… No, he's left it too late. Forced to go off the track, yet again the Spaniard gives way under the pressure from Rossi, who made no bones about saying, stifling a smile, that "Yes, a mistake by one of my adversaries turned to my advantage." For sure, Gibernau, seated alongside him as protocol requires, would have liked to have been miles away from that spot…

GERMANY MOTO GP

STILL ROSSI, ANOTHER BLUNDER BY GIBERNAU, IN A RACE IN TWO STAGES.

A STRONG LINE-UP
A third Kawasaki was lined up for Olivier Jacque, the hero of Shanghai. For the remainder: nothing to report..

QUALIFYINGS
The Yamaha riders were none too comfortable on the German merry-go-round, Hayden treated himself to a nice pole position, ahead of Gibernau and Barros. So Rossi was "only" starting in the second row.

START
Superb reflexes from Hayden, ahead of Barros, Rossi and Capirossi. The first bend claimed its victims: Byrne and two out of the three Kawasaki riders (Jacque and Hofmann, though the German got back onto the track). First time past the line, Hayden had a 0.853 sec lead over Rossi.

LAP 3
Rossi has come back to just 0.231 sec behind Hayden. A second crash for Hofmann, and a crash for Bayliss..

LAP 6
A terrible somersault from John Hopkins, landing heavily on his back. The red flag went up, but John was able to go back to his stand, where he waved to the camera with a broad smile.

SECOND START
Off they went again for 25 laps. A new holeshot for Hayden, ahead of Rossi, Gibernau who slipped in, and Barros. At the end of the first lap, Hayden had a 0.161 sec lead over Rossi, who would soon pass. Gibernau kept up, Barros wasn't far behind.

LAP 2
Gibernau took the lead (by 0.157 sec).

LAP 5
Checa crashed. Gibernau had a 0.328 sec lead over Rossi (Hayden and Barros were right behind).

MID-RACE (LAP 12)
Still Gibernau, who now had a 0.542 sec lead over Rossi (passed by Hayden just after the line). Barros was fourth at 0.774 sec, Biaggi was at 1.2 sec and spotted approaching Nakano, who at this point was the fastest man on the track

LAP 18
Sete has had a perfect race. His lead now increased to 0.563 sec over Hayden. Behind him, the places were unchanged (Nakano gave way, gradually losing ground behind Biaggi).

LAP 19
Rossi passed Hayden, off in pursuit of his favourite prey, Sete Gibernau.

LAP 20
Gibernau - Rossi = 0.419 sec.

LAP 23
Biaggi passed Barros for fourth place, Rossi gained ground to 0.287 sec.

FINISH (25 LAPS)
0.163 sec going into the last lap, Sete misjudged the first bend, Rossi took advantage of this. His 76th win, now he's gone down in legend alongside Mike Hailwood, receiving a flag to commemorate the event..

CHAMPIONSHIP
120-point lead for Rossi: for a long time now, the question was no longer "if", but "when" Rossi would be crowned. Now it could be at Motegi… in Honda's own back yard. A nice touch, don't you think?

Rossi in the lead, and a green altercation (Jacque-Hofmann) at the first turn. Or, how to quickly eliminate two Kawasakis…

GP GERMANY | 31st July 2005 | Sachsenring | 3.671 m

STARTING GRID
1	69	N. Hayden	Honda	1'22.785
2	15	S. Gibernau	Honda	1'22.889
3	4	A. Barros	Honda	1'22.932
4	46	V. Rossi	Yamaha	1'22.973
5	33	M. Melandri	Honda	1'23.051
6	3	M. Biaggi	Honda	1'23.054
7	5	C. Edwards	Yamaha	1'23.130
8	65	L. Capirossi	Ducati	1'23.174
9	10	K. Roberts	Suzuki	1'23.212
10	21	J. Hopkins	Suzuki	1'23.296
11	7	C. Checa	Ducati	1'23.341
12	56	S. Nakano	Kawasaki	1'23.382
13	66	A. Hofmann	Kawasaki	1'23.405
14	19	O. Jacque	Kawasaki	1'23.715
15	6	M. Tamada	Honda	1'23.860
16	12	T. Bayliss	Honda	1'23.916
17	24	T. Elias	Yamaha	1'24.421
18	11	R. Xaus	Yamaha	1'24.605
19	77	J. Ellison	Blata	1'24.988
20	44	R. Rolfo	Ducati	1'25.011
21	67	S. Byrne	Proton KR	1'25.713
22	27	F. Battaini	Blata	1'26.154

RACE: 25 laps = 91.775 km (*)
1	Valentino Rossi	35'04.434 (156.1997 km/h)
2	Sete Gibernau	+ 0''685
3	Nicky Hayden	+ 0''885
4	Massimiliano Biaggi	+ 2''365
5	Alex Barros	+ 2''855
6	Shinya Nakano	+ 4''557
7	Marco Melandri	+ 12''269
8	Colin Edwards	+ 14''849
9	Loris Capirossi	+ 23''489
10	Makoto Tamada	+ 27''829
11	Kenny Roberts	+ 42''099
12	Toni Elias	+ 47''304
13	Ruben Xaus	+ 1'00.175
14	Roberto Rolfo	+ 1'07.714
15	Franco Battaini	+ 1 lap

(*): Race was red flagged after the fall of John Hopkins (USA, Suzuki). A second start is given for the 25 laps.

Fastest lap
Gibernau, in 1'23.705 (157.883 km/h). New record. Previous record: Barros, in 1'24.056 (157.223 km/h/2004).

Outright fastest lap
Biaggi, in 1'22.756 (159.693 km/h/2004).

CHAMPIONSHIP
1	V. Rossi	236 (8 wins)
2	M. Melandri	116
3	S. Gibernau	115
4	C. Edwards	114
5	M. Biaggi	113
6	A. Barros	101 (1 win)
7	N. Hayden	101 (1 win)
8	L. Capirossi	72
9	S. Nakano	65
10	C. Checa	51

10 · 250cc GERMANY

PEDROSA CAN STAND UP TO ANYTHING... EVEN JORGE LORENZO, A COMPLETELY UNINHIBITED FIGHTER!

A STRONG LINE-UP
Still Cajback for Todorov at Yamaha-Kurz. This is the second GP for the KTM 250 cc. Guest riders: Molina and Polzer (two old hands) and the Germans Aschenbrenner and Walter

QUALIFYING
Alex de Angelis has always been at ease on this rather particular circuit, and achieved the best times just as well on Saturday as on Friday. Pedrosa was beaten by just 0·096 sec. Lorenzo and Porto completed the front row.

START
A strange start, with Takahashi trying to pass everybody, but forgetting to turn, and Lorenzo who took the lead ahead of Aoyama. First time past the line, the two men had a 0·7 second lead over the rest of the pack, led by De Angelis, and comprising Pedrosa, Dovizioso, Porto, De Puniet and company.

LAP 3
A severe crash by Locatelli, left unconscious in the sand trap. Aoyama took the lead, De Angelis was second.

LAP 5
A crash by Lorenzo, in a fight with his sworn "enemy" Dani Pedrosa, whose exhaust got bent in this daring manœuvre.

LAP 7
Dovizioso passed De Angelis to take second place. Aoyama was still ahead, Pedrosa came back into the leading trio..

LAP 8
De Angelis took the lead... but not for long, Aoyama soon claimed his own property back.

LAP 10
De Angelis again. The first six (De Angelis, Dovizioso, Aoyama, Pedrosa, Porto and De Puniet) are all within a second of each other (0·949 sec, to be exact).

LAP 12
Pedrosa took things in hand, De Puniet passed Porto.

MID-RACE (LAP 15)
The World Champion stepped up the pace, Pedrosa had a 0·802 sec lead over De Angelis. Aoyama was third, within a second of the citizen of the Principality of San Marino, Dovizioso snapping at his heels. Porto got the better of his team-mate Randy de Puniet.

LAP 17
Dovizioso passed Aoyama into third place

LAP 21
Aoyama back on the virtual podium again.

LAP 24
Pedrosa still ahead. The fight for fourth place started to get interesting, as Porto had just caught Dovizioso by surprise, but he soon reclaimed his own property.

FINISH (29 LAPS)
Like Rossi in MotoGP, Pedrosa is just too strong in 250 cc, winning with an almost 8 second lead over De Angelis; his team-mate Aoyama managed to save his third place against Dovizioso. West's KTM is once again in the points (tenth).

CHAMPIONSHIP
An exactly 50-point lead for Daniel Pedrosa over Casey Stoner (only seventh in this race), giving the World Champion two GPs in hand.

The Sachsenring also means some surprising viewpoints (left, Sylvain Guintoli). Top right, Pedrosa, with a bent exhaust, makes his mark. Bottom, Dovizioso uses his knee.

GP GERMANY | 31st July 2005 | Sachsenring | 3.671 m

STARTING GRID

1	5	A. De Angelis	Aprilia	1'24.618
2	1	D. Pedrosa	Honda	1'24.714
3	48	J. Lorenzo	Honda	1'24.905
4	19	S. Porto	Aprilia	1'25.193
5	73	H. Aoyama	Honda	1'25.433
6	55	Y. Takahashi	Honda	1'25.469
7	27	C. Stoner	Aprilia	1'25.470
8	7	R. De Puniet	Aprilia	1'25.617
9	80	H. Barbera	Honda	1'25.643
10	34	A. Dovizioso	Honda	1'25.669
11	15	R. Locatelli	Aprilia	1'26.139
12	14	A. West	KTM	1'26.278
13	50	S. Guintoli	Aprilia	1'26.303
14	24	S. Corsi	Aprilia	1'26.320
15	57	C. Davies	Aprilia	1'26.360
16	17	S. Jenkner	Aprilia	1'26.449
17	25	A. Baldolini	Aprilia	1'26.507
18	28	D. Heidolf	Honda	1'26.512
19	96	J. Smrz	Honda	1'26.841
20	32	M. Giansanti	Aprilia	1'26.845
21	6	A. Debon	Honda	1'26.983
22	38	G. Leblanc	Aprilia	1'27.678
23	44	T. Sekiguchi	Aprilia	1'27.950
24	8	A. Ballerini	Aprilia	1'27.954
25	64	R. Rous	Honda	1'28.105
26	36	M. Cardeñas	Aprilia	1'28.522
27	21	A. Vincent	Fantic	1'28.691
28	41	A. Molina	Aprilia	1'28.979
29	26	A. Martensson	Yamaha	1'29.672
30	16	F. Aschenbrenner	Honda	1'29.769
31	23	N. Cajback	Yamaha	1'30.093
32	52	T. Walter	Honda	1'30.502

Not qualified:
	53	P. Lakerveld	Honda	1'30.630
	42	Y. Polzer	Aprilia	1'30.812
	20	G. Ferro	Fantic	1'31.136

RACE: 29 vueltas = 106.459 km

1	Daniel Pedrosa	41'35.089 (153.602 km/h)
2	Alex de Angelis	+ 7''940
3	Hiroshi Aoyama	+ 11''171
4	Andrea Dovizioso	+ 11''346
5	Sebastian Porto	+ 11''444
6	Randy De Puniet	+ 17''536
7	Casey Stoner	+ 17''949
8	Hector Barbera	+ 22''193
9	Yuki Takahashi	+ 42''288
10	Anthony West	+ 42''696
11	Sylvain Guintoli	+ 51''283
12	Alex Debon	+ 1'01.959
13	Dirk Heidolf	+ 1'03.260
14	Steve Jenkner	+ 1'13.348
15	Martin Cardeñas	+ 1'13.813
16	Jakub Smrz	+ 1'13.876
17	Mirko Giansanti	+ 1'14.151
18	Taru Sekiguchi	+ 1'18.289
19	Alvaro Molina	+ 1 lap
20	Radomil Rous	+ 1 lap
21	Andreas Martensson	+ 1 lap
22	Nicolas Cajback	+ 1 lap
23	Thomas Walter	+ 2 laps

Fastest lap
Pedrosa, in 1'25.327 (154.881 km/h).
Record: Porto, in 1'25.118 (155.262 km/h/2004).

Outright fastest lap
De Angelis, in 1'24.618 (156.179 km/h/2005).

CHAMPIONSHIP

1	D. Pedrosa	181 (5 wins)
2	C. Stoner	131 (2 wins)
3	A. Dovizioso	124
4	S. Porto	96 (1 win)
5	R. De Puniet	89 (1 win)
6	A. De Angelis	87
7	H. Aoyama	87
8	J. Lorenzo	78
9	H. Barbera	59
10	S. Corsi	54

GERMANY 125cc

THE RACE IS INTERRUPTED AFTER A CRASH BY POGGIALI. KALLIO, LÜTHI AND SIMONCELLI DON'T GET ANY DESSERT.

A STRONG LINE-UP
Sascha Hommel was back at last with Malaguti (having got back in form by taking part in a few European Championship races), Mateo Tuñez was still replacing Julian Miralles. Five riders held wild cards, including the German hopeful Stefan Bradl and his Austrian team-mate Michael Ranseder (they'll be moving on to GP in 2006).

QUALIFYINGS
Who else but Kallio for pole? No-one. For the sixth time this season, the Finn from KTM had the best time in the qualifying. The "greats" in the class are the front-runners, with Simoncelli, Lüthi (the most consistent performer) and Pasini in the front row, Simón and Talmacsi just behind.

START
The best start from Simoncelli and Lüthi, who went ahead in the turn. As usual, there was some damage in the first bend (Kuzuhara, Pirro, Terol, Bautista). First time over the line, Lüthi was 0·014 sec ahead of Lai, who would soon take over the lead. Simoncelli was third

LAP 2
Simoncelli ahead. Faubel and Iannone crashed

LAP 3
Lüthi again (0·247 sec ahead of Lai). Simoncelli, Talmacsi, Pasini, Kallio and Simón were following..

LAP 5
Gadea crashed. Lüthi 0·415 sec ahead of Simoncelli.

LAP 7
Simoncelli now ahead, Kallio, Pasini and Lüthi right on his heels.

LAP 8
Kallio ahead.

LAP 9
Pasini crashed. Kallio leading, ahead of Lüthi and Talmacsi.

MID-RACE (LAP 13)
Six were fighting it out for victory, with a spread of just 0·854 sec: Kallio, Lüthi, Talmacsi, Simón, Pesek and Simoncelli, in that order.

LAP 17
Di Meglio and Koyama crashed. Kallio and Lüthi gained a 0·5 sec lead over Simoncelli.

LAP 20
Kallio, Lüthi, Simoncelli and Talmacsi: there were now four of them within 0·481 sec of each other. Simón and Pesek got left behind.

LAP 21
Poggiali crashed, his bike staying on the track, the red flag went up. The placings from the previous lap were taken: Kallio won, ahead of Lüthi and Simoncelli. The spectators and observers were frustrated: the battle promised for the final didn't happen. The people involved viewed it differently: "Of course, we all had plans for a final attack, but given where Poggiali's bike was, it was just too dangerous", Lüthi confided.

CHAMPIONSHIP
After Mugello, this is the second time in his career that the Swiss Thomas Lüthi found himself leading the world championships. His lead? Three points ahead of Mika Kallio, six ahead of Talmacsi.

The duel of the year: Mika Kallio (36) against Thomas Lüthi (12). Poggiali's crash (above) put a stop to the race, handing victory to the Finn (right).

GP GERMANY | 31st July 2005 | Sachsenring | 3.671 m

STARTING GRID

1	36	M. Kallio	KTM	1'27.965
2	58	M. Simoncelli	Aprilia	1'28.182
3	12	T. Lüthi	Honda	1'28.240
4	75	M. Pasini	Aprilia	1'28.353
5	60	J. Simón	KTM	1'28.375
6	71	T. Koyama	Honda	1'28.563
7	52	L. Pesek	Derbi	1'28.605
8	14	G. Talmacsi	KTM	1'28.631
9	55	H. Faubel	Aprilia	1'28.635
10	33	S. Gadea	Aprilia	1'28.735
11	41	A. Espargaro	Honda	1'28.736
12	8	L. Zanetti	Aprilia	1'28.917
13	32	F. Lai	Honda	1'29.025
14	29	A. Iannone	Aprilia	1'29.116
15	11	S. Cortese	Honda	1'29.145
16	9	T. Kuzuhara	Honda	1'29.167
17	6	J. Olivé	Aprilia	1'29.175
18	22	P. Nieto	Derbi	1'29.179
19	19	A. Bautista	Honda	1'29.182
20	63	M. Di Meglio	Honda	1'29.254
21	54	M. Poggiali	Gilera	1'29.329
22	43	M. Hernandez	Aprilia	1'29.465
23	45	I. Toth	Aprilia	1'29.468
24	7	A. Masbou	Honda	1'29.480
25	35	R. De Rosa	Aprilia	1'29.535
26	77	S. Bradl	KTM	1'29.565
27	76	M. Ranseder	KTM	1'29.569
28	28	J. Carchano	Aprilia	1'29.906
29	25	D. Giuseppetti	Aprilia	1'30.058
30	44	K. Abraham	Aprilia	1'30.234
31	16	R. Schouten	Honda	1'30.298
32	15	M. Pirro	Malaguti	1'30.350
33	47	A. Rodriguez	Honda	1'30.389
34	18	N. Terol	Derbi	1'30.464
35	10	F. Sandi	Honda	1'30.508
36	86	M. Tuñez	Aprilia	1'30.613
37	13	P. Unger	Aprilia	1'31.076
38	31	S. Hommel	Malaguti	1'31.221
39	26	V. Braillard	Aprilia	1'31.379
40	78	H. Van den berg	Aprilia	1'31.460
41	98	M. Mickan	Honda	1'31.924

RACE: 20 laps = 73.420 km (*)

1	Mika Kallio	29'46.795 (147.925 km/h)	
2	Thomas Lüthi	+ 0''134	
3	Marco Simoncelli	+ 0''288	
4	Gabor Talmacsi	+ 0''481	
5	Julian Simón	+ 1''435	
6	Lukas Pesek	+ 1''628	
7	Fabrizio Lai	+ 15''039	
8	Joan Olivé	+ 15''256	
9	Aleix Espargaro	+ 15''305	
10	Pablo Nieto	+ 15''524	
11	Manuel Poggiali	+ 15''577	
12	Michael Ranseder	+ 20''873	
13	Lorenzo Zanetti	+ 21''045	
14	Sandro Cortese	+ 21''186	
15	Raffaele De Rosa	+ 25''343	
16	Stefan Bradl	+ 26''261	
17	Karel Abraham	+ 27''185	
18	Dario Giuseppetti	+ 31''138	
19	Mateo Tuñez	+ 32''802	
20	Imre Toth	+ 33''272	
21	Patrick Unger	+ 34''418	
22	Vincent Braillard	+ 44''072	
23	Manuel Hernandez	+ 48''367	
24	Manuel Mickan	+ 1'06.745	
25	Hugo Van den Berg	+ 1'06.857	
26	Jordi Carchano	+ 2 laps	

(*): Race was red flagged after Manuel Poggiali having fallen. As a sufficiency distance had been covered, the ranking was established the lap before the accident.

Fastest lap
Kallio, in 1'28.522 (149.291 km/h).
Record: Barbera, in 1'27.680 (150.725 km/h/2004).

Outright fastest lap
Barbera, in 1'27.680 (150.725 km/h/2004).

CHAMPIONSHIP

1	T. Lüthi	119 (1 win)
2	M. Kallio	116 (2 wins)
3	G. Talacsi	113 (2 wins)
4	M. Simoncelli	101 (1 win)
5	M. Pasini	100 (2 wins)
6	J. Simón	91 (1 win)
7	F. Lai	88
8	M. Poggiali	64
9	T. Koyama	52
10	H. Faubel	50

Valentino Rossi, all alone. The soon-to-be seven-time world champion no longer has any competitors of his stature on two wheels.

11

28th August 2005

CZECH REPUBLIC BRNO

Clouds, smiles and glints of sunlight: Brno 2005 in two images.

ROSSI
AND HIS RED LOVES

ALL ALONE ON THE TRACK, VALENTINO ROSSI SET FIRE TO THE PADDOCK WHEN HE ARRIVED IN THE ZECH REPUBLIC: SOMETHING RELATED TO THE CONTINUATION OF HIS FLIRTATION WITH AN ALL-RED, VERY ITALIAN FORMULA 1 SINGLE-SEATER…

MOTO GP CZECH REPUBLIC

THE RACE

VALENTINO ROSSI IS STILL A MOTORCYCLE RIDER, BUT, THIS SUMMER, SOMETHING CHANGED IN HIS SPIRIT.

Not content with getting himself talked about every time he climbs onto his bike (and hence, wins…), Valentino Rossi made the most of his holidays, sparking a new flurry of media attention surrounding his holy person: "But I didn't do anything. Ferrari just invited me for a second test, this time a real working session, over two days; as I was on holiday, and had nothing else to do, I couldn't say no. It's not the sort of invitation you can refuse…"

No sooner had Valentino Rossi arrived in the Brno paddock than he set off a deluge of questions over his medium-term future.

His time behind the wheel of the "rossa"? "I can't talk about the times, Ferrari doesn't want me to. But at the end of the test, I realized that I had improved a lot compared with the first time: it's true, I think that from now on I can also be very fast with the F1." Just as fast? At the same time, a indiscrete remark from la Scuderia chief Jean Todt let slip that "Valentino still has a problem when braking, but in the bends he is as fast as Schumacher…" Ouch!

Is Valentino about to go off to F1?
The whole paddock was shaking; the bosses at Yamaha can no longer be holding out high hopes for the long term. As for Rossi, he repeats that "this test was organized in order to verify certain things", but he doesn't say which things. Be that as it may, something in his thinking has changed over this Summer. Even if he still says loud and clear that motorbikes are the best thing in the world, even though he will look you straight in the eye and insist that F1 is just another adventure like any other, nothing really serious, we can guess that the operation "Rossi-Ferrari" is now officially launched.

The number 1 proof? Still in Brno, Rossi set off another earthquake, this time within the Yamaha team, by announcing that next year he no longer wants to ride under the colours of a cigarette manufacturer (Gauloises, this year). In fact, Rossi would like to form his own team, with his own colours. His own team? "Yes, quite simply so as to be able to organize his timetable more easily, to be able to fit as many F1 tests as he wants into his diary next year. We know, everyone is scared here, but there's nothing we can do to change things", explained a member of the Yamaha team in confidence.

Valentino won't say any more himself, so as not to upset anyone. He even toned down his speech a bit two weeks later, in Japan, to calm down his immediate entourage. But the fact remains that his mind seems to be made up this time: a new challenge, worthy of the figure that he is, awaits him in 2007.

And while we're waiting? Valentino Rossi won this Czech Republic GP, once again after a superb duel with Sete Gibernau. His adversary? Ran out of petrol a few hundred metres short of the finish! Or: how the insolent success of the one contrasts with the henceforth chronic misfortune of the other…

Rossi under a barrage of questions, and in the middle of some acrobatics on the track: we'll miss him, when he moves on to other obsessions.

CZECH REPUBLIC MOTO GP

Sete Gibernau (left) had a remarkable race… until his Honda stopped in the final lap, to the great delight of Loris Capirossi on his Ducati, who came in second.

THE ROSSI-GIBERNAU DUEL ENDED WITH AN EMPTY TANK!

A STRONG LINE-UP
There was a major shake-up between Kenny Roberts and KTM, the Austrian maker having decided to end its (technical and financial) collaboration with Proton. As a result, Kenny has got out his own V5s again. Dorna boss Carmelo Ezpeleta put pressure on KTM, and some engines did finally arrive in Brno as an emergency. At the handlebars, Jeremy McWilliams replaces Shane Byrne (who up till now had been paid by KTM).

QUALIFYINGS
Sete Gibernau intended putting pressure on Rossi, and dominated the qualifyings (Valentino "only" came 4th)

START
Gibernau, Rossi and Melandri set off in the lead. Rossi didn't even wait for the end of the first lap to take the lead ahead of Gibernau, who would hang on his tail..

LAP 3
A superb duel between the two fraternal enemies: Gibernau took the king by surprise, Rossi countered coming out of the straight. Behind, Melandri was already at 0.7 sec, soon to be passed by Hayden.

LAP 4
A rare event: an error by Rossi. Gibernau passed, with a half-second lead at the line.

LAP 7
0.311 sec between Gibernau and Rossi. Hayden was third, 1.349 sec behind the World Champion, ahead of Melandri. Barros passed Capirossi for fifth place, McWilliams stops.

LAP 9
Barros took Melandri by surprise, he was 0.469 sec behind Nicky Hayden. In front, there was 0.589 sec between Gibernau and Rossi.

MID-RACE (LAP 11)
Gibernau still hanging on: the Spaniard had a 0.140 sec lead over Rossi. Third, Hayden saw himself overtaken by Barros in fine form. Capirossi took Melandri by surprise for fifth place

LAP 12
Rossi was ahead

LAP 13
Rossi's lead was 0.2 sec

LAP 17
Gibernau was still in Rossi's slipstream, Capirossi passed Hayden.

LAP 18
Sete took back the lead, Barros and Capirossi were closing: now there were four of them within less than a second of each other.

LAP 20
Six riders within 2.137 sec (Biaggi passed Hayden), everyone's having a good time. Gibernau holds out, Capirossi hangs on.

FINISH (22 LAPS)
Rossi passed one lap from the finish (a gap of just 0.055 sec), managing to forge a 0.4 sec lead over a single section. Sete was taking every imaginable risk… but his bike stopped in the last lap, out of petrol. So it was that Capirossi found himself on the second step of the podium.

CHAMPIONSHIP
261 for Valentino Rossi, 129 for his new would-be successor, Max Biaggi: that makes a 132-point lead. All he needs to do is come second in Japan (assuming Max wins there), in order to be crowned in Honda's own back yard

---

GP CZECH REPUBLIC | 28th August 2005 | Brno | 5.403 m

STARTING GRID

1	15	S. Gibernau	Honda	1'57.504
2	69	N. Hayden	Honda	1'57.551
3	65	L. Capirossi	Ducati	1'57.685
4	46	V. Rossi	Yamaha	1'57.875
5	33	M. Melandri	Honda	1'57.999
6	7	C. Checa	Ducati	1'58.185
7	4	A. Barros	Honda	1'58.223
8	21	J. Hopkins	Suzuki	1'58.277
9	5	C. Edwards	Yamaha	1'58.323
10	3	M. Biaggi	Honda	1'58.337
11	56	S. Nakano	Kawasaki	1'58.490
12	6	M. Tamada	Honda	1'58.610
13	12	T. Bayliss	Honda	1'58.662
14	66	A. Hofmann	Kawasaki	1'58.793
15	24	T. Elias	Yamaha	1'58.815
16	9	N. Aoki	Suzuki	1'59.495
17	10	K. Roberts	Suzuki	1'59.734
18	77	J. Ellison	Blata	2'00.529
19	44	R. Rolfo	Ducati	2'00.879
20	11	R. Xaus	Yamaha	2'01.535
21	27	F. Battaini	Blata	2'02.585
22	99	J. McWilliams	Proton KR	2'04.663

RACE: 22 laps = 118.866 km

1	Valentino Rossi	43'56.539 (162.302 km/h)
2	Loris Capirossi	+ 1''837
3	Massimiliano Biaggi	+ 3''444
4	Alex Barros	+ 4''148
5	Nicky Hayden	+ 4''363
6	Marco Melandri	+ 11''150
7	Colin Edwards	+ 13''532
8	Carlos Checa	+ 19''331
9	Troy Bayliss	+ 27''125
10	Makoto Tamada	+ 27''248
11	Kenny Roberts	+ 27''684
12	Shinya Nakano	+ 27''803
13	John Hopkins	+ 28''278
14	Toni Elias	+ 28''571
15	Alex Hofmann	+ 29''768
16	Nobuatsu Aoki	+ 41''778
17	Roberto Rolfo	+ 57''800
18	Ruben Xaus	+ 1'08.082
19	James Ellison	+ 1'42.169
20	Franco Battaini	+ 1'54.784

Fastest lap
Rossi, in 1'58.787 (163.745 km/h). New record.
Previous record: Barros, en 1'59.302 (163.038 km/h/2004).

Outright fastest lap
Gibernau, in 1'57.504 (165.533 km/h/2004).

CHAMPIONSHIP

1	V. Rossi	261 (9 wins)
2	M. Biaggi	129
3	M. Melandri	126
4	C. Edwards	123
5	S. Gibernau	115
6	A. Barros	114 (1 win)
7	N. Hayden	112 (1 win)
8	L. Capirossi	92
9	S. Nakano	69
10	C. Checa	59

250cc CZECH REPUBLIC

DESPITE LORENZO'S INCREASINGLY OBVIOUS AMBITIONS, PEDROSA GAVE A FORCEFUL DEMONSTRATION

A STRONG LINE-UP
Not a lot to report in this class. Worth noting was the presence once again of Spaniard Alvaro Molina, one of the regular players in the European Championships. One Czech rider was invited: Michal Filla, 24, a young man born in Brno who had already been seen on this track last year..

QUALIFYINGS
Now Spain is getting excited over a new duel, almost as heated as the one seen in the 80s between Sito Pons and Juan Garriga. This time, it's Jorge Lorenzo, a laid-back young man, who decided a long time ago not to kick up a fuss opposite outgoing champion Pedrosa. The two men had already crossed swords at the Sachsenring; here they were fighting to the 1/1000th of a second (0·003 sec in Lorenzo's favour after the deciding session). Stoner and Dovizioso rounded off the front row. Ferro and Tedorov didn't make it through qualification.

START
Takahashi and Barbera made contact during the first lap, Corsi crashed, De Puniet completely lost the plot.

LAP 3
The Japanese Aoyama led ahead of Alex de Angelis. Lorenzo, Stoner, Dovizioso and Pedrosa are right behind them. Guintoli (who became the father of a little girl Alicia during the break) was a brilliant seventh.

LAP 5
Lorenzo took matters in hand, but Aoyama and De Angelis wouldn't let go of their leading positions.

MID-RACE (LAP 10)
Still Lorenzo, 0·184 sec ahead of De Angelis. The Aprilia rider led a pack comprising Pedrosa, Aoyama, Stoner and Dovizioso. Porto, seventh, is within 7 seconds of the 125 cc title-holder.

LAP 11
Pedrosa was second, within 0·351 sec of Lorenzo. People were already relishing the explanations to come between the two Spaniards.

LAP 14
Lorenzo, De Angelis and Pedrosa: all three within 0·395 sec of each other, Casey Stoner right up there with them. Behind the Australian, a little gap had opened with Dovizioso, while Aoyama gave way.

LAP 16
Pedrosa was once again second, De Angelis made a mistake and immediately dropped back. Coming out of the straight, Pedrosa took the lead; Lorenzo countered the first time, but not the second.

LAP 18
0·470 sec lead for Pedrosa over Lorenzo. With third place at stake, Stoner passed De Angelis.

FINISH (20 LAPS)
Strong, very strong, too strong: Pedrosa won once again. Lorenzo came second, Stoner putting an Aprilia on the podium; Aoyama had the last word against Dovizioso

CHAMPIONSHIP
59-point lead for Pedrosa over Stoner, putting the outgoing champion more than two races ahead.

Lorenzo led the pack in the first metres... but Daniel Pedrosa (below left, under a threatening sky) wasn't going to get pushed around. Right, Arnaud Vincent, 25th in the qualifiers.

GP CZECH REPUBLIC | 28th August 2005 | Brno | 5.403 m

STARTING GRID
1	48	J. Lorenzo	Honda	2'02.261
2	1	D. Pedrosa	Honda	2'02.264
3	27	C. Stoner	Aprilia	2'02.468
4	34	A. Dovizioso	Honda	2'02.493
5	7	R. De Puniet	Aprilia	2'02.813
6	19	S. Porto	Aprilia	2'02.822
7	5	A. De Angelis	Aprilia	2'02.851
8	73	H. Aoyama	Honda	2'03.131
9	55	Y. Takahashi	Honda	2'03.529
10	50	S. Guintoli	Aprilia	2'03.759
11	15	R. Locatelli	Aprilia	2'03.851
12	80	H. Barbera	Honda	2'03.973
13	24	S. Corsi	Aprilia	2'04.302
14	96	J. Smrz	Honda	2'04.486
15	57	C. Davies	Aprilia	2'04.674
16	8	A. Ballerini	Aprilia	2'05.224
17	25	A. Baldolini	Aprilia	2'05.360
18	64	R. Rous	Honda	2'05.368
19	6	A. Debon	Honda	2'05.448
20	28	D. Heidolf	Honda	2'05.458
21	32	M. Giansanti	Aprilia	2'05.574
22	17	S. Jenkner	Aprilia	2'05.590
23	14	A. West	KTM	2'05.621
24	44	T. Sekiguchi	Aprilia	2'05.774
25	21	A. Vincent	Fantic	2'06.558
26	38	G. Leblanc	Aprilia	2'07.431
27	36	M. Cardeñas	Aprilia	2'08.388
28	70	M. Filla	Aprilia	2'08.816
29	41	A. Molina	Aprilia	2'09.287
30	23	N. Cajback	Yamaha	2'10.123
Not qualified:				
	20	G. Ferro	Fantic	2'11.336
	22	A. Todorov	Yamaha	2'13.084

RACE: 20 laps = 108.060 km
1	Daniel Pedrosa	41'24.944 (156.549 km/h)
2	Jorge Lorenzo	+ 1''303
3	Casey Stoner	+ 4''253
4	Alex de Angelis	+ 5''326
5	Hiroshi Aoyama	+ 8''392
6	Andrea Dovizioso	+ 8''471
7	Sebastian Porto	+ 25''545
8	Randy De Puniet	+ 32''159
9	Roberto Locatelli	+ 33''969
10	Sylvain Guintoli	+ 35''544
11	Jakub Smrz	+ 51''827
12	Anthony West	+ 52''049
13	Alex Debon	+ 58''214
14	Radomil Rous	+ 58''604
15	Steve Jenkner	+ 58''911
16	Andrea Ballerini	+ 1'06.203
17	Mirko Giansanti	+ 1'14.453
18	Arnaud Vincent	+ 1'27.753
19	Martin Cardeñas	+ 1'28.522
20	Alvaro Molina	+ 1'48.266
21	Gregory Leblanc	+ 1'49.455
22	Michal Filla	+ 1 tour
23	Alex Baldolini	+ 1 tour
24	Nicolas Cajback	+ 1 tour

Fastest lap
Pedrosa, in 2'02.554 (158.712 km/h). New record.
Previous record: Pedrosa, in 2'03.332 (157.710 km/h/2004).

Outright fastest lap
Lorenzo, in 2'02.261 (159.261 km/h/2005).

CHAMPIONSHIP
1	D. Pedrosa	206 (6 wins)
2	C. Stoner	147 (2 wins)
3	A. Dovizioso	134
4	S. Porto	105 (1 win)
5	A. De Angelis	100
6	J. Lorenzo	98
7	H. Aoyama	98
8	R. De Puniet	97 (1 win)
9	H. Barbera	59
10	S. Corsi	54

CZECH REPUBLIC 125cc

THOMAS LÜTHI'S SECOND VICTORY, AFTER A RISKY FINAL LAP.

A STRONG LINE-UP
A brave return by Julian Miralles Junior (seriously injured at Mugello). David Bonache appeared in the LG Mobile Galicia team, replacing his compatriot Angel Rodriguez. Amongst the wild cards were the two riders from the KTM Junior team (Ranseder and Bradl), along with three young Czechs (Vostarek, Razek and Mayer).

QUALIFYINGS
The tension mounted between the contesters for the title. On the Friday, at the end of the final lap, Kallio pulled back in dangerously onto Lüthi as they crossed the line; luckily, no harm was done. On the Saturday, Thomas Lüthi dominated the two sessions, earning himself the second pole position of his career, after Le Mans.

START
A few drops of rain fell on the riders just before taking to the grid. Lüthi took the lead right away. Lai worked his way in, but the Swiss reclaimed his property, crossing the line with a 0·274 sec lead over Kallio. Then came Lai, Pasini, Talmacsi and the rest of the pack.

LAP 2
0·961 sec over Lüthi.

LAP 5
The Swiss rider's advantage increased to 1·162 sec (3rd lap), Pasini was now second at 0·413 sec, Kallio and Zanetti right behind him. Simoncelli was a second behind the group.

LAP 6
Still Lüthi ahead of Pasini. Masbou, Koyama and Ranseder crashed.

LAP 8
Kallio found his opening. Right on the line, the Finn, the Swiss and Pasini lay within 0·147 sec of each other (Pasini took the lead coming out of the straight). Zanetti and Simoncelli kept up; behind them, the gap had already widened.

MID-RACE (LAP 10)
Pasini and Lüthi were neck and neck (0·44 sec), Kallio is at 0·2 sec, Zanetti at 0·5 sec. Pesek (Derbi) crashed..

LAP 11
Lüthi passed. The first five are within 0·663 sec of each other.

LAP 13
Zanetti is left behind, Lüthi still in front, by just 0·2 sec.

LAP 15
The cards were completely shuffled around. Now it was Pasini, Kallio, Simoncelli and Lüthi, all within less than 0·4 sec of each other.

LAP 17
Lüthi took back the lead, at a time when the sky looked increasingly threatening: 0·518 sec lead over Kallio, Pasini and Simoncelli.

FINISH (19 LAPS)
With it raining more heavily at one point on the circuit, Pasini crashed. Lüthi had a 1·485 sec lead going into the last lap, earning himself his second victory at the highest level. Even the excellent (but hard-to-please) Italian magazine "Motosprint" awarded him the top mark (10) for his perfect weekend.

CHAMPIONSHIP
Lüthi increased his lead over Kallio by 5 little points. Pasini was the great loser of the weekend

Hansueli Lüthi, Thomas' father, managed to persuade the track marshals to let him step over the barriers. He can proudly hand a Swiss flag to his son.

GP CZECH REPUBLIC | 28th August 2005 | Brno | 5.403 m

STARTING GRID

1	12	T. Lüthi	Honda	2'08.638
2	75	M. Pasini	Aprilia	2'08.670
3	36	M. Kallio	KTM	2'08.875
4	58	M. Simoncelli	Aprilia	2'08.953
5	14	G. Talmacsi	KTM	2'09.045
6	11	S. Cortese	Honda	2'09.205
7	32	F. Lai	Honda	2'09.472
8	52	L. Pesek	Derbi	2'09.533
9	71	T. Koyama	Honda	2'09.807
10	35	R. De Rosa	Aprilia	2'09.896
11	7	A. Masbou	Honda	2'09.905
12	76	M. Ranseder	KTM	2'09.998
13	60	J. Simón	KTM	2'10.049
14	54	M. Poggiali	Gilera	2'10.057
15	8	L. Zanetti	Aprilia	2'10.128
16	55	H. Faubel	Aprilia	2'10.176
17	63	M. Di Meglio	Honda	2'10.184
18	29	A. Iannone	Aprilia	2'10.227
19	22	P. Nieto	Derbi	2'10.287
20	33	S. Gadea	Aprilia	2'10.350
21	19	A. Bautista	Honda	2'10.499
22	43	M. Hernandez	Aprilia	2'10.587
23	41	A. Espargaro	Honda	2'10.787
24	44	K. Abraham	Aprilia	2'11.315
25	45	I. Toth	Aprilia	2'11.339
26	77	S. Bradl	KTM	2'11.400
27	16	R. Schouten	Honda	2'11.485
28	9	T. Kuzuhara	Honda	2'11.723 (*)
29	25	D. Giuseppetti	Aprilia	2'11.848
30	15	M. Pirro	Malaguti	2'12.110
31	18	N. Terol	Derbi	2'12.320
32	6	J. Olivé	Aprilia	2'12.328
33	26	V. Braillard	Aprilia	2'12.831
34	87	P. Vostarek	Honda	2'12.936
35	10	F. Sandi	Honda	2'13.107
36	28	J. Carchano	Aprilia	2'13.433
37	31	S. Hommel	Malaguti	2'13.603
38	99	T. Mayer	Aprilia	2'14.191
39	48	D. Bonache	Honda	2'14.771
40	84	J. Miralles	Aprilia	2'15.130
41	97	L. Razek	Honda	2'15.603

(*): Having fallen 2 times on Saturday, T. Kuzuhara (J, Honda) is forced to pull out with a broken right collarbone.

RACE: 19 laps = 102.657 km

1	Thomas Lüthi	41'32.409 (148.176 km/h)
2	Mika Kallio	+ 3''212
3	Marco Simoncelli	+ 3''326
4	Sergio Gadea	+ 7''754
5	Lorenzo Zanetti	+ 14''453
6	Fabrizio Lai	+ 25''156
7	Mike di Meglio	+ 25''247
8	Manuel Poggiali	+ 25''509
9	Gabor Talmacsi	+ 25''773
10	Julian Simón	+ 26''066
11	Andrea Iannone	+ 28''977
12	Alvaro Bautista	+ 30''360
13	Aleix Espargaro	+ 30''375
14	Sandro Cortese	+ 30''759
15	Stefan Bradl	+ 33''726
16	Pablo Nieto	+ 36''880
17	Raffaele De Rosa	+ 38''339
18	Imre Toth	+ 38''415
19	Nicolas Terol	+ 41''510
20	Manuel Hernandez	+ 44''672
21	Vincent Braillard	+ 47''255
22	Joan Olivé	+ 1'02.693
23	Sascha Hommel	+ 1'32.186
24	Thomas Mayer	+ 1'32.368
25	Julian Miralles	+ 2'09.147
26	David Bonache	+ 2'17.127

Fastest lap
Gadea, in 2'08.931 (150.862 km/h).
Record: Cecchinello, in 2'07.836 (152.154 km/h/2003).

Outright fastest lap
Cecchinello, in 2'07.836 (152.154 km/h/2003).

CHAMPIONSHIP

1	T. Lüthi	144 (2 wins)
2	M. Kallio	136 (2 wins)
3	G. Talmacsi	120 (2 wins)
4	M. Simoncelli	117 (1 win)
5	M. Pasini	100 (2 wins)
6	F. Lai	98
7	J. Simón	97 (1 win)
8	M. Poggiali	72
9	M. di Meglio	54
10	T. Koyama	52

John Hopkins qualified on his Suzuki, fitted with Bridgestone tyres, to place in the first row.

12

17th September 2005

JAPAN MOTEGI

The accident that would cause a lot of ink to be spilled: Lüthi fell, Koyama avoided him, Gadea hit his ankle and used the Swiss rider's machine as a springboard: the red flags went up to stop the race, and the ranking in the previous lap was taken into account. Lüthi, groggy but not seriously hurt, thus recovered the 20 points for second place.

WHERE'S THE SPORT,
IN ALL THIS?

GP WAS A STRANGE WEEKEND, WHERE THE PROCEEDINGS WERE MARKED BY COMPLAINTS AND PROTESTS, AND WHERE PEOPLE FORGOT THAT IN THE 125CC, TWO YOUNG LADS - LÜTHI AND GADEA - COULD HAVE BEEN SERIOUSLY INJURED.

MOTO GP JAPAN

THE RACE

THE BUMP BETWEEN ROSSI AND MELANDRI ENRAGED HRC. ONE MORE COMPLAINT FOR THIS ODD WEEKEND

We were probably all expecting too much. Such a fine celebration, one of those thumbed noses that Valentino Rossi is so good at: winning his second title in a row for Yamaha, on the Honda circuit, built by Honda, for Honda, in front of a museum to the glory of Honda, watched by a party of Honda employees, turned up in Hondas to watch Hondas.

Alas, that scenario was too piquant: the formidable Valentino Rossi winning machine committed two errors this weekend: on Saturday, by taking a few seconds too many fitting the last set of qualification tyres; and on Sunday, when he was caught out by Marco Melandri's early braking (so Vale says…), and the two men found themselves on the ground. Not that it makes any difference, for Rossi is still going to be World Champion for the seventh time.

No, after this weekend at Motegi, an odd feeling has invaded people's minds, an almost universal malaise in the face of an unfortunate new trend in modern racing (run by commercial interests): the use of legal means to try and influence sporting results.

With six races in the space of eight weekends, three world titles at stake, and interests amounting to millions in the top class surrounding the Valentino Rossi phenomenon, Autumn 2005 in Motorcycle GP couldn't help but be played out under extreme tension.

And right from the first act of this explosive final, this tension, this pressure, relegated the sporting gesture,

Max Biaggi was no longer enough, HRC needed other weapons to beat Rossi.

human values, into second place. The 125 cc race? Instead of thanking God for having spared Swiss Thomas Lüthi and Spaniard Sergio Gadea the worst, the paddock, this astonishing microcosm of 2,000 people who live together for eight months out of the year, flew into a fury over the point of rules that allowed Lüthi to keep his 20 points for second place. The 250 cc race and the demonstration of a still almost unknown Japanese rider, Hiroshi Aoyama? Wiped out by the "affair" of the day, in which the too-fiery Spaniard Jorge Lorenzo was obliged to pass a one-race suspension (in Malaysia) for driving judged dangerous.

The race of races, reserved for the stars of the MotoGP class? A shame for Loris Capirossi, for Ducati and for Bridgestone: their feat of the day was totally overshadowed by the threat hanging for a few hours over Valentino Rossi, whom certain parties (the HRC, on behalf of all the Honda teams) would have liked to have seen given a one-race suspension after his "right on the limit" attack on Marco Melandri. Valentino Rossi's too strong? Let's try and muzzle him! Because motorcycle sport is constantly growing, with more and more people taking an interest in it - and hence, it's generating increasing financial interest - from now on they'll be trying anything.

In this highly-charged atmosphere, it only remains to be seen who will keep a cool head the longest. And whether, unfortunately, we will not soon be regretting having gone too far in this incitement to hatred.

Valentino Rossi moved up into the wake of Marco Melandri's Honda. A few kilometres further on, at a braking point, the world champion tangled with his compatriot's bike

JAPAN MOTO GP 12

ROSSI'S BLUNDER MEANT THE SECOND CORONATION OF THE CAPIROSSI-DUCATI PAIRING.

A STONG LINE-UP
Injured during motocross in Australia, Bayliss was replaced by Tohru Ukawa. The Proton KR team was not present, but Kenny Roberts and his second, Chuck Aksland, did make the trip to Motegi: they had meetings with the HRC, with the aim of obtaining some Honda V5s for 2006. As anticipated, Moriwaki was present (with Naoki Matsudo).

ESSAIS
Capirossi was on demonstration, on the circuit where it can be guessed (Tamada the winner last year, Nakano third) that the Bridgestones are one length ahead. Besides, another rider using Japanese tyres (Hopkins) made the second-fastest time. Rossi only came eleventh, as - short of a few seconds - he wasn't able to use his last set of qualification tyres.

START
Super start for Melandri, ahead of Biaggi, Capirossi, Hopkins and Tamada. First time across the line, Melandri had a 0.770 sec lead over Capirossi. Rossi was already seventh. Matsudo went off into the sand trap.

LAP 2
Rossi was fifth.

LAP 3
Hofmann crashed, injuring himself and taking Rolfo down with him. Capirossi got back to within 0.241 sec of Melandri, Rossi was still being blocked by Tamada.

LAP 4
Rossi was fourth, 1.088 behind Biaggi

LAP 7
Melandri, Capirossi and Biaggi were within 0.323 sec of each other. Rossi just had an alert, he was within 0.299 sec of Max.

LAP 9
Nakano abandoned the race (engine broken).

LAP 10
Attack by Capirossi, who got scared… and dropped one place. Melandri was now 0.199 sec ahead of Biaggi. Rossi was fourth.

MID-RACE (LAP 12)
Gibernau crashed. Biaggi took over the lead, 0.373 sec ahead of Capirossi. Melandri was third. Rossi made a come-back.

LAP 13
Rossi wanted to surprise Melandri at the moment of braking; he touched him, and both men ended up on the ground. Melandri was injured (a foot-rest from Rossi's Yamaha went through his boot). Valentino's coronation is put back a few days.

LAP 15
Barros crashed.

LAP 18
0.212 sec lead for Biaggi over Capirossi, who got past a little further on.

LAP 19
Capirossi gained a 0.312 sec lead.

FINISH (24 LAPS)
The second victory for the Capirossi-Ducati combination, a second success in a row for Bridgestone tyres at Motegi. Biaggi came second, theoretically still in the running for the title. There were only eleven of them left at the finish of this peculiar race.

CHAMPIONSHIP
261 points for Rossi, 149 for Biaggi = Valentino can afford to lose 12 in Malaysia (if Biaggi wins, "Vale" will have to settle for fourth place).

A glorious day for European motorcycling, in Honda's back yard: Loris Capirossi (on the podium with his boss, Livio Suppo) and Ducati had written a perfect story.

GP JAPAN | 17th September 2005 | Motegi | 4.801 m

STARTING GRID				
1	65	L. Capirossi	Ducati	1'46.363
2	21	J. Hopkins	Suzuki	1'46.861
3	33	M. Melandri	Honda	1'46.867
4	6	M. Tamada	Honda	1'47.043
5	3	M. Biaggi	Honda	1'47.089
6	69	N. Hayden	Honda	1'47.166
7	15	S. Gibernau	Honda	1'47.168
8	10	K. Roberts	Suzuki	1'47.257
9	7	C. Checa	Ducati	1'47.323
10	4	A. Barros	Honda	1'47.562
11	46	V. Rossi	Yamaha	1'47.563
12	66	A. Hofmann	Kawasaki	1'47.594
13	5	C. Edwards	Yamaha	1'47.678
14	56	S. Nakano	Kawasaki	1'47.787
15	72	T. Ukawa	Honda	1'48.194
16	44	R. Rolfo	Ducati	1'48.733
17	24	T. Elias	Yamaha	1'48.861
18	45	N. Matsudo	Moriwaki	1'49.734
19	11	R. Xaus	Yamaha	1'49.969
20	27	F. Battaini	Blata	1'51.902
21	77	J. Ellison	Blata	1'51.972

RACE 24 laps = 115.224 km		
1	Loris Capirossi	43'30.499 (158.499 km/h)
2	Massimiliano Biaggi	+ 1''479
3	Makoto Tamada	+ 16''227
4	Carlos Checa	+ 22''148
5	John Hopkins	+ 33''212
6	Colin Edwards	+ 34''915
7	Nicky Hayden	+ 45''894
8	Kenny Roberts	+ 56''498
9	Toni Elias	+ 1'12.037
10	Ruben Xaus	+ 1'34.927
11	Franco Battaini	+ 1 tour

Fastest lap
Capirossi, in 1'47.968 (160.080 km/h). New record. Previous record: Tamada, in 1'48.524 (159.260 km/h/2004).

Outright fastest lap
Capirossi, in 1'46.363 (162.496 km/h/2005).

CHAMPIONSHIP		
1	V. Rossi	261 (9 wins)
2	M. Biaggi	149
3	C. Edwards	133
4	M. Melandri	126
5	N. Hayden	121 (1 win)
6	L. Capirossi	117 (1 win)
7	S. Gibernau	115
8	A. Barros	114 (1 win)
9	C. Checa	72
10	S. Nakano	69

12 250cc JAPAN

In the lead from the start, Hiroshi Aoyama was to have a perfect run: his first GP win. Further back, things were trickier for the German rider, Heidolf (28), and the Czech, Smrz (on the ground).

A FIRST FOR HIROSHI AOYAMA, AND A PUNISHMENT FOR JORGE LORENZO.

A STRONG LINE-UP
There was a change in the France-Scrab Equipe GP team, as Gregory Leblanc was replaced by the young Mathieu Gines (not yet 17), this year's 125 cc Champion of France. Five Japanese riders held wild cards, including Shuhei Aoyama, the brother of Pedrosa's team-mate

QUALIFYING
Talking of Pedrosa: the World Champion has already had some problems at Motegi over the last few years, and he had three crashes during the qualifyings; as a result: he only managed the seventh time and was placed in row two. His team-mate Aoyama had the last word, opposite the ever-more fiery Lorenzo.

START
Super start by Aoyama, who was soon passed by Lorenzo and De Angelis. Lorenzo ended the first lap with a 0.368 lead over Aoyama. De Angelis is right behind, Pedrosa a little further behind.

LAP 3
First West crashed, then the brilliant guest rider Shuhei Aoyama. Lorenzo was still in front, the first nine were within less than 2 sec.

LAP 5
Hiroshi Aoyama took matters in hand, ahead of De Angelis, Lorenzo and Dovizioso. There were still ten within less than 2 sec.

LAP 7
Dovizioso had just made the best time, he was second, 0.435 sec ahead of Aoyama

LAP 11
A crash from Porto. Now it was De Angelis who was trying to hang on Aoyama's tail.

MID-RACE (LAP 12)
Aoyama had a 0.432 sec lead over De Angelis. Dovizioso was third (0.485 sec off the Aprilia rider), ahead of Stoner, Lorenzo, Takahashi, Pedrosa and De Puniet, eighth.

LAP 14
Pedrosa was fifth, having just completed the best lap of the race..

LAP 17
In front, Aoyama and De Angelis were within a fraction over 0.3 sec; further off, Dovizioso led the pack comprising Stoner and Pedrosa. Lorenzo and the others were left behind.

LAP 19
Aoyama made the break: a 1.218 sec lead over a trio formed by De Angelis, Dovizioso and Pedrosa.

LAP 21
With second place at stake, a superb heated exchange between De Angelis, Pedrosa and Dovizioso.

FINISH (23 LAPS)
Aoyama gained his first success, but everyone was laughing at him. The fight between De Angelis and Pedrosa was crazy, all the more so because Lorenzo came back up, but made contact: first he touched Pedrosa's bike, then he crashed, taking De Angelis with him (who got back on the track). Judged dangerous, Lorenzo's driving earned him a one-race suspension (Malaysia).

CHAMPIONSHIP
Pedrosa has made one step closer to the title. His lead is now 63 points over Stoner, i.e. more than two races in hand.

GP JAPAN | 17th September 2005 | Motegi | 4.801 m

STARTING GRID

1	73	H. Aoyama	Honda	1'51.843
2	48	J. Lorenzo	Honda	1'51.859
3	75	S. Aoyama	Honda	1'52.374
4	5	A. De Angelis	Aprilia	1'52.408
5	34	A. Dovizioso	Honda	1'52.603
6	55	Y. Takahashi	Honda	1'52.634
7	1	D. Pedrosa	Honda	1'52.662
8	7	R. De Puniet	Aprilia	1'52.890
9	27	C. Stoner	Aprilia	1'52.923
10	19	S. Porto	Aprilia	1'52.966
11	50	S. Guintoli	Aprilia	1'53.768
12	44	T. Sekiguchi	Aprilia	1'53.868
13	80	H. Barbera	Honda	1'53.925
14	14	A. West	KTM	1'53.970
15	17	S. Jenkner	Aprilia	1'54.060
16	6	A. Debon	Honda	1'54.245
17	15	R. Locatelli	Aprilia	1'54.345
18	78	R. Yokoe	Yamaha	1'54.435
19	96	J. Smrz	Honda	1'54.458
20	28	D. Heidolf	Honda	1'54.512
21	32	M. Giansanti	Aprilia	1'54.539
22	64	R. Rous	Honda	1'55.006
23	57	C. Davies	Aprilia	1'55.065
24	24	S. Corsi	Aprilia	1'55.105
25	79	M. Tokudome	Yamaha	1'55.206
26	8	A. Ballerini	Aprilia	1'55.240
27	25	A. Baldolini	Aprilia	1'55.789
28	93	K. Takahashi	Honda	1'55.815
29	36	M. Cardeñas	Aprilia	1'55.986
30	77	M. Akiya	Yamaha	1'56.647
31	21	A. Vincent	Fantic	1'56.936
32	56	M. Gines	Aprilia	1'56.955

Not qualified:

	23	N. Cajback	Yamaha	1'59.899
	20	G. Ferro	Fantic	2'02.055
	22	A. Todorov	Yamaha	2'03.740

RACE: 23 laps = 110.423 km

1	Hiroshi Aoyama	43'52.454 (151.008 km/h)
2	Daniel Pedrosa	+ 5''313
3	Casey Stoner	+ 7''781
4	Yuki Takahashi	+ 10''222
5	Randy De Puniet	+ 10''763
6	Andrea Dovizioso	+ 11''054
7	Alex de Angelis	+ 19''199
8	Hector Barbera	+ 24''665
9	Alex Debon	+ 37''683
10	Sylvain Guintoli	+ 38''122
11	Simone Corsi	+ 38''194
12	Steve Jenkner	+ 53''211
13	Mirko Giansanti	+ 56''364
14	Alex Baldolini	+ 1'08.640
15	Radomil Rous	+ 1'09.205
16	Kouki Takahashi	+ 1'17.982
17	Martin Cardeñas	+ 1'25.096
18	Dirk Heidolf	+ 1'26.088
19	Mamoru Akiya	+ 1'33.286
20	Masaki Tokudome	+ 1'35.598
21	Mathieu Gines	+ 1'37.552

Fastest lap
Pedrosa, in 1'53.199 (152.683 km/h).
Record: Nakano, in 1'52.253 (153.970 km/h/2000).

Outright fastest lap
H. Aoyama, in 1'51.843 (154.534 km/h/2005).

CHAMPIONSHIP

1	D. Pedrosa	226 (6 wins)
2	C. Stoner	163 (2 wins)
3	A. Dovizioso	144
4	H. Aoyama	123 (1 win)
5	A. De Angelis	109
6	R. De Puniet	108 (1 win)
7	S. Porto	105 (1 win)
8	J. Lorenzo	98
9	H. Barbera	67
10	S. Corsi	59

JAPAN 125cc

KALLIO BEAT LÜTHI, WHO WAS ABSENT FROM THE PODIUM. AND FOR GOOD REASON... HE WAS IN THE HOSPITAL.

A STRONG LINE-UP
Poor Julian Miralles Junior: severely injured in Italy, the Spaniard had made a brave comeback in the Czech Republic; sadly, he was injured again during a training session (motocross). He was replaced by Mateo Tuñez, who achieved the best time in the race before crashing. For Derbi, Enrique Jerez used the bike normally ridden by Nicolas Terol, and for Molenaar, the Japanese Takumi Takahashi took the place of Raymond Schouten.

QUALIFYINGS
Who but Kallio in pole position? But no: not Kallio, but his KTML team-mate Gabor Talmacsi. The Finn (5th) and Lüthi (7th), the two strong men of the championship, found themselves in the second row, preceded by Pasini and Simoncelli, as well as surprise guest Koyama, on the Honda-Ajo.

START
Best start from Pasini, taking the lead ahead of Kallio, Koyama, Talmacsi and Lüthi. Simón didn't finish the first lap. First time over the line, Pasini, Kallio, Talmacsi and Lüthi all lay within 0·512 sec of each other.

LAP 3
Best lap from Lüthi, returning to third position

LAP 5
In a single manœuvre, Lüthi passed both Kallio and Talmacsi, who had temporarily taken the lead

LAP 7
Pasini took the lead. Lüthi was 0·126 sec behind, Talmacsi and Kallio sticking close behind, along with Faubel, Poggiali and Koyama.

LAP 8
Frenzy on the track between Pasini, Talmacsi, Kallio, Lüthi and Faubel. Tuñez, who had been making a strong comeback, crashed.

MID-RACE (LAP 10)
Simoncelli crashed. Nine of them were within 1·372 sec: Talmacsi, Pasini, Kallio, Lüthi, Faubel, Koyama, Poggiali, Nieto and Gadea, in that order.

LAP 12
Kallio and Lüthi (0·103 sec between them) built a 0·3 sec lead over Pasini.

LAP 14
Talmacsi, who had been third, crashed. Kallio and Lüthi were still neck and neck (only 0·178 sec between them). Faubel was now third, more than 1·5 sec behind.

LAP 16
Coming into the straight, Lüthi had a terrible crash, his bike cut in two by Gadea's Aprilia. The red flag went up to stop the race. The placings from the previous lap were taken into account: Kallio won, ahead of Lüthi and Faubel

FINISH
Only two of them on the podium, as Lüthi is in the medical centre (dislocated right shoulder, contusions to both ankles).

CHAMPIONSHIP
Although injured, Lüthi keeps his first place in the Championship. He still has a 3-point lead over Kallio; below that, there's a big gap, as Talmacsi is 44 points behind the leader.

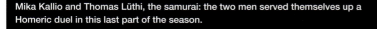
Mika Kallio and Thomas Lüthi, the samurai: the two men served themselves up a Homeric duel in this last part of the season.

GP JAPAN | 17th September 2005 | Motegi | 4.801 m

STARTING GRID

1	14	G. Talmacsi	KTM	1'58.653
2	71	T. Koyama	Honda	1'58.920
3	75	M. Pasini	Aprilia	1'58.970
4	58	M. Simoncelli	Aprilia	1'59.038
5	36	M. Kallio	KTM	1'59.137
6	55	H. Faubel	Aprilia	1'59.143
7	12	T. Lüthi	Honda	1'59.363
8	54	M. Poggiali	Gilera	1'59.460
9	19	A. Bautista	Honda	1'59.539
10	33	S. Gadea	Aprilia	1'59.596
11	60	J. Simón	KTM	1'59.660
12	63	M. Di Meglio	Honda	1'59.724
13	22	P. Nieto	Derbi	1'59.874
14	32	F. Lai	Honda	1'59.982
15	46	M. Tuñez	Aprilia	2'00.106
16	11	S. Cortese	Honda	2'00.181
17	51	E. Jerez	Derbi	2'00.281
18	8	L. Zanetti	Aprilia	2'00.287
19	29	A. Iannone	Aprilia	2'00.288
20	9	T. Kuzuhara	Honda	2'00.301
21	7	A. Masbou	Honda	2'00.436
22	35	R. De Rosa	Aprilia	2'00.453
23	52	L. Pesek	Derbi	2'00.750
24	41	A. Espargaro	Honda	2'00.754
25	45	I. Toth	Aprilia	2'00.756
26	43	M. Hernandez	Aprilia	2'01.015
27	6	J. Olivé	Honda	2'01.126
28	25	D. Giuseppetti	Aprilia	2'01.788
29	20	T. Takahashi	Honda	2'01.974
30	44	K. Abraham	Aprilia	2'02.043
31	68	H. Kuzuhara	Honda	2'02.080
32	64	Y. Hamamoto	Honda	2'02.224
33	66	A. Mori	Honda	2'02.274
34	10	F. Sandi	Honda	2'02.663
35	65	H. Iwata	Honda	2'02.664
36	28	J. Carchano	Aprilia	2'02.770
37	15	M. Pirro	Malaguti	2'02.885
38	26	V. Braillard	Aprilia	2'03.341
39	48	D. Bonache	Honda	2'03.463
40	31	S. Hommel	Malaguti	2'04.379
41	67	K. Hanafusa	Honda	2'04.673

RACE: 15 laps = 72.015 km (*)

1	Mika Kallio	30'10.854 (143.166 km/h)
2	Thomas Lüthi	+ 0''111
3	Hector Faubel	+ 1''517
4	Tomoyoshi Koyama	+ 2''349
5	Mattia Pasini	+ 2''406
6	Manuel Poggiali	+ 2''619
7	Sergio Gadea	+ 2''761
8	Pablo Nieto	+ 2''961
9	Alvaro Bautista	+ 3''720
10	Fabrizio Lai	+ 9''936
11	Mike Di Meglio	+ 14''546
12	Aleix Espargaro	+ 14''693
13	Andrea Iannone	+ 15''699
14	Toshihisa Kuzuhara	+ 20''833
15	Enrique Jerez	+ 22''562
16	Raffaele De Rosa	+ 24''038
17	Lorenzo Zanetti	+ 25''907
18	Joan Olivé	+ 27''014
19	Manuel Hernandez	+ 27''502
20	Alexis Masbou	+ 27''548
21	Imre Toth	+ 47''987
22	Hiroaki Kuzuhara	+ 48''337
23	Federico Sandi	+ 48''524
24	Yuki Hamamoto	+ 51''086
25	Takumi Takahashi	+ 53''530
26	Arata Mori	+ 53''610
27	Vincent Braillard	+ 54''652
28	Karel Abraham	+ 55''454
29	Kazuki Hanafusa	+ 1'03.564
30	Jordi Carchano	+ 2 laps

(*): Race was red flagged, after the fall off of Thomas Lüthi and Sergio Gadea. As a sufficiency distance had been covered, the ranking was established the lap before the accident.

Fastest lap
Tuñez, in 1'59.018 (145.218 km/h).
Record: Pedrosa, in 1'58.354 (146,033 km/h/2002).

Outright fastest lap
Pedrosa, in 1'57.736 (146.799 km/h/2003).

CHAMPIONSHIP

1	T. Lüthi	164 (2 wins)
2	M. Kallio	161 (3 wins)
3	G. Talmacsi	120 (2 wins)
4	M. Simoncelli	117 (1 win)
5	M. Pasini	111 (2 wins)
6	F. Lai	104
7	J. Simón	97 (1 win)
8	M. Poggiali	82
9	H. Faubel	66
10	T. Koyama	65

And seven... dwarves for seven titles.

13

25th September 2005
MALAYSIA SEPANG

Love and (hot) kisses from Malaysia.

ROSSI AND THE SEVEN DWARVES

A SEVENTH TITLE IS WELL WORTH A LITTLE CELEBRATION. VALENTINO ROSSI DIDN'T HESITATE, FINDING, IN HIS LAP OF HONOUR, SEVEN DWARVES AND, NATURALLY, SNOW WHITE.

MOTO GP MALAYSIA

THE RACE

VALENTINO ROSSI, BEATEN, BUT THE CHAMPION, RECEIVES A KISS FROM SNOW WHITE

The doctor calls: Rossi takes his seventh world title.

Calendar co-incidence: while the World Motorcycle Championship was going through its most intense period between Japan, Malaysia, Qatar, Australia and Turkey, the great circus of Formula 1 had stopped off for the final in Brazil. Now, thanks to (or maybe it's the fault of…) Valentino Rossi, these two worlds are increasingly close. And from now on, the year's achievements (in the motorcycle GP world) are going to be talked about in the other. So it was that, tired of seeing Rossi asserting himself as "the" best-known sports personality in Italy, Flavio Briatore, head of the twice World Champion Renault F1 team, dared to express a value judgement: "Just let Rossi go on monkeying around in his kids' playground of motorcycle GP. When he grows up, he'll come over to Formula 1. Then we'll see…"
We can well imagine that this attack has delighted the Italian press; and even more so, that Valentino Rossi was obliged to respond. With his talent on the track - a seventh World Champion title, although for the first time "Vale" didn't win what was the decisive race for his coronation - just as much as with the pleasure he gets celebrating his triumph on each great occasion with his pals, he came up with a comical idea for his lap of honour - a fresh stroke of genius from the man who this Summer was made a Doctor of Science in communication. On his lap of honour, Rossi stopped at a point on the circuit where there some figures worthy of a children's playground were waiting for him: seven little dwarves (for seven world titles) and a delicious Snow White, delighted to be kissing her hero. Who was hiding behind the figure: his mum Stefania, always there for important races? His fiancée Arianna, increasingly in evidence? "No, it was the real Snow White", answered a beaming Valentino.
True to form, he soon put aside the joking to launch into a cold analysis: "You know that it's not the way I think, but this second place, it's like a win for me. Which means that everyone needs to keep on working: Michelin, to counter the increasingly impressive progress from Bridgestone, as well as Yamaha, as the competition are getting their acts together."
On the evening of this seventh title, when he might have been able to let his hair down a bit and celebrate, he set off instead for a few days in Italy. He took advantage of the journey to speak about the elements he needed to improve: "Last year, after my first title with Yamaha, it was regarded as the victory of man over machine. This year, they were waiting round the corner for me, and I won; that was the fruit of two years of enormous work… but don't let's kid ourselves: it's not by dozing off now that we're going to stay at the best level in the future."
That's the way Valentino Rossi is. He always wants more, and those at his side are well rewarded for this tenacity. As for his adversaries…

MALAYSIA MOTO GP 13

The (futile, for once) race run by Valentino Rossi behind Loris Capirossi. Checa joined the two Italians on the podium..

THE SECOND VICTORY IN A ROW FOR CAPIROSSI. ROSSI WINS THE CHAMPIONSHIP. TWO DUCATIS MAKE THE PODIUM.

A STRONG LINE-UP
The Japanese GP had left its marks, as Olivier Jacque was called in an emergency to make up for the absence of Alexander Hofmann (multiple fracture of one foot). In the Camel Honda team, it was the turn of British rider Shane Byrne (freed up by Proton, who are no longer there) to take over Troy Bayliss's RC211 V. Despite thirty-odd stitches in his right foot, Marco Melandri kept his place.

QUALIFYINGS
Bridgestone's spectacular progress was confirmed in the first free trials, with Kenny Roberts, John Hopkins, and of course Loris Capirossi taking it in turns at the summit of the hierarchy. Moreover, the latter picked up pole position. Rossi was seventh, but his theoretical adversaries for the title (Biaggi, Edwards) were further back still.

START
A perfect start by Capirossi. First time across the line, Capirossi had a lead of 0.231 sec over Nakano. Melandri was third, Hayden fourth, ahead of Gibernau and Rossi.

LAP 2
Things were changing fast on the track; Gibernau and Nakano found themselves off the track in the hairpin just before the straight.

LAP 4
Still Capirossi. Hayden was 0.356 sec behind, Rossi was third: this time, he passed Melandri without problem. Olivier Jacque went back to his stand.

LAP 6
Capirossi, Hayden and Rossi were all within 0.538 sec of each other.

LAP 8
Rossi passed Hayden, Checa took Melandri by surprise for fourth place.

MID-RACE (LAP 11)
Rossi took the lead, but took the last hairpin too wide; once again, Capirossi took the lead at the line by 0.154 sec. Hayden was third, Checa - the fastest man on the track at this point in the race - was fourth, 1.757 behind his team-mate.

LAP 12
This time, Rossi is in front, but Capirossi and Hayden are hanging on his tail.

LAP 14
Superb Capirossi took back the lead (0.309 sec at the line).

LAP 16
Capirossi broke away (0.658 sec). For the second time, Checa puts the attack on Hayden; for the second time, he fails

LAP 17
Checa found the opening: now there were two Ducatis on the virtual podium.

FINISH (21 LAPS)
A lead of more than 2 sec for Capirossi, the race was won. Interest switched to the struggle for second place, as Checa was again snapping at Rossi's heels; he failed by just 0.070 sec.

CHAMPIONSHIP
Rossi is champion and gets a kiss from Snow White with the seven dwarves (seven titles) looking on; Capirossi is now third.

GP MALAYSIA | 25th septembre 2005 | Sepang | 5.548 m

#	No	STARTING GRID	Bike	Time
1	65	L. Capirossi	Ducati	2'01.731
2	15	S. Gibernau	Honda	2'01.867
3	21	J. Hopkins	Suzuki	2'02.017
4	56	S. Nakano	Kawasaki	2'02.178
5	10	K. Roberts	Suzuki	2'02.215
6	69	N. Hayden	Honda	2'02.377
7	46	V. Rossi	Yamaha	2'02.412
8	7	C. Checa	Ducati	2'02.419
9	33	M. Melandri	Honda	2'02.660
10	5	C. Edwards	Yamaha	2'02.805
11	4	A. Barros	Honda	2'03.013
12	3	M. Biaggi	Honda	2'03.210
13	19	O. Jacque	Kawasaki	2'03.364
14	24	T. Elias	Yamaha	2'03.397
15	6	M. Tamada	Honda	2'03.974
16	11	R. Xaus	Yamaha	2'04.010
17	44	R. Rolfo	Ducati	2'05.092
18	67	S. Byrne	Honda	2'06.493
19	27	F. Battaini	Blata	2'07.492
20	77	J. Ellison	Blata	2'08.352

RACE: 24 laps = 116.508 km

#	Rider	Time/Gap
1	Loris Capirossi	43'27.523 (160.853 km/h)
2	Valentino Rossi	+ 1''999
3	Carlos Checa	+ 2''069
4	Nicky Hayden	+ 9''227
5	Marco Melandri	+ 15''886
6	Massimiliano Biaggi	+ 16''826
7	Kenny Roberts	+ 17''249
8	Alexandre Barros	+ 18''221
9	John Hopkins	+ 20''125
10	Colin Edwards	+ 22''275
11	Toni Elias	+ 29''856
12	Makoto Tamada	+ 51''672
13	Roberto Rolfo	+ 1'05.365
14	Shane Byrne	+ 1'19.106
15	Ruben Xaus	+ 1'19.356
16	Franco Battaini	+ 1'55.882

Fastest lap
Hayden, in 2'02.993 (162.389 km/h). New record.
Previous record: Rossi, en 2'03.253 (162.047 km/h/2004).
Outright fastest lap
Capirossi, in 2'01.731 (164.073 km/h/2005).

CHAMPIONSHIP

#	Rider	Points
1	V. Rossi	281 (9 wins)
2	M. Biaggi	159
3	L. Capirossi	142 (2 wins)
4	C. Edwards	139
5	M. Melandri	137
6	N. Hayden	134 (1 win)
7	A. Barros	122 (1 win)
8	S. Gibernau	115
9	C. Checa	88
10	S. Nakano	69

13 250cc MALAYSIA

CELEBRATION FOR CASEY STONER AND A CRASH BY DANIEL PEDROSA: WHAT IF THE CHAMPIONSHIP WAS RELAUNCHED?

FORCES EN PRÉSENCE
So Jorge Lorenzo was suspended for one race - he spent his time in the Pan Pacific hotel gym, determined to show what he's made of in Qatar, in a week's time (should be good!) The Frenchman Erwan Nigon replaced Bulgarian Todorov, in the Kurz team - people are beginning to wonder how it can keep changing riders in this way… paying. The Zonghsen Team of China team was present with two Aprilias, for Zhu Wang and Zheng Peng Li (neither of whom qualified).

QUALIFYINGS
A lively session for Hiroshi Aoyama, the winner at Motegi. On Saturday afternoon, the Japanese started out by crashing, he went back to his stand, where he later remarked: "I've changed bikes and tactics: I've gone back to the track knowing that I had nothing more to lose." At the line, Aoyama was 0·081 sec ahead of his leader Dani Pedrosa, behind whom he had been hiding in order to pull off his performance. De Angelis and Stoner were alongside them, De Puniet (7th) crashed and slightly injured his left hand.

START
Pedrosa pulled off the best start, but Stoner took over the lead before the end of the first lap. Dovizioso took a fall in the middle of the bunch, and Debon too was eliminated before the end of this initial lap.

"Gone out for a second. Be back in Qatar" read the sign in pride of place behind Lorenzo's chair: he was suspended for this race. Below, Mathieu Gines and Casey Stoner, the man who completely dominated the race

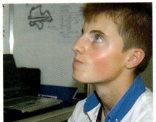

LAP 2
World Champion Daniel Pedrosa crashed, shaking his head as he got up. Stoner had a 0·776 sec lead over De Angelis. Aoyama was third, Porto, De Puniet and Barbera hot on their heels.

LAP 5
There was now 1·580 sec between Stoner and De Angelis. De Puniet had just helped himself to third place; further off, Porto took Aoyama by surprise too.

LAP 8
Corsi crashed.

MID-RACE (LAP 10)
Stoner was dominating his field, with a 3·573 sec lead over De Angelis. On the other hand, the struggle for third place between De Puniet, Porto and Aoyama was interesting. Behind them was a great void: Barbera was already 15·173 sec behind the leader.

LAP 12
Porto passed his team-mate De Puniet, who was suffering from the onset of engine seizure.

FINISH (20 LAPS)
We were - how can we put it politely? -a bit bored during this race. Stoner didn't make any mistakes, De Angelis indulged himself with a few stylish figures, and Porto took advantage of his team-mate Randy De Puniet's technical problems. So the first three were all Aprilias. In ninth place, Guintoli was once again the best private contestant in the class.

CHAMPIONSHIP
Casey Stoner climbs to just 38 points short of title-holder Dani Pedrosa, the great loser of the weekend. There are still 100 points up for grabs.

GP MALAYSIA | 25th septembre 2005 | Sepang | 5.548 m

STARTING GRID

1	73	H. Aoyama	Honda	2'07.860
2	1	D. Pedrosa	Honda	2'07.941
3	5	A. De Angelis	Aprilia	2'08.195
4	27	C. Stoner	Aprilia	2'08.286
5	19	S. Porto	Aprilia	2'08.436
6	34	A. Dovizioso	Honda	2'08.523
7	7	R. De Puniet	Aprilia	2'08.762
8	80	H. Barbera	Honda	2'09.552
9	50	S. Guintoli	Aprilia	2'09.891
10	24	S. Corsi	Aprilia	2'09.998
11	8	A. Ballerini	Aprilia	2'10.039
12	6	A. Debon	Honda	2'10.138
13	96	J. Smrz	Honda	2'10.164
14	15	R. Locatelli	Aprilia	2'10.212
15	28	D. Heidolf	Honda	2'10.279
16	64	R. Rous	Honda	2'10.304
17	14	A. West	KTM	2'10.330
18	55	Y. Takahashi	Honda	2'10.448
19	25	A. Baldolini	Aprilia	2'10.786
20	57	C. Davies	Aprilia	2'10.858
21	32	M. Giansanti	Aprilia	2'10.888
22	17	S. Jenkner	Aprilia	2'11.033
23	44	T. Sekiguchi	Aprilia	2'11.542
24	36	M. Cardeñas	Aprilia	2'12.195
25	63	E. Nigon	Yamaha	2'12.369
26	56	M. Gines	Aprilia	2'12.509
27	21	A. Vincent	Fantic	2'12.537
28	23	N. Cajback	Yamaha	2'15.560
Not qualified:				
	20	G. Ferro	Fantic	2'17.579
	60	Z. Wang	Aprilia	2'17.690
	61	T. Li	Aprilia	2'17.780

RACE: 20 laps = 110.960 km

1	Casey Stoner	43'23.138 (153.451 km/h)
2	Alex de Angelis	+ 3''133
3	Sebastian Porto	+ 4''111
4	Randy De Puniet	+ 7''569
5	Hiroshi Aoyama	+ 10''109
6	Hector Barbera	+ 26''123
7	Yuki Takahashi	+ 27''301
8	Roberto Locatelli	+ 28''006
9	Sylvain Guintoli	+ 59''478
10	Taro Sekiguchi	+ 59''579
11	Dirk Heidolf	+ 1'01.437
12	Chaz Davies	+ 1'04.004
13	Mirko Giansanti	+ 1'04.803
14	Steve Jenkner	+ 1'12.500
15	Martin Cardeñas	+ 1'21.073
16	Erwan Nigon	+ 1'31.925
17	Mathieu Gines	+ 1'51.975
18	Nicklas Cajback	+ 1 lap
19	Jakub Smrz	+ 1 lap

Fastest lap
Stoner, in 2'08.853 (155.004 km/h).
Record: Pedrosa, in 2'08.015 (156.019 km/h/2004).

Outright fastest lap
Porto, in 2'06.940 (157.340 km/h/2004).

CHAMPIONSHIP

1	D. Pedrosa	226 (6 wins)
2	C. Stoner	188 (3 wins)
3	A. Dovizioso	144
4	H. Aoyama	134 (1 win)
5	A. De Angelis	129
6	R. De Puniet	121 (1 win)
7	S. Porto	121 (1 win)
8	J. Lorenzo	98
9	H. Barbera	77
10	S. Guintoli	62

MALAYSIA 125cc 13

JUST ONE WEEK AFTER HIS TERRIBLE ACCIDENT IN MOTEGI, THOMAS LÜTHI WON BY 2 THOUSANDTHS OF A SECOND.

A STRONG LINE-UP
Suffering from numerous contusions to both feet, the result of his accident at Motegi, the Swiss World Championship leader Thomas Lüthi was present (his right shoulder is still painful). Tuñez was still replacing Miralles, and Jerez rode Terol's Derbi. In the Molenaar team Chinese rider Wai On Cheung (already seen at Shanghai) took the place of Schouten, whilst Indonesian Doni Tata Pradita held a wild card (with a Yamaha).

QUALIFYINGS
The first day belonged to Honda... and to Mike Di Meglio: the Frenchman dominated both sessions, he was still to be seen Saturday morning, but he handled the afternoon session badly. The opposite of Thomas Lüthi, who achieved a time in his third qualifying lap that would no-one could get close to. Pasini was second, Talmacsi and Kallio (crashed during the Sunday morning warm-up) completed the first row.

START
Kallio, Pasini and Lüthi were ahead at the first braking point, the Swiss took the lead a few metres further on. First time across the line, the World Championship leader had a 0·803 sec lead over Simón. Then came Pasini, Kallio and Talmacsi.

LAP 3

Alone against the KTM armada, the Swiss rider Thomas Lüthi would stamp his authority on the race, despite the still-painful memories of his accident at the Japanese GP. The photo finish would be required…

Still Lüthi, 0·628 sec ahead of the orange train, the KTMs of Simón, Kallio and Talmacsi. Pasini had already been left well behind.

LAP 4
Kallio was second, 1·173 behind the leader.

MID-RACE (LAP 10)
Lüthi was still holding out, with a lead of 0·865 sec over Kallio, who had broken away from his stable companions. Talmacsi was third, 2·454 sec behind the leader, with Simón snapping at his heels. Pasini was all alone out in sixth place

LAP 13
Kallio has come back to just 0·446 sec. Behind, the KTM duo saw Pasini swoop down on them, passing both Simón and Talmacsi together.

LAP 16
It was Faubel's turn to make a comeback and pass the Talmacsi-Simón duo. In front, Lüthi and Kallio were within 0·127 sec of each other.

FINISH (19 LAPS)
0·169 sec between the two men going into the last lap. Kallio appeared to be better placed, as he could take advantage of Lüthi's slipstream. The Swiss, who had deliberately been saving his effort in the two previous laps, didn't make that mistake: Kallio was beaten at the line, by just 0·002 sec.

CHAMPIONSHIP
Once again, an 8-point lead for Lüthi over Kallio, the two strong men of the closing stages of the championship, who've been hogging the two top places for the last four races. Behind them, Talmacsi is now 50 points behind his team-mate Kallio.

GP MALAYSIA | 25th septembre 2005 | Sepang | 5.548 m

STARTING GRID

1	12	T. Lüthi	Honda	2'14.546
2	75	M. Pasini	Aprilia	2'14.837
3	14	G. Talmacsi	KTM	2'14.903
4	36	M. Kallio	KTM	2'14.964
5	58	M. Simoncelli	Aprilia	2'15.047
6	52	L. Pesek	Derbi	2'15.187
7	54	M. Poggiali	Gilera	2'15.257
8	60	J. Simón	KTM	2'15.326
9	55	H. Faubel	Aprilia	2'15.343
10	63	M. Di Meglio	Honda	2'15.349
11	71	T. Koyama	Honda	2'15.594
12	6	J. Olivé	Aprilia	2'15.635
13	32	F. Lai	Honda	2'15.750
14	41	A. Espargaro	Honda	2'15.833
15	7	A. Masbou	Honda	2'15.864
16	35	R. De Rosa	Aprilia	2'16.231
17	51	E. Jerez	Derbi	2'16.277
18	33	S. Gadea	Aprilia	2'16.406
19	8	L. Zanetti	Aprilia	2'16.559
20	19	A. Bautista	Honda	2'16.796
21	43	M. Hernandez	Aprilia	2'17.094
22	11	S. Cortese	Honda	2'17.511
23	22	P. Nieto	Derbi	2'17.670
24	29	A. Iannone	Aprilia	2'17.672
25	25	D. Giuseppetti	Aprilia	2'17.799
26	45	I. Toth	Aprilia	2'17.876
27	9	T. Kuzuhara	Honda	2'17.997
28	28	J. Carchano	Aprilia	2'18.159
29	48	D. Bonache	Honda	2'18.290
30	15	M. Pirro	Malaguti	2'18.623
31	46	M. Tuñez	Aprilia	2'18.679
32	26	V. Braillard	Aprilia	2'18.984
33	44	K. Abraham	Aprilia	2'18.996
34	10	F. Sandi	Honda	2'19.039
35	31	S. Hommel	Malaguti	2'20.354
36	72	D. Padrita	Yamaha	2'21.017
37	38	W. Cheung	Honddda	2'21.576

RACe: 19 laps = 105.412 km

1	Thomas Lüthi	43'02.214 (146.960 km/h)
2	Mika Kallio	+ 0''002
3	Mattia Pasini	+ 9''684
4	Hector Faubel	+ 9''709
5	Gabor Talmacsi	+ 9''892
6	Julian Simón	+ 11''936
7	Fabrizio Lai	+ 19''632
8	Manuel Poggiali	+ 19''755
9	Marco Simoncelli	+ 19''967
10	Tomoyoshi Koyama	+ 20''071
11	Mike Di Meglio	+ 20''158
12	Lukas Pesek	+ 20''427
13	Pablo Nieto	+ 21''178
14	Alexis Masbou	+ 24''199
15	Aleix Espargaro	+ 24''266
16	Sergio Gadea	+ 24''481
17	Joan Olivé	+ 24''615
18	Andrea Iannone	+ 48''038
19	Enrique Jerez	+ 48''157
20	Lorenzo Zanetti	+ 49''207
21	Sandro Cortese	+ 49''207
22	Imre Toth	+ 1'02.994
23	Dario Giuseppetti	+ 1'03.000
24	Manuel Hernandez	+ 1'03.756
25	Mateo Tuñez	+ 1'11.588
26	Alvaro Bautista	+ 1'20.152
27	David Bonache	+ 1'23.094
28	Jordi Carchano	+ 1'32.733
29	Wai On Cheung	+ 1'47.362
30	Sascha Hommel	+ 1'47.672
31	Doni Tata Pradita	+ 2'20.854

Fastest lap
Talmacsi, in 2'14.839 (148.123 km/h).
Record: Cecchinello, in 2'13.919 (149.140 km/h/2002).

Outright fastest lap
Dovizioso, in 2'12.684 (150.529 km/h/2004).

CHAMPIONSHIP

1	T. Lüthi	189 (3 wins)
2	M. Kallio	181 (3 wins)
3	G. Talmacsi	131 (2 wins)
4	M. Pasini	127 (2 wins)
5	M. Simoncelli	124 (1 win)
6	F. Lai	113
7	J. Simón	107 (1 win)
8	M. Poggiali	90
9	H. Faubel	79
10	T. Koyama	71

Rossi, Melandri and Hayden neck and neck, then… nothing (sorry, Colin Edwards, who was watching the battle from afar): it's the image of this end of season which dominates.

14

1st October 2005

QATAR LOSAIL

Elias progresses and Carlos Checa discovers a new passion...

MELANDRI-HAYDEN:
CHARGE AFTER ROSSI!

CROWNED WORLD CHAMPION THE WEEK BEFORE, VALENTINO ROSSI MADE THE RACE HIS ONCE AGAIN. BUT THE NEW WAVE WERE PRESSING MORE AND MORE.

14 MOTO GP QATAR

THE RACE

ROSSI SETTLES SCORES AT OK-LOSAIL, BEFORE BECOMING A PASSENGER LIKE ANY OTHER...

Valentino Rossi had a score to settle with the Losail circuit in Qatar. Well, that's that done, then!

The three key men battling it out. Each day Marco Melandri establishes himself a little more as Rossi's opponent.

The scene takes place on the evening of Saturday 1st October at Doha International Airport in Qatar. It'll soon be 11 o'c, and the man who is henceforth the prince of this desert of sand and oil, Valentino Rossi, is queuing up with all the other people going through passport control. In mufti, the henceforth famous ear-ring dangling from one ear, he sighs to his accomplice Uccio, his shadow: "Well, the people in my queue have chosen badly. If they'd known I was the slowest man in the world... when it comes to picking the right queue." Uccio, more voluble, takes up the game. Pretending not to understand what a police officer is trying to explain to him, he slips across into the next queue, meant for local people only. In just a few minutes, he was through. Valentino hasn't moved. Ahead of him, the customs officer is turning the pages of a tourist's passport back and forth, asking questions, consulting with his boss next door. "What did I tell you: I've lost again", says Rossi, enjoying this little game.

A bit further on, other representatives of the formidable Italian GP colony are laughing openly: away from the circuits, in mufti, Valentino Rossi is an ordinary chap just like anyone else.

His weekend in Qatar went as he'd been hoping. As he'd wanted it to. Having already secured the title week before, the World Champion went home to Italy before going to the Arab peninsula. Demotivated? That word's not in his vocabulary. Especially here, on this Losail circuit with which he has a score to settle. Or, to be more exact, on which he has never yet won - for it was here, just 12 months before, that he had ended up in pickle, a crash putting a premature end to an outstanding climb-back from the back row of the starting grid. Yes, it was here in 2004 that the "affair" blew up: claims by Honda against his team, accused of having swept his space on the starting grid, and a win for Gibernau, who that day became the traitor, the enemy, the man to be beaten.

Ever since then, Sete has not won the least race. And Rossi has sworn that it'll stay like that for as long as he, the Motorcycle King, is on the starting line. So this victory in the desert has a particular flavour to it. Not just because it was won at the end of a fine duel with Marco Melandri, increasingly present, increasingly insistent; but above all because it was marked by a fresh error by Gibernau, who ended up fifth - once again dominated, once again beaten by the new guard at Honda (his own team-mate, Marco Melandri and the American Nicky Hayden). In a nutshell, a perfect scenario for this passenger just like any other, who each week becomes a little bit more a rider unlike any other: "This race was lacking from my list of wins, so I did what had to be done to put that right", he would say after the race. He didn't actually say "to put right this injustice" - but he sure was thinking it!

QATAR MOTO GP

MELANDRI IS MORE AND MORE THREATENING, BUT ROSSI WINS AGAIN...

A STRONG LINE-UP
World Champion Valentino Rossi had gone back to Italy for a few days. As for the rest, nothing to report: Jacque once again replaced Hofmann for Kawasaki, and Byrne was still on Troy Bayliss's Honda.

QUALIFYINGS
Not much luck for Olivier Jacque, who crashed in the first session of free trials; he went back onto the track before going to see the doctors: suffering in his lower back, he was evacuated to a hospital in Doha, before taking the plane back to Europe, all trussed up in a protective corset. Capirossi picked up a fresh pole position, at the end of a lap where he fought like a condemned man: superb to watch. Gibernau and Rossi completed the first row.

START
Super start from Capirossi, ahead of Gibernau, Rossi and Hayden. First time over the line, Capirossi had a 0·054 sec lead over Gibernau, who would pass him coming out of the straight..

LAP 2
Gibernau was leading, Rossi hard on his heels, Hayden not far behind.

LAP 4
Gibernau had gained a 0·738 sec lead over a group consisting of Rossi, Hayden, Edwards and Melandri. Capirossi was sixth, more than a second behind.

LAP 6
Still Gibernau. Rossi was at 0·734 sec, battling with a very aggressive Melandri..

LAP 7
Biaggi abandoned..

LAP 8
Capirossi went off to play in the sand. Rossi got back to 0·460 sec, Melandri still snapping at his heels.

LAP 10
Melandri passed Rossi, Hopkins went back to his stand to change a wheel. Gibernau has a 0·721 sec lead over his team-mate.

MID-RACE (LAP 11)
There was no holding Gibernau: a 0·894 sec lead over Rossi, who passed Melandri again at the line. Hayden was 0·5 sec from the two Italians

LAP 14
A 0·683 sec lead for Gibernau

LAP 16
Gibernau, Rossi and Melandri crossed the line within 0·133 sec of each other. A little further on, Rossi was passed by Melandri, then had a serious alert (the two men managed to avoid making contact).

LAP 18
A super duel between Melandri and Gibernau, who made the mistake and went off the track at high speed into the sand trap (ending up fifth).

LAP 20
Rossi had just taken the lead, by 0·012 sec over Melandri. Hayden was third, and now out on his own.

FINISH (22 LAPS)
0·041 sec behind going into the last lap, Melandri attempted a daring attack on Rossi, but had to deviate from his trajectory. The World Champion won, but it was a great achievement for Melandri.

CHAMPIONSHIP
From now on, interest is focussed on the battle for second place: there's an 11-point gap between Biaggi (2nd) and Capirossi (6th).

Opposite, the first few hundred metres of the race: Capirossi got the best start, ahead of Gibernau and Rossi, Melandri (33) not far behind. Above: Shinya Nakano and Nicky Hayden.

GP QATAR | 1st October 2005 | Losail | 5.380 m

STARTING GRID

1	65	L. Capirossi	Ducati	1'56.917
2	15	S. Gibernau	Honda	1'56.996
3	46	V. Rossi	Yamaha	1'57.360
4	5	C. Edwards	Yamaha	1'57.447
5	33	M. Melandri	Honda	1'57.468
6	7	C. Checa	Ducati	1'57.481
7	56	S. Nakano	Kawasaki	1'57.697
8	69	N. Hayden	Honda	1'57.872
9	24	T. Elias	Yamaha	1'57.902
10	6	M. Tamada	Honda	1'58.317
11	10	K. Roberts	Suzuki	1'58.329
12	21	J. Hopkins	Suzuki	1'58.527
13	3	M. Biaggi	Honda	1'58.622
14	4	A. Barros	Honda	1'59.084
15	44	R. Rolfo	Ducati	1'59.392
16	11	R. Xaus	Yamaha	1'59.482
17	67	S. Byrne	Honda	2'00.097
18	77	J. Ellison	Blata	2'00.909
19	27	F. Battaini	Blata	2'01.678

RACE: 22 laps = 118.360 km

1	Valentino Rossi	43'33.759 (163.020 km/h)
2	Marco Melandri	+ 1''670
3	Nicky Hayden	+ 5''536
4	Colin Edwards	+ 14''737
5	Sete Gibernau	+ 20''431
6	Carlos Checa	+ 31''432
7	Shinya Nakano	+ 32''983
8	Toni Elias	+ 39''888
9	Alexandre Barros	+ 41''792
10	Loris Capirossi	+ 44''252
11	Kenny Roberts	+ 48''745
12	Roberto Rolfo	+ 1'01.991
13	Shane Byrne	+ 1'04.805
14	Ruben Xaus	+ 1'13.824
15	James Ellison	+ 2'08.642
16	Franco Battaini	+ 1 lap
17	John Hopkins	+ 1 lap

Fastest lap
Hayden, in 1'57.903 (164.270 km/h). New record.
Previous: Edwards, en 1'59.293 (162.356 km/h/2004).

Outright fastest lap
Capirossi, in 1'56.917 (165.655 km/h/2005).

CHAMPIONSHIP

1	V. Rossi	306 (10 wins)
2	M. Biaggi	159
3	M. Melandri	157
4	C. Edwards	152
5	N. Hayden	150 (1 win)
6	L. Capirossi	148 (2 wins)
7	A. Barros	129 (1 win)
8	S. Gibernau	126
9	C. Checa	98
10	S. Nakano	78

14 250cc QATAR

STONER CONTINUES TO CREEP UP ON DANIEL PEDROSA IN POINTS.

A STRONG LINE-UP
Nothing new in the class compared with the Malaysian GP.. well, hardly anything! Nigon was still riding the Kurz team's second Yamaha, but the main thing to note was the return of Lorenzo after his one-race suspension at Sepang; he'd taken advantage of the opportunity to further recharge his batteries… one guesses they must already have been seriously full. Showtime in sight!

QUALIFYINGS
Lorenzo delivered what he promised: the young Spaniard picked up pole position ahead of De Angelis and Stoner. Pedrosa, who was 20 on the first day of the qualifyings ("I'm here to work, not to party", he lost no time in emphasizing) was fourth. The first seven were all within 0.674 sec; the eighth, Randy De Puniet (one crash), was already at more than 2 sec!

START
Holeshot by Stoner, who led the turn into the first bend, ahead of Pedrosa and Lorenzo. West was not there at the start with the KTM 250, officially for safety reasons - the proto-Austrian having experienced engine problems during the qualifyings. The truth was different: Stoner had given Harald Bartol a stern talking-to on the Saturday evening…

LAP 2
Stoner no longer had any choice: he had to play an attacking race. He was already 1.658 sec ahead of his first pursuer, Lorenzo.

LAP 3
An alert for Stoner (some serious skidding), but the Australian mastered the situation.

LAP 6
Having made it back into the pack, Alex De Angelis crashed.

LAP 7
Locatelli crashed.

MID-RACE (LAP 10)
Stoner was now 3.508 ahead of the pursuit, still including Lorenzo, along with Dovizioso, Porto and Pedrosa. Aoyama was all alone in sixth position..

LAP 12
De Puniet was idling, left behind in eighteenth position. Stoner's lead over Lorenzo settled at just under 3 sec (2.982).

14° TOUR
De Puniet went back to the stands (sparking plug).

FINISH (20 LAPS)
Things were clear for the first two places: Stoner had completed the race without fault, and Lorenzo broke out of the pack at just the right moment. The remaining question was what was going to happen in the battle for third place between Pedrosa and Dovizioso; it was the 125 cc title-holder who had the last word, proving here too that team orders can only exist when different teams are up against one another.

CHAMPIONNAT
In six days (Malaysia and Qatar GPs), Stoner claimed back 37 points from Pedrosa. The Australian has come back to within 26 lengths of the World Champion, three races from the end. The next one, which looks very promising, is at Phillip Island, home territory for Casey.

Daniel Pedrosa (right) is a champion on the defensive faced with Casey Stoner (top left). Sylvain Guintoli (bottom left) is still the best private team rider.

GP QATAR | 1st October 2005 | Losail | 5.380 m

STARTING GRID

1	48	J. Lorenzo	Honda	2'02.154
2	5	A. De Angelis	Aprilia	2'02.303
3	27	C. Stoner	Aprilia	2'02.473
4	1	D. Pedrosa	Honda	2'02.544
5	19	S. Porto	Aprilia	2'02.704
6	34	A. Dovizioso	Honda	2'02.715
7	73	H. Aoyama	Honda	2'02.828
8	7	R. De Puniet	Aprilia	2'04.219
9	80	H. Barbera	Honda	2'04.282
10	55	Y. Takahashi	Honda	2'04.327
11	50	S. Guintoli	Aprilia	2'04.419
12	15	R. Locatelli	Aprilia	2'04.485
13	14	A. West	KTM	2'04.594
14	96	J. Smrz	Honda	2'04.816
15	8	A. Ballerini	Aprilia	2'04.964
16	32	M. Giansanti	Aprilia	2'04.999
17	17	S. Jenkner	Aprilia	2'05.033
18	6	A. Debon	Honda	2'05.039
19	44	T. Sekiguchi	Aprilia	2'05.296
20	24	S. Corsi	Aprilia	2'05.313
21	57	C. Davies	Aprilia	2'05.600
22	36	M. Cardeñas	Aprilia	2'05.796
23	28	D. Heidolf	Honda	2'06.036
24	63	E. Nigon	Yamaha	2'06.179
25	25	A. Baldolini	Aprilia	2'06.190
26	21	A. Vincent	Fantic	2'06.669
27	64	R. Rous	Honda	2'07.557
28	56	M. Gines	Aprilia	2'07.712

Not qualified:
	20	G. Ferro	Fantic	2'12.646
	23	N. Cajback	Yamaha	2'12.962

RACE: 20 laps = 107.600 km

1	Casey Stoner	41'22.628 (156.028 km/h)
2	Jorge Lorenzo	+ 1''566
3	Andrea Dovizioso	+ 2''603
4	Daniel Pedrosa	+ 2''659
5	Sebastian Porto	+ 4''867
6	Hiroshi Aoyama	+ 29''971
7	Hector Barbera	+ 32''708
8	Yuki Takahashi	+ 46''470
9	Sylvain Guintoli	+ 46''849
10	Taro Sekiguchi	+ 1'01.682
11	Alex Debon	+ 1'01.696
12	Mirko Giansanti	+ 1'01.780
13	Martin Cardeñas	+ 1'02.795
14	Steve Jenkner	+ 1'03.952
15	Andrea Ballerini	+ 1'04.917
16	Chaz Davies	+ 1'06.194
17	Simone Corsi	+ 1'21.004
18	Dirk Heidolf	+ 1'36.546
19	Mathieu Gines	+ 1'51.045
20	Alex Baldolini	+ 2'02.105

Fastest lap
Pedrosa, in 2'03.301 (157.079 km/h).
Record: De Angelis, in 2'03.015 (157.444 km/h/2004).

Outright fastest lap
Lorenzo, in 2'02.154 (158.553 km/h/2005).

CHAMPIONSHIP

1	D. Pedrosa	239 (6 wins)
2	C. Stoner	213 (4 wins)
3	A. Dovizioso	160
4	H. Aoyama	144 (1 win)
5	S. Porto	132 (1 win)
6	A. De Angelis	129
7	R. De Puniet	121 (1 win)
8	J. Lorenzo	118
9	H. Barbera	86
10	S. Guintoli	69

QATAR 125cc

HARA-KIRI FOR KTM: TALMACSI SURPRISES MIKA KALLIO ON THE LINE!

A STRONG LINE-UP

The 125 cc field changed yet again: injured (a broken toe, suspected fracture of the right navicular) Swiss Vincent Braillard had gone home, replaced in the Toth team by Angel Rodriguez. Hommel lost his place with Malaguti (Pellino coming to the rescue), but picked up the Molenaar team's Honda.

ESSAIS

Heat and sand: like last year, grip was precarious on the first day of the qualifyings. World Championship leader Thomas Lüthi found this out the hard way (without coming to any harm). On Friday, the KTM armada got its three soldiers (Kallio in pole, ahead of Talmacsi, Simón fourth) in the first row, while Lüthi was "only" ninth.

START

The orange train got going as soon as the lights went green: Kallio immediately took the lead, ahead of Talmacsi, Simón and Mike Di Meglio. First time over the line, the Kallio-Talmacsi duo already had a 1·301 sec lead over the pursuit (Lüthi was eighth).

LAP 3

A lead of more than 2 sec for the two leading men: everyone was raving about the tactical lesson given by KTM. Behind, Pasini, Poggiali, Simón, Di Meglio, Simoncelli, Lai, and Lüthi were fighting it out

LAP 4

Pesek crashed.

6ᵉ TOUR

Nothing much to report from up front. With third place at stake, Simoncelli had a few hundred metres lead - at this point he was the fastest rider on the track.

MID-RACE (LAP 9)

0·024 sec between Kallio and Talmacsi - the KTM demonstration was continuing. Simoncelli was now third at 3·684 sec. For fourth place (1·393 sec behind Simoncelli), things are still hot between Poggiali, Pasini, Di Meglio, Simón, and Lüthi.

12ᵉ TOUR

Alert on the track: coming out of the straight, Lüthi and Pasini make contact. The two men stayed on their bikes (miraculously, in Pasini's case), Simón had to avoid them

ARRIVÉE (18 TOURS)

0·073 sec between Kallio and Talmacsi going into the last lap, the Hungarian was better positioned (thanks to the slipstream), but no-one imagined that he would dare to entrap his own leader… except him: he took Kallio by surprise right on the line! Back at KTM, he got a frosty reception: Harald Bartol cried treachery and lying (at first, Talmacsi explained that he thought he still had a lap to go…), but there was a great sigh of relief in Lüthi's camp (finished sixth).

CHAMPIONSHIP

Kallio takes back the lead in the Championship, but only by 2 points, whereas logically he should have had a 7-point lead over Lüthi.

The three main players in an astonishing weekend: after have played eagle-tamer, Thomas Lüthi will appreciate Gabor Talmacsi's win over Kallio, the Swiss rider's opponent…

GP QATAR | 1st October 2005 | Losail | 5.380 m

STARTING GRID

1	36	M. Kallio	KTM	2'09.455
2	14	G. Talmacsi	KTM	2'09.601
3	75	M. Pasini	Aprilia	2'09.653
4	60	J. Simón	KTM	2'09.680
5	32	F. Lai	Honda	2'09.699
6	54	M. Poggiali	Gilera	2'09.718
7	58	M. Simoncelli	Aprilia	2'09.850
8	47	A. Rodriguez	Aprilia	2'09.962
9	12	T. Lüthi	Honda	2'10.010
10	63	M. Di Meglio	Honda	2'10.024
11	55	H. Faubel	Aprilia	2'10.075
12	19	A. Bautista	Honda	2'10.282
13	6	J. Olivé	Aprilia	2'10.415
14	35	R. De Rosa	Aprilia	2'10.432
15	7	A. Masbou	Honda	2'10.444
16	71	T. Koyama	Honda	2'10.489
17	41	A. Espargaro	Honda	2'10.728
18	33	S. Gadea	Aprilia	2'11.094
19	22	P. Nieto	Derbi	2'11.176
20	29	A. Iannone	Aprilia	2'11.411
21	11	S. Cortese	Honda	2'11.455
22	8	L. Zanetti	Aprilia	2'11.485
23	52	L. Pesek	Derbi	2'11.498
24	51	E. Jerez	Derbi	2'11.618
25	42	G. Pellino	Malaguti	2'11.784
26	43	M. Hernandez	Aprilia	2'12.032
27	25	D. Giuseppetti	Aprilia	2'12.032
28	46	M. Tuñez	Aprilia	2'12.313
29	28	J. Carchano	Aprilia	2'12.355
30	15	M. Pirro	Malaguti	2'12.392
31	10	F. Sandi	Honda	2'12.588
32	44	K. Abraham	Aprilia	2'13.224
33	48	D. Bonache	Honda	2'13.283
34	9	T. Kuzuhara	Honda	2'13.491
35	45	I. Toth	Aprilia	2'13.679
36	31	S. Hommel	Honda	2'14.299

RACE: 18 laps = 96.840 km

1	Gabor Talmacsi	39'23.248 (147.519 km/h)
2	Mika Kallio	+ 0''017
3	Marco Simoncelli	+ 9''571
4	Mike Di Meglio	+ 11''815
5	Hector Faubel	+ 12''169
6	Thomas Lüthi	+ 12''303
7	Manuel Poggiali	+ 12''317
8	Julian Simón	+ 12''565
9	Mattia Pasini	+ 17''571
10	Fabrizio Lai	+ 19''757
11	Joan Olivé	+ 22''037
12	Sergio Gadea	+ 24''205
13	Raffaele De Rosa	+ 25''342
14	Tomoyoshi Koyama	+ 27''965
15	Enrique Jerez	+ 37''241
16	Lorenzo Zanetti	+ 43''704
17	Sandro Cortese	+ 44''855
18	Aleix Espargaro	+ 44''870
19	Andrea Iannone	+ 45''521
20	Alexis Masbou	+ 49''011
21	Dario Giuseppetti	+ 50''024
22	Alvaro Bautista	+ 50''059
23	Gioele Pellino	+ 50''299
24	Mateo Tuñez	+ 56''956
25	Jordi Carchano	+ 57''020
26	Federico Sandi	+ 1'14.927
27	Toshihisa Kuzuhara	+ 1'29.137
28	Karel Abraham	+ 1'29.158
29	Imre Toth	+ 1'39.784

Fastest lap
Simoncelli, in 2'10.515 (148.396 km/h).
Record: Lorenzo, in 2'09.569 (149.480 km/h/2004).

Outright fastest lap
Kallio, in 2'09.455 (149.611 km/h/2005).

CHAMPIONSHIP

1	M. Kallio	201 (3 wins)
2	T. Lüthi	199 (3 wins)
3	G. Talmacsi	156 (3 wins)
4	M. Simoncelli	140 (1 win)
5	M. Pasini	134 (2 wins)
6	F. Lai	119
7	J. Simón	115 (1 win)
8	M. Poggiali	99
9	H. Faubel	90
10	M. Di Meglio	77

The setting at Phillip Island is unique, magical. And Valentino Rossi is absolutely unique. Magic...

15

16th October 2005

AUSTRALIA PHILLIP ISLAND

The astonishing Australian version of the "Beauty and the Beast" story.

TOWARDS THE END OF A CYCLE

VALENTINO ROSSI WON AGAIN, BUT THE THREAT EMBODIED BY MARCO MELANDRI AND NICKY HAYDEN WAS BECOMING CLEARER.

15 MOTO GP **AUSTRALIA**

THE RACE

DISAPPOINTMENT UPON DISAPPOINTMENT FOR THE FROGS WHO WANTED TO PUFF THEMSELVES UP BIGGER THAN THE BULL, AND WOULD SOON HAVE TO GO AND CROAK ELSEWHERE...

Rossi, Melandri, Hayden: the king now had a lot to do

Alexandre Barros passed, Massimiliano Biaggi went down: the times were getting hard for the veterans.

Marco Melandri in Qatar and Nicky Hayden at Phillip Island: as the season draws to a close, the ambitious young hounds are now sharpening their claws on Valentino Rossi's armour. And those others, who have so dreamed of beating the master one day? From now on they're going to be nicknamed the "human riders" (as distinct from the "extra-terrestrial" Valentino), and they'll be playing the demanding, greedy barons for a bit longer yet.
In fact, it's a bit like Lafontaine's fable of the frog who wanted to be bigger than the ox - but with one important difference: in this pond - the paddock - there is an abnormal phenomenon: one frog that can jump higher, further, faster and longer than the others. A frog who can turn into a Prince Charming, and who doesn't fail to go and kiss Snow White a few seconds after bagging his seventh world title - to the great delight of the seven conniving dwarves. You've guessed it, this superior frog is Valentino Rossi, whom all his fellows seek to emulate. But there you have it: through wanting too much to be like him, they often end up getting a mouthful. Just so long as they don't drown...
That said, you don't become a frog (sorry, rider) without being a bit headstrong. So, they persist. And the years pass. And Valentino Rossi picks up title after title and pulls in the crowds. Meantime, the star frog (Gibernau) has got close to a top model and thinks he too is obliged to hold a rôle in this artificial world; there's the frog Biaggi, who for years has been croaking because he never has the right bike and because he's never in the right place at the right time. There's the worker frog (the unfortunate Loris Capirossi), fearless and unreproachful; the veteran frog (Alexandre Barros) and the tubby old ex-serviceman frog (Kenny Roberts). There are a few experienced frogs who'd very much like it to be known (Colin Edwards and Carlos Checa), and a few promising, ambitious ones (Nicky Hayden, Marco Melandri and Toni Elias).
Yet none of them manages to give the master much to worry about over the whole length of the championship - despite the resources employed, despite their ever-increasing financial demands. But exceptional beings are not made of bank-notes. For the moment, everything's still going very well, because Super-Frog is there, to give us all something to dream about. But in a year's time, he'll be off to ponds new. Within the same space of time, the current bikes will be packed off to the museum. So the frogs who wanted to be as big as the ox will be forced to realize that they've gone too far. There's nothing left for them to do except to find a lily-pad big enough for their egos, and leave the pond to those who are still only trainee newts. Some (Pedrosa and Stoner, soon Lorenzo and Dovizioso) already have clearly visible back legs. Then the GPs will have moved into a new era - but are we going to find a new Super-Frog there?

AUSTRALIA MOTO GP 15

ROSSI'S VICTORY HAS NOT WIPED OUT THE FEAR CAUSED BY LORIS CAPIROSSI'S TERRIBLE ACCIDENT.

A STONG LINE-UP
The attraction of the weekend was the presence of the young Australian Chris Vermeulen, former World Supersport Champion and rough diamond that Honda is forging for World Superbike. He picked up the Sito Pons team's second RC211V.

QUALIFYINGS
Nicky Hayden's superb performance was rather overshadowed, because the trials were marked by Loris Capirossi's terrible crash on the Friday morning. The Italian, suffering from a pneumothorax, was first evacuated to a hospital in Dandenong, before heading off to Melbourne. Short of a miracle, the season is over for him. The year 2005 is also over for Kenny Roberts: the former World Champion fractured his left navicular.

START
Hayden turned in the lead, ahead of Rossi and Checa. Max Biaggi didn't finish the first lap, which Hayden ended with a lead of 0·038 sec over Rossi and 0·156 over Checa.

LAP 3
Rossi had taken matters in hand, Hayden and Melandri in his wake. Checa was still keeping up, Edwards and Gibernau rather less so.

LAP 5
Rossi had gained a half-second lead over Melandri, now second.

LAP 8
Rossi and Hayden are within 0·168 sec of each other. Melandri slipped back to

Rossi in action (top) and Loris Capirossi, a few minutes before the most serious accident of his career.

1·010 sec. A little further back, Gibernau was back on Checa's tail.

LAP 10
Gibernau has just taken Checa by surprise. Hayden was still less than 0·2 sec from Rossi.

LAP 12
Checa took back his property from Gibernau

MID-RACE (LAP 13)
Rossi made a 0·377 sec lead over Hayden. Melandri was third at 2·163 sec. Checa and Gibernau were sticking to each other like leeches. Barros was sixth, but already almost 10 sec behind Rossi.

LAP 16
Super Hayden, who took the lead in the straight. Behind, Melandri was now being directly threatened by Checa.

LAP 17
The cards were re-shuffled: Hayden, Rossi, Melandri and Checa were all within 0·721 sec of each other.

LAP 20
Rossi took charge of operations again, in the space of two laps forging a 1·266 sec lead over the trio of Hayden, Melandri, Checa. Gibernau wasn't able to keep up the pace.

LAP 24
Spectacular crash by Barros, who had been sixth. Rossi had a 1·010 sec lead over Hayden, who had left Melandri behind.

FINISH (27 LAPS)
The gap between Rossi and Hayden was 0·758 sec, the World Champion did not make a mistake. For third place, Checa took Melandri by surprise right on the line (by 0·017 sec).

CHAMPIONSHIP
The battle for second place is closer than ever. Hayden and Melandri are level (170 points), Edwards 8 lengths behind, and Biaggi 11

GP AUSTRALIA | 16th October 2005 | Phillip Island | 4.448 m

STARTING GRID
1	69	N. Hayden	Honda	1'29.337
2	46	V. Rossi	Yamaha	1'29.443
3	15	S. Gibernau	Honda	1'29.729
4	7	C. Checa	Ducati	1'29.775
5	5	C. Edwards	Yamaha	1'29.943
6	3	M. Biaggi	Honda	1'30.070
7	24	T. Elias	Yamaha	1'30.094
8	33	M. Melandri	Honda	1'30.322
9	6	M. Tamada	Honda	1'30.624
10	56	S. Nakano	Kawasaki	1'30.628
11	21	J. Hopkins	Suzuki	1'30.667
12	4	A. Barros	Honda	1'30.757
13	19	O. Jacque	Kawasaki	1'31.079
14	17	C. Vermeulen	Honda	1'31.654
15	11	R. Xaus	Yamaha	1'31.728
16	44	R. Rolfo	Ducati	1'33.495
17	77	J. Ellison	Blata	1'33.673
Not qualified:				
	27	F. Battaini	Blata	1'35.933

RACE: 27 laps = 120.096 km
1	Valentino Rossi	41'08.542	(175.142 km/h)
2	Nicky Hayden	+ 1''007	
3	Carlos Checa	+ 4''215	
4	Marco Melandri	+ 4''232	
5	Sete Gibernau	+ 14''088	
6	Colin Edwards	+ 33''200	
7	Shinya Nakano	+ 45''055	
8	Makoto Tamada	+ 45''103	
9	Toni Elias	+ 45''104	
10	John Hopkins	+ 50''260	
11	Chris Vermeulen	+ 50''697	
12	Ruben Xaus	+ 1'08.324	
13	Roberto Rolfo	+ 1'31.737	
14	James Ellison	+ 1 lap	
15	Franco Battaini	+ 1 lap	
16	Olivier Jacque	+ 2 laps	

Fastest lap
Melandri, in 1'30.332 (177.266 km/h). New record.
Previous: Capirossi, in 1'31.102 (175.767 km/h/2004).

Outright fastest lap
Hayden, en 1'29.337 (179.240 km/h/2005).

CHAMPIONSHIP
1	V. Rossi	331 (11 wins)
2	N. Hayden	170 (1 win)
3	M. Melandri	170
4	C. Edwards	162
5	M. Biaggi	159
6	L. Capirossi	148 (2 wins)
7	S. Gibernau	137
8	A. Barros	129 (1 win)
9	C. Checa	114
10	S. Nakano	87

15 250cc AUSTRALIA

CASEY STONER FELL, DANIEL PEDROSA TOOK THE RACE BY 27 THOUSANDTHS OF A SECOND: THE SPANIARD SUCCESSFULLY DEFENDED HIS WORLD TITLE.

A STRONG LINE-UP
As we thought in the evening at Qatar, no sign of the KTM 250… nor of Anthony West. The Australian had a right old set-to with Harald Bartol. At Würth Honda BQR, the Spaniard Arturo Tizon, who has been dominating the Spanish Supersport Championship, had left Albacete on Sunday evening to go to Australia; he replaced the Czech Radomil Rous.

QUALIFYINGS
We know that Dani Pedrosa, the World Championship leader, has some painful memories of Phillip Island, and we guessed that Casey Stoner, on home ground, would try to lay on the pressure right from the first trials. We weren't wrong. Amazingly calm, ignoring the media interest that now surrounds him, Stoner took pole ahead of Lorenzo (despite a high-speed crash), De Angelis and Porto. Pedrosa was "only" sixth.

START
Stoner made the best start and finished the first lap in the lead, ahead of a tight group consisting of Lorenzo, De Angelis, Porto, Pedrosa, Dovizioso, Aoyama and Barbera..

LAP 4
Stoner crashed at the bottom of the toboggan, De Angelis went flying over the Australian's bike, but miraculously landed on his two wheels (though he still had to abandon the race). Lorenzo took the lead, Porto and Pedrosa hard on his heels. If the world title-holder could assert his position, that would be one more crown for him.

LAP 8
Porto was now in front, Pedrosa just 0·063 sec behind. Stoner had gone back to his stand. Dovizioso was third, 1·665 sec behind Pedrosa and is battling it out with Lorenzo.

LAP 10
Lorenzo had passed Dovizioso, he was third, 2 sec behind Pedrosa.

LAP 12
Takahashi abandoned, after going off the track.

MID-RACE (LAP 13)
Porto was still ahead by 0·136 sec over Pedrosa. Lorenzo was third at 3·766 sec, having shaken off Dovizioso. Barbera and Aoyama were fighting it out for fifth place.

LAP 20
Pedrosa was still well hidden in Porto's wake, and when he took the latter by surprise coming out of the straight, the Spaniard allowed him to take over. Behind them, Barbera was now fourth, ahead of Dovizioso and Aoyama.

FINISH (25 LAPS)
0·076 sec between them going into the final lap, Pedrosa had got out of Porto's wake at just the right moment. By just 0·027 sec, he is World Champion for the third year running.

CHAMPIONSHIP
We can't hold it against Casey Stoner. For a long time the young Australian no longer had any choice, he had to take every risk going. Hats off to Dani Pedrosa, who has not made a single mistake. And welcome to MotoGP next year!

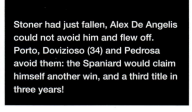

Stoner had just fallen, Alex De Angelis could not avoid him and flew off. Porto, Dovizioso (34) and Pedrosa avoid them: the Spaniard would claim himself another win, and a third title in three years!

GP AUSTRALIA | 16th October 2005 | Phillip Island | 4.448 m

STARTING GRID

1	27	C. Stoner	Aprilia	1'32.756
2	48	J. Lorenzo	Honda	1'32.843
3	5	A. De Angelis	Aprilia	1'32.882
4	19	S. Porto	Aprilia	1'33.117
5	80	H. Barbera	Honda	1'33.624
6	1	D. Pedrosa	Honda	1'33.691
7	34	A. Dovizioso	Honda	1'33.733
8	73	H. Aoyama	Honda	1'34.134
9	7	R. De Puniet	Aprilia	1'34.341
10	15	R. Locatelli	Aprilia	1'34.715
11	55	Y. Takahashi	Honda	1'34.739
12	17	S. Jenkner	Aprilia	1'34.998
13	6	A. Debon	Honda	1'35.028
14	50	S. Guintoli	Aprilia	1'35.087
15	44	T. Sekiguchi	Aprilia	1'35.104
16	24	S. Corsi	Aprilia	1'35.225
17	57	C. Davies	Aprilia	1'35.710
18	25	A. Baldolini	Aprilia	1'35.761
19	96	J. Smrz	Honda	1'35.891
20	8	A. Ballerini	Aprilia	1'36.107
21	28	D. Heidolf	Honda	1'36.192
22	32	M. Giansanti	Aprilia	1'36.318
23	36	M. Cardeñas	Aprilia	1'36.547
24	33	A. Tizon	Honda	1'36.631
25	21	A. Vincent	Fantic	1'36.756
26	63	E. Nigon	Yamaha	1'37.463
27	56	M. Gines	Aprilia	1'37.611

Not qualified:
	82	M. Kelly	Honda	1'39.266
	23	N. Cajback	Yamaha	1'39.507
	81	M. Rowling	Yamaha	1'42.395
	20	G. Ferro	Fantic	1'59.674

RACE: 25 laps = 111.200 km

1	Daniel Pedrosa	39'18.195	(169.756 km/h)
2	Sebastian Porto	+ 0''027	
3	Jorge Lorenzo	+ 8''674	
4	Hector Barbera	+ 24''838	
5	Andrea Dovizioso	+ 24''868	
6	Hiroshi Aoyama	+ 24''872	
7	Randy De Puniet	+ 37''274	
8	Roberto Locatelli	+ 47''013	
9	Alex Debon	+ 56''602	
10	Sylvain Guintoli	+ 56''747	
11	Chaz Davies	+ 1'09.126	
12	Dirk Heidolf	+ 1'09.796	
13	Jakub Smrz	+ 1'09.830	
14	Steve Jenkner	+ 1'14.472	
15	Andrea Ballerini	+ 1'14.497	
16	Simone Corsi	+ 1'14.771	
17	Martin Cardeñas	+ 1'22.080	
18	Mirko Giansanti	+ 1 lap	
19	Arturo Tizon	+ 1 lap	
20	Mathieu Gines	+ 1 lap	

Fastest lap
Porto, in 1'33.503 (171.254 km/h).
Record: Porto, in 1'33.381 (171.478 km/h/2004).

Outright fastest lap
Porto, in 1'32.099 (173.865 km/h/2004).

CHAMPIONSHIP

1	D. Pedrosa	264 (7 wins)
2	C. Stoner	213 (4 wins)
3	A. Dovizioso	171
4	H. Aoyama	154 (1 win)
5	S. Porto	152 (1 win)
6	J. Lorenzo	134
7	R. De Puniet	130 (1 win)
8	A. De Angelis	129
9	H. Barbera	99
10	S. Guintoli	75

AUSTRALIA 125cc

THOMAS LÜTHI CAME, HE SAW... AND HE CONQUERED!

A STRONG LINE-UP
Terol took back the handlebars of the second Derbi, that he had handed over to Enrique Jerez. The Swiss Vincent Braillard was still not there, and it was still Rodriguez who showed up with the Toth team's Aprilia (he had the best time in the race).

QUALIFYINGS
The KTMs domination was less impressive than usual, despite some innovations (a more discrete, Honda-style fairing). On the first day, the championship leader, Mika Kallio, complained of engine problems (he was only 18th), and on the Saturday, only Talmacsi (third) managed to qualify in the first row. Pole went to Thomas Lüthi, who has experienced some problems at Phillip Island these last two years; for him, the 2003 and 2004 seasons are certainly something to be filed away and forgotten.

START
Lüthi made a success of his start, as did Talmacsi, who attempted to block the Swiss on the outside; Kallio made the most of this to press forward from his second row position, but Lüthi showed he's the boss by braking later than everyone else, allowing him to take the lead in the first bend. First time over the line, the Swiss had a 0·967 sec lead over a pack where Kallio, Pasini, Talmacsi, Simoncelli and Lai were giving each other a run for their money..

LAP 5
Lüthi was still in front, now with a 1·894 sec lead over Pasini, who is in front of Kallio, Simoncelli, Simón, Talmacsi and Faubel.

LAP 8
Simón, who had been seventh, crashed (fracturing his right wrist). Lüthi is king: a 3·414 sec lead over his new heir apparent, Marco Simoncelli

LAP 9
Pesek crashed.

MID-RACE (LAP 12)
A perfect scenario for Lüthi. He now had a 3·861 sec lead over the pack, where Pasini, Simoncelli, Koyama and Rodriguez were now ahead of the World Championship leader, Mika Kallio. Faubel was keeping up, just like Talmacsi... who this time didn't dare to try anything against his leader

LAP 17
Still Lüthi, by 3·840 sec. Simoncelli was second, Koyama and Faubel hard on his heels.

LAP 19
Kallio broke away from the group, crossing the line 3·947 sec behind his great rival for the title, Thomas Lüthi.

FINISH (23 LAPS)
3·296 sec ahead going into the last lap, Lüthi did not make the slightest mistake. Excitement mounted over the battle for second place, and it was Koyama who had the last word, just 0·002 sec ahead of Simoncelli. Kallio "only" came fifth.

CHAMPIONSHIP
Lüthi reclaims the lead, by 12 points. The Swiss found himself some convenient allies at just the right moment…

The day before the race, someone told Thomas Lüthi that it was impossible, for a 125 cc rider, to break away on the Phillip Island circuit. Being the perfectionist that he is, the Swiss rider wanted to make sure…

GP AUSTRALIA | 16th October 2005 | Phillip Island | 4.448 m

STARTING GRID

1	12	T. Lüthi	Honda	1'37.543
2	75	M. Pasini	Aprilia	1'37.704
3	14	G. Talmacsi	KTM	1'37.731
4	58	M. Simoncelli	Aprilia	1'37.796
5	36	M. Kallio	KTM	1'37.906
6	71	T. Koyama	Honda	1'37.930
7	63	M. Di Meglio	Honda	1'37.983
8	52	L. Pesek	Derbi	1'38.177
9	32	F. Lai	Honda	1'38.182
10	6	J. Olivé	Aprilia	1'38.208
11	60	J. Simón	KTM	1'38.239
12	47	A. Rodriguez	Aprilia	1'38.449
13	55	H. Faubel	Aprilia	1'38.649
14	35	R. De Rosa	Aprilia	1'38.734
15	54	M. Poggiali	Gilera	1'38.968
16	11	S. Cortese	Honda	1'39.020
17	7	A. Masbou	Honda	1'39.107
18	19	A. Bautista	Honda	1'39.107
19	41	A. Espargaro	Honda	1'39.249
20	18	N. Terol	Derbi	1'39.368
21	45	I. Toth	Aprilia	1'39.578
22	33	S. Gadea	Aprilia	1'39.610
23	8	L. Zanetti	Aprilia	1'39.656
24	28	J. Carchano	Aprilia	1'39.701
25	22	P. Nieto	Derbi	1'39.953
26	9	T. Kuzuhara	Honda	1'39.963
27	44	K. Abraham	Aprilia	1'40.082
28	43	M. Hernandez	Aprilia	1'40.272
29	42	G. Pellino	Malaguti	1'40.412
30	10	F. Sandi	Honda	1'40.418
31	46	M. Tuñez	Aprilia	1'40.678
32	15	M. Pirro	Malaguti	1'40.936
33	48	D. Bonache	Honda	1'41.172
34	29	A. Iannone	Aprilia	1'41.814
35	25	D. Giuseppetti	Aprilia	1'42.145
36	69	B. Leigh-Smith	Honda	1'43.269
37	31	S. Hommel	Honda	1'43.285
38	81	T. Hatton	Honda	1'43.320
Not qualified:				
	70	B. Rigoli	Honda	1'45.550
	83	R. Moller	Honda	1'46.071
	82	C. Scott	Honda	1'47.132

RACE: 23 laps = 102.304 km

1	Thomas Lüthi	38'00.352	(161.507 km/h)
2	Tomoyoshi Koyama	+ 2''663	
3	Marco Simoncelli	+ 2''665	
4	Mattia Pasini	+ 2''673	
5	Mika Kallio	+ 2''860	
6	Hector Faubel	+ 2''945	
7	Gabor Talmacsi	+ 2''950	
8	Angel Rodriguez	+ 3''386	
9	Sergio Gadea	+ 10''546	
10	Alexis Masbou	+ 10''551	
11	Raffaele De Rosa	+ 10''851	
12	Fabrizio Lai	+ 11''071	
13	Manuel Poggiali	+ 11''133	
14	Mike Di Meglio	+ 11''629	
15	Joan Olivé	+ 15''048	
16	Alvaro Bautista	+ 30''883	
17	Aleix Espargaro	+ 30''884	
18	Pablo Nieto	+ 49''058	
19	Sandro Cortese	+ 49''131	
20	Lorenzo Zanetti	+ 49''170	
21	Toshihisa Kuzuhara	+ 50''660	
22	Manuel Hernandez	+ 51''027	
23	Mateo Tuñez	+ 1'07.317	
24	Gioele Pellino	+ 1'09.832	
25	Jordi Carchano	+ 1'21.312	
26	Dario Giuseppetti	+ 1'28.227	
27	David Bonache	+ 1 tour	
28	Blake Leigh-Smith	+ 2 tours	

Fastest lap
Rodriguez, in 1'38.054 (163.305 km/h).
Record : Pedrosa, in 1'37.983 (163.424 km/h/2002).

Outright fastest lap
Perugini, in 1'37.342 (164.500 km/h/2003).

CHAMPIONSHIP

1	T. Lüthi	224 (4 wins)
2	M. Kallio	212 (3 wins)
3	G. Talmacsi	165 (3 wins)
4	M. Simoncelli	156 (1 win)
5	M. Pasini	147 (2 wins)
6	F. Lai	123
7	J. Simón	115 (1 win)
8	M. Poggiali	102
9	H. Faubel	100
10	T. Koyama	93

Dream architecture for an exceptionally beautiful circuit.

16
23rd October 2005
TURKEY ISTANBUL PARK

Hayden in pursuit of Melandri: a spell-binding show.

THE REVOLT
OF THE YOUNG WOLVES

THE PROGRESS OF THE NEW GUARD IS CONFIRMED: MARCO MELANDRI CLAIMS HIS FIRST WIN IN THE TOP CATEGORY.

MOTO GP TURKEY

THE RACE

AMONG THE GENERAL INERTIA, MARCO MELANDRI IS THE PERFECT EMBODIMENT OF HOW POWER IS PASSING FROM ONE GENERATION OF RIDERS TO THE NEXT.

The accumulated fatigue of the past six weeks - five GPs on the calendar, from Japan to Turkey, via Malaysia, Qatar and Australia - has left its mark on everyone. And on hearts even more than on bodies.
In this jolly large paddock of Istanbul's superb new circuit, it suddenly seems as if there's something missing: excitement! Sure, there was the duel at the top - the last one that counts - between Thomas Lüthi and Mika Kallio, with the 125 cc title at stake, but in 250 cc and MotoGP, minds are already elsewhere - thinking about holidays, about the new challenges that await certain of the World Championship players in 2006… and about retirement, for a few of the legendary figures in the paddock.
Yet in this torpor, the new young hounds have shown their teeth. Marco Melandri, of course, who has been recognized during this year's racing as becoming great, and who has had his first success in the premier category; and also Toni Elias, his season too progressing from strength to strength, who was the author of a race of rare intensity in Istanbul.
Just as important, for the very future of the World Championship itself: on the eve of this penultimate race of the year, we learnt that the Australian Chris Vermeulen had just turned his back on Honda, who were offering him a new contract in World Superbike, in order to accept Suzuki's offer that will enable him to become a MotoGP rider from next year.
Don't let's kid ourselves. This rebellion by the up-and-coming young riders is only a foretaste of a movement that is going to gain still more impetus in 12 months' time, when the MotoGP 1000 ccs are going to be replaced with bikes that are lighter and smaller (800 cc), and hence more suitable for the youngsters who have finished their training (Pedrosa and Stoner), or who are still going to be polishing up their talent next year (Dovizioso, Lorenzo) in 250 cc, before moving up to the next class.
The old school are going to have to make room for these go-getters, this new generation of riders. Kenny Roberts, still injured, will no longer be riding with Suzuki… and may not even be riding at all next year; and in the duo of Alexandre Barros and Massimiliano Biaggi, there's one candidate too many for the last Sito Pons bike (the other one is being entrusted to Checa).

Marco Melandri's war-cry, and gesture: the Italian rider was perfect throughout the weekend in Turkey.

2006 is the last year the premier category will be led by Valentino Rossi. Carlos Checa, Edwards, and Capirossi will still be in it; but most of all it will belong to the young go-getters who have cut their teeth this year, like Melandri, Hayden and Elias. Young riders who have had enough of being satisfied with the crumbs that fall - those that Valentino Rossi drops for them. Nicky Hayden in Laguna Seca and Marco Melandri in Istanbul have both proved that under certain specific conditions, the king Valentino can be found wanting. It only remains now for these youngsters to try to achieve the same thing throughout the whole length of a championship. For that's what it's going to take for one of them to become, in 12 months' time, the pretender to the king's throne.

TURKEY MOTO GP 16

A NEW BLUNDER BY GIBERNAU, CELEBRATION BY MELANDRI: ROSSI WAS NOT AT ALL UNHAPPY WITH HIS WEEKEND.

A STRONG LINE-UP
As expected, Loris Capirossi had been transferred to Italy, where he is being treated by Dr Claudio Costa; the Italian was replaced by Shinichi Ito, Ducati-Bridgestone's test rider. Chris Vermeulen was still riding Bayliss's Honda, Jacque once again replaced Hofmann. Roberts was not replaced (just one Suzuki on the track).

QUALIFYINGS
The two riders from Fausto Gresini's team dominated each session, especially Marco Melandri, in very fine form; sadly for him, in the last few minutes he was robbed of pole by his team-mate Gibernau. Hayden completed the first row. There were three Yamahas in the second row (Rossi, Edwards and Elias, making progress). There was much talk of a deal, as Suzuki announced that Kenny Roberts's contract will not be extended… and still didn't make Vermeulen's arrival official.

START
Super start by Melandri, but not by Rossi, who was only seventh at the first checkpoint. Gibernau was right away at his team-mate's heels. Hayden was third, ahead of Edwards and Elias.

LAP 3
A false start was signalled for Ito, who had to make the detour via the stand lane. Melandri and Gibernau were still in front (in 0·248 sec), Rossi made the best time, he was fourth, 1·968 sec behind the leader.

LAP 4
Gibernau took the lead, Rossi was now directly threatening Hayden.

LAP 6
Gibernau made his bloomer of the day, finding himself in the sand trap. Melandri then has a 0·8 sec lead over Hayden, whom Rossi was following..

LAP 8
Ito was stopped at the black flag for having failed to carry out his punishment. Rossi grabbed second place, 1·018 sec behind Melandri.

MID-RACE (LAP 11)
Still Melandri, who resisted Rossi's attempted comeback (the World Champion was 1·298 sec behind his compatriot). Hayden was third, half a second from Rossi. Gibernau, fourth, was all on his own. In crisis as usual, Biaggi was in fourteenth position.

LAP 14
There was no holding super Melandri. His lead over Rossi was now 1·652 sec.

LAP 16
A new record for Melandri.

LAP 19
Revolt, and follow-up: while Melandri was still dominating up front, Toni Elias, who had gone off the track a few laps earlier, passed Tamada and Barros together, in the battle for seventh place.

FINISH (22 LAPS)
A first victory - what panache, what domination! - in the premier class by Marco Melandri, who had beaten the king Rossi.

CHAMPIONSHIP
Melandri alone - deservedly - now occupies second place. But Hayden hasn't had his last say yet.

A walk in the sand for Sete Gibernau... which seems to amuse Rossi. Right, Marco Melandri's triumphant finish.

GP TURKEY | 23rd October 2005 | Istanbul Park | 5.340 m

STARTING GRID

1	15	S. Gibernau	Honda	1'52.334
2	33	M. Melandri	Honda	1'52.463
3	69	N. Hayden	Honda	1'52.976
4	46	V. Rossi	Yamaha	1'53.177
5	5	C. Edwards	Yamaha	1'53.219
6	24	T. Elias	Yamaha	1'53.230
7	6	M. Tamada	Honda	1'53.667
8	4	A. Barros	Honda	1'53.719
9	7	C. Checa	Ducati	1'53.836
10	56	S. Nakano	Kawasaki	1'54.023
11	17	C. Vermeulen	Honda	1'54.217
12	3	M. Biaggi	Honda	1'54.358
13	19	O. Jacque	Kawasaki	1'54.407
14	21	J. Hopkins	Suzuki	1'54.434
15	23	S. Ito	Ducati	1'54.669
16	11	R. Xaus	Yamaha	1'55.414
17	44	R. Rolfo	Ducati	1'55.838
18	77	J. Ellison	Blata	1'56.576
19	27	F. Battaini	Blata	1'58.417

RACE: 22 laps = 117.480 km

1	Marco Melandri	41'44.139	(168.891 km/h)
2	Valentino Rossi	+ 1''513	
3	Nicky Hayden	+ 6''873	
4	Sete Gibernau	+ 12''420	
5	Carlos Checa	+ 26''963	
6	Toni Elias	+ 29''105	
7	Colin Edwards	+ 29''255	
8	Makoto Tamada	+ 33''345	
9	Alexandre Barros	+ 33''790	
10	Shinya Nakano	+ 44''225	
11	Chris Vermeulen	+ 46''099	
12	Massimiliano Biaggi	+ 50''184	
13	Olivier Jacque	+ 56''766	
14	Ruben Xaus	+ 1'01.360	
15	John Hopkins	+ 1'03.391	
16	Roberto Rolfo	+ 1'17.654	
17	Franco Battaini	+ 1 lap	
18	James Ellison	+ 1 lap	

Fastest lap
Melandri, in 1'53.111 (169.956 km/h).
New record (new circuit).

Outright fastest lap
Gibernau, in 1'52.334 (171.132 km/h/2005).

CHAMPIONSHIP

1	V. Rossi	351 (11 wins)
2	M. Melandri	195 (1 win)
3	N. Hayden	186 (1 win)
4	C. Edwards	171
5	M. Biaggi	163
6	S. Gibernau	150
7	L. Capirossi	148 (2 wins)
8	A. Barros	136 (1 win)
9	C. Checa	125
10	S. Nakano	93

16 250cc TURKEY

A LAST-DITCH STAND BY CASEY STONER, WHO BEAT THE WORLD CHAMPION BY 93 THOUSANDTHS OF A SECOND.

A STRONG LINE-UP
Spaniard Arturo Tizon was still riding the second Honda BQR. Zonghsen Team of China was there, with Zhu Wang and Zheng Peng Li, both holding wild cards for their Aprilias.

QUALIFYINGS
Things moved fast in the qualifyings, and pole went to Alex De Angelis, who is however not the happiest of chaps: the representative of the Principality of San Marino feels betrayed by Aprilia (Barbera and Lorenzo have been announced for next year at Noale!) Aoyama and Pedrosa completed the first row. For Fantic, former World 125 cc Champion Arnaud Vincent learnt officially on Thursday evening that the Italian challenge is going to finish at the end of a season that will have been a jolly difficult one.

START
Super start by Casey Stoner. Randy De Puniet crashed in the first bend. The Australian finished the first lap with a 0_378 sec lead over Jorge Lorenzo. Alex De Angelis and Dovizioso were hard on the heels of the fiery Spaniard.

LAP 2
Sebastian Porto crashed (a tough day for the team managed by Aspar Martinez!)

LAP 3
Sekiguchi crashed. Stoner has a 0_727 sec lead over De Angelis.

LAP 4
Jenkner abandoned.

LAP 5
Cardeñas crashed. A major scare for Alex De Angelis, who had got to within 0_2 sec of Stoner. Crossing the line, the Australian's lead was once again 0_756 sec.

LAP 6
Though Stoner was king up front (a lead of 1_445 sec), the battle for second place was worthy… of the 125 cc class, between Pedrosa, De Angelis, Dovizioso and Aoyama.

MID-RACE (LAP 10)
Corsi crashed. Stoner held a 1_136sec lead over Pedrosa, who had shaken off Alex De Angelis (Aoyama was hard on the heels of the Aprilia rider). Dovizioso was fifth, at 1_715 sec. A fine scrap between Lorenzo and Barbera.

LAP 12
Pedrosa came back to within 0_683 sec of Stoner. With third place at stake, a superb duel between De Angelis and Aoyama.

LAP 15
0_258 sec between Stoner and Pedrosa. Aoyama was more than 7 sec behind, still battling it out with De Angelis.

FINISH (20 LAPS)
0_165 sec between them going into the last lap, the Australian held out right until the line. De Angelis fell in the final bend, ending up rescuing seventh place. Aoyama was third, Lorenzo just made fourth, ahead of Dovizioso.

CHAMPIONSHIP
It was already clear who the champion (Pedrosa) and vice-champion (Stoner) were going to be, though there was still an arithmetic doubt over the third place on the final podium, between Dovizioso and Aoyama, who has come back to just 12 points from the man who is still the world 125 cc title holder.

The last moments of the race in two images: Pedrosa doesn't manage to make up all the distance between him and Stoner, while De Angelis fell in the final chicane. This was Stoner's fifth win.

GP TURKEY | 23rd October 2005 | Istanbul Park | 5.340 m

STARTING GRID

1	5	A. De Angelis	Aprilia	1'56.930
2	27	C. Stoner	Aprilia	1'57.071
3	73	H. Aoyama	Honda	1'57.198
4	1	D. Pedrosa	Honda	1'57.390
5	19	S. Porto	Aprilia	1'57.408
6	80	H. Barbera	Honda	1'57.969
7	48	J. Lorenzo	Honda	1'58.093
8	34	A. Dovizioso	Honda	1'58.107
9	15	R. Locatelli	Aprilia	1'58.421
10	7	R. De Puniet	Aprilia	1'58.437
11	55	Y. Takahashi	Honda	1'58.678
12	6	A. Debon	Honda	1'59.074
13	50	S. Guintoli	Aprilia	1'59.129
14	17	S. Jenkner	Aprilia	1'59.167
15	24	S. Corsi	Aprilia	1'59.296
16	25	A. Baldolini	Aprilia	1'59.325
17	57	C. Davies	Aprilia	1'59.750
18	36	M. Cardeñas	Aprilia	1'59.757
19	96	J. Smrz	Honda	1'59.948
20	44	T. Sekiguchi	Aprilia	1'59.951
21	28	D. Heidolf	Honda	2'00.007
22	8	A. Ballerini	Aprilia	2'00.147
23	32	M. Giansanti	Aprilia	2'00.180
24	33	A. Tizon	Honda	2'00.677
25	56	M. Gines	Aprilia	2'01.217
26	63	E. Nigon	Yamaha	2'02.817
27	21	A. Vincent	Fantic	2'02.819
28	61	Z. Li	Aprilia	2'04.091
29	60	Z. Wang	Aprilia	2'04.265
30	23	N. Cajback	Yamaha	2'05.062
Not qualified:				
	20	G. Ferro	Fantic	2'08.940

RACE: 20 laps = 106.800 km

1	Casey Stoner	39'28.243	(162.348 km/h)
2	Daniel Pedrosa	+ 0''093	
3	Hiroshi Aoyama	+ 11''647	
4	Jorge Lorenzo	+ 21''861	
5	Andrea Dovizioso	+ 21''940	
6	Hector Barbera	+ 22''258	
7	Alex De Angelis	+ 43''755	
8	Roberto Locatelli	+ 44''105	
9	Sylvain Guintoli	+ 48''918	
10	Chaz Davies	+ 54''376	
11	Alex Baldolini	+ 54''651	
12	Alex Debon	+ 59''791	
13	Andrea Ballerini	+ 1'00.082	
14	Mirko Giansanti	+ 1'00.225	
15	Jakub Smrz	+ 1'00.338	
16	Dirk Heidolf	+ 1'28.084	
17	Mathieu Gines	+ 1'34.665	
18	Arturo Tizon	+ 1'45.487	
19	Erwan Nigon	+ 1 lap	
20	Zheng Peng Li	+ 1 lap	
21	Nicklas Cajback	+ 1 lap	

Fastest lap
Pedrosa, in 1'57.595 (163.476 km/h).
New record (new circuit).

Outright fastest lap
De Angelis, in 1'56.930 (164.406 km/h/2005).

CHAMPIONSHIP

1	D. Pedrosa	284 (7 wins)
2	C. Stoner	238 (5 wins)
3	A. Dovizioso	182
4	H. Aoyama	170 (1 win)
5	S. Porto	152 (1 win)
6	J. Lorenzo	147
7	A. De Angelis	138
8	R. De Puniet	130 (1 win)
9	H. Barbera	109
10	S. Guintoli	82

TURKEY 125cc

A MISTAKE BY KALLIO, A GOOD DEAL FOR LÜTHI AND, ABOVE ALL, A FIRST WIN FOR MIKE DI MEGLIO.

A STRONG LINE-UP
Simón had joined Braillard and Miralles in the family of injured riders; he was not replaced. So there were only two KTMs in the running. Other changes to note: Manuel Hernandez has been thrown out by the management of the Totti Top Sport team, he was replaced by his compatriot Daniel Saez… and he bounced back into the Angaia team in place of the Japanese Kuzuhara, who has also been fired. First GP for the young Frenchman Jules Cluzel (for Malaguti, in place of Pirro).

QUALIFYINGS
In the whole paddock, there are only two riders still involved in the world title in this 125 cc class: Swiss Thomas Lüthi and Finn Mika Kallio. Kallio put th pressure on right from the first day, but Lüthi pulled off the perfect lap on Saturday afternoon, landing his fifth pole position. On Sunday morning, during the warm-up, Kallio took back the upper hand, making the best time, 0_4 sec faster than his great adversary's pole.

START
Super start for Kallio but, just as in Australia, Lüthi took matters in hand in the first bends. After one lap, Kallio had a 0_096 sec lead over the Swiss. Gadea, Di Meglio and the rest were just behind.

LAP 2
Di Meglio was in the lead, ahead of Kallio, Talmacsi, Lüthi and Gadea.

LAP 3
Nine of them were within 1_521 sec of each other. Di Meglio was leading, ahead of Kallio and Lüthi.

LAP 4
The two KTMs were in front. Faubel and Gadea crashed, there are only five left in the battle: Kallio, Talmacsi, Di Meglio, Lüthi and Pasini.

LAP 5
Following a superb manœuvre, Lüthi took back the lead

LAP 7
The group of five were all within 0_774 sec of each other (Kallio, Lüthi, Talmacsi, Pasini and Di Meglio, in that order).

LAP 9
Now Pasini was in front by 0_503 sec. Kallio, Lüthi and Talmacsi followed

MI-COURSE (10 TOURS)
A Dante-esque spectacle: Pasini, Kallio, Lüthi, Di Meglio and Talmacsi were all within less than 0_7 sec (0_651, to be exact).

LAP 11
Koyama was back up there with the rest. Now there were six of them wheel-to-wheel, separate by just 0_9 sec

LAP 13
Di Meglio was leading.

LAP 15
Lüthi made two minor errors one after the other, and found himself sixth..

LAP 17
Les than 0_9 sec between the six leaders (so Lüthi had pulled back).

FINISH (19 LAPS)
Kallio crashed three bends from the finish, Mike Di Meglio won his first GP. Thomas Lüthi finished fifth.

CHAMPIONSHIP
Lüthi has a 23-point lead over Kallio before the Valencia final. So the Finn has got to win; if he wins, Lüthi will have to make do with thirteenth place

What a final: the French rider Mike Di Meglio (63) would finally have the last word against Mattia Pasini (75). Above: Mike smiles, and Thomas Lüthi concentrates, approaching the title.

GP TURKEY | 23rd October 2005 | Istanbul Park | 5.340 m

STARTING GRID

1	12	T. Lüthi	Honda	2'03.585
2	55	H. Faubel	Aprilia	2'04.064
3	36	M. Kallio	KTM	2'04.115
4	75	M. Pasini	Aprilia	2'04.179
5	33	S. Gadea	Aprilia	2'04.833
6	63	M. Di Meglio	Honda	2'04.888
7	71	T. Koyama	Honda	2'05.026
8	14	G. Talmacsi	KTM	2'05.107
9	58	M. Simoncelli	Aprilia	2'05.300
10	52	L. Pesek	Derbi	2'05.368
11	32	F. Lai	Honda	2'05.511
12	35	R. De Rosa	Aprilia	2'05.519
13	7	A. Masbou	Honda	2'05.643
14	6	J. Olivé	Aprilia	2'05.845
15	47	A. Rodriguez	Aprilia	2'05.864
16	19	A. Bautista	Honda	2'05.902
17	54	M. Poggiali	Gilera	2'06.186
18	8	L. Zanetti	Aprilia	2'06.243
19	18	N. Terol	Derbi	2'06.303
20	22	P. Nieto	Derbi	2'06.345
21	29	A. Iannone	Aprilia	2'06.455
22	44	K. Abraham	Aprilia	2'06.654
23	41	A. Espargaro	Honda	2'06.727
24	28	J. Carchano	Aprilia	2'06.787
25	11	S. Cortese	Honda	2'07.007
26	25	D. Giuseppetti	Aprilia	2'07.243
27	45	I. Toth	Aprilia	2'07.293
28	89	J. Cluzel	Malaguti	2'07.861
29	10	F. Sandi	Honda	2'07.937
30	43	M. Hernandez	Honda	2'08.143
31	49	D. Saez	Aprilia	2'08.290
32	46	M. Tuñez	Aprilia	2'08.443
33	42	G. Pellino	Malaguti	2'08.680
34	48	D. Bonache	Honda	2'09.432
35	31	S. Hommel	Honda	2'09.597

RACE: 19 laps = 101.460 km

1	Mike Di Meglio	39'50.377	(152.802 km/h)
2	Mattia Pasini	+ 0''105	
3	Tomoyoshi Koyama	+ 0''156	
4	Gabor Talmacsi	+ 0''271	
5	Thomas Lüthi	+ 0''417	
6	Marco Simoncelli	+ 5''752	
7	Fabrizio Lai	+ 6''148	
8	Angel Rodriguez	+ 6''294	
9	Joan Olivé	+ 6''611	
10	Andrea Iannone	+ 17''119	
11	Manuel Poggiali	+ 17''554	
12	Alvaro Bautista	+ 21''232	
13	Lukas Pesek	+ 21''466	
14	Sandro Cortese	+ 42''207	
15	Dario Giuseppetti	+ 42''798	
16	Nicolas Terol	+ 47''875	
17	Aleix Espargaro	+ 47''915	
18	Karel Abraham	+ 48''240	
19	Jordi Carchano	+ 48''367	
20	Pablo Nieto	+ 48''693	
21	Mateo Tuñez	+ 48''940	
22	Jules Cluzel	+ 1'07.174	
23	Gioele Pellino	+ 1'07.453	
24	Imre Toth	+ 1'12.930	
25	Manuel Hernandez	+ 1'13.742	
26	Sascha Hommel	+ 1'36.276	

Fastest lap
Lüthi, in 2'04.428 (154.498 km/h).
New record (new circuit).

Outright fastest lap
Lüthi, in 2'03.585 (155.552 km/h/2005).

CHAMPIONSHIP

1	T. Lüthi	235 (4 wins)
2	M. Kallio	212 (3 wins)
3	G. Talmacsi	178 (3 wins)
4	M. Pasini	167 (2 wins)
5	M. Simoncelli	166 (1 win)
6	F. Lai	132
7	J. Simón	115 (1 win)
8	T. Koyama	109
9	M. Poggiali	107
10	M. Di Meglio	104 (1 win)

Melandri and Hayden put on a show, with Rossi as a backdrop: what if 2006 looks like this?

17

6th November 2005
VALENCIA CHESTE

For this last GP of the season, there was clearly Miss... and Miss!

SO THAT TOMORROW
IS ANOTHER DAY...

24 HOURS AFTER MARCO MELANDRI'S VICTORY, THE 2006 SEASON BEGAN AT VALENCIA.

MOTORCYCLE YEARBOOK 2005 **167**

17 MOTO GP VALENCIA

THE RACE

A SPECTACULAR FINAL AND A CELEBRATORY OUTCOME WITH LOTS OF LESSONS TO BE LEARNED: WHEN THE CHAMPIONSHIP TIPS OVER FROM ONE YEAR INTO THE NEXT.

The crowd to witness the Melandri-Hayden duel... and the calm the next day for first Randy De Puniet's outing on the saddle of a Kawasaki MotoGP..

Valencia, 7th November. There's surely nothing more sad than the final Grand Prix of a season, when everyone says goodbye, when whole teams don't know if they'll be coming back the following year, when everyone's glad of their few weeks' break - and yet very disappointed to be parting. That's the way it is, every 12 months, in the life of these nomadic racing folk.

These feelings are stronger than ever at the end of this year 2005, with the very clear impression that we are witnessing the end of a reign, with the certainty now that some of the significant figures from the last ten years will no longer be on the track next year.

But everybody knows, the end of one adventure is also the beginning of a new one. And the demonstration of strength, the confirmation of the arrival of Marco Melandri and Nicky Hayden are surely guarantees of a happy future.

All the more so because, the day after the World Championship final, when some people were still bleary-eyed from the excesses (controlled, you can be assured!) of the night before, the 2006 championship has already started. Toni Elias moving from Yamaha to Honda, new colours for the Gresini team's bikes, Randy De Puniet's first outing on the Kawasaki MotoGP, Daniel Pedrosa's impatience to mount the Honda RC211V that is to be his future - everything started with a rush. Just like Casey Stoner's first outing with the greats, Sete Gibernau's first impressions moving to Ducati, all these other new things that promise us a Winter full of lessons. Just a few questions: will Valentino Rossi, who at that very moment was already in Italy where three days of trials at the wheel of the F1 Ferrari awaited him, also be sovereign again? Are Marco Melandri and Nicky Hayden going to be able to maintain the same level they've managed over the last two months for the whole length of a season? Is Toni Elias, like Melandri 12 months ago, going to move in one fell swoop from promising youngster to the status of real opponent, now he has a Honda to ride? Will Sete Gibernau stand comparison with Loris Capirossi, the fearless and unreproachful knight at Ducati? Can Chris Vermeulen climb from game entry to the level of John Hopkins at Suzuki? What is De Puniet going to do at Kawasaki? And Pedrosa, little (in height) Pedrosa: is he going to be able to take up the most important challenge of his career, as he becomes "on paper" the Number 1 in Honda's future?

So many questions, the answers to which will unfold as the weeks go by, as the- very numerous - trials take place, as the surprises - nice and nasty - are sprung. The life of these racing nomads is such that, after the fatigue and discontent that invade the paddock during the final GPs, everybody is already eager to dive into the future - be they the winners who jolly well intend to remain so, or those who have been beaten and dream of revenge. It's true, in this world too, tomorrow is another day…

VALENCIA MOTO GP

AND TWO FOR MARCO MELANDRI, WHO CONTAINED HAYDEN UNTIL THE END.

A STRONG LINE-UP
Look what's new! First of all, we must applaud the lesson in courage from Loris Capirossi, back again after his serious injury during qualifying for the Australian GP. Next, it was the turn of Japanese Ryuichi Kiyonari, 2nd in this season's British Superbike, to find himself astride the Camel team's second Honda. For Suzuki, test rider Nobuatsu Aoki replaced Kenny Roberts, Hofmann was back for Kawasaki, and Kurtis Roberts came over from the States to ride his father's Proton KR.

QUALIFYINGS
A thunderbolt on the Saturday afternoon: in difficulties right from the start of the weekend, Valentino Rossi crashed 12 minutes from the end, when he had just fitted his first set of qualification tyres; the World Champion set off again with his second bike, but had to be content with fifteenth position. Out in front, it was a Gibernau fiesta.

START
Melandri led the turn, ahead of Hayden, Gibernau and Biaggi. Rolfo crashed, Rossi ended the first lap in eighth position, 2·769 sec behind Melandri.

LAP 3
Melandri had built a 0·672 sec lead over Hayden.

LAP 4
Gibernau retired (engine problems). Melandri made another best lap, Hayden was 0·7 sec behind, Rossi was fifth.

LAP 6
Setting off from fifteenth position, Rossi only took six laps to gain a place on the podium!

LAP 9
Aoki retired.

LAP 12
Hayden was still hard on Melandri's heels (0·519 sec). For third place, Checa was sticking close to Rossi's tail, but both men were almost 6 sec behind the leader.

MID-RACE (LAP 15)
Melandri and Hayden were neck-and-neck (0·254 sec). Rossi gained a few metres' lead over Checa, 5·789 sec behind Melandri, from whom he had just snatched 0·8 sec in a single lap.

LAP 16
Kurtis Roberts retired.

20° TOUR
The front positions were set, but not the rear, as Barros was back on Biaggi's tail.

23° TOUR
Hayden took advantage of Battaini's passing (he lost a lap) to get closer to Melandri (0·238 sec). Rossi got back to within 3·886 sec of the head of the race.

FINISH (30 LAPS)
The gap between Melandri and Hayden was 0·355 sec at the penultimate line. Melandri wasn't about to make a mistake at the end of an impressive final lap: this was his second win in succession. Hats off to Capirossi, seventh.

CHAMPIONSHIP
Melandri ensured his final second place in the championship in the finest possible manner: Rossi is going to have him to reckon with next year.

Three men, three destinies: Marco Melandri (left), the rider for tomorrow; Valentino Rossi (above), still undeniably the king; and Massimiliano Biaggi: was Sunday the last GP start for the Roman?

GP VALENCIA | 6th November 2005 | Cheste | 4.005 m

STARTING GRID

1	15	S. Gibernau	Honda	1'31.874
2	33	M. Melandri	Honda	1'32.111
3	69	N. Hayden	Honda	1'32.217
4	7	C. Checa	Ducati	1'32.374
5	3	M. Biaggi	Honda	1'32.384
6	5	C. Edwards	Yamaha	1'32.456
7	65	L. Capirossi	Ducati	1'32.482
8	4	A. Barros	Honda	1'32.518
9	56	S. Nakano	Kawasaki	1'32.663
10	6	M. Tamada	Honda	1'32.682
11	21	J. Hopkins	Suzuki	1'32.785
12	66	A. Hofmann	Kawasaki	1'32.966
13	24	T. Elias	Yamaha	1'33.005
14	9	N. Aoki	Suzuki	1'33.393
15	46	V. Rossi	Yamaha	1'33.503
16	54	R. Kiyonari	Honda	1'33.846
17	11	R. Xaus	Yamaha	1'34.874
18	44	R. Rolfo	Ducati	1'34.978
19	77	J. Ellison	Blata	1'35.158
20	80	Ku. Roberts	Proton KR	1'35.374
21	27	F. Battaini	Blata	1'35.712

RACE: 30 laps = 120.150 km

1	Marco Melandri	46'58.152 (153.483 km/h)
2	Nicky Hayden	+ 0''097
3	Valentino Rossi	+ 2''959
4	Carlos Checa	+ 18''718
5	Alexandre Barros	+ 20''706
6	Massimiliano Biaggi	+ 21''254
7	Loris Capirossi	+ 23''142
8	Colin Edwards	+ 25''678
9	Makoto Tamada	+ 36''710
10	Toni Elias	+ 39''116
11	Shinya Nakano	+ 41''136
12	Ryuichi Kiyonari	+ 45''691
13	John Hopkins	+ 46''507
14	Alex Hofmann	+ 49''856
15	Ruben Xaus	+ 1'19.443
16	Franco Battaini	+ 1 lap

Fastest lap
Melandri, in 1'33.043 (154.960 km/h). New record.
Previous: Rossi, in 1'33.317 (154.505 km/h/2003).

Outright fastest lap
Gibernau, in 1'31.874 (156.932 km/h/2005).

CHAMPIONSHIP

1	V. Rossi	367 (11 wins)
2	M. Melandri	220 (2 wins)
3	N. Hayden	206 (1 win)
4	C. Edwards	179
5	M. Biaggi	173
6	L. Capirossi	157 (2 wins)
7	S. Gibernau	150
8	A. Barros	147 (1 win)
9	C. Checa	138
10	S. Nakano	98

17 250cc VALENCIA

A STRONG DISPLAY BY DANIEL PEDROSA, FOR HIS FAREWELL TO THE 250CC CATEGORY.

A STRONG LINE-UP
A new GP for the Zonghsen Team of China (Wang and Li). Another wild card for European Champion Alvaro Molina. As for the rest, no change from the last GPs. On the eve of the race, official confirmation of what had been guessed ever since the Turkish GP: the team managed by Dani Amatriain (Lorenzo and Barbera) is leaving Honda to go and join Aprilia.

QUALIFYINGS
A demonstration of the strength of World Champion Daniel Pedrosa, ahead of his compatriot Hector Barbera, who has found himself right at the end of the season. Lots of crashes on the Saturday (Stoner, De Puniet and Porto, in particular).

START
Having crashed the day before, Sebastián Porto did not take part in the warm-up, and pulled out of the start of the race. After the first few metres, a group of seven split off, up to Randy de Puniet. Following a 'right on the limit' manœuvre by Barbera, Dovizioso carried straight on at the first bend, just avoiding making contact with Alex de Angelis. He ended this first lap in last place.

LAP 2
Barbera in the lead, ahead of his team-mate Lorenzo, who had just taken Pedrosa by surprise.

LAP 3
There was no holding Lorenzo, he passed Barbera.

LAP 4
Pedrosa took Barbera by surprise and clung directly into Lorenzo's wake.

LAP 6
Lorenzo and Pedrosa forged a lead of a few metres.

LAP 8
Stoner passed Barbera to grab third place.

MID-RACE (LAP 13)
Lorenzo and Pedrosa were within 0·082 sec of each other, keeping up the battle they'd started in the third lap. Stoner was at 3·185, Barbera was fourth, fighting it out with De Angelis.

LAP 15
Best lap for Pedrosa, who'd built a lead of over 0·6 sec, an advantage he doubled one lap later with another perfect lap: the World Champion had decided to leave the class with a flourish.

LAP 17
Another new record. Pedrosa's lead over Lorenzo was now 2·203 sec, the die was cast.

FINIS (27 LAPS)
Pedrosa dominated the field like the champion he is: he won the last 250 cc GP of his career with the best time in qualifying and the best race time (a new record). That's what you call a flourish!

CHAMPIONSHIP
Eight wins out of 16 races, over 50 points lead: Daniel Pedrosa didn't do things by half measures this year. A phenomenon of the times: Porto, De Angelis and De Puniet, the "seniors" in the class, have suffered faced with the "new wave": the 2004 World 125 cc Champion (Dovizioso) is third, Lorenzo fifth and Barbera ends his season on a rising note.

Daniel Pedrosa (left) storms on to another win. Above, an impressive battle between Stoner and Barbera while, right, makes a scene in the sand trap: next year he'll be with Aprilia.

GP VALENCIA | 6th November 2005 | Cheste | 4.005 m

STARTING GRID
1	1	D. Pedrosa	Honda	1'35.298
2	80	H. Barbera	Honda	1'35.530
3	5	A. De Angelis	Aprilia	1'35.768
4	48	J. Lorenzo	Honda	1'35.942
5	34	A. Dovizioso	Honda	1'35.995
6	73	H. Aoyama	Honda	1'36.038
7	27	C. Stoner	Aprilia	1'36.143
8	55	Y. Takahashi	Honda	1'36.284
9	19	S. Porto	Aprilia	1'36.522
10	7	R. De Puniet	Aprilia	1'36.537
11	96	J. Smrz	Honda	1'36.742
12	28	D. Heidolf	Honda	1'36.840
13	6	A. Debon	Honda	1'36.870
14	44	T. Sekiguchi	Aprilia	1'36.973
15	25	A. Baldolini	Aprilia	1'37.025
16	15	R. Locatelli	Aprilia	1'37.106
17	50	S. Guintoli	Aprilia	1'37.183
18	17	S. Jenkner	Aprilia	1'37.559
19	36	M. Cardeñas	Aprilia	1'37.577
20	57	C. Davies	Aprilia	1'37.639
21	8	A. Ballerini	Aprilia	1'37.746
22	33	A. Tizon	Honda	1'38.325
23	56	M. Gines	Aprilia	1'38.530
24	41	A. Molina	Aprilia	1'38.536
25	24	S. Corsi	Aprilia	1'38.544
26	21	A. Vincent	Fantic	1'38.638
27	32	M. Giansanti	Aprilia	1'39.127
28	63	E. Nigon	Yamaha	1'39.324
29	60	Z. Wang	Aprilia	1'40.548
30	61	Z. Li	Aprilia	1'41.390

Not qualified:
	23	N. Cajback	Yamaha	1'42.096
	20	G. Ferro	Fantic	1'43.778

RACE: 27 laps = 108.135 km
1	Daniel Pedrosa	43'33.395 (148.957 km/h)
2	Jorge Lorenzo	+ 3''448
3	Casey Stoner	+ 14''372
4	Alex De Angelis	+ 17''771
5	Hector Barbera	+ 26''233
6	Hiroshi Aoyama	+ 31''244
7	Yuki Takahashi	+ 35''518
8	Randy De Puniet	+ 36''488
9	Andrea Dovizioso	+ 43''129
10	Roberto Locatelli	+ 43''960
11	Alex Debon	+ 55''494
12	Jakub Smrz	+ 57''265
13	Martin Cardeñas	+ 58''185
14	Sylvain Guintoli	+ 58''545
15	Taro Sekiguchi	+ 1'01.485
16	Chaz Davies	+ 1'12.112
17	Steve Jenkner	+ 1'23.475
18	Alex Baldolini	+ 1'30.535
19	Mirko Giansanti	+ 1'31.957
20	Mathieu Gines	+ 1 lap
21	Zheng Peng Li	+ 1 lap

Fastest lap
Pedrosa, in 1'35.792 (150.513 km/h). New record.
Previous: Nakano, in 1'36.398 (149.567 km/h/2000).

Outright fastest lap
Pedrosa, in 1'35.298 (151.293 km/h/2005).

CHAMPIONSHIP
1	D. Pedrosa	309 (8 wins)
2	C. Stoner	254 (5 wins)
3	A. Dovizioso	189
4	H. Aoyama	180 (1 win)
5	J. Lorenzo	167
6	S. Porto	152 (1 win)
7	A. De Angelis	151
8	R. De Puniet	138 (1 win)
9	H. Barbera	120
10	S. Guintoli	84

VALENCIA 125cc

MIKA KALLIO WINS... BUT THOMAS LÜTHI IS WORLD CHAMPION

A STRONG LINE-UP
Julian Simón was back, as was Swiss Vincent Braillard (and hence Rodriguez found himself taking an enforced break). A second GP for Jules Cluzel, with Malaguti. This time, Enrique Jerez held a wild card (so there were three Derbis racing), as did his compatriot Esteve Rabat.

QUALIFYINGS
Kallio needed to put the pressure on Lüthi, Lüthi couldn't afford to be too far from Kallio, the Spaniards were eager to do well in front of their home crowd, Pasini was still very fast: quite enough to guarantee an exciting race ! Gadea grabbed pole position, just 0·003 sec ahead of Pasini. Kallio and Lüthi completed the front row, the 14 frontrunners were all within 0·995 sec of each other.

START
Gadea made the best start, ahead of Faubel, Kallio, Talmacsi. Giuseppetti didn't finish the first lap, which local hero Gadea completed with a 1·013 sec lead over his team-mate Faubel. Pasini was third, ahead of Kallio, Talmacsi, Lai and Lüthi, 7th.

LAP 3
Gadea was still in the lead, by 0·310 sec from Pasini. Kallio was third, Lüthi still seventh

LAP 5
Pasini took over the lead, 0·262 sec ahead of Pasini. Kallio, third, had just notched up the best time. Lüthi was sixth.

LAP 6
Istanbul winner Di Meglio crashed.

LAP 8
Pasini, Gadea, Kallio and Talmacsi: the first four were within 0·645 sec of each other. Faubel, Lai and Lüthi were almost 3 sec behind them.

MID-RACE (LAP 12)
Pasini, Gadea, Kallio and Talmacsi were within 0·424 sec. Faubel was fifth, 2·836 behind the leader, Lüthi sixth, more than 6 sec from Pasini; the Swiss is just doing his job

LAP 13
Gadea took back the lead.

LAP 16
Gadea built a lead of 0·785 sec over Kallio, who temporarily took second place. Lüthi still sixth.

LAP 17
Poggiali crashed.

LAP 18
Cortese crashed.

LAP 19
With a 1·428 lead over Pasini, Gadea crashed. Pasini, Kallio and Talmacsi were within 0·190 sec of each other. Lüthi now seventh.

LAP 23
Still the same three in front, Lüthi settled at the rear of his group, in ninth position.

FINISH (24 TOURS)
Mika Kallio took Pasini by surprise in the final bend, he tried to beat him off and committed an error; Talmacsi took advantage of this to make it a KTM double. Kallio did what he had to do, he only had to look round to see that Lüthi, ninth, was World Champion.

CHAMPIONSHIP
Lüthi, whom we've seen full of panache, has shown that he also knows how to calculate his risks. Bravo!

The Spaniard, Gadea (33), couldn't be held back at the start of the race, but was to crash. In the final lap, Kallio (opposite: Kallio at the head of the pack chasing the frontrunning duo, Gadea and Pasini) found his opening and snatched the win. Behind, Lüthi (above) has calculated it right: in ninth, he was world champion.

GP VALENCIA | 6th November 2005 | Cheste | 4.005 m

STARTING GRID

1	33	S. Gadea	Aprilia	1'39.830
2	75	M. Pasini	Aprilia	1'39.833
3	36	M. Kallio	KTM	1'39.899
4	12	T. Lüthi	Honda	1'39.994
5	32	F. Lai	Honda	1'40.101
6	55	H. Faubel	Aprilia	1'40.114
7	11	S. Cortese	Honda	1'40.177
8	14	G. Talmacsi	KTM	1'40.222
9	71	T. Koyama	Honda	1'40.256
10	63	M. Di Meglio	Honda	1'40.502
11	58	M. Simoncelli	Aprilia	1'40.530
12	60	J. Simón	KTM	1'40.643
13	52	L. Pesek	Derbi	1'40.674
14	41	A. Espargaro	Honda	1'40.825
15	54	M. Poggiali	Gilera	1'41.033
16	29	A. Iannone	Aprilia	1'41.033
17	89	J. Cluzel	Malaguti	1'41.133
18	7	A. Masbou	Honda	1'41.351
19	43	M. Hernandez	Honda	1'41.521
20	8	L. Zanetti	Aprilia	1'41.534
21	35	R. De Rosa	Aprilia	1'41.557
22	19	A. Bautista	Honda	1'41.714
23	28	J. Carchano	Aprilia	1'41.752
24	22	P. Nieto	Derbi	1'41.855
25	10	F. Sandi	Honda	1'41.913
26	18	N. Terol	Derbi	1'41.982
27	6	J. Olivé	Aprilia	1'41.983
28	46	M. Tuñez	Aprilia	1'42.095
29	48	D. Bonache	Honda	1'42.289
30	25	D. Giuseppetti	Aprilia	1'42.335
31	45	I. Toth	Aprilia	1'42.574
32	49	D. Saez	Aprilia	1'42.587
33	44	K. Abraham	Aprilia	1'42.604
34	42	G. Pellino	Malaguti	1'42.627
35	59	E. Rabat	Honda	1'42.788
36	51	E. Jerez	Derbi	1'42.805
37	84	J. Miralles	Aprilia	1'43.201
38	26	V. Braillard	Aprilia	1'43.215
39	31	S. Hommel	Honda	1'44.682

RACE: 24 laps = 96.120 km

1	Mika Kallio	40'26.640 (142.597 km/h)
2	Gabor Talmacsi	+ 0''237
3	Mattia Pasini	+ 0''367
4	Hectór Faubel	+ 12''401
5	Marco Simoncelli	+ 17''009
6	Tomoyoshi Koyama	+ 20''635
7	Fabrizio Lai	+ 20''670
8	Julian Simón	+ 20''809
9	Thomas Lüthi	+ 23''517
10	Pablo Nieto	+ 32''805
11	Aleix Espargaro	+ 35''930
12	Alvaro Bautista	+ 36''015
13	Raffaele De Rosa	+ 43''436
14	Joan Olivé	+ 47''651
15	Andrea Iannone	+ 49''387
16	Nicolas Terol	+ 53''187
17	Jordi Carchano	+ 57''976
18	Enrique Jerez	+ 1'00.860
19	Manuel Hernandez	+ 1'01.055
20	Mateo Tuñez	+ 1'06.276
21	Imre Toth	+ 1'06.915
22	Gioele Pellino	+ 1'08.479
23	Vincent Braillard	+ 1'13.289
24	Esteve Rabat	+ 1'22.682
25	Julian Miralles	+ 1'23.174
26	Sascha Hommel	+ 1'39.732

Fastest lap
Gadea, in 1'40.286 (143.768 km/h).
Record: Jenkner, in 1'40.252 (143.817 km/h/2002).

Outright fastest lap
Pedrosa, in 1'39.426 (145.012 km/h/2002).

CHAMPIONSHIP

1	T. Lüthi	242 (4 wins)
2	M. Kallio	237 (4 wins)
3	G. Talmacsi	198 (3 wins)
4	M. Pasini	183 (2 wins)
5	M. Simoncelli	177 (1 win)
6	F. Lai	141
7	J. Simón	123 (1 win)
8	T. Koyama	119
9	H. Faubel	113
10	M. Poggiali	107

CLASSIFICATION & STATISTICS — MOTO GP

1	2	3	4	5	6	7	8	9	10
1 ROSSI VALENTINO	ITA	367	17	5	9	11	16	16	1	1
2 MELANDRI MARCO	ITA	220	17	-	9	2	7	14	1	3
3 HAYDEN NICKY	USA	206	17	3	6	1	6	15	1	2
4 EDWARDS COLIN	USA	179	17	-	1	-	3	17	2	-
5 BIAGGI MAX	ITA	173	17	-	1	-	4	14	2	3
6 CAPIROSSI LORIS	ITA	157	15	3	5	2	4	15	1	-
7 GIBERNAU SETE	ESP	150	17	5	14	-	4	10	2	7
8 BARROS ALEX	BRÉ	147	17	1	3	1	2	13	1	4
9 CHECA CARLOS	ESP	138	17	-	1	-	2	13	3	4
10 NAKANO SHINYA	JAP	98	17	-	-	-	-	13	4	-
11 TAMADA MAKOTO	JAP	91	14	-	-	-	1	12	3	2
12 ELIAS TONI	ESP	74	14	-	-	-	-	14	6	-
13 ROBERTS KENNY	USA	63	14	-	-	-	1	11	2	2
14 HOPKINS JOHN	USA	63	17	-	2	-	-	12	5	3
15 BAYLISS TROY	AUS	54	11	-	-	-	-	8	6	3
16 XAUS RUBEN	ESP	52	17	-	-	-	-	14	10	1
17 JACQUE OLIVIER	FRA	28	6	-	-	-	1	3	2	2
18 ROLFO ROBERTO	ITA	25	17	-	-	-	-	9	10	3
19 HOFMANN ALEX	ALL	24	10	-	-	-	-	6	8	3
20 VD GOORBERGH JURGEN	HOL	12	2	-	-	-	-	2	6	-
21 VERMEULEN CHRIS	AUS	10	2	-	-	-	-	2	11	-
22 BATTAINI FRANCO	ITA	7	17	-	-	-	-	3	11	3
23 ELLISON JAMES	GB	7	16	-	-	-	-	4	13	6
24 BYRNE SHANE	GB	6	12	-	-	-	-	3	13	4
25 KIYONARI RYUICHI	JAP	4	1	-	-	-	-	1	12	-
26 CHECA DAVID	ESP	4	3	-	-	-	-	2	13	-
27 UKAWA TOHRU	JAP	1	2	-	-	-	-	1	15	-

1 Final Championship Classification **2** Number of points **3** Number of qualifications (out of 17 GP) **4** Number of pole positions **5** Number of front row starts **6** Number of victories **7** Number of podiums **8** Score points (top 15) **9** Best race finish **10** Number of retirements

FINAL CONSTRUCTOR'S WORLDS CHAMPIONSHIP CLASSIFICATION

1	YAMAHA	381
2	HONDA	341
3	DUCATI	202
4	KAWASAKI	126
5	SUZUKI	100
6	BLATA	13
7	PROTON KR	1
8	MORIWAKI	1

ROOKIE OF THE YEAR

1	ELIAS TONI	ESP	71
2	ROLFO ROBERTO	ITA	24
3	BATTAINI FRANCO	ITA	7

FINAL TEAMS WORLDS CHAMPIONSHIP CLASSIFICATION

1	GAULOISES YAMAHA	546
2	REPSOL HONDA	379
3	MOVISTAR HONDA	370
4	DUCATI MARLBORO	295
5	CAMEL HONDA	220
6	KAWASAKI RACING	150
7	FORTUNA YAMAHA	130
8	SUZUKI MOTOGP	126
9	KONICA MINOLTA HONDA	103
10	D'ANTIN PRAMAC	25
11	BLATA WCM	14
12	TEAM ROBERTS	1

CLASSIFICATION & STATISTICS 250cc

1	2	3	4	5	6	7	8	9	10
1 PEDROSA DANIEL	SPA	309	16	5	13	8	11	15	1	1
2 STONER CASEY	AUS	254	16	2	10	5	10	14	1	2
3 DOVIZIOSO ANDREA	ITA	189	16	-	5	-	5	15	2	1
4 AOYAMA HIROSHI	JAP	180	16	2	3	1	4	14	1	2
5 LORENZO JORGE	ESP	167	15	4	12	-	6	12	2	3
6 PORTO SEBASTIAN	ARG	152	15	-	7	1	4	11	1	4
7 DE ANGELIS ALEX ST-M		151	16	2	8	-	4	11	2	5
8 DE PUNIET RANDY	FRA	138	16	1	4	1	3	11	1	4
9 BARBERA HECTOR	ESP	120	16	-	1	-	-	13	4	2
10 GUINTOLI SYLVAIN	FRA	84	16	-	-	-	-	14	8	2
11 TAKAHASHI YUKI	JAP	77	16	-	-	-	-	10	4	6
12 DEBON ALEX	ESP	67	16	-	-	-	-	13	8	3
13 LOCATELLI ROBERTO	ITA	61	16	-	-	-	-	10	7	5
14 CORSI SIMONE	ITA	59	16	-	-	-	-	8	5	5
15 GIANSANTI MIRKO	ITA	36	16	-	-	-	-	9	9	1
16 DAVIES CHAZ	GB	32	16	-	-	-	-	7	10	7
17 WEST ANTHONY	AUS	30	7	-	-	-	1	3	2	3
18 BALDOLINI ALEX	ITA	25	16	-	-	-	-	7	10	6
19 BALLERINI ANDREA	ITA	19	16	-	-	-	-	7	10	6
20 SMRZ JAKUB	TCH	19	16	-	-	-	-	6	11	5
21 SEKIGUCHI TARO	JAP	13	9	-	-	-	-	3	10	5
22 HEIDOLF DIRK	ALL	13	15	-	-	-	-	4	11	6
23 JENKNER STEVE	ALL	13	14	-	-	-	-	6	12	5
24 ROUS RADOMIL	TCH	11	11	-	-	-	-	5	12	3
25 CARDEÑAS MARTIN	COL	9	14	-	-	-	-	5	13	3
26 LEBLANC GREGORY	FRA	6	10	-	-	-	-	4	14	3
27 NIGON ERWAN	FRA	3	7	-	-	-	-	1	13	3
28 MARCHAND HUGO	FRA	3	4	-	-	-	-	2	14	2

1 Final Championship Classification **2** Number of points **3** Number of qualifications (out of 17 GP) **4** Number of pole positions **5** Number of front row starts **6** Number of victories **7** Number of podiums **8** Score points (top 15) **9** Best race finish **10** Number of retirements

FINAL CONSTRUCTOR'S WORLDS CHAMPIONSHIP CLASSIFICATION

1	HONDA	349
2	APRILIA	339
3	KTM	30

ROOKIE OF THE YEAR

1	DOVIZIOSO ANDREA	ITA	189
2	LORENZO JORGE	ESP	167
3	BARBERA HECTOR	ESP	120
4	TAKAHASHI YUKI	JAP	77
5	CORSI SIMONE	ITA	59
6	GIANSANTI MIRKO	ITA	36
7	BALLERINI ANDREA	ITA	19
8	JENKNER STEVE	ALL	13
9	ROUS RADOMIL	TCH	11
10	CARDEÑAS MARTIN	COL	9
11	LEBLANC GREGORY	FRA	6

MICHEL MÉTRAUX TROPHY (BEST PRIVATE RIDER)

1	GUINTOLI SYLVAIN	FRA	84
2	DEBON ALEX	ESP	67
3	GIANSANTI MIRKO	ITA	36
4	DAVIES CHAZ	GB	32
5	BALDOLINI ALEX	ITA	25
6	BALLERINI ANDREA	ITA	19
7	SMRZ JAKUB	TCH	19
8	SEKIGUCHI TARO	JAP	13
9	HEIDOLF DIRK	ALL	13
10	JENKNER STEVE	ALL	13
11	ROUS RADOMIL	TCH	11
12	CARDEÑAS MARTIN	COL	9
13	LEBLANC GREGORY	FRA	6

CLASSIFICATION & STATISTICS | 125cc

1			2	3	4	5	6	7	8	9	10
1	LÜTHI THOMAS	SUI	242	16	5	11	4	8	14	1	1
2	KALLIO MIKA	FIN	237	16	8	13	4	10	13	1	3
3	TALMACSI GABOR	HON	198	16	1	8	3	5	13	1	3
4	PASINI MATTIA	ITA	183	16	-	13	2	6	12	1	3
5	SIMONCELLI MARCO	ITA	177	16	1	10	1	6	13	1	2
6	LAI FABRIZIO	ITA	141	16	-	1	-	3	14	2	1
7	SIMÓN JULIAN	ESP	123	16	-	1	1	1	13	1	2
8	KOYAMA TOMOYOSHI	JAP	119	16	-	1	-	2	11	2	5
9	FAUBEL HECTOR	ESP	113	16	-	4	-	3	9	2	7
10	POGGIALI MANUEL	ST-M	107	16	-	-	-	-	14	5	1
11	DI MEGLIO MIKE	FRA	104	16	-	-	1	2	11	1	3
12	GADEA SERGIO	ESP	68	16	1	1	-	1	8	2	5
13	NIETO PABLO	ESP	64	16	-	-	-	-	10	5	2
14	OLIVÉ JOAN	ESP	60	16	-	-	-	1	10	3	2
15	BAUTISTA ALVARO	ESP	47	16	-	-	-	-	8	4	4
16	ESPARGARO ALEIX	ESP	36	16	-	-	-	-	9	7	2
17	ZANETTI LORENZO	ITA	30	14	-	1	-	-	6	5	3
18	MASBOU ALEXIS	FRA	28	16	-	-	-	-	5	5	8
19	PESEK LUKAS	TCH	25	16	-	-	-	-	5	6	11
20	IANNONE ANDREA	ITA	20	16	-	-	-	-	5	10	3
21	KUZUHARA TOSHIHISA	JAP	17	12	-	-	-	-	4	9	4
22	RODRIGUEZ ANGEL	ESP	16	12	-	-	-	-	2	8	7
23	DE ROSA RAFFAELE	ITA	13	16	-	-	-	-	5	11	4
24	HERNANDEZ MANUEL	ESP	12	16	-	-	-	-	4	10	3
25	RANSEDER MICHAEL	AUT	12	4	-	-	-	-	3	12	1
26	CORTESE SANDRO	ALL	8	16	-	-	-	-	5	14	4
27	LINFOOT DAN	GB	7	1	-	-	-	-	1	9	-
28	TOTH IMRE	HON	7	16	-	-	-	-	1	9	2
29	CARCHANO JORDI	ESP	6	16	-	-	-	-	2	13	2
30	CONTI MICHELE	ITA	5	1	-	-	-	-	1	11	-
31	ELKIN CHRISTIAN	GB	4	1	-	-	-	-	1	12	-
32	GIUSEPPETTI DARIO	ALL	4	16	-	-	-	-	2	13	6
33	PIRRO MICHELE	ITA	3	14	-	-	-	-	1	13	11
34	JEREZ ENRIQUE	ESP	2	4	-	-	-	-	2	15	-
35	BRADL STEFAN	ALL	1	3	-	-	-	-	1	15	-
36	TEROL NICOLAS	ESP	1	13	-	-	-	-	1	15	3

1 Final Championship Classification **2** Number of points **3** Number of qualifications (out of 17 GP) **4** Number of pole positions **5** Number of front row starts **6** Number of victories **7** Number of podiums **8** Score points (top 15) **9** Best race finish **10** Number of retirements

FINAL CONSTRUCTOR'S WORLDS CHAMPIONSHIP CLASSIFICATION

1	KTM	332
2	HONDA	304
3	APRILIA	296
4	GILERA	107
5	DERBI	73
6	MALAGUTI	3

ROOKIE OF THE YEAR

1	KOYAMA TOMOYOSHI	JAP	119
2	FAUBEL HECTOR	ESP	113
3	ESPARGARO ALEIX	ESP	36
4	ZANETTI LORENZO	ITA	30
5	MASBOU ALEXIS	FRA	28
6	IANNONE ANDREA	ITA	20
7	KUZUHARA TOSHIHISA	JAP	17
8	DE ROSA RAFFAELE	ITA	13
9	HERNANDEZ MANUEL	ESP	12
10	CORTESE SANDRO	ALL	8
11	PIRRO MICHELE	ITA	3
12	TEROL NICOLAS	ESP	1

MICHEL MÉTRAUX TROPHY (BEST PRIVATE RIDER)

1	LÜTHI THOMAS	SUI	242
2	PASINI MATTIA	ITA	183
3	SIMONCELLI MARCO	ITA	177
4	LAI FABRIZIO	ITA	141
5	KOYAMA TOMOYOSHI	JAP	119
6	FAUBEL HECTOR	ESP	113
7	DI MEGLIO MIKE	FRA	104
8	GADEA SERGIO	ESP	68
9	OLIVÉ JOAN	ESP	60
10	BAUTISTA ALVARO	ESP	47
11	ESPARGARO ALEIX	ESP	36
12	ZANETTI LORENZO	ITA	30
13	MASBOU ALEXIS	FRA	28
14	IANNONE ANDREA	ITA	20
15	KUZUHARA TOSHIHISA	JAP	17
16	RODRIGUEZ ANGEL	ESP	16
17	DE ROSA RAFFAELE	ITA	13
18	HERNANDEZ MANUEL	ESP	12
19	CORTESE SANDRO	ALL	8
20	TOTH IMRE	HON	7
21	CARCHANO JORDI	ESP	6
22	GIUSEPPETTI DARIO	ALL	4

THE RESULTS
OF THE CHAMPIONSHIPS

THE MOST EXTENSIVE STATISTICS SECTION ON THE MARKET, FROM THE SUPERBIKE WORLD CHAMPIONSHIP TO THE SWISS CHAMPIONSHIP, VIA GERMANY, FRANCE, ITALY, THE UNITED STATES, GREAT BRITAIN AND SPAIN.

THE RESULTS OF THE OTHER CHAMPIONSHIPS

SUPERBIKE WORLD CHAMPIONSHIP

26th February - Losail - Qatar

Race I: 1. T. Corser (AUS, Suzuki), 18 tours, 37'10.394 (156.306 km/h); 2. Y. Kagayama (J, Suzuki), 3''065; 3. R. Laconi (F, Ducati), 3''496; 4. A. Pitt (AUS, Yamaha), 14''714; 5. N. Haga (J, Yamaha), 20''300; 6. J. Toseland (GB, Ducati), 20''562; 7. I. Silva (E, Yamaha), 22''031; 8. C. Vermeulen (AUS, Honda), 22''188; 9. K. Muggeridge (AUS, Honda), 26''929; 10. N. Abé (J, Yamaha), 27''231; 11. G. Bussei (I, Kawasaki), 38''995; 12. M. Borciani (I, Yamaha), 42''208; 13. F. Gonzales-Nieto (E, Ducati), 43''494; 14. C. Walker (GB, Kawasaki), 44''894; 15. S. Martin (AUS, Petronas FP1), 49''673. 20 finishers.
Fastest lap: Y. Kagayama (J, Suzuki), 2'02''135 (158.579 km/h).
Race II: 1. Y. Kagayama (J, Suzuki), 18 tours, 37'00.062 (157.033 km/h); 2. R. Laconi (F, Ducati), 2''454; 3. T. Corser (Aus, Suzuki), 5''959; 4. C. Vermeulen (AUS, Honda), 7''245; 5. P. Chili (I, Honda), 8''600; 6. J. Toseland (GB, Ducati), 8''601; 7. N. Abé (J, Yamaha), 9''731; 8. M. Neukirchner (D, Honda), 11''501; 9. A. Pitt (AUS, Yamaha), 11''790; 10. S. Gimbert (F, Yamaha), 11''808; 11. N. Haga (J, Yamaha), 21''364; 12. L. Lanzi (I, Ducati), 25''875; 13. F. Gonzales-Nieto (E, Ducati), 34''084; 14. G. Bussei (I, Kawasaki), 34''119; 15. M. Sanchini (I, Kawasaki), 47''446. 18 finishers.
Fastest lap: S. Gimbert (F, Yamaha), 2'01''852 (158.947 km/h).

3rd April - Phillip Island - Australia

Race I: 1. T. Corser (AUS, Suzuki), 22 tours, 35'15.199 (166.435 km/h); 2. Y. Kagayama (J, Suzuki), 8''279; 3. C. Vermeulen (AUS, Honda), 12''551; 4. M. Neukirchner (D, Honda), 12''761; 5. A. Pitt (AUS), Yamaha, 13''204; 6. N. Abé (J, Yamaha), 15''116; 7. R. Laconi (F, Ducati), 17''195; 8. K. Muggeridge (AUS, Honda). 33''821; 9. C. Walker (GB, Kawasaki), 34''010; 10. G. Bussei (I, Kawasaki), 42''594; 11. S. Gimbert (F, Yamaha), 42''851; 12. M. Sanchini (I, Kawasaki), 44''556; 13. I. Clementi (I, Kawasaki), 44''804; 14. J. Toseland (GB, Ducati), 1'01.011; 15. A. Stroud (NZ, Suzuki), 1'32.156. 16 finishers.
Fastest lap: T. Corser (AUS, Suzuki), 1'34.917 (168.589 km/h).
Race II: 1. T. Corser (AUS, Suzuki), 22 tours, 37'34.183 (156.174 km/h); 2. Y. Kagayama (J, Suzuki), 5''822; 3. M. Neukirchner (D, Honda), 10''897; 4. C. Vermeulen (AUS, Honda), 18''757; 5. F. Gonzales-Nieto (E, Ducati), 53''089; 6. A. Corradi (I, Ducati), 54''127; 7. R. Laconi (F, Ducati), 58''076; 8. A. Abé (J, Yamaha), 1'03.328; 9. G. Bussei (I, Kawasaki), 1'04.355; 10. M. Sanchini (I, Kawasaki), 1'08,754; 11. B. Bostrom (USA, Honda), 1'14.447; 12. A. Stroud (NZ, Suzuki), 1'16.710; 13. L. Lanzi (I, Ducati), 1'20.004; 14. M. Praia (POR, Yamaha), 2'44.473. 14 finishers.
Fastest lap: T. Corser (AUS, Suzuki), 1'34.979 (168.479 km/h).

24th April - Valencia - Spain

Race I: 1. T. Corser (AUS, Suzuki), 23 tours, 37'31.052 (147.315 km/h); 2. C. Vermeulen (AUS, Honda), 9''116; 3. Y. Kagayama (J, Suzuki), 12''788; 4. C. Walker (GB, Kawasaki), 16''867; 5. N. Haga (J, Yamaha), 17''882; 6. S. Gimbert (F, Yamaha), 26''495; 7. P. Chili (I, Honda), 28''784; 8. J. Toseland (GB, Ducati), 36''604; 9. S. Fuertes (E, Suzuki), 39''524; 10. D. Checa (E, Yamaha), 39''775; 11. I. Clementi (I, Kawasaki), 40''047; 12. B. Bostrom (USA, Honda), 41''941; 13. G. Bussei (I, Kawasaki), 47''505; 14. L. Alfonsi (I, Yamaha), 47''585; 15. I. Silva (E, Yamaha), 48''993. 19 finishers.
Fastest lap: T. Corser (AUS, Suzuki), 1'36.721 (149.068 km/h).
Race II: 1. T. Corser (AUS, Suzuki), 23 tours, 37'52.057 (145.953 km/h); 2. C. Vermeulen (AUS, Honda), 5''361; 3. C. Walker (GB, Kawasaki), 7''184; 4. N. Haga (J, Yamaha), 10''600; 5. N. Abé (J, Yamaha), 11''903; 6. B. Bostrom (USA, Honda), 19''200; 7. Y. Kagayama (J, Suzuki), 19''345; 8. A. Pitt (AUS, Yamaha), 23''246; 9. D. Checa (E, Yamaha), 24''787; 10. P. Chili (I, Honda), 25''299; 11. S. Gimbert (F, Yamaha), 25''495; 12. M. Neukirchner (D, Honda), 27''833; 13. I. Clementi (I, Kawasaki), 31''339; 14. G. Vizziello (I, Yamaha), 33''013; 15. L. Alfonsi (I, Yamaha), 34''024. 19 finishers.
Fastest lap: T. Corser (AUS, Suzuki), 1'37.756 (147.490 km/h).

8th May - Monza - Italy

Race I: 1. T. Corser (AUS, Suzuki), 18 tours, 32'40.906 (191.435 km/h); 2. Y. Kagayama (J, Suzuki), 0''985; 3. J. Toseland (GB, Ducati), 1''040; 4. R. Laconi (F, Ducati), 1''757; 5. A. Pitt (AUS, Yamaha), 8''609; 6. K. Muggeridge (AUS, Honda), 12''435; 7. P. Chili (I, Honda), 12''628; 8. C. Walker (GB, Kawasaki), 16''656; 9. G. Nannelli (I, Ducati), 20''481; 10. N. Abé (J, Yamaha), 21''119; 11. N. Haga (J, Yamaha), 23''169; 12. M. Borciani (I, Ducati), 39''874; 13. G. Bussei (I, Kawasaki), 40''080; 14. M. Sanchini (I, Kawasaki), 41''484; 15. I. Clementi (I, Kawasaki), 41''955. 25 finishers.
Fastest lap: Y. Kagayama (J, Suzuki), 1'48.082 (192.953 km/h).
Race II: 1. C. Vermeulen (AUS, Honda), 17 tours, 30'49.758 (191.664 km/h); 2. R. Laconi (F, Ducati), 0''582; 3. T. Corser (AUS, Suzuki), 2''458; 4. K. Muggeridge (AUS, Honda), 3''379; 5. J. Toseland (GB, Ducati), 9''901; 6. A. Pitt (AUS, Yamaha), 10''076; 7. P. Chili (I, Honda), 11''116; 8. C. Walker (GB, Kawasaki), 11''587; 9. N. Haga (J, Yamaha), 26''936; 10. G. Nannelli (I, Ducati), 33''459; 11. G. Bussei (I, Kawasaki), 35''184; 12. N. Abé (J, Yamaha), 35''612; 13. M. Sanchini (I, Kawasaki), 36''817; 14. L. Conforti (I, Ducati), 45''473; 15. I. Clementi (I, Kawasaki), 47''350. 21 finishers.
Fastest lap: C. Vermeulen (AUS, Honda), 1'48.233 (192.684 km/h).

29th May - Silverstone - Great Britain

Race I: 1. R. Laconi (F, Ducati), 28 tours, 40'58.899 (145.979 km/h); 2. T. Corser (AUS, Suzuki), 0''096; 3. J. Toseland (GB, Ducati), 1''136; 4. C. Vermeulen (AUS, Honda), 11''285; 5. P. Chili (I, Honda), 14''649; 6. C. Walker (GB, Kawasaki), 16''461; 7. M. Neukirchner (D, Honda), 40''465; 8. G. Bussei (I, Kawasaki), 43''265; 9. J. Cardoso (E. Yamaha), 46''411; 10. K. Muggeridge (AUS, Honda), 49''211; 11. Y. Kagayama (J, Suzuki), 51''706; 12. M. Sanchini (I, Kawasaki), 56''374; 13. A. Pitt (AUS, Yamaha), 1'11.602; 14. A. Velini (I, Ducati), 1'25.186; 15. M. Praia (POR, Yamaha), 1'25.974. 16 finishers.
Fastest lap: R. Laconi (F, Ducati), 1'21.130 (147.132 km/h).
Race II: 1. J. Toseland (GB, Ducati), 28 tours, 40'55.190 (146.200 km/h); 2. T. Corser (AUS, Suzuki), 0''473; 3. N. Haga (J, Yamaha), 3''187; 4. C. Vermeulen (AUS, Honda), 6''691; 5. P. Chili (I, Honda), 16''923; 6. C. Walker (GB, Kawasaki), 17''057; 7. Y. Kagayama (J, Suzuki), 28''248; 8. N. Abé (J, Yamaha), 31''760; 9. A. Pitt (AUS, Yamaha), 32''084; 10. K. Muggeridge (AUS, Honda), 36''492; 11. L. Lanzi (I, Ducati), 39''470; 12. I. Clementi (I, Ducati), 40''182; 13. G. McCoy (AUS, Petronas FP1), 41''325; 14. B. Bostrom (USA, Honda), 46''096; 15. M. Roccoli (I, Yamaha), 56''251. 21 finishers.
Fastest lap: T. Corser (AUS, Suzuki), 1'27.166 (147.071 km/h).

26th June - Misano - Italy

Race I: 1. R. Laconi (F, Ducati), 24 tours, 39'07.157 (149.451 km/h); 2. C. Vermeulen (AUS, Honda), 4''439; 3. T. Corser (AUS, Suzuki), 8''043; 4. J. Toseland (GB, Ducati), 10''198; 5. L. Lanzi (I, Ducati), 14''105; 6. N. Haga (J, Yamaha), 16''841; 7. P. Chili (I, Honda), 18''000; 8. C. Walker (GB, Kawasaki), 20''110; 9. A. Gonzales-Nieto (E, Ducati), 21''468; 10. K. Muggeridge (AUS, Honda), 22''590; 11. S. Martin (AUS, Petronas FP1), 24''800; 12. M. Sanchini (I, Kawasaki), 26''201; 13. J. Cardoso (E, Yamaha), 27''795; 14. B. Bostrom (USA, Honda), 31''185; 15. I. Clementi (I, Ducati), 34''975. 20 finishers.
Fastest lap: C. Vermeulen (AUS, Honda), 1'36.666 (151.201 km/h).
Race II: 1. R. Laconi (F, Ducati), 25 tours, 40'46.260 (149.371 km/h); 2. C. Vermeulen (AUS, Honda), 1''491; 3. T. Corser (AUS, Suzuki), 3''143; 4. J. Toseland (GB, Ducati), 14''562; 5. P. Chili (I, Honda), 16''291; 6. N. Haga (J, Yamaha), 18''600; 7. K. Muggeridge (AUS, Honda), 24''065; 8. S. Martin (AUS, Petronas FP1), 24''503; 9. L. Lanzi (I, Ducati), 25''865; 10. G. Bussei (I, Kawasaki), 28''458; 11. C. Walker (GB, Kawasaki), 28''522; 12. Y. Kagayama (J, Suzuki), 31''223; 13. M. Sanchini (I, Kawasaki), 33''345; 14. L. Alfonsi (I, Yamaha), 35''792; 15. N. Abé (J, Yamaha), 39''660. 18 finishers.
Fastest lap: R. Laconi (F, Ducati), 1'36.806 (150.982 km/h).

17th July - Brno - Czech Republic

Race I: 1. T. Corser (AUS, Suzuki), 20 tours, 41'42.829 (155.431 km/h); 2. J. Toseland (GB, Ducati), 6''592; 3. R. Laconi (F, Ducati), 7''477; 4. C. Walker (GB, Kawasaki), 9''060; 5. P. Chili (I, Honda), 9''183; 6. L. Lanzi (I, Ducati), 10''778; 7. N. Haga (J, Yamaha), 13''760; 8. C. Vermeulen (GB, Honda), 15''069; 9. N. Abé (J, Yamaha), 16''320; 10. A. Pitt (Aus, Yamaha), 19''676; 11. Y. Kagayama (J, Suzuki), 21''822; 12. F. Gonzales-Nieto (E, Ducati), 24''782; 13. K. Muggeridge (AUS, Honda), 25''830; 14. M. Neukirchner (D, Honda), 27''486; 15. D. Checa (E, Yamaha), 31''003. 28 finishers.
Fastest lap: T. Corser (AUS, Suzuki), 2'03.812 (157.099 km/h).
Race II: 1. N. Haga (J, Yamaha), 20 tours, 41'43.525 (155.387 km/h); 2. T. Corser (AUS, Suzuki), 3''233; 3. C. Vermeulen (AUS, Honda), 11''012; 4. N. Abé (J, Yamaha), 12''268; 5. P. Chili (I, Honda), 12''361; 6. L. Lanzi (I, Ducati), 13''511; 7. R. Laconi (F, Ducati), 14''141; 8. J. Toseland (GB, Ducati), 16''439; 9. K. Muggeridge (AUS, Honda), 16''820; 10. C. Walker (GB, Kawasaki), 19''737; 11. Y. Kagayama (J, Suzuki), 24''777; 12. F. Gonzales-Nieto (E, Ducati), 25''244; 13. I. Clementi (I, Ducati), 26''700; 14. D. Checa (E, Yamaha), 28''119; 15. G. Bussei (I, Kawasaki), 42''082. 24 finishers.
Fastest lap: N. Haga (J, Yamaha), 2'03.747 (157.182 km/h).

7th August - Brands Hatch - Great Britain

Race I: 1. T. Corser (AUS, Suzuki), 25 tours, 36'45.074 (171.300 km/h); 2. N. Haga (J, Yamaha), 0''186; 3. R. Laconi (F, Ducati), 1''976; 4. C. Vermeulen (AUS, Honda), 4''590; 5. C. Walker (GB, Kawasaki), 5''746; 6. K. Muggeridge (AUS, Honda), 8''428; 7. A. Pitt (AUS, Yamaha), 8''598; 8. L. Lanzi (I, Ducati), 15''628; 9. Y. Kagayama (J, Suzuki), 15''671; 10. M. Neukirchner (D, Honda), 28''250; 11. N. Abé (J, Yamaha), 32''470; 12. B. Bostrom (USA, Honda), 32''500; 13. D. Hobbs (GB, Yamaha), 32''683; 14. P. Riba Cabana (E, Kawasaki), 32''885; 15. S. Martin (AUS, Petronas FP1), 35''171. 20 finishers.
Fastest lap: N. Haga (J, Yamaha), 1'27.489 (172.698 km/h).
Race II: 1. N. Haga (J, Yamaha), 25 tours, 36'39.815 (171.710 km/h); 2. T. Corser (AUS, Suzuki), 2''686; 3. C. Vermeulen (AUS, Honda), 8''062; 4. C. Walker (GB, Kawasaki), 12''053; 5. R. Laconi (F, Ducati), 13''044; 6. A. Pitt (AUS, Yamaha), 13''184; 7. J. Toseland (GB, Ducati), 14''215; 8. L. Lanzi (I, Ducati), 21''026; 9. Y. Kagayama (J, Suzuki), 21''175; 10. B. Bostrom (USA, Honda), 21''257; 11. M. Neukirchner (D, Honda), 29''315; 12. P. Riba Cabana (E, Kawasaki), 30''591; 13. P. Chili (I, Honda), 34''619; 14. S. Gimbert (F, Yamaha), 39''732; 15. D. Hobbs (GB, Yamaha), 39''879. 18 finishers.
Fastest lap: Haga (J, Yamaha), 1'27.272 (173.128 km/h).

4th September - Assen - Netherlands

Race I: 1. C. Vermeulen (AUS, Honda), 16 tours, 33'36.029 (171.340 km/h); 2. J. Toseland (GB, Ducati), 3''396; 3. N. Haga (J, Yamaha), 4''876; 4. T. Corser (AUS, Suzuki), 6''815; 5. A. Pitt (AUS, Yamaha), 10''075; 6. Y. Kagayama (J, Suzuki), 12''526; 7. L. Lanzi (I, Ducati), 12''661; 8. M. Neukirchner (D, Honda), 20''595; 9. K. Muggeridge (AUS, Honda), 20''872; 10. P. Chili (I, Honda), 27''691; 11. I. Clementi (I, Ducati), 36''444; 12. S. Gimbert (F, Yamaha), 36''844; 13. G. McCoy (AUS, Petronas FP1), 37''012; 14. S. Martin (AUS, Petronas FP1), 39''262; 15. G. Bussei (I, Kawasaki), 39''339. 23 finishers.
Fastest lap: C. Vermeulen (AUS, Honda), 2'04.685 (173.150 km/h).
Race II: 1. C. Vermeulen (AUS, Honda), 16 tours, 33'34.053 (171.508 km/h); 2. N. Haga (J, Yamaha), 0''085; 3. J. Toseland (GB, Ducati), 3''318; 4. T. Corser (AUS, Suzuki), 5''938; 5. A. Pitt (AUS, Yamaha), 6''394; 6. L. Lanzi (I, Ducati), 16''480; 7. M. Neukirchner (D, Honda), 17''255; 8. K. Muggeridge (AUS, Honda), 22''338; 9. N. Abé (J, Yamaha), 30''801; 10. B. Bostrom (USA, Honda), 34''071; 11. Y. Kagayama (J, Suzuki), 36''480; 12. G. McCoy (AUS, Petronas FP1), 36''658; 13. S. Gimbert (F, Yamaha), 37''165; 14. P. Chili (I, Honda), 37''888; 15. G. Bussei (I, Kawasaki), 38''414. 22 finishers.
Fastest lap: N. Haga (J, Yamaha), 2'04.799 (172.992 km/h).

11th September - Lausitz - Germany

Race I: 1. C. Vermeulen (AUS, Honda), 20 tours (*), 33'36.341 (152.296 km/h); 2. N. Haga (J, Yamaha), 0''269; 3. T. Corser (AUS, Suzuki), 2''299; 4. J. Toseland (GB, Ducati), 7''058; 5. Y. Kagayama (J, Suzuki), 12''708; 6. A. Pitt (AUS, Yamaha), 14''053; 7. M. Neukirchner (D, Honda), 16''616; 8. L. Lanzi (I, Ducati), 19''023; 9. N. Abé (J, Yamaha), 24''651; 10. B. Bostrom (USA, Honda), 34''354; 11. G. McCoy (AUS, Petronas FP1), 44''385; 12. G. Bussei (I, Kawasaki), 45''020; 13. J. Cardoso (E, Yamaha), 51''811; 14. N. Brignola (I, Ducati), 51''943; 15. S. Cruciani (I, Kawasaki), 1'04.111. 18 finishers.
Fastest lap: N. Haga (J, Yamaha), 1'39.828 (153.805 km/h).
(*): Race arrêtée au drapeau rouge.
Race II: 1. L. Lanzi (I, Ducati), 24 tours, 40'20.947 (152.212 km/h); 2. C. Vermeulen (AUS, Honda), 0''840; 3. N. Haga (J, Yamaha), 4''598; 4. Y. Kagayama (J, Suzuki), 5''291; 5. K. Muggeridge (AUS, Honda), 16''236; 6. A. Pitt (AUS, Yamaha), 18''362; 7. M. Neukirchner (D, Honda), 26''360; 8. N. Abé (J, Yamaha), 26''453; 9. S. Martin (AUS, Petronas FP1), 27''076; 10. P. Chili (I, Honda), 37''303; 11. J. Toseland (GB, Ducati), 40''997; 12. G. Bussei (I, Kawasaki), 44''309; 13. T. Corser (AUS, Suzuki), 44''485; 14. S. Gimbert (F, Yamaha), 48''459; 15. B. Bostrom (USA, Honda), 53''264. 18 finishers.
Fastest lap: N. Haga (J, Yamaha), 1'39.790 (153.863 km/h).

25th September - Imola - Italy

Race I: 1. C. Vermeulen (AUS, Honda), 21 tours, 39'35.789 (156.973 km/h); 2. T. Corser (AUS, Suzuki), 0''297; 3. N. Haga (J, Yamaha), 8''313; 4. J. Toseland (GB, Ducati), 15''339; 5. S. Martin (AUS, Petronas FP1), 49''638; 6. C. Walker (GB, Kawasaki), 50''072; 7. M. Neukirchner (D, Honda), 52''175; 8. S. Gimbert (F, Yamaha), 52''381; 9. R. Laconi (F, Ducati), 57''834; 10. G. Vizziello (I, Yamaha), 1'05.727; 11. G. Bussei (I, Kawasaki), 1'08.332; 12. M. Sanchini (I, Kawasaki), 1'10.289; 13. B. Bostrom (USA, Honda), 1'10.786; 14. M. Borciani (I, Ducati), 1'27.905; 15. Y. Kagayama (J, Suzuki), 1'33.440. 17 finishers. **Fastest lap:** T. Corser (AUS, Suzuki), 1'50.632 (160.521 km/h).
Race II: Annulée en raison de pluies torrentielles.

9th October - Magny-Cours - France

Race I: 1. C. Vermeulen (AUS, Honda), 23 tours, 39'03.405 (155.855 km/h); 2. Y. Kagayama (J, Suzuki), 8''200; 3. J. Toseland (GB, Ducati), 13''336; 4. K. Muggeridge (AUS, Honda), 13''887; 5. T. Corser (AUS, Suzuki), 14''299; 6. A. Pitt (AUS, Yamaha), 15''270; 7. C. Walker (GB, Kawasaki), 16''136; 8. M. Neukirchner (D, Honda), 16''616; 9. L. Lanzi (I, Ducati), 18''201; 10. N. Abé (J, Yamaha), 31''100; 11. D. Checa (E, Yamaha), 34''310; 12. B. Bostrom (USA, Honda), 34''493; 13. G. Bussei (I, Kawasaki), 38''601; 14. A. Gonzales-Nieto (E, Kawasaki), 38''914; 15. S. Gimbert (F, Yamaha), 40''508. 19 finishers.
Fastest lap: C. Vermeulen (AUS, Honda), 1'40.985 (157.247 km/h).
Race II: 1. L. Lanzi (I, Ducati), 23 tours, 39'01.858 (155.958 km/h); 2. Y. Kagayama (J, Suzuki), 6''662; 3. N. Haga (J, Yamaha), 10''722; 4. T. Corser (AUS, Suzuki), 13''457; 5. C. Walker (GB, Kawasaki), 16''651; 6. J. Toseland (GB, Ducati), 17''006; 7. A. Pitt (AUS, Yamaha), 20''863; 8. M. Neukirchner (D, Honda), 22''280; 9. N. Abé (J, Yamaha), 22''713; 10. P. Chili (I, Honda), 31''108; 11. B. Bostrom (USA, Honda), 32''271; 12. D. Checa (E, Yamaha), 38''195; 13. A. Gonzales-Nieto (E, Kawasaki), 45''314; 14. J. Da Costa (F, Yamaha), 46''922; 15. G. Vizziello (I, Yamaha), 50''604. 21 finishers.
Fastest lap: L. Lanzi (I, Ducati), 1'40.601 (157.847 km/h).

FINAL CLASSIFICATION

1. Troy Corser (AUS)	Suzuki	433
2. Chris Vermeulen (AUS)	Honda	379
3. Noriyuki Haga (J)	Yamaha	271

4. J. Toseland (GB, Ducati), 254; 5. Y. Kagayama (J, Suzuki), 252; 6. R. Laconi (F, Ducati), 221; 7. C. Walker (GB, Kawasaki), 160; 8. A. Pitt (AUS, Yamaha), 156; 9. L. Lanzi (I, Ducati), 150; 10. P. Chili (I, Honda), 131. 40 finishers.

CONSTRUCTORS

1. Suzuki	468
2. Honda	403
3. Ducati	385

4. Yamaha, 322; 5. Kawasaki, 183; 6. Petronas, 48.

SUPERSPORT WORLD CHAMPIONSHIP

26th February - Losail - Qatar

1. K. Fujiwara (J, Honda), 18 tours, 37'54.414 (153.281 km/h); 2. S. Charpentier (F, Honda), 5''462; 3. M. Fabrizio (I, Honda), 13''970; 4. K. Curtain (AUS, Yamaha), 28''713; 5. F. Foret (F, Honda), 31''316; 6. B. Parkes (AUS, Yamaha), 32''459; 7. S. Chambon (F, Honda), 36''842; 8. J. Fores (E, Suzuki), 42''491; 9. G. Nannelli (I, Ducati), 54''930; 10. T. Lauslehto (SF, Honda), 59''092; 11. A. Berta (I, Ducati), 1'31.728; 12. T. Miksovsky (CZ, Honda), 1'36.071; 13. P. Szkopek (POL, Honda), 1'47.590; 14. M. Baiocco (I,

THE RESULTS OF THE OTHER CHAMPIONSHIPS

Kawasaki), 1 tour. 14 finishers. **Fastest lap:** S. Charpentier (F, Honda), 2'04.686 (155.334 km/h).

3rd April - Phillip Island - Australia

1. S. Charpentier (F, Honda), 21 tours, 34'28.920 (162.424 km/h); 2. K. Curtain (AUS, Yamaha), 3''595; 3. F. Foret (F, Honda), 9''641; 4. K. Fujiwara (J, Honda), 9''664; 5. J. Van Den Goorbergh (NL, Ducati), 29''602; 6. J. Stigefelt (S, Honda), 34''168; 7. B. Parkes (AUS, Yamaha), 42''695; 8. S. Chambon (F, Honda), 46''360; 9. T. Lauslehto (SF, Honda), 48''976; 10. C. Cogan (F, Suzuki), 56''859; 11. J. Fores (E, Suzuki), 1'20.356; 12. D. Garcia (E, Kawasaki), 1'20.461; 13. T. Miksovsky (CZ, Honda), 1'28.701; 14. P. Szkopek (POL, Honda), 1 tour. 14 finishers.
Fastest lap: S. Charpentier (F, Honda), 1'37.438 (164.228 km/h).

24th April - Valencia - Spain

1. S. Charpentier (F, Honda), 23 tours, 38'27.276 (143.725 km/h); 2. K. Fujiwara (J, Honda), 0''844; 3. K. Curtain (AUS, Yamaha), 21''382; 4. M. Fabrizio (I, Honda), 25''602; 5. F. Foret (F, Honda), 31''478; 6. B. Parkes (AUS, Yamaha), 32''837; 7. B. Veneman (NL, Suzuki), 36''134; 8. G. Nannelli (I, Ducati), 38''076; 9. S. Chambon (F, Honda), 38''297; 10. J. Stigefelt (S, Honda), 38''750; 11. J. Fores (E, Suzuki), 44''507; 12. W. Daemen (B, Honda), 45''628; 13. S. Legrelle (B, Honda), 52''390; 14. A. Tizon (E, Yamaha), 52''463; 15. T. Lauslehto (SF, Honda), 53''109. 19 finishers.
Fastest lap: S. Charpentier (F, Honda), 1'38.976 (145.672 km/h).

8th May - Monza - Italy

1. K. Fujiwara (J, Honda), 16 tours, 30'15.930 (183.750 km/h); 2. S. Charpentier (F, Honda), 0''036; 3. G. Nannelli (I, Ducati), 2''726; 4. M. Fabrizio (I, Honda), 8''043; 5. K. Curtain (AUS, Yamaha), 8''163; 6. T. Lauslehto (SF, Honda), 26''566; 7. B. Parkes (AUS, Yamaha), 26''632; 8. S. Chambon (F, Honda), 26''940; 9. I. Goi (I, Yamaha), 37''497; 10. S. Le Grelle (B, Honda), 37''686; 11. J. Fores (E, Suzuki), 37''943; 12. B. Veneman (NL, Suzuki), 44''198; 13. J. Stigefelt (S, Honda), 47''954; 14. T. Miksovsky (CZ, Honda), 57''562; 15. M. Baiocco (I, Kawasaki), 1'05.958. 19 finishers.
Fastest lap: S. Charpentier (F, Honda), 1'52.726 (185.004 km/h).

29th May - Silverstone - Great Britain

1. S. Charpentier (F, Honda), 28 tours, 41'53.540 (142.806 km/h); 2. K. Curtain (AUS, Yamaha), 2''843; 3. F. Foret (F, Honda), 20''405; 4. S. Chambon (F, Honda), 22''363; 5. B. Parkes (AUS, Yamaha), 24''823; 6. B. Veneman (NL, Suzuki), 32''010; 7. G. Nannelli (I, Ducati), 33''642; 8. A. Corradi (I, Ducati), 37''326; 9. K. Fujiwara (J, Honda), 37''789; 10. T. Lauslehto (SF, Honda), 37''828; 11. S. Legrelle (B, Honda), 47''018; 12. J. Fores (E, Suzuki), 47''498; 13. J. Da Costa (F, Kawasaki), 48''495; 14. T. Tunstall (GB, Honda), 50''780; 15. J. Jansen (NL, Suzuki), 52''972. 20 finishers.
Fastest lap: S. Charpentier (F, Honda), 1'29.027 (143.997 km/h).

26th June - Misano - Italy

1. S. Charpentier (F, Honda), 23 tours, 38'14.344 (146.520 km/h); 2. F. Foret (F, Honda), 0''496; 3. K. Fujiwara (J, Honda), 4''981; 4. K. Curtain (AUS, Yamaha), 13''367; 5. B. Parkes (AUS, Yamaha), 19''396; 6. S. Sanna (I, Honda), 22''277; 7. J. Fores (E, Suzuki), 26''558; 8. A. Antonello (I, Kawasaki), 26''871; 9. C. Migliorati (I, Kawasaki), 26''901; 10. T. Lauslehto (SF, Honda), 27''564; 11. R. Harms (DK, Honda), 31''558; 12. B. Veneman (NL, Suzuki), 36''341; 13. J. Stigefelt (S, Honda), 37''712; 14. C. Mariottini (I, Honda), 38''284; 15. S. Chambon (F, Honda), 40''437. 26 finishers.
Fastest lap: S. Charpentier (F, Honda), 1'38.821 (147.904 km/h).

17th July - Brno - Czech Republic

1. S. Charpentier (F, Honda), 18 tours, 38'44.765 (150.602 km/h); 2. M. Fabrizio (I, Honda), 4''429; 3. G. Nannelli (I, Ducati), 5''366; 4. R. Harms (DK, Honda), 7''973; 5. J. Fores (E, Suzuki), 9''589; 6. C. Jones (GB, Honda), 9''782; 7. S. Chambon (F, Honda), 18''814; 8. A. Corradi (I, Ducati), 22''238; 9. W. Daemen (B, Honda), 22''409; 10. B. Veneman (NL, Suzuki), 24''494; 11. J. Stigefelt (S, Honda), 25''446; 12. T. Lauslehto (SF, Honda), 25''762; 13. C. Migliorati (I, Kawasaki), 36''836; 14. M. Lagrive (F, Suzuki), 38''506; 15. S. Le Grelle (B, Honda), 41''909. 27 finishers.
Fastest lap: S. Charpentier (F, Honda), 2'07.316 (152.776 km/h).

7th August - Brands Hatch - Great Britain

1. S. Charpentier (F, Honda), 23 tours, 34'33.153 (167.625 km/h); 2. M. Fabrizio (I, Honda), 0''985; 3. K. Curtain (AUS, Yamaha), 1''173; 4. S. Chambon (F, Honda), 7''317; 5. F. Foret (F, Honda), 7''777; 6. K. Fujiwara (J, Honda), 17''008; 7. A. Corradi (I, Ducati), 18''416; 8. C. Jones (GB, Honda), 21''131; 9. M. Lagrive (F, Suzuki), 28''218; 10. C. Crutchlow (GB, Honda), 28''788; 11. J. Fores (E, Suzuki), 29''853; 12. T. Tunstall (GB, Honda), 30''065; 13. R. Harms (DK, Honda), 30''382; 14. T. Lauslehto (SF, Honda), 30''699; 15. J. Stigefelt (S, Honda), 33''175. 23 finishers.
Fastest lap: S. Charpentier (F, Honda), 1'39.380 (169.045 km/h).

4th September - Assen - Netherlands

1. F. Foret (F, Honda), 16 tours, 34'37.800 (166.247 km/h); 2. S. Charpentier (F, Honda), 0''258; 3. M. Fabrizio (I, Honda), 1''109; 4. K. Curtain (AUS, Yamaha), 1''380; 5. K. Fujiwara (J, Honda), 5''490; 6. R. Harms (DK, Honda), 10''430; 7. B. Parkes (AUS, Yamaha), 16''765; 8. S. Chambon (F, Honda), 25''592; 9. T. Lauslehto (SF, Honda), 25''648; 10. J. Fores (E, Suzuki), 25''656; 11. M. Lagrive (F, Suzuki), 25''870; 12. J. Stigefelt (S, Honda), 26''015; 13. A. Vos (NL, Honda), 26''017; 14. J. Jansen (NL, Suzuki), 37''278; 15. V. Kallio (SF, Yamaha), 38''087. 23 finishers.
Fastest lap: K. Fujiwara (J, Honda), 2'08.865 (167.533 km/h).

11th September - Lausitz - Germany

1. K. Curtain (AUS, Yamaha), 23 tours, 39'39.394 (148,417 km/h); 2. B. Parkes (AUS, Yamaha), 2''578; 3. F. Foret (F, Honda), 12''033; 4. K. Fujiwara (J, Honda), 18''284; 5. M. Fabrizio (I, Honda), 25''996; 6. S. Chambon (F, Honda), 26''016; 7. A. Corradi (I, Ducati), 29''150; 8. J. Stigefelt (S, Honda), 32''326; 9. T. Lauslehto (SF, Honda), 34''636; 10. W. Daemen (B, Honda), 35''957; 11. A. Tode (D, Honda), 36''379; 12. K. Andersen (N, Kawasaki), 39''176; 13. R. Harms (DK, Honda), 46''478; 14. J. Fores (E, Suzuki), 53''369; 15. J. Jansen (NL, Suzuki), 1'10.252. 22 finishers.
Fastest lap: K. Curtain (AUS, Yamaha), 1'42.438 (149.886 km/h).

25th September - Imola - Italy

1. G. Nannelli (I, Ducati), 21 tours, 42'55.695 (144.790 km/h); 2. K. Curtain (AUS, Yamaha), 2''452; 3. A. Corradi (I, Ducati), 4''201; 4. M. Fabrizio (I, Honda), 7''965; 5. B. Parkes (AUS, Yamaha), 10''506; 6. A. Antonello (I, Kawasaki); 7. A. Vos (NL, Honda), 41''764; 8. J. Stigefelt (S, Honda), 47''274; 9. C. Mariottini (I, Honda), 48''496; 10. M. Lagrive (F, Suzuki), 1'03.068; 11. F. Foret (F, Honda), 1'14.967; 12. J. Enjolras (F, Yamaha), 1'15.858; 13. T. Miksovsky (CZ, Honda), 1'15.904; 14. S. Penna (SF, Honda), 1'21.678; 15. N. Canepa (I, Kawasaki), 1'25.763. 20 finishers.
Fastest lap: M. Fabrizio (I, Honda), 1'52.646 (157.651 km/h).

9th October - Magny-Cours - France

1. B. Parkes (AUS, Yamaha), 23 tours, 40'12.350 (151.400 km/h); 2. K. Curtain (AUS, Yamaha), 0''750; 3. M. Fabrizio (I, Honda), 1''215; 4. F. Foret (F, Honda), 4''098; 5. J. Fores (E, Suzuki), 21''623; 6. J. Stigefelt (S, Honda), 23''448; 7. K. Fujiwara (J, Honda), 30''108; 8. S. Chambon (F, Honda), 32''144; 9. G. Nannelli (I, Ducati), 32''408; 10. M. Lagrive (F, Suzuki), 44''378; 11. A. Vos (NL, Honda), 49''939; 12. T. Lauslehto (SF, Honda), 50''269; 13. I. Goi (I, Yamaha), 1'01.701; 14. J. Janssen (NL, Suzuki), 1'10.471; 15. S. Penna (SF, Honda), 1'11.325. 19 finishers.
Fastest lap: M. Fabrizio (I, Honda), 1'44.071 (152.584 km/h).

FINAL CLASSIFICATION

1. Sébastien Charpentier (F)	Honda	210
2. Kevin Curtain (AUS)	Yamaha	187
3. Katsuaki Fujiwara (J)	Honda	149

4. F. Foret (F, Honda), 144; 5. M. Fabrizio (I, Honda), 138; 6. B. Parkes (AUS, Yamaha), 125; 7. S. Chambon (F, Honda), 94; 8. G. Nannelli (I, Ducati), 88; 9. J. Fores (E, Suzuki), 71; 10. T. Lauslehto (SF, Honda), 60.

CONSTUCTORS

1. Honda	270
2. Yamaha	192
3. Ducati	117

4. Suzuki, 90; 5. Kawasaki, 35.

ENDURANCE WORLD CHAMPIONSHIP

28th March - 500 km of Assen - Netherlands

1. Philippe/Kitagawa (F/J, Suzuki), 130 tours, 3 h 33'42''965 (140.550 km/h); 2. Kellenberger/Morillon/Mizera (CH/F/F, Kawasaki), 2 tours; 3. Hutchins/Falcke/Mizera (GB/D/F, Kawasaki), 3 tours; 4. Cudlin/Notman/Nowland (GB/GB/AUS, Yamaha), 4 tours; 5. Jerman/Giabbani (SLO/F, Yamaha); 6. Andersson/Minim/Carlberg (S, Suzuki), 5 tours; 7. Rothlaan/Wylie/Hogan (GB, Yamaha); 8. Tessari/Ricci (I, Yamaha); 9. Jennes/Bruning/Roth (D, Kawasaki); 10. Veneman/Janssen/van Steinbergen (NL, Suzuki).

21st May - 8 Hours of Albacete - Spain

1. Philippe/Kitagawa/Four (F/J/F, Suzuki), 299 tours, 8 h 00'08''820 (132.220 km/h); 2. Ribalta/Noyes/Riba Cabana (E, Yamaha), 3 tours; 3. Jerman/Giabbani/Hinterreiter (SLO/F/A, Yamaha), 5 tours; 4. Kellenberger/Morillon/Mizera (CH/F/F, Kawasaki), 6 tours; 5. Cudlin/Notman/Nowland (GB/GB/AUS, Yamaha), 11 tours; 6. Molinier/Pailoux/Grelaud (F, Suzuki), 12 tours; 7. Rothlaan/Wylie/Hogan (GB, Yamaha); 8. Mizera/Hutchins/Falcke (F/GB/D, Kawasaki); 9. Ruozi/De Matteis/Giachino (I, Suzuki), 15 tours; 10. Monot/A. Santos/M. Santos (F, Suzuki), 17 tours.

31st July - 8 Hours of Suzuka - Japan

1. Ukawa/Kiyonari (J, Honda), 204 tours, 8 h 01'22''351 (148.010 km/h); 2. Vermeulen/Fujiwaea (AUS/J, Honda), 3 tours; 3. Aoki/Yasuda (J, Honda), 4 tours; 4. Deguchi/Teshima (J, Honda), 5 tours; 5. Tokudome/Yamaguchi (J, Honda), 6 tours; 6. Sugai/Brookes (J/AUS, Honda), 7 tours; 7. Philippe/Kagayama (F/J, Suzuki), 8 tours; 8. Kawase/Tamitsuji (J, Suzuki), 9 tours; 9. Giabbani/Jerman/Saiger (F/SLO/A, Yamaha), 10 tours; 10. Kagayama/Watanabe (J, Suzuki), 11 tours.

13-14th August - 24 Hours of Oschersleben - Germany

1. Philippe/Lagrive/Kitagawa (F/F/J, Suzuki), 855 tours, 24 h 00'42''339 (130.573 km/h); 2. Kellenberger/Morillon/Stamm (CH/F/CH, Kawasaki), 23 tours; 3. Hutchins/Mizera/Baker (GB/F/GB, Kawasaki), 30 tours; 4. Giachino/Ruozi/Monot (I/I/F, Suzuki), 43 tours; 5. Röthig/Strauch/Heiler (D, Suzuki), 44 tours; 6. Klein/Bitter/Marjan (A/H/SLO, Suzuki), 50 tours; 7. Pellizzon/Aliverti/Veghini (I, Aprilia), 61 tours; 8. Hulth/Agombar/Carlberg (S, Suzuki); 9. Marceletti/Schönfelder/Walter (D, Suzuki), 65 tours; 10. Kittel/König/Steinebach (D, Yamaha), 66 tours.

25th September - 200 Miles of Vallelunga - Italy

1. Philippe/Kagayama/Lagrive (F/J/F, Suzuki), 79 tours; 2. Nowland/Cudlin (AUS/GB, Yamaha), 1'29.236; 3. Jerman/Hinterreiter (SLO/A, Yamaha), 1 tour; 4. Kellenberger/Morillon (CH/F, Kawasaki); 5. Colombo/Mauri/Gennari (I, Ducati), 2 tours; 6. Notman/Carlbark (GB, Suzuki) ; 7. Hogan/Rothlaan/Wylle (GB, Yamaha) ; 8. Tessari/Ricci/Clementini (I, Yamaha) ; 9. Ruozi/Giachino/Codeluppi (I, Suzuki), 3 tours ; 10. Flückiger/Roth/Wildisen (D/D/CH, Kawasaki).

FINAL CLASSIFICATION

1. Suzuki Castrol	134
2. Bolliger Switzerland	77
3. Yamaha Austria	62

4. Yamaha Phase One, 57 ; 5. Diablo 666 Kawasaki, 48 ; 6. Shell Endurance Yamaha, 47 ; 7. No Limits Suzuki, 43 ; 8. Seven Stars Honda 7, 30 ; 9. Folch Endurance Yamaha, 24 ; 10. Seven Stars Honda 11, 24.

MASTERS

16-17th April - Le Mans 24 Hours - France

1. Gimbert/Costes/D. Checa (F/F/E, Yamaha), 830 tours; 2. Kitagawa/Chambon/Lagrive (J/F/F, Suzuki), 20''459; 3. Dietrich/Four/Coxhell (F/F/AUS, Suzuki), 7 tours; 4. Giabbani/Scarnato/Jerman (F/F/SLO, Honda), 21 tours; 5. Fastre/Weynand/Fissette (B, Yamaha), 28 tours; 6. Kellenberger/Morillon/Stamm (CH/F/CH, Kawasaki), 35 tours; 7. Hars/Lalevée/Hernandez (F, Suzuki), 37 tours; 8. Baratin/Thuret/Cheron (F, Suzuki), 39 tours; 9. Baker/Cuzin/Giles (GB/F/GB, Yamaha), 43 tours; 10. Mizera/F. Jond/S. Jond (F, Honda), 44 tours.

17-18th September - Bol d'Or - France

1. Lagrive/Kitagawa/Philippe (F/J/F, Suzuki), 806 tours, 24 h 01'29.009 (147.980 km/h); 2. Gimbert/Costes/D. Checa (F/F/E, Yamaha), 4 tours; 3. Dietrich/Four/Ribalta Bosch (F/F/E, Suzuki), 6 tours; 4. Da Costa/Cogan/Moreira (F, Kawasaki), 9 tours; 5. Bonhuil/Donischal/Giabbani (F, Honda), 15 tours; 6. Fouloi/Metro/Cabana (F/F/E, Suzuki), 40 tours; 7. Hogan/Wylie/Minin (GB/GB/S, Yamaha), 46 tours; 8. Baker/Cuzin/Giles (GB/F/GB, Yamaha); 9. Haquin/Guerouah/Labussière (F, Kawasaki), 48 tours; 10. Baratin/Thuret/Cheron (F, Suzuki), 50 tours.

FIM SUPERSTOCK CUP 1000

24th April - Valencia - Spain

1. K. Sofuoglu (TUR, Yamaha), 13 tours, 21'42.070 (143.951 km/h); 2. D. Van Keymeulen (B, Yamaha), 3''876; 3. M. Roccoli (I, Yamaha), 5''027; 4. W. De Angelis (RSM, Yamaha), 5''203; 5. C. Coxhell (AUS, Suzuki), 6''564; 6. F. De Marco (I, MV-Agusta), 13''936; 7. I. Dionisi (I, Suzuki), 22''396; 8. H. Gantner (CH, Yamaha), 24''228; 9. A. Badovini (I, MV-Agusta), 25''219; 10. R. Cooper (GB, Honda), 25''485; 11. P. Lerat-Vanstaen (F, Suzuki), 29''217; 12. D. Sacchetti (I, Kawasaki), 32''641; 13. J. Mazuecos (E, Yamaha), 32''656; 14. S. Vermonden (B, Suzuki), 32''985; 15. P. Solli (NOR, Yamaha), 34''615. 28 finishers.
Fastest lap: M. Roccoli (I, Yamaha), 1'39.034 (145.586 km/h).

8th May - Monza - Italy

1. K. Sofuoglu (TUR, Yamaha), 11 tours, 20'37.642 (185.355 km/h); 2. M. Roccoli (I, Yamaha), 0''156; 3. C. Coxhell (AUS, Suzuki), 0''214; 4. R. Chiarello (I, Suzuki), 3''054; 5. D. Van Keymeulen (B, Yamaha), 3''294; 6. A. Martinez (E, Yamaha), 9''904; 7. A. Polita (I, Suzuki), 12''831; 8. D. Sacchetti (I, Kawasaki), 12''872; 9. R. Cooper (GB, Honda), 14''264; 10. S. Vermonden (B, Suzuki), 15''466; 11. V. Iannuzzo (I, MV-Agusta), 15''470; 12. F. De Marco (I, MV-Agusta), 17''955; 13. I. Dionisi (I, Suzuki), 22''757; 14. M. Jerman (SLO, Suzuki), 29''107; 15. G. Romanelli (I, Yamaha), 29''530. 24 finishers.
Fastest lap: M. Roccoli (I, Yamaha), 1'51,619 (186.839 km/h).

29th May - Silverstone - Great Britain

1. M. Roccoli (I, Yamaha), 15 tours, 22'40.167 (141.375 km/h); 2. C. Coxhell (AUS, Suzuki), 0''218; 3. K. Sofuoglu (TUR, Yamaha), 0''708; 4. D. Van Keymeulen (B, Yamaha), 3''790; 5. W. De Angelis (RSM, Yamaha), 8''175; 6. E. Rocamora (E, Suzuki), 9''037; 7. A. Martinez (E, Yamaha), 9''472; 8. L. Scassa (I, Yamaha), 10''253; 9. V. Iannuzzo (I, MV-Agusta), 15''612; 10. A. Polita (I, Suzuki), 18''134; 11. D. Sacchetti (I, Kawasaki), 18''349; 12. F. De Marco (I, MV-Agusta), 18''994; 13. H. Gantner (CH, Yamaha), 19''559; 14. V. Cox (GB, Suzuki), 19''894; 15. M. Jerman (SLO, Suzuki), 25''803. 25 finishers.
Fastest lap: M. Roccoli (I, Yamaha), 1'29.615 (143.052 km/h).

26th June - Misano - Italy

1. R. Chiarello (I, Suzuki), 15 tours, 24'57.938 (146.361 km/h); 2. D. Van Keymeulen (B, Yamaha), 0''666; 3. V. Iannuzzo (I, MV-Agusta), 5''079; 4. M. Roccoli (I, Yamaha), 5''513; 5. A. Polita (I, Suzuki), 5''747; 6. C. Coxhell (AUS, Suzuki), 9''117; 7. L. Scassa (I, Yamaha), 11''671; 8. W. De Angelis (RSM, Yamaha), 11''805; 9. I. Dionisi (I, Suzuki), 15''015; 10. A. Martinez (E, Yamaha), 19''097; 11. D. Sacchetti (I, Kawasaki), 27''729; 12. A. Badovini (I, MV-Agusta), 28''012; 13. H. Gantner (CH, Yamaha), 28''412; 14. R. Cooper (GB, Honda), 31''592; 15. M. Jerman (SLO, Suzuki), 41''451. 21 finishers.
Fastest lap: V. Iannuzzo (I, MV-Agusta), 1'38.235 (148.786 km/h).

THE RESULTS OF THE OTHER CHAMPIONSHIPS

17th July - Brno - Czech Republic

1. C. Coxhell (AUS, Suzuki), 12 tours, 25'42.576 (151.312 km/h); 2. K. Sofuoglu (TUR, Yamaha), 0''649; 3. M. Roccoli (I, Yamaha), 0''830; 4. D. Van Keymeulen (B, Yamaha), 0''902; 5. P. Solli (NOR, Yamaha), 16''085; 6. A. Polita (I, Suzuki), 15''539; 7. R. Chiarello (I, Suzuki), 16''857; 8. I. Dionisi (I, Suzuki), 16''988; 9. E. Rocamora (E, Suzuki), 18''645; 10. R. Cooper (GB, Honda), 18''709; 11. W. De Angelis (RSM, Yamaha), 18''842; 12. A. Badovini (I, MV-Agusta), 23''157; 13. A. Martinez (E, Yamaha), 25''144; 14. V. Iannuzzo (I, MV-Agusta), 25''626; 15. L. Scassa (I, Yamaha), 26''464. 30 finishers.
Fastest lap: D. Van Keymeulen (B, Yamaha), 2'06.980 (153.180 km/h).

7th August - Brands Hatch - Great Britain

1. K. Sofuoglu (TUR, Yamaha), 15 tours, 22'38.518 (166.827 km/h); 2. L. Scassa (I, Yamaha), 5''249; 3. A. Polita (I, Suzuki), 5''644; 4. R. Chiarello (I, Suzuki), 7''391; 5. C. Coxhell (AUS, Suzuki), 7''461; 6. A. Martinez (E, Yamaha), 8''138; 7. A. Badovini (I, MV-Agusta), 11''991; 8. I. Dionisi (I, Suzuki), 12''238; 9. E. Rocamora (E, Suzuki), 21''833; 10. O. Bridewell (GB, Kawasaki), 21''877; 11. D. Van Keymeulen (B, Yamaha), 22''528; 12. J. Laverty (IRL, Suzuki), 23''768; 13. R. Cooper (GB, Honda), 24''872; 14. J. Mazuecos (E, Yamaha), 26''813; 15. G. Sanders (GB, Kawasaki), 33''117. 29 finishers.
Fastest lap: K. Sofuoglu (TUR, Yamaha), 1'29.569 (168.688 km/h).

4th September - Assen - Netherlands

1. A. Polita (I, Suzuki), 11 tours, 23'51-323 (165.917 km/h); 2. D. Van Keymeulen (B, Yamaha), 1''508; 3. K. Sofuoglu (TUR, Yamaha), 6''754; 4. M. Roccoli (I, Yamaha), 9''215; 5. A. Badovini (I, MV-Agusta), 14''956; 6. E. Rocamora (E, Suzuki), 15''095; 7. I. Dionisi (I, Suzuki), 15''655; 8. A. Martinez (E, Yamaha), 16''836; 9. W. De Angelis (RSM, Yamaha), 21''505; 10. R. Chiarello (I, Suzuki), 25''927; 11. C. Coxhell (AUS, Suzuki), 27''399; 12. R. Van Steenbergen (NL, Suzuki), 30''317; 13. S. Vermonden (B, Suzuki), 31''509; 14. N. Saelens (B, Suzuki), 32''227; 15. R. Cooper (GB, Honda), 32''864. 27 finishers.
Fastest lap: A. Polita (I, Suzuki), 2'08.422 (168.111 km/h).

11th September - Lausitz - Germany

1. D. Van Keymeulen (B, Yamaha), 14 tours, 24'11.899 (148.052 km/h); 2. L. Scassa (I, Yamaha), 9''153; 3. R. Chiarello (I, Suzuki), 16''200; 4. A. Polita (I, Suzuki), 16''700; 5. C. Coxhell (AUS, Suzuki), 16''745; 6. K. Sofuoglu (TUR, Yamaha), 19''452; 7. E. Rocamora (E, Suzuki), 26''963; 8. A. Badovini (I, MV-Agusta), 26''999; 9. R. Cooper (GB, Honda), 29''581; 10. W. De Angelis (RSM, Yamaha), 32''177; 11. J. Mazuecos (E, Yamaha), 36''210; 12. E. Pasini (I, Suzuki), 38''842; 13. H. Gantner (CH, Yamaha), 44''544; 14. P. Solli (N, Yamaha), 46''155; 15. M. Jerman (SLO, Suzuki), 48''306. 24 finishers.
Fastest lap: K. Sofuoglou (TUR, Yamaha), 1'42.612 (149.632 km/h).

25th September - Imola - Italy

1. R. Chiarello (I, Suzuki), 13 tours, 29'26.347 (130.702 km/h); 2. A. Polita (I, Suzuki), 0''209; 3. C. Coxhell (AUS, Suzuki), 9''812; 4. I. Dionisi (I, Suzuki), 28''064; 5. D. Van Keymeulen (B, Yamaha), 28''173; 6. L. Scassa (I, Yamaha), 28''877; 7. J. Mazuecos (E, Yamaha), 38''223; 8. R. Cooper (GB, Honda), 45''084; 9. M. Roccoli (I, Yamaha), 48''016; 10. A. Martinez (E, Yamaha), 51''316; 11. R. Lunadei (I, Yamaha), 52''291; 12. G. Romanelli (I, Yamaha), 1'01.199; 13. J. Laverty (IRL, Suzuki), 1'03.312; 14. A. Badovini (I, MV-Agusta), 1'04.023; 15. G. Rapicavoli (I, MV-Agusta), 1'07.011. 28 finishers.
Fastest lap: R. Chiarello (I, Suzuki), 2'09.871 (136.742 km/h).

9th October - Magny-Cours - France

1. D. Van Keymeulen (B, Yamaha), 14 tours, 24'36.343 (150.585 km/h); 2. K. Sofuoglu (TUR, Yamaha), 0''453; 3. S. Nebel (D, Yamaha), 0''877; 4. I. Dionisi (I, Suzuki), 2''171; 5. A. Polita (I, Suzuki), 4''182; 6. L. Scassa (I, Yamaha), 5''328; 7. M. Roccoli (I, Yamaha), 5''757; 8. E. Rocamora (E, Suzuki), 6''121; 9. W. De Angelis (RSM, Yamaha), 6''713; 10. R. Chiarello (I, Suzuki), 11''060; 11. J. Laverty (IRL, Suzuki), 11''222; 12. P. Solli (NOR, Yamaha), 19''128; 13. A. Martinez (E, Yamaha), 20''631; 14. R. Cooper (GB, Honda), 20''934; 15. D. Sacchetti (I, Kawasaki), 26''391. 27 finishers.
Fastest lap: A. Polita (I, Suzuki), 1'44.445 (152.038 km/h).

FINAL CLASSIFICATION

1. Didier Van Keymeulen (B)	Yamaha	163
2. Kevin Sofuoglu (TUR)	Yamaha	157
3. Chris Coxhell (AUS)	Suzuki	125

4. A. Polita (I, Suzuki), 121; 5. M. Roccoli (I, Yamaha), 119; 6. R. Chiarello (I, Suzuki), 113; 7. L. Scassa (I, Yamaha), 78; 8. I. Dionisi (I, Suzuki), 70; 9. W. De Angelis (RSM, Yamaha), 57; 10. A. Martinez (E, Yamaha), 55.

CONSTRUCTORS

1. Yamaha	221
2. Suzuki	192
3. MV-Agusta	72

4. Honda, 42; 5. Kawasaki, 29.

SIDE-CARS WORLD CUP

8th May - Brands Hatch - Great Britain

Race I : 1. Webster/Woodhead (GB, LCR-Suzuki), 5 tours, 4'05.756; 2. Ti. Reeves/Tr. Reeves (GB, LCR-Suzuki), 0''546; 3. J. Steinhausen/Hopkinson (D/GB, LCR-Suzuki), 6''452; 4. Laidlow/Farrance (GB, LCR-Suzuki), 7''699; 5. Morrisey/R. Biggs (GB, LCR-Suzuki), 9''693; 6. Philp/Long (GB, LCR-Yamaha), 9''702. 6 finishers.
Race II : 1. Webster/Woodhead (GB, LCR-Suzuki), 14 tours, 11'19.823; 2. Ti. Reeves/Tr. Reeves (GB, LCR-Suzuki), 2''368; 3. J. Steinhausen/Hopkinson (D/GB, LCR-Suzuki), 19''898; 4. Gatt/Randall (GB, LCR-Suzuki), 10''980; 5. Laidlow/Farrance (GB, LCR-Suzuki), 20''537; 6. Pedder/Steadman (GB, LCR-Suzuki), 20''662; 7. Philp/Long (GB, LCR-Yamaha), 26''539; 8. Morrisey/R. Biggs (GB, LCR-Yamaha), 26''539; 9. Norbury/Parnell (GB, Yamaha), 32''134; 10. Gällros/Briggs (S/GB, LCR-Suzuki), 35''100; 11. M. Van Gils/T. Van Gils (NL, LCR-Suzuki), 35''758; 12. Roscher/Hänni (D/CH, Suzuki), 35''964; 13. Lambert/Murray (GB, Suzuki), 36''534; 14. Manninen/Kuismanen (SF, LCR-Suzuki), 36''664; 15. Paivärinta/Wall (SF/GB, LCR-Suzuki), 36''779.
Race III : 1. Ti. Reeves/Tr. Reeves /GB, LCR-Suzuki), 30 tours, 24'27.719; 2. Gatt/Randall (GB, LCR-Suzuki), 24''268; 3. Steinhausen/Hopkinson (D/GB, LCR-Suzuki), 34''141; 4. Pedder/Steadman (GB, LCR-Suzuki), 37''692; 5. Laidlow/Farrance (GB, LCR-Suzuki), 44''442; 6. Morrisey/R. Biggs (GB, LCR-Yamaha), 1 tour; 7. Paivärinta/Wall (SF/GB, LCR-Suzuki); 8. Gällros/Briggs (S/GB, LCR-Suzuki); 9. Knight/Knight (GB, LCR-Suzuki); 10. M. Van Gils/T. Van Gils (NL, LCR-Suzuki); 11. Roscher/Hänni (D/CH, Suzuki); 12. Manninen/Kuismanen (SF, LCR-Suzuki); 13. Gray/Pointer (GB, Yamaha); 14. Foukal/Perlicek (CZ, Yamaha), 2 tours; 15. J. Cluze/C. Cluze (F, LCR-Suzuki), 3 tours.

29th May - Hungaroring - Hungary

1. Ti. Reeves/Tr. Reeves (GB, LCR-Suzuki), 19 tours, 37'19.981 (133.778 km/h); 2. Roscher/Hänni (D/CH, Suzuki), 16''266; 3. M. Van Gils/T. Van Gils (NL, LCR-Suzuki), 20''826; 4. J. Steinhausen/Hopkinson (D/GB, LCR-Suzuki), 33''477; 5. Gällros/Briggs (S/GB, LCRSuzuki), 38''041; 6. Paivärinta/Wall (SF/GB, LCR-Suzuki), 47''676; 7. Morrissey/R. Biggs (GB, LCR-Suzuki), 47''881; 8. Manninen/Kuismanen (SF, LCR-Suzuki), 48''108; 9. Pedder/Steadman (GB, LCR-Suzuki), 58''314; 10. Doppler/Wagner (A, LCR-Yamaha), 1'19.513; 11. Foukal/Pertlicek (CZ, Yamaha), 1 tour; 12. J. Cluze/G. Cluze (F, LCR-Suzuki). 12 finishers.

19th June - Nürburgring - Germany

1. Steinhausen/Hopkinson (D/GB, LCR-Suzuki), 23 tours, 35'43.844 (139.735 km/h); 2. Ti. Reeves/Tr. Reeves (GB, LCR-Suzuki), 0''190; 3. Laidlow/Farrance (GB, LCR-Suzuki), 21''310; 4. M. Van Gils/T. Van Gils (NL, LCR-Suzuki), 54''675; 5. G. Knight/D. Knight (GB, LCR-Suzuki); 6. Moser/Wäfler (A/CH, LCR-Honda), 1'02.106; 7. Gällros/Briggs (S/GB, LCR-Suzuki), 1'04.093; 8. Philp/Long (GB, LCR-Yamaha), 1'09.593; 9. Manninen/Kuismanen (SF, LCR-Suzuki), 1'16.441; 10. Norbury/Cox (GB, Windle-Suzuki), 1'23.155; 11. Morrissey/R. Biggs (GB, LCR-Suzuki), 1 tour; 12. Peach/Webb (GB, LCR-Suzuki); 13. Hainbucher/Adelsberger (A/D, RSR-Suzuki); 14. M. Grabmüller/B. Grabmüller (A, LCR-Yamaha); 15. Nicholson/Van Lith (GB/NL, RCN- Yamaha).

10th July - Schleiz - Germany

Race I : 1. Ti. Reeves/Tr. Reeves (GB, LCR-Suzuki), 11 tours, 16'55.002; 2. J. Steinhausen/Hopkinson (D/GB, LCR-Suzuki), 0''130; 3. Päivärinta/Wall (SF/S, LCR-Suzuki), 12''271; 4. Manninen/Kuismanen (SF, LCR-Suzuki), 12''432; 5. Muldoon/Knapton (GB, LCR-Suzuki), 22''723; 6. Pedder/Steadman (GB, LCR-Suzuki), 23''744; 7. M. Van Gils/T. Van Gils (NL, LCR-Suzuki), 28''193; 8. Moser/Wäfler (A/CH, LCR-Honda), 34''286; 9. Gällros/Briggs (S/GB, LCR-Suzuki), 37''643; 10. Doppler/Wagner (A, LCR-Yamaha), 40''882; 11. G. Knight/D. Knight (GB, LCR-Suzuki), 41''222; 12. Foukal/Pertlicek (CZ, LCR-Yamaha), 1'03.818; 13. Norbury/Cox (GB, Windle-Yamaha), 1'08.288; 14. Morrissey/R. Biggs (GB, LCR-Suzuki), 1'16.943; 15. Bevers/Verbrugge (NL/B, RCN-Yamaha), 1 tour.
Race II: 1. Ti. Reeves/Tr. Reeves (GB, LCR-Suzuki), 22 tours, 33'55.657; 2. Manninen/Kuismanen (SF, LCR-Suzuki), 39''502; 3. Pedder/Steadman (GB, LCR-Suzuki), 41''042; 4. G. Knight/D. Knight (GB, LCR-Suzuki), 50''266; 5. M. Van Gils/T. Van Gils (NL, LCR-Suzuki), 50''436; 6. Gällros/Briggs (S/GB, LCR-Suzuki), 58''590; 7. Moser/Wäfler (A/CH, LCR-Honda), 1'08.341; 8. Doppler/Wagner (A, LCR-Yamaha), 1 tour; 9. Foukal/Pertlicek (CZ, LCR-Yamaha); 10. J. Cluze/G. Cluze (F, LCR-Suzuki); 11. Bevers/Verbrugge (NL/B, RCN-Yamaha), 2 tours; 12. Laidlow/Farrance (GB, LCR-Suzuki), 5 tours. 12 finishers.

7th August - Salzburgring - Austria

1. Ti. Reeves/Tr. Reeves (GB, LCR-Suzuki), 19 tours, 27'11.044 (178,400 km/h); 2. J. Steinhausen/Hopkinson (D/GB, LCR-Suzuki), 0''70; 3. Laidlow/Farrance (GB, LCR-Suzuki), 32''58; 4. Muldoon/Knapton (GB, LCR-Suzuki), 43''66; 5. Manninen/Kuismanen (SF, LCR-Suzuki), 44''41; 6. M. Van Gils/T. Van Gils (NL, LCR-Suzuki), 46''01; 7. Päivärinta/Wall (SF/S, LCR-Suzuki), 51''36; 8. G. Knight/D. Knight (GB, LCR-Suzuki), 51''96; 9. Doppler/Wagner (A, LCR-Yamaha), 51''96; 10. Morrisey/R. Biggs (GB, LCR-Suzuki), 1'16.33; 11. Gällros/Briggs (S/GB, LCR-Suzuki), 1 tour; 12. Foukal/Pertlicek (CZ, LCR-Yamaha); 13. J. Cluze/G. Cluze (F, LCR-Suzuki); 14. Nicholson/Ban Lith (GB/NL, RCN-Yamaha); 15. Bevers/Verbruggen (NL/B, RCN-Yamaha).

21st August - Rijeka - Croatia

Race I: 1. Päivärinta/Wall (SF/S, LCR-Suzuki), 10 tours, 16''00.438; 2. J. Steinhausen/Hopkinson (D/GB, LCR-Suzuki), 3''457; 3. Gällros/Briggs (S/GB, LCR-Suzuki), 4''096; 4. Manninen/Kuismanen (SF, LCR-Suzuki), 11''393; 5. Laidlow/Farrance (GB, LCR-Suzuki), 11''679; 6. Hanks/P. Biggs (GB, LCR-Suzuki), 13''586; 7. Norbury/Cox (GB, LCR-Yamaha), 20''109; 8. Ti. Reeves/Tr. Reeves (GB, LCR-Suzuki), 22''433; 9. G. Knight/D. Knight (GB, Windle-Yamaha), 23''433; 10. Roscher/Hänni (D/CH, LCR-Suzuki), 24''090; 11. Doppler/Wagner (A, LCR-Yamaha), 24''342; 12. Foukal/Pertlicek (CZ, LCR-Yamaha), 48''534; 13. J. Cluze/G. Cluze (F, LCR-Suzuki), 1'16.307; 14. Dagnino/Hildebrand (I/D, LCR-Suzuki), 1'36.910. 14 finishers.
Race II : 1. Päivärinta/Wall (SF/S, LCR-Suzuki), 10 tours, 16'22.023; 2. Ti. Reeves/Tr. Reeves (GB, LCR-Suzuki), 3''330; 3. Manninen/Kuismanen (SF, LCR-Suzuki), 4''565; 4. Gällros/Briggs (S/GB, LCR-Suzuki), 11''915; 5. Laidlow/Farrance (GB, LCR-Suzuki), 31''362; 6. Norbury/Cox (GB, LCR-Yamaha), 41''379; 7. G. Knight/D. Knight (GB, Windle-Yamaha), 47''020; 8. Doppler/Wagner (A, LCR-Yamaha), 58''436; 9. Morrissey/R. Biggs (GB, LCR-Suzuki), 58''421; 10. Hanks/P. Biggs (GB, LCR-Suzuki), 59''221; 11. J. Cluze/G. Cluze (F, LCR-Suzuki), 1'24.747; 12. Dagnino/Hildebrand (I/D, LCR-Suzuki), 2'31.597; 13. Foukal/Pertlicek (CZ, LCR-Yamaha), 1 tour; 14. Roscher/Hänni (D/CH, LCR-Suzuki). 14 finishers.

4th September - Assen - Netherlands

1. Ti. Reeves/Tr. Reeves (GB, LCR-Suzuki), 14 tours, 31'07.761; 2. Laidlow/Farrance (GB, LCR-Suzuki), 21''315; 3. Hanks/Biggs (GB, LCR-Suzuki), 22''612; 4. Manninen/Kuismanen (SF, LCR-Suzuki), 27''963; 5. Muldoon/Knapton (GB, LCR-Suzuki), 34''855; 6. M. Van Gils/T. Van Gils (NL, LCR-Suzuki), 35''872; 7. Gällros/Briggs (S/GB, LCR-Suzuki), 50''481; 8. G. Knight/D. Knight (GB, LCR-Suzuki), 53''708; 9. B. Birchall/T. Birchall (GB, Windle-Yamaha), 53''832; 10. Päivärinta/Wall (SF/S, LCR-Suzuki), 1'00.641; 11. Roscher/Hänni (D/CH, LCR-Suzuki), 1'01.202; 12. Philp/Long (GB, LCR-Yamaha), 1'03.850; 13. Delannoy/Bidault (F, LCR-Suzuki), 1'15.017; 14. Norbury/Parnell (GB, Windle-Suzuki), 1'21.517; 15. Peach/Lawrence (GB, LCR-Suzuki), 1'22.330.

18th September - Sachsenring - Germany

Race I: 1. Ti. Reeves/Tr. Reeves (GB, LCR-Suzuki), 10 tours, 15'13.302 (144.66 km/h); 2. Manninen/Kuismanen (SF, LCR-Suzuki), 10''409; 3. Gällros/Briggs (S/GB, LCR-Suzuki), 16''097; 4. Päivärinta/Wall (SF/S, LCR-Suzuki), 16''265; 5. Muldoon/Knapton (GB, LCR-Suzuki)., 27''169; 6. Hanks/Biggs (GB, LCR-Suzuki), 28''154; 7. Delannoy/Bidault (F, LCR-Suzuki), 29''555; 8. M. Van Gils/T. Van Gils (NL, LCR-Suzuki), 30''941; 9. Doppler/Wagner (A, LCR-Yamaha), 32''229; 10. Norbury/Cox (GB, Windle-Suzuki), 38''576; 11. Roscher/Hänni (D/CH, LCR-Suzuki), 39''265; 12. G. Knight/D. Knight (GB, LCR-Suzuki), 40''994; 13. Göttlich/Höss (D, LCR-Suzuki), 42''405; 14. Laidlow/Farrance (GB, LCR-Suzuki), 57''205; 15. J. Cluze/G. Cluze (F, LCR-Suzuki), 1'11.154.
Race II: 1. Ti. Reeves/Tr. Reeves (GB, LCR-Suzuki), 22 tours, 33'36.111 (144.17 km/h); 2. Manninen/Kuismanen (SF, LCR-Suzuki), 8''757; 3. Delannoy/Bidault (F, LCR-Suzuki), 18''572; 4. Hanks/Biggs (GB, LCR-Suzuki), 32''000; 5. Gällros/Briggs (S/GB, LCR-Suzuki), 32''123; 6. Laidlow/Farrance (GB, LCR-Suzuki), 37''448; 7. Roscher/Hänni (D/CH, LCR-Suzuki), 37''709; 8. M. Van Gils/T. Van Gils (NL, LCR-Suzuki), 39''741; 9. Päivärinta/Wall (SF/S, LCR-Suzuki), 44''332; 10. Foukal/Pertlicek (CZ, LCR-Yamaha), 1'19.791; 11. Doppler/Wagner (A, LCR-Yamaha), 1'24.383; 12. G. Knight/D. Knight (GB, LCR-Suzuki), 1 tour; 13. Schröder/Burkard (CH, LCR-Suzuki); 14. J. Cluze/G. Cluze (F, LCR-Suzuki); 15. Bevers/Verbrugge (NL/B, RCN-Yamaha).

FINAL CLASSIFICATION

1. Tim Reeves/Tristan Reeves (GB)	LCR-Suzuki	334
2. Tero Manninen/Pekka Kuismanen (SF)	LCR-Suzuki	211
3. Jörg Steinhausen/Trevor Hopkinson (D/GB)	LCR-Suzuki	181

4. Päivärinta/Wall (SF/S, LCR-Suzuki), 165; 5. Laidlow/Farrance (GB, LR-Suzuki), 157; 6. Gällros/Briggs (S/GB, LCR-Suzuki), 153; 7. G. Knight/D. Knight (GB, LCR-Suzuki), 110; 8. M. Van Gils/T. Van Gils (NL, LCR-Suzuki), 106; 9. Hanks/Biggs (GB, LCR-Suzuki), 82; 10. Roscher/Hänni (D/CH, LCR-Suzuki), 78.

EUROPEAN CHAMPIONSHIP
125 CC

28th March - Assen - Netherlands

1. Ranseder (A, KTM), 18 tours, 25'22.541 (154.219 km/h); 2. Kalab (CZ, Aprilia), 0''282; 3. Conti (I, Honda), 5''893; 4. Mickan (D, Honda), 33''731; 5. Van den Berk (NL, Aprilia), 33''807; 6. Litjens (NL, Honda), 34''104; 7. A. Boscoscuro (I, Honda), 39''232; 8. Eitzinger (A, Honda), 46''008; 9. Van den Dragt (NL, Honda), 47''556; 10. Den Bekker (NL, Honda), 52''861; 11. Van Daalen (NL, Honda), 1'04.865; 12. Mayer (D, Aprilia), 1'10.159; 13. Kaulamo (SF, Honda), 1'10.298; 14. Verhoeff (NL, Honda), 1'10.643; 15. Friedricks (NL, Honda), 1'19.197.

15th May - Vallelunga - Italy

1. Baroni (I, Aprilia), 19 tours, 26'06.197 (141.630 km/h); 2. Conti (I, Honda), 0''101; 3. Palumbo (I, Aprilia), 7''560; 4. Vivarelli (I, Honda), 16''313; 5. Van den Berk (NL, Aprilia), 28''448; 6. Biliotti (I, Aprilia), 29''372; 7. G. Gnani (I, Gnani), 37''167; 8. Kaulamo (SF, Honda), 47''950; 9. A. Boscoscuro (I, Honda), 49''652; 10. Mayer (D, Aprilia), 50''042; 11. Milovanovic (S, Honda), 51''844; 12. Litjens (NL, Honda), 56''427; 13. Verdini (I, Aprilia), 57''350; 14. Dubbink (NL, Honda), 1 tour ; 15. Mariotti (I, Honda).

29th May - Hungaroring - Hungary

1. Ranseder (A, KTM), 15 tours, 29'30.159 (133.545 km/h); 2. Conti (I, Honda), 7''382; 3. Kalab (CZ, Aprilia), 10''126; 4. S. Bradl (D, KTM), 19''951; 5. A. Boscoscuro (I, Honda), 20''197; 6. Eitzinger (A, Honda), 20''594; 7. Litjens (NL, Honda), 29''206; 8. Van den Dragt (NL, Honda), 37''522; 9. Wirsing (D, KTM), 39''210; 10. Razek (CZ, Honda), 39''427; 11. Rabat (E, Honda), 41''215; 12. Vostarek (CZ, Honda), 41''607; 13. Lasser (D, KTM), 48''906; 14. Aegerter (CH, Honda), 1'01.071; 15. Mauresan (ROU, Honda), 1'03.717.

THE RESULTS OF THE OTHER CHAMPIONSHIPS

12th June - Rijeka - Croatia

1. Kalab (CZ, Aprilia), 15 tours, 23'53.012 (157.062 km/h); 2. G. Gnani (I, Gnani), 10''674; 3. Litjens (NL, Honda), 19''200; 4. Bergada (E, Honda), 24''076; 5. Magda (H, FGR), 24''392; 6. Mayer (D, Aprilia), 28''2268; 7. M. Conti (I, Honda), 33''101; 8. R. Filice (I, Honda), 48''491; 9. Kaulamo (SF, Honda), 48''538; 10. Razek (CZ, Honda), 50''019; 11. Gyorfi (H, Honda), 52''286; 12. Vostarek (CZ, Honda), 1'07.752; 13. A. Boscoscuro (I, Honda), 1'16.925; 14. Hosek (CZ, Honda), 1'21.642; 15. Sembera (CZ, Honda), 1'27.741.

10th July - Most - Czech Republic

1. Fröhlich (D, Honda), 17 tours, 30'28.732 (141.193 km/h); 2. Vostarek (CZ, Honda), 4''018; 3. Eitzinger (A, Honda), 4''042; 4. Hommel (D, Honda), 4''347; 5. Gnani (I, Gnani), 12''859; 6. R. Filice (I, Honda), 13''188; 7. Aegerter (CH, Honda), 14''189; 8. Van den Dragt (NL, Honda), 14''227; 9. Kaulamo (SF, Honda), 14''271; 10. Litjens (NL, Honda), 19''235; 11. Magda (H, FGR), 28''554; 12. Gyoerfi (H, Honda), 29''090; 13. Razek (CZ, Honda), 29''407; 14. Rebien (DK, Honda), 29''428; 15. Hübsch (D, Honda), 31''191.

28th August - Schleiz - Germany

1. Fröhlich (D, Honda), 15 tours, 23'56.144 (143.070 km/h); 2. Baroni (I, Aprilia), 3''779; 3. A. Boscoscuro (I, Honda), 7''451; 4. Aegerter (CH, Honda), 11''128; 5. Litjens (NL, Honda), 12''838; 6. Hübsch (D, Honda), 16''642; 7. Bergada (E, Honda), 19''348; 8. Vostarek (CZ, Honda), 19''624; 9. Conti (I, Honda), 23''636; 10. Michels (D, Honda), 27''605; 11. Milovanovic (S, Aprilia), 439''602; 12. Verhoeff (NL, Honda), 42''688; 13. Van den Dragt (NL, Honda), 45''146; 14. R. Filice (I, Honda), 47''917; 15. Mayer (D, Aprilia), 49''498.

9h October - Braga - Portugal

1. Baroni (I, Aprilia), 22 tours, 30'03.782 (132.601 km/h); 2. Conti (I, Honda), 14''702; 3. Sancioni (I, Aprilia), 15''197; 4. Kalab (CZ, Aprilia), 26''719; 5. Magda (H, FGR), 33''430; 6. Litjens (NL, Honda), 53''919; 7. A. Boscoscuro (I, Honda), 53''957; 8. Kaulamo (SF, Honda), 54''442; 9. Ferreira (POR, Honda), 1 tour; 10. Kovacs (H, Honda); 11. Hosek (CZ, Honda). 11 finishers.

16th October - Cartagena - Spain

1. Baroni (I, Aprilia), 20 tours, 33'10.895 (126.790 km/h); 2. Kalab (CZ, Aprilia), 13''142; 3. Fröhlich (D, Honda), 19''916; 4. Sancioni (Aprilia), 22''288; 5. Eitzinger (A, Honda), 22''322; 6. Vostarek (CZ, Honda), 33''612; 7. Conti (I, Honda), 36''529; 8. A. Boscoscuro (I, Honda), 36''583; 9. Lombardi (I, Aprilia), 46''561; 10. Hübsch (D, Honda), 48''270; 11. Litjens (NL, Honda), 51''960; 12. Kaulamo (SF, Honda), 52''089; 13. Bordonado (E, Aprilia), 1'38.548; 14. Rebien (DK, Honda), 1 tour; 15. Hosek (CZ, Honda).

FINAL CLASSIFICATION

1. Michele Conti (I)	Honda	101
2. Lorenzo Baroni (I)	Aprilia	95
3. Igor Kalab (CZ	Aprilia	94

4. J. Litjens (NL, Honda), 71; 5. G. Fröhlich (D, Honda), 66; 6. A. Boscoscuro (I, Honda), 63; 7. M. Ranseder (A, KTM), 50; 8. P. Vostarek (CZ, Honda), 46; 9. P. Eitzinger (A, Honda), 45; 10. G. Gnani (I, Gnani), 40. 47 finishers.

250 CC

15th May - Vallelunga - Italy

1. Molina (E, Aprilia), 22 tours, 30'05.105 (142.288 km/h); 2. Martensson (S, Honda), 6''005; 3. Polzer (A, Aprilia), 8''665; 4. Lagerveld (NL, Honda), 15''451; 5. Zanette (I, Yamaha), 30''988; 6. Walther (D, Honda), 34''156; 7. Menghi (I, Honda), 35''201; 8. Aschenbrenner (D, Honda), 37''860; 9. Cajback (S, Yamaha), 37''925; 10. Todorov (BG, Yamaha), 38''192; 11. Ronzoni (I, Yamaha), 38''937; 12. Rank (D, Honda), 39''151; 13. Mariotti (I, Honda), 55''736; 14. Heierli (CH, Honda), 57''283; 15. Bork (D, Yamaha), 1'06.937.

29th May - Hungaroring - Hungary

1. Molina (E, Aprilia), 16 tours, 31'02.059 (135.520 km/h); 2. Lakerveld (NL, Honda), 4''062; 3. Polzer (A, Aprilia), 14''167; 4. Zanette (I, Yamaha), 16''554; 5. Lindfors (S, Aprilia), 25''318; 6. Aggerholm (DK, Yamaha), 25''606; 7. Filla (CZ, Yamaha), 33''399; 8. Rank (D, Honda), 35''912; 9. Walther (D, Honda), 36''246; 10. Ronzoni (I, Yamaha), 36''800; 11. Matikainen (SF, Honda), 37''037; 12. Heierli (CH, Honda), 37''517; 13. Cerny (SLO, Yamaha), 39''874; 14. Binucci (I, Yamaha), 59''283; 15. Martensson (S, Yamaha), 1'14.466.

12th June - Rijeka - Croatia

1. Molina (E, Aprilia), 17 tours, 26'31.918 (160.235 km/h); 2. Polzer (A, Aprilia), 3''043; 3. Todorov (BUL, Yamaha), 3''455; 4. Cajback (S, Yamaha), 7''885; 5. Lakerveld (NL, Honda), 12''628; 6. Lindfors (S, Aprilia), 21''581; 7. Zanette (I, Yamaha), 23''450; 8. Martensson (S, Yamaha), 29''046; 9. Filla (CZ, Yamaha), 29''235; 10. Walhter (D, Honda), 29''468; 11. Rank (D, Honda), 29''830; 12. Heierli (CH, Honda), 49''023; 13. Litjens (NL, Yamaha), 56''711; 14. Binucci (I, Yamaha), 57''406; 15. Mayer (D, Honda), 59''586.

25th June - Assen - Netherlands

1. Molina (E, Aprilia), 14 tours, 31'12.434 (161.420 km/h); 2. Lakerveld (NL, Honda), 6''031; 3. Aggerholm (DK, Yamaha), 16''180; 4. Martensson (S, Yamaha), 35''476; 5. Filla (CZ, Yamaha), 44''620; 6. Walther (D, Honda), 49''807; 7. Rank (D, Honda), 50''378; 8. Aschenbrenner (D, Honda), 1'02.797; 9. Heierli (CH, Honda), 1'03.335; 10. Maikanen (SF, Honda), 1'03.457; 11. Binucci (I, Yamaha), 1'05.182; 12. Persson (S, Yamaha), 1'05.687; 13. Sjostrom (S, ISR), 1'10.180; 14. Appelo (NL, Honda), 1'14.793; 15. Dobrich (S, Aprilia), 1'20.837.

10th July - Most - Czech Republic

1. Lakerveld (NL, Honda), 18 tours, 30'51.921 (147.626 km/h); 2. Smees (NL, Aprilia), 2''742; 3. Molina (E, Aprilia), 9''079; 4. Aggerholm (DK, Yamaha), 14''029; 5. Gevers (NL, Aprilia), 18''724; 6. Martensson (S, Yamaha), 25''911; 7. Roelofs (NL, Yamaha), 32''138; 8. Filla (CZ, Yamaha), 32''149; 9. Matikainen (SF, Honda), 42''928; 10. Menghi (I, Honda), 47''998; 11. Markham (GB, Yamaha), 50''560; 12. Sjöström (S, ISR), 56''667; 13. Appelo (NL, Honda), 57''391; 14. Scaccia (F, Yamaha), 1'05.051; 15. Aschenbrenner (D, Honda), 1'05.429.

28th August - Schleiz - Germany

1. Molina (E, Aprilia), 21 tours, 32'25.548 (147.854 km/h); 2. Polzer (A, Aprilia), 0''156; 3. Smees (NL, Aprilia), 2''698; 4. Martensson (S, Yamaha), 18''423; 5. Aggerholm (DK, Yamaha), 18''725; 6. Walther (D, Honda), 20''274; 7. Menghi (I, Honda), 31''185; 8. Lindfors (S, Aprilia), 31''315; 9. Lakerveld (NL, Honda), 31''485; 10. Filla (CZ, Yamaha), 31''728; 11. Zappa (I, Yamaha), 34''148; 12. Rank (D, Honda), 47''571; 13. Gevers (NL, Aprilia), 48''081; 14. Roelofs (NL, Yamaha), 48''651; 15. Matikainen (SF, Honda), 51''498.

9th October - Braga - Portugal

1. Molina (E, Aprilia), 28 tours, 37'52.776 (133.940 km/h); 2. Morelli (I, Aprilia), 11''782; 3. Martensson (S, Yamaha), 23''067; 4. Lakerveld (NL, Honda), 38''296; 5. Zanette (I, Yamaha), 44''160; 6. Planas Comes (E, Honda), 47''344; 7. Walther (D, Honda), 54''535; 8. Polzer (A, Aprilia), 59''945; 9. Matikainen (SF, Honda), 1'07.248; 10. Rank (D, Honda), 1'10.901; 11. Lindfors (S, Aprilia), 1'13.353; 12. Postmus (NL, Yamaha), 1 tour; 13. Menghi (I, Honda); 14. Voit (D, Aprilia); 15. Sjöström (S, ISR).

16th October - Cartagena - Spain

1. Molina (E, Aprilia), 24 tours, 39'17.371 (128.490 km/h); 2. Morelli (I, Aprilia), 5''193; 3. Aggerholm (DK, Yamaha), 25''611; 4. Watz (S, Yamaha), 30''584; 5. Filla (CZ, Yamaha), 40''059; 6. Zanette (I, Yamaha), 57''984; 7. Planas Comes (E, Honda), 1'00.252; 8. Walther (D, Honda), 1'00.596; 9. Rank (D, Honda), 1'06.344; 10. Aschenbrenner (D, Honda), 1'06.418; 11. Lindfors (S, Aprilia), 1'39.538; 12. Heierli (CH, Honda), 1'42.468; 13. Matikainen (SF, Honda), 1 tour; 14. Aubry (F, Honda); 15. Sjöström (S, ISR).

FINAL CLASSIFICATION

1. Alvaro Molina (E)	Aprilia	191
2. Patrick Lakerveld (Nö)	Honda	109
3. Andreas Martensson (S)	Yamaha	81

4. Y. Polzer (A, Aprilia), 80; 5. K. Aggerholm (DK, Yamaha), 66; 6. T. Walther (D, Honda), 60; 7. C. Zanette (I, Yamaha), 54; 8. M. Filla (CZ, Yamaha), 52; 9. N. Rank (D, Honda), 43; 10. L. Morelli (I, Aprilia), 40. 39 finishers.

SUPERSPORT 600

15th May - Vallelunga - Italy

1. Boccolini (I, Kawasaki), 25 tours, 34'25.900 (141.279 km/h); 2. Proietto (I, Kawasaki), 6''215; 3. Tarizzo (I, Honda), 11''911; 4. Anello (I, Honda), 29''715; 5. A. Aldrovandi (I, Honda), 30''025 ; 6. Valjan (CRO, Honda), 34''130; 7. Barone (I, Honda), 37''259; 8. Almeda (E. Yamaha), 41''591; 9. Manici (I, Yamaha), 1'01.790; 10. Abellan (E, Yamaha), 1 tour; 11. Roncoroni (I, Yamaha); 12. Aromaa (SF, Honda); 13. Boaretto (I, Yamaha); 14. Zannini (I, Yamaha); 15. Vanoni (I, Honda), 2 tours.

29th May - Hungaroring - Hungary

1. Tarizzo (I, Honda), 16 tours, 31'08.944 (135.020 km/h); 2. Boccolini (I, Kawasaki), 0''031; 3. Székely (H, Honda), 12''876; 4. A. Aldrovandi (I, Honda), 17''577; 5. Jesek (CZ, Kawasaki), 20''143; 6. Manici (I, Yamaha), 32''510; 7. Pintar (SLO, Yamaha), 40''715; 8. Valjan (CRO, Honda), 46''490; 9. Aromaa (SF, Honda), 1'14.122; 10. Roncoroni (I, Yamaha), 1'38.662; 11. Vanoni (I, Honda), 1 tour.

12th June - Rijeka - Croatia

1. Valjan (CRO, Honda), 17 tours, 26'32.467 (160.180 km/h); 2. Tarizzo (I, Honda), 0''178; 3. Pintar (SLO, Yamaha), 17''268; 4. A. Aldrovandi (I, Honda), 27''564; 5. Barone (I, Honda), 33''141; 6. Broz (CZ, Kawasaki), 1'20.213; 7. Kaldowski (POL, Yamaha), 1'24.880; 8. Bianchi (I, Honda), 1'28.876; 9. Bittman (CZ, Honda), 2'01.005; 10. Roncoroni (I, Yamaha), 1 tour. 10 finishers.

10th July - Most - Czech Republic

1. Boccolini (I, Kawasaki), 21 tours, 36'14.335 (146.692 km/h); 2. A. Aldrovandi (I, Honda), 0''298; 3. Valjan (CR, Honda), 39''292; 4. Bittman (CZ, Honda), 39''573; 5. Seidel (D, Honda), 39''969; 6. Jesek (CZ, Kawasaki), 56''787; 7. Broz (CZ, Kawasaki), 57''373; 8. Kaldowski (POL, Yamaha), 1'05.127; 9. Heyndrickx (B, Honda), 1'06.510; 10. Kerkhoven (NL, Suzuki), 1'12.763; 11. Lukaseder (A, Honda), 1'14.087; 12. Puccetti (I, Kawasaki), 1.15.308; 13. Bock (D, Yamaha), 1'18.996; 14. Manici (I, Yamaha), 1'25.184; 15. Pajic (NL, Kawasaki), 1 tour.

28th August - Schleiz - Germany

1. A. Aldrovandi (I, Honda), 19 tours, 29'26.529 (147.329 km/h); 2. Boccolini (I, Kawasaki), 3''801; 3. Ahnendrop (NL, Honda), 18''457; 4. Kerkhoven (NL, Suzuki), 30''039; 5. Valjan (CR, Honda), 31''453; 6. Manici (I, Yamaha), 37''667; 7. Pajic (NL, Kawasaki), 52''054; 8. Janz (D, Honda), 59''931; 9. Pintar (SLO, Yamaha), 1'03.597; 10. Brandt (D, Honda), 1'03.889; 11. Roncoroni (I, Yamaha), 1'20.351; 12. Lenters (NL, Yamaha), 1'32.354; 13. Broz (CZ, Kawasaki), 1'44.586; 14. Kaldowski (POL, Yamaha), 1'47.874; 15. Vanoni (I, Honda), 1'48.619.

4th September - Assen - Netherlands

1. Le Grelle (B, Honda); 2. V. Kallio (SF, Yamaha); 3. Veijer (NL, Honda); 4. A. Aldrovandi (I, Honda); 5. Opheij (NL, Yamaha); 6. Boccolini (I, Kawasaki); 7. Pekkanen (SF, Honda); 8. Van Kleef (NL, Honda); 9. Van de Lagemaat (NL, Honda); 10. Valtonen (SF, Honda); 11. Heyndrickx (B, Honda); 12. Bittman (CZ, Honda); 13. Pronk (NL, Kawasaki); 14. Ivanov (RUS, Kawasaki); 15. Lenters (NL, Yamaha).

9th October - Braga - Portugal

1. Boccolini (I, Kawasaki), 28 tours, 38'11.239 (132.861 km/h); 2. Valjan (CR, Honda), 15''422; 3. Valtonen (SF, Honda), 39''772; 4. Manici (I, Yamaha), 52''963; 5. Roncoroni (I, Yamaha), 55''070. 5 finishers.

16th October - Cartagena - Spain

1. A. Aldrovandi (I, Honda), 24 tours, 39'58.021 (126.320 km/h); 2. Boccolini (I, Kawasaki), 5''897; 3. Moral (E, Yamaha), 7''549; 4. Aguilar (E, Yamaha), 9''841; 5. Hodt (N. Yamaha), 23''507; 6. Barone (I, Honda), 23''707; 7. Aromaa (SF, Honda), 56''393; 8. Valtonen (SF, Honda), 1'00.512; 9. Puccetti (I, Kawasaki), 1'02.832; 10. Valjan (CR, Honda), 1'09.776; 11. Manici (I, Yamaha), 1'15.605; 12. Abellan (E, Yamaha), 1'16.176; 13. Roncoroni (I, Yamaha), 1'21.813; 14. Planas (E, Yamaha), 1'39.255; 15. Lopez (E, Yamaha), 1 tour.

FINAL CLASSIFICATION

1. Gilles Boccolini (I)	Kawasaki	145
2. Alessio Aldrovandi (I)	Honda	120
3. Loris Valjan (CR)	Honda	94

4. G. Tarizzo (I, Honda), 61; 5. A. Manici (I, Yamaha), 45; 6. M. Roncoroni (I, Yamaha), 34; 7. B. Pintar (SLO, Yamaha), 32; 8. G. Barone (I, Honda), 30; 9. V. Valtonen (SF, Honda), 29; 10. S. Le Grelle (B, Honda), 25. 47 finishers.

SUPERSTOCK 600

24th April - Valencia - Spain

1. Tiberio (F, Honda), 11 tours, 19'10.867 (137.807 km/h); 2. Corti (I, Yamaha), 0''122; 3. X. Simeon (B, Suzuki), 4''242; 4. Canepa (I, Kawasaki), 7''880; 5. Perez-Muñoz (E, Honda), 11''588; 6. Berger (F, Honda), 16''078; 7. Hidalgo (E, Honda), 17''560; 8. Wimbauer (USA, Suzuki), 25''367; 9. Beretta (I, Kawasaki), 27''340; 10. Chmielewski (POL, Yamaha), 28''636; 11. Taipale (SF, Honda), 43''284; 12. Polita (I, Suzuki), 43''969; 13. Burrell (GB, Honda), 44''069; 14. Van Looy (B, Suzuki), 44''338; 15. Caldart (I, Yamaha), 1'04.530.

8th May - Monza - Italy

1. Corti (I, Yamaha), 9 tours, 17'47.228 (175.870 km/h); 2. Tiberio (F, Honda), 0''102; 3. Berger (F, Honda), 5''565; 4. Canepa (I, Kawasaki), 6''948; 5. X. Simeon (B, Suzuki), 16''324; 6. Perez-Muñoz (E, Honda), 22''599; 7. J. Gallina (I, Honda), 28''950; 8. Chmielewski (POL, Yamaha), 31''914; 9. McDougall (GB, Suzuki), 32''309; 10. Rivas (E, Honda), 36''007; 11. De Boer (NL, Honda), 36''027; 12. Villar-Machado (E, Honda), 38''486; 13. Pelliccioni (I, Yamaha), 39''615; 14. Perri (I, Kawasaki), 41''700; 15. Ten Napel (NL, Honda), 42''573.

29th May - Silverstone - Great Britain

1. Corti (I, Yamaha), 14 tours, 21'52.823 (136.709 km/h); 2. Tiberio (F, Honda), 4''113; 3. Berger (F, Honda), 5''731; 4. Canepa (I, Kawasaki); 5. Napoleone (F, Kawasaki), 26''486; 6. Antonelli (I., Kawasaki), 26''830; 7. Forner (E, Honda), 41''857; 8. Perez Munoz (E, Honda), 45''090; 9. Taipale (SF, Honda), 45''605; 10. McDougall (GB, Suzuki), 46''160; 11. Ter Braake (NL, Honda), 46''675; 12. Hidalgo (E, Honda), 49''890; 13. Wimbauer (USA, Suzuki), 50''284; 14. Villar-Machado (E, Honda), 51''895; 15. J. Gallina (I, Honda), 55''531.

26th June - Misano - Italy

1. Corti (I, Yamaha), 12 tours, 20'34.449 (142.081 km/h); 2. Tiberio (F, Honda), 0''136; 3. Colatosti (I, Honda), 8''239; 4. Antonelli (I, Kawasaki), 17''763; 5. Lorenzetti (I, Yamaha), 24''036; 6. Colucci (I, Suzuki), 24''931; 7. Di Stefano (I, Yamaha), 29''408; 8. Rivas (E, Honda), 29''923; 9. Magnoni (I, Yamaha), 30''050; 10. Canepa (I, Kawasaki), 31''031; 11. Hidalgo (E, Honda), 32''801; 12. Wimbauer (USA, Suzuki), 35''190; 13. Ter Braake (NL, Honda), 38''957; 14. Forner (E, Honda), 39''924; 15. Villar-Machado (E, Honda), 45''418.

17th July - Brno - Czech Republic

1. Tiberio (F, Honda), 10 tours, 22'28.626 (144.227 km/h); 2. Canepa (I, Kawasaki), 7''252; 3. Corti (I, Yamaha), 13''068; 4. Forner (E, Honda), 17''248; 5. Taipale (SF, Honda), 21''606; 6. Rivas Fernandez (E, Honda), 21''662; 7. Chmielewski (POL, Yamaha), 22''745; 8. Jezek (CZ, Kawasaki), 27''812; 9. Beretta (I, Kawasaki), 28''279; 10. J. Gallina (I, Honda), 28''483; 11. Ten Napel (NL, Honda), 29''388; 12. De Boer (NL, Honda), 33''751; 13. Villar-Machado (E, Honda), 35''761; 14. Wimbauer (USA, Suzuki), 36''612; 15. Van Looy (B, Suzuki), 36''801.

THE RESULTS OF THE OTHER CHAMPIONSHIPS

7th August - Brands Hatch - Great Britain

1. Corti (I, Yamaha), 12 tours, 18'52.018 (160.166 km/h); 2. Canepa (I, Kawasaki), 0''529; 3. Berger (F, Honda), 2''580; 4. Simeon (B, Suzuki), 14''133; 5. Antonelli (I, Kawasaki), 14''183; 6. Wimbauer (USA, Suzuki), 14''416; 7. McDougall (GB, Suzuki), 14''525; 8. Villar Machado (E, Honda), 21''201; 9. Rivas Fernandez (E, Honda), 22''490; 10. Jezek (CZ, Kawasaki), 23''147; 11. Napoleone (F, Kawasaki), 23''865; 12. Forner (E, Honda), 23''994; 13. Van Looy (B, Suzuki), 25''206; 14. Colucci (I, Suzuki), 25''157; 15. De Boer (NL, Honda), 25''594.

4th September - Assen - Netherlands

1. Corti (I, Yamaha), 9 tours, 20'30.263 (157.936 km/h); 2. Forner (E, Honda), 6''859; 3. Antonelli (I, Kawasaki), 7''037; 4. Simeon (B, Suzuki), 7''082; 5. Ter Braake (NL, Honda), 10''681; 6. Rivas Fernandez (E, Honda), 18''240; 7. De Boer (NL, Honda), 19''581; 8. Napoleone (F, Kawasaki), 19''591; 9. Jesek (CZ, Kawasaki), 19''789; 10. Chmielewski (POL, Yamaha), 21''283; 11. McDougall (GB, Suzuki), 25''570; 12. Bovee (NL, Honda), 30''918; 13. Villar Machado (E, Honda), 32''541; 14. Berger (F, Honda), 38''310; 15. Perez Muñoz (E, Honda), 38''494.

11th September - Lausitz - Germany

1. Berger (F, Honda), 12 tours, 21'50.636 (140.579 km/h); 2. Tiberio (F, Honda), 7''537; 3. X. Simeon (B, Suzuki), 9''170; 4. Antonelli (I, Kawasaki), 13''586; 5. Jesek (CZ, Kawasaki), 16''844; 6. Ten Napel (NL, Honda), 17''036; 7. Napoleone (F, Kawasaki), 17''965; 8. De Boer (NL, Honda), 17''970; 9. Corti (I, Yamaha), 18''313; 10. Chmielewski (POL, Yamaha), 21''727; 11. Rivas Fernandez (E, Honda), 31''260; 12. Lundh (S, Honda), 32''148; 13. Burrell (GB, Honda), 32''501; 14. J. Gallina (I, Honda), 32''905; 15. Beretta (I, Kawasaki), 35''594.

25th September - Imola - Italy

1. Tiberio (F, Honda), 10 tours, 19'45.147 (149.845 km/h); 2. Berger (F, Honda), 1''661; 3. Antonelli (I, Kawasaki), 7''049; 4. X. Simeon (B, Suzuki), 7''301; 5. Corti (I, Yamaha), 15''250; 6. Napoleone (F, Kawasaki), 17''026; 7. Colucci (I, Suzuki), 18''463; 8. Lorenzetti (I, Honda), 18''918; 9. Jezek (CZ, Kawasaki), 26''254; 10. Rivas Fernandez (E, Honda), 27''063; 11. Forner (E, Honda), 27''517; 12. Beretta (I, Kawasaki), 33''789; 13. Villar Machado (E, Honda), 33''985; 14. Burrell (GB, Honda), 44''009; 15. Piermaria (I, Yamaha), 49''189.

9th October - Magny-Cours - France

1. Tiberio (F, Honda), 11 tours, 19'54.688 (146.210 km/h); 2. Canepa (I, Kawasaki), 2''834; 3. Berger (F, Honda), 3''582; 4. X. Simeon (B, Suzuki), 20''744; 5. Antonelli (I, Kawasaki), 25''285; 6. F. Millet (F, Honda), 26''258; 7. Corti (I, Yamaha), 31''500; 8. Colucci (I, Suzuki), 32''499; 9. Taipale (SF, Honda), 32''709; 10. Rivas Fernandez (E, Honda), 44''430; 11. Van Looy (B, Suzuki), 46''203; 12. Chmielewski (POL, Yamaha), 46''345; 13. Villar Machado (E, Honda), 47''187; 14. Wimbauer (USA, Suzuki), 48''057; 15. Ten Nappel (NL, Honda), 49''018.

FINAL CLASSIFICATION

1. Claudio Corti (I)	Yamaha	188
2. Yann Tiberio (F)	Honda	180
3. Maxime Berger (F)	Honda	121

4. N. Canepa (I, Kawasaki), 105; 5. X. Simeon (B, Suzuki), 95; 6. A. Antonelli (I, Kawasaki), 90; 7. D. Rivas Fernandez (E, Honda), 58; 8. G. Forner (E, Honda), 53; 9. L. Napoleone (F. Kawasaki), 43; 10. O. Jesek (CZ, Kawasaki), 39.

USA CHAMPIONSHIP

SUPERSPORT

12th March - Daytona

1. T. Hayden (Kawasaki); 2. Hacking (Yamaha); 3. Di Salvo (Yamaha); 4. Spies (Suzuki); 5. Aa. Gobert (AUS, Yamaha); 6. Jensen (Yamaha); 7. Barnes (Yamaha); 8. May (Suzuki); 9. Picotte (Yamaha); 10. Eslick (Suzuki).

24th April - Birmingham

1. Hacking (Yamaha); 2. T. Hayden (Kawasaki); 3. R.-L. Hayden (Kawasaki); 4. Di Salvo (Yamaha); 5. Aa. Gobert (AUS, Yamaha); 6. D. Buckmaster (AUS, Yamaha); 7. Jensen (Yamaha); 8. Attard (Kawasaki); 9. Peris (Yamaha); 10. Spies (Suzuki).

1st May - Fontana

1. Hacking (Yamaha); 2. T. Hayden (Kawasaki); 3. R.-L. Hayden (Kawasaki); 4. Di Salvo (Yamaha); 5. Aa. Gobert (AUS, Yamaha); 6. Spies (Suzuki); 7. Attard (Kawasaki); 8. May (Suzuki); 9. Peris (Yamaha); 10. Moore (Yamaha).

15th May - Sonoma

1. T. Hayden (Kawasaki); 2. Di Salvo (Yamaha); 3. Hacking (Yamaha); 4. R.-L. Hayden (Kawasaki); 5. Spies (Suzuki); 6. D. Buckmaster (AUS, Yamaha); 7. Attard (Kawasaki); 8. May (Suzuki); 9. Perris (Yamaha); 10. Eslick (Suzuki).

22nd May - Fountain

1. R.-L. Hayden (Kawasaki); 2. T. Hayden (Kawasaki); 3. Hacking (Yamaha); 4. Aa. Gobert (AUS, Yamaha); 5. Attard (Kawasaki); 6. Peris (Yamaha); 7. Spies (Suzuki); 8. Eslick (Suzuki); 9. D. Buckmaster (AUS, Yamaha); 10. May (Suzuki).

5th June - Elkhart Lake

1. T. Hayden (Kawasaki); 2. R.-L. Hayden (Kawasaki); 3. Di Salvo (Yamaha); 4. Aa. Gobert (AUS, Yamaha); 5. Spies (Suzuki); 6. May (Suzuki); 7. D. Buckmaster (AUS, Yamaha); 8. Peris (Yamaha); 9. Jensen (Yamaha); 10. Conrad (Kawasaki).

10th July - Laguna Seca

1. Di Salvo (Yamaha); 2. R.-L. Hayden (Kawasaki); 3. Aa. Gobert (AUS, Yamaha); 4. Spies (Suzuki); 5. May (Suzuki); 6. T. Hayden (Kawasaki); 7. D. Buckmaster (AUS, Yamaha); 8. Peris (Yamaha); 9. Moore (Yamaha); 10. Young (Suzuki).

24th July - Lexington

1. R.-L. Hayden (Kawasaki); 2. T. Hayden (Kawasaki); 3. Attard (Kawasaki); 4. Di Salvo (Yamaha); 5. Spies (Suzuki); 6. Jensen (Yamaha); 7. Peris (Yamaha); 8. D. Buckmaster (AUS, Yamaha); 9. Aa. Gobert (AUS, Yamaha); 10. Eslick (Suzuki).

28th August - Alton

1. R.-L. Hayden (Kawasaki); 2. T. Hayden (Kawasaki); 3. Di Salvo (Yamaha); 4. Attard (Kawasaki); 5. D. Buckmaster (AUS, Yamaha); 6. Aa. Gobert (AUS, Yamaha); 7. May (Suzuki); 8. Moore (Yamaha); 9. Knapp (Yamaha); 10. Young (Suzuki).

4th September - Braselton

1. R.-L. Hayden (Kawasaki); 2. Di Salvo (Yamaha); 3. Attard (Kawasaki); 4. D. Buckmaster (AUS, Yamaha); 5. T. Hayden (Kawasaki); 6. Jensen (Yamaha); 7. Spies (Suzuki); 8. May (Suzuki); 9. Acree (Suzuki); 10. Young (Suzuki).

FINAL CLASSIFICATION

1. Tommy Hayden	Kawasaki	327
2. Roger-Lee Hayden	Kawasaki	308
3. Jason Di Salvo	Yamaha	272

4. B. Spies (Suzuki), 231; 5. G. May (Suzuki), 228; 6. Aa. Gobert (AUS, Yamaha), 222; 7. D. Buckmaster (AUS, Yamaha), 215; 8. B. Attard (Kawasaki), 201; 9. R. Jensen (Yamaha), 199; 10. C. Peris (Yamaha), 187.

SUPERSTOCK

12th March - Daytona

1. Haskovec (Suzuki); 2. Yates (Suzuki); 3. Pridmore (Suzuki); 4. Hacking (Yamaha); 5. Di Salvo (Yamaha); 6. May (Suzuki); 7. T. Hayden (Kawasaki); 8. Rapp (Suzuki); 9. George (Suzuki); 10. Holden (Suzuki).

24th April - Birmingham

1. T. Hayden (Kawasaki); 2. Di Salvo (Yamaha); 3. Yates (Suzuki); 4. Hacking (Yamaha); 5. Haskovec (Suzuki); 6. Rapp (Suzuki); 7. Aa. Gobert (AUS, Yamaha); 8. R.-L. Hayden (Kawasaki); 9. D. Buckmaster (AUS, Yamaha); 10. Holden (Suzuki).

1st May - Fontana

1. Di Salvo (Yamaha); 2. Hacking (Yamaha); 3. Rapp (Suzuki); 4. T. Hayden (Kawasaki); 5. Haskovec (Suzuki); 6. Aa. Gobert (Yamaha); 7. Haner (Suzuki); 8. Holden (Suzuki); 9. Wood (Suzuki); 10. Yates (Suzuki).

15th May - Sonoma

1. Yates (Suzuki); 2. Hacking (Yamaha); 3. Di Salvo (Yamaha); 4. Rapp (Suzuki); 5. T. Hayden (Kawasaki); 6. Aa. Gobert (AUS, Yamaha); 7. R.-L. Hayden (Kawasaki); 8. Holden (Suzuki); 9. Haner (Suzuki); 10. D. Buckmaster (AUS, Yamaha).

22nd May - Fountain

1. Hacking (Yamaha); 2. Yates (Suzuki); 3. T. Hayden (Kawasaki); 4. Di Salvo (Yamaha); 5. Barnes (Suzuki); 6. Rapp (Suzuki); 7. R.-L. Hayden (Kawasaki); 8. Haner (Suzuki); 9. May (Suzuki); 10. Holden (Suzuki).

5th June - Elkhart Lake

1. Yates (Suzuki); 2. May (Suzuki); 3. Di Salvo (Yamaha); 4. R.-L. Hayden (Kawasaki); 5. T. Hayden (Kawasaki); 6. Barnes (Suzuki); 7. Aa. Gobert (AUS, Yamaha); 8. Rapp (Suzuki); 9. D. Buckmaster (AUS, Yamaha); 10. Holden (Suzuki).

10th July - Laguna Seca

1. Yates (Suzuki); 2. Di Salvo (Yamaha); 3. R.-L. Hayden (Kawasaki); 4. Holden (Suzuki); 5. Haner (Suzuki); 6. Rapp (Suzuki); 7. Aa. Gobert (AUS, Yamaha); 8. D. Buckmaster (Yamaha); 9. George (Suzuki); 10. Moore (Suzuki).

24th July - Lexington

1. Yates (Suzuki); 2. Di Salvo (Yamaha); 3. Rapp (Suzuki); 4. Holden (Suzuki); 5. R.-L. Hayden (Kawasaki); 6. Pridmore (Suzuki); 7. Barnes (Suzuki); 8. D. Buckmaster (AUS, Yamaha); 9. Haner (Suzuki); 10. May (Suzuki).

28th August - Alton

1. Yates (Suzuki); 2. R.-L. Hayden (Kawasaki); 3. Di Salvo (Yamaha); 4. D. Buckmaster (AUS, Yamaha); 5. May (Suzuki); 6. Aa. Gobert (AUS, Yamaha); 7. Rapp (Suzuki); 8. Pridmore (Suzuki); 9. Haner (Suzuki); 10. Barnes (Suzuki).

4th September - Braselton

1. R.-L. Hayden (Kawasaki); 2. Di Salvo (Yamaha); 3. May (Suzuki); 4. D. Buckmaster (AUS, Yamaha); 5. Haner (Suzuki); 6. Rapp (Suzuki); 7. Barnes (Suzuki); 8. Pridmore (Suzuki); 9. Yates (Suzuki); 10. Perez (Yamaha).

FINAL CLASSIFICATION

1. Aaron Yates	Suzuki	323
2. Jason Di Salvo	Yamaha	314
3. Steve Rapp	Suzuki	255

4. R.-L. Hayden (Kawasaki), 241; 5. J. Haner (Suzuki), 222; 6. J. Holden (Suzuki), 195; 7. D. Buckmaster (AUS, Yamaha), 192; 8. G. May (Suzuki), 189; 9. Aa. Gobert (AUS, Yamaha), 187; 10. T. Hayden (Kawasaki), 168.

SUPERBIKE

12th March - Daytona

1. Mladin (AUS, Suzuki); 2. Hodgson (GB, Ducati); 3. Spies (Suzuki); 4. Yates (Suzuki); 5. Zemke (Honda); 6. Mi. Duhamel (CAN, Honda); 7. Pridmore (Suzuki); 8. May (Suzuki); 9. Ku. Roberts (Honda); 10. Rapp (Suzuki).

24th April - Birmingham

Race I: 1. Mladin (AUS, Suzuki); 2. Yates (Suzuki); 3. Spies (Suzuki); 4. Hodgson (GB, Ducati); 5. Mi. Duhamel (CAN, Honda); 6. Pridmore (Suzuki); 7. Rapp (Suzuki); 8. E. Bostrom (Ducati); 9. Haskovec (Suzuki); 10. Craggill (AUS, Suzuki).
Race II: 1. Mladin (AUS, Suzuki); 2. Hodgson (GB, Ducati); 3. Spies (Suzuki); 4. Mi. Duhamel (Honda); 5. E. Bostrom (Ducati); 6. Hayes (Kawasaki); 7. Haskovec (Suzuki); 8. Yates (Suzuki); 9. Craggill (AUS, Suzuki); 10. Haner (Suzuki).

1st May - Fontana

Race I: 1. Spies (Suzuki); 2. Yates (Suzuki); 3. Hodgson (GB, Ducati); 4. Mi. Duhamel (CAN, Honda); 5. E. Bostrom (Ducati); 6. Zemke (Honda); 7. Hayes (Kawasaki); 8. Rapp (Suzuki); 9. Craggill (AUS, Suzuki); 10. Haskovec (Suzuki).
Race II: 1. Mladin (AUS, Suzuki); 2. Spies (Suzuki); 3. Yates (Suzuki); 4. E. Bostrom (Ducati); 5. Hodgson (GB, Ducati); 6. Zemke (Honda); 7. Rapp (Suzuki); 8. Craggill (AUS, Suzuki); 9. McBain (Suzuki); 10. Pegram (Honda).

15th May - Sonoma

Race I: 1. Mladin (AUS, Suzuki); 2. Yates (Suzuki); 3. Hodgson (GB, Ducati); 4. Spies (Suzuki); 5. Hayes (Kawasaki); 6. Rapp (Suzuki); 7. Holden (Suzuki); 8. Pegram (Honda); 9. Craggill (AUS, Suzuki); 10. E. Bostrom (Ducati).
Race II: 1. Mladin (AUS, Suzuki); 2. Yates (Suzuki); 3. Spies (Suzuki); 4. Zemke (Honda); 5. Hodgson (GB, Ducati); 6. Mi. Duhamel (CAN, Honda); 7. E. Bostrom (Ducati); 8. Hayes (Kawasaki); 9. Craggill (AUS, Suzuki); 10. Pegram (Honda).

22nd May - Fountain

1. E. Bostrom (Ducati); 2. Yates (Suzuki); 3. Spies (Suzuki); 4. Mladin (AUS, Suzuki); 5. Hayes (Kawasaki); 6. Rapp (Suzuki); 7. Ledesma (Honda); 8. Haner (Suzuki); 9. Mi. Duhamel (CAN, Honda); 10. George (Suzuki).

5th June - Elkhart Lake

Race I: 1. Hodgson (GB, Ducati); 2. Mladin (AUS, Suzuki); 3. Hayes (Kawasaki); 4. Spies (Suzuki); 5. Craggill (Suzuki); 6. Zemke (Honda); 7. Mi. Duhamel (CAN, Honda); 8. Pegram (Honda); 9. Haner (Suzuki); 10. Tamitsuji (J, Suzuki).
Race II: 1. Mladin (AUS, Suzuki); 2. Spies (Suzuki); 3. Zemke (Honda); 4. E. Bostrom (Ducati); 5. Yates (Suzuki); 6. Hayes (Kawasaki); 7. Ku. Roberts (Honda); 8. Rapp (Suzuki); 9. Acree (Suzuki); 10. McBain (Suzuki).

10th July - Laguna Seca

1. E. Bostrom (Ducati); 2. Mladin (AUS, Suzuki); 3. Yates (Suzuki); 4. Spies (Suzuki); 5. Zemke (Honda); 6. Mi. Duhamel (CAN, Honda); 7. Ku. Roberts (Honda); 8. Rapp (Suzuki); 9. Holden (Suzuki); 10. Pridmore (Suzuki).

24th July - Lexington

Race I: 1. Mladin (AUS, Suzuki); 2. Spies (Suzuki); 3. E. Bostrom (Ducati); 4. Mi. Duhamel (CAN, Honda); 5. Hodgson (GB, Ducati); 6. Hayes (Kawasaki); 7. Ku. Roberts (Honda); 8. Pridmore (Suzuki); 9. Holden (Suzuki); 10. Craggill (AUS, Suzuki).

THE RESULTS OF THE OTHER CHAMPIONSHIPS

Race II: 1. E. Bostrom (Ducati); 2. Mi. Duhamel (CAN, Honda); 3. Spies (Suzuki); 4. Hodgson (GB, Ducati); 5. Ku. Roberts (Honda); 6. Rapp (Suzuki); 7. Pridmore (Suzuki); 8. Holden (Suzuki); 9. Yates (Suzuki); 10. Pegram (Honda).

28th August - Alton
Race I: 1. Mladin (AUS, Suzuki); 2. Spies (Suzuki); 3. Yates (Suzuki); 4. Zemke (Honda); 5. Mi. Duhamel (CAN, Honda); 6. E. Bostrom (Ducati); 7. Hayes (Kawasaki); 8. Craggill (AUS, Suzuki); 9. Toye (Honda); 10. Acree (Suzuki).
Race II: 1. Mladin (AUS, Suzuki); 2. Yates (Suzuki); 3. Spies (Suzuki); 4. Mi. Duhamel (CAN, Honda); 5. Hodgson (Ducati); 6. Hayes (Kawasaki); 7. E. Bostrom (Ducati); 8. Pridmore (Suzuki); 9. Rapp (Suzuki); 10. C.-D. West (Suzuki).

4th September - Braselton
Race I: 1. Mladin (AUS, Suzuki); 2. Spies (Suzuki); 3. Mi. Duhamel (CAN, Honda); 4. Hodgson (GB, Ducati); 5. E. Bostrom (Ducati); 6. Hayes (Kawasaki); 7. Pridmore (Suzuki); 8. Ku. Roberts (Honda); 9. Craggill (AUS, Suzuki); 10. Acree (Suzuki).
Race II: 1. Yates (Suzuki); 2. Spies (Suzuki); 3. Hodgson (GB, Ducati); 4. Mladin (AUS, Suzuki); 5. Zemke (Honda); 6. Hayes (Kawasaki); 7. Pridmore (Suzuki); 8. E. Bostrom (Ducati); 9. Mi. Duhamel (CAN, Honda); 10. Rapp (Suzuki).

FINAL CLASSIFICATION
1. Mathew Mladin (AUS)   Suzuki   536
2. Ben Spies   Suzuki   514
3. Eric Bostrom   Ducati   431

4. A. Yates (Suzuki), 414; 5. M. Duhamel (CAN, Honda), 392; 6. N. Hodgson (GB, Ducati), 384; 7. M. Cragill (AUS, Suzuki), 331; 8. S. Rapp (Suzuki), 305; 9. L. Acree (Suzuki), 301; 10. J. Zemke (Honda), 265.

XTREME

12th March
1. Mi. Duhamel (CAN, Honda); 2. Ku. Roberts (Honda); 3. Zemke (Honda); 4. Eslick (Suzuki); 5. Peris (Yamaha); 6. Perez (Yamaha); 7. Barnes (Yamaha); 8. Howard (Yamaha); 9. Knapp (Yamaha); 10. Turner (IRL, Yamaha).

24th April - Birmingham
1. Zemke (Honda); 2. Mi. Duhamel (CAN, Honda); 3. Haskovec (Suzuki); 4. Attard (Kawasaki); 5. Peris (Yamaha); 6. Picotte (Yamaha); 7. Crevier (Honda); 8. Moore (Yamaha); 9. Caylor (Suzuki); 10. Andrews (Ducati).

1st May - Fontana
1. Zemke (Honda); 2. Mi. Duhamel (CAN, Honda); 3. Haskovec (Suzuki); 4. Eslick (Suzuki); 5. Moore (Yamaha); 6. Caylor (Suzuki); 7. Al. Gobert (AUS, Honda); 8. Small (Yamaha); 9. Andrews (Ducati); 10. J.-L. Filice (Honda).

15th May - Sonoma
1. Zemke (Honda); 2. Mi. Duhamel (CAN, Honda); 3. Attard (Kawasaki); 4. Jensen (Yamaha); 5. Peris (Yamaha); 6. Eslick (Suzuki); 7. Al. Gobert (AUS, Honda); 8. McBain (Yamaha); 9. Caylor (Suzuki); 10. Lacombe (Suzuki).

22nd May - Fountain
1. Zemke (Honda); 2. Mi. Duhamel (CAN, Honda); 3. Attard (Kawasaki); 4. Peris (Yamaha); 5. Eslick (Suzuki); 6. Barnes (Suzuki); 7. Moore (Yamaha); 8. Al. Gobert (AUS, Honda); 9. Andrews (Ducati); 10. Ferrer (Yamaha).

5th June - Elkhart Lake
1. Mi. Duhamel (CAN, Honda); 2. Zemke (Honda); 3. Barnes (Suzuki); 4. Attard (Kawasaki); 5. Eslick (Suzuki); 6. Al. Gobert (AUS, Honda); 7. Hale (Honda); 8. Jensen (Yamaha); 9. Chirinos (Yamaha); 10. J.-L. Filice (Honda).

24th July - Lexington
1. Zemke (Honda); 2. Mi. Duhamel (CAN, Honda); 3. Ku. Roberts (Honda); 4. Barnes (Suzuki); 5. Attard (Kawasaki); 6. Howard (Yamaha); 7. Jensen (Yamaha); 8. Peris (Yamaha); 9. Eslick (Suzuki); 10. Caylor (Suzuki).

28th August - Alton
1. Mi. Duhamel (CAN, Honda); 2. Zemke (Honda); 3. Jensen (Yamaha); 4. Attard (Kawasaki); 5. Barnes (Suzuki); 6. Caylor (Suzuki); 7. Moore (Yamaha); 8. Andrews (Ducati); 9. Hale (Honda); 10. Yonce (Yamaha).

4th September - Braselton
1. Mi. Duhamel (CAN, Honda); 2. Attard (Kawasaki); 3. Barnes (Suzuki); 4. D. Eslick (Suzuki); 5. Jensen (Yamaha); 6. Peris (Yamaha); 7. Caylor (Suzuki); 8. Andrews (Ducati); 9. Al. Gobert (AUS, Honda); 10. Hale (Honda).

FINAL CLASSIFICATION
1. Miguel Duhamel (CAN)   Honda   314
2. Joshua Zemke   Honda   295
3. Danny C. Eslick   Suzuki 198

4. B. Attard (Kawasaki), 187; 5. Al. Gobert (AUS, Honda), 175; 6. M. Barnes (Suzuki), 160; 7. C. Peris (Yamaha), 160; 8. N. Moore (Yamaha), 158; 9. O. Caylor (Suzuki), 139; 10. T. Knapp (Yamaha), 139.

GERMANY CHAMPIONSHIP

125

15th May - Lausitz
1. Ranseder (A, KTM); 2. S. Bradl (KTM); 3. Mickan (Honda); 4. R. Krummenacher (CH, Honda); 5. Fröhlich (Honda); 6. Eitzinger (A, Honda); 7. Van den Dragt (NL, Honda); 8. Aegerter (CH, Honda); 9. Lässer (KTM); 10. Kaulbach (Honda).

5th June - Pannoniaring - Hongrie
1. S. Bradl (KTM); 2. Ranseder (A, KTM); 3. Kalab (CZ, Aprilia); 4. Unger (Aprilia); 5. Wirsing (KTM); 6. Vostarek (CZ, Honda); 7. Michels (Honda); 8. R. Krummenacher (CH, Honda); 9. Mickan (Honda); 10. Aegerter (CH, Honda).

19th June - Nürburgring
1. Ranseder (A, KTM); 2. R. Krummenacher (CH, Honda); 3. Unger (Aprilia); 4. Kalab (CZ, Aprilia); 5. S. Bradl (KTM); 6. Lässer (KTM); 7. Eitzinger (A, Honda); 8. Mickan (Honda); 9. Vostarek (CZ, Honda); 10. Fröhlich (Honda).

3rd July - Salzburgring - Austria
1. Ranseder (A, KTM); 2. S. Bradl (KTM); 3. Unger (Aprilia); 4. Kalab (CZ, Aprilia); 5. Mickan (Honda); 6. Aegerter (CH, Honda); 7. Eitzinger (A, Honda); 8. Fröhlich (Honda); 9. R. Krummenacher (CH, Honda); 10. Vostarek (CZ, Honda).

7th August - Schleiz
1. Bradl (KTM); 2. Fröhlich (Honda); 3. Ranseder (A, KTM); 4. Unger (Aprilia); 5. Mickan (Honda); 6. Minnerop (Honda); 7. Aegerter (CH, Honda); 8. Litjens (NL, Honda); 9. Puffe (Honda); 10. Kalab (CZ, Aprilia).

4th September - Oschersleben
1. Ranseder (A, KTM); 2. Fröhlich (Honda); 3. S. Bradl (KTM); 4. Unger (Aprilia); 5. Eitzinger (A, Hnda); 6. Mickan (Honda); 7. Hübsch (Honda); 8. Litjens (NL, Honda); 9. Aegerter (CH, Honda); 10. Michels (Honda).

18th September - Sachsenring
1. S. Bradl (KTM); 2. Unger (Aprilia); 3. Fröhlich (Honda); 4. Kalab (CZ, Aprilia); 5. Van den Berg (NL, Aprilia); 6. Eitzinger (A, Honda); 7. Lässer (KTM); 8. R. Krummenacher (CH, Honda); 9. Minnerop (Honda); 10. Aegerter (CH, Honda).

2nd October - Hockenheim
1. Ranseder (A, KTM); 2. S. Bradl (KTM); 3. Fröhlich (Honda); 4. Kalab (CZ, Aprilia); 5. Minnerop (Honda); 6. Michels (Honda); 7. Eitzinger (A, Honda); 8. Lässer (KTM); 9. R. Krummenacher (CH, Honda); 10. Mayer (Aprilia).

FINAL CLASSIFICATION
1. Stefan Bradl   KTM   162
2. Michael Ranseder (A)   KTM   161
3. Patrick Unger   Aprilia 107

4. G. Fröhlich (Honda), 96; 5. I. Kalab (CZ, Aprilia), 78; 6. R. Krummenacher (CH, Honda), 63; 7. M. Mickan (Honda), 60; 8. P. Eitzinger (A, Honda), 59; 9. D. Aegerter (CH, Honda), 54 ; 10. R. Lässer (KTM), 49.

SUPERSPORT

15th May - Lausitz
1. Tode (Honda); 2. Andersen (N, Kawasaki); 3. Kaufmann (Yamaha); 4. Günther (Honda); 5. Solberg (N, Yamaha); 6. Raschle (CH, Honda); 7. Prinz (Yamaha); 8. Seidel (Honda); 9. Richter (Yamaha); 10. Jesek (CZ, Kawasaki).

5th June - Pannoniaring - Hungary
1. Andersen (N, Kawasaki); 2. Damen (B, Honda); 3. Kerbl (A, Honda); 4. Solberg (N, Yamaha); 5. Richter (Yamaha); 6. Fzekely (H, Honda); 7. Maehr (A, Suzuki); 8. Prinz (Yamaha); 9. Seidel (Honda); 10. Bildl (Kawasaki).

19th June - Nürburgring
1. Andersen (N, Kawasaki); 2. Daemen (B, Honda); 3. Tode (Honda); 4. Kaufmann (Yamaha); 5. Stamm (CH, Suzuki); 6. Günther (Honda); 7. Richter (Yamaha); 8. Solberg (N, Yamaha); 9. Seidel (Honda); 10. Van de Lagemaat (NL, Honda).

3rd July - Salzburgring - Austria
1. Kaufmann (Yamaha); 2. Kerbl (A, Honda); 3. Solberg (N, Yamaha); 4. Mähr (A, Suzuki); 5. Günther (Honda); 6. Stamm (CH, Suzuki); 7. Mayrhofer (Yamaha); 8. Ahnendorp (NL, Honda); 9. Lukaseder (A, Honda); 10. Bergau (Honda).

7th August - Schleiz
1. Kaufmann (Yamaha); 2. Andersen (N, Kawasaki); 3. Daemen (B, Honda); 4. Stamm (CH, Suzuki); 5. Richter (Yamaha); 6. Tode (Honda); 7. Günther (Honda); 8. Ahnendorp (NL, Honda); 9. Mähr (A, Suzuki); 10. Seidel (Honda).

4th September - Oschersleben
1. Kaufmann (Yamaha); 2. Stamm (CH, Suzuki); 3. Günther (Honda); 4. Solberg (N, Yamaha); 5. Richter (Yamaha); 6. Ivanov (Rus, Yamaha); 7. Ahnendrop (NL, Honda); 8. Andersen (N, Kawasaki); 9. Prinz (Yamaha); 10. Bergau (Honda).

18th September - Sachsenring
1. Andersen (N, Kawasaki); 2. Tode (Honda); 3. Stamm (CH, Suzuki); 4. Kaufmann (Yamaha); 5. Günther (Honda); 6. Solberg (N, Yamaha); 7. Johnson (AUS, Yamaha); 8. Prinz (Yamaha); 9. Ahnendrop (NL, Honda); 10. Mähr (A, Suzuki).

2nd October - Hockenheim
1. Andersen (N, Kawasaki); 2. Tode (Honda); 3. Stamm (CH, Suzuki); 4. Solberg (N, Yamaha); 5. Kaufmann (Yamaha); 6. Günther (Honda); 7. Ahnendrop (NL, Honda); 8. Prinz (Yamaha); 9. Mähr (A, Suzuki); 10. Ivanov (RUS, Yamaha).

FINAL CLASSIFICATION
1. Kai Borre Andersen (N)   Kawasaki   148
2. Herbert Kaufmann   Yamaha   128
3. Arne Tode   Honda   98

4. T. Solberg (N, Yamaha), 92; 5. R. Stamm (CH, Suzuki), 87; 6. J. Günther (Honda), 82; 7. R. Mähr (A, Suzuki), 80; 8. W. Daemen (B, Honda), 56; 9. N. Prinz (Yamaha), 52; 10. R. Richter (Yamaha), 51.

SUPERBIKE

15th May - Lausitz
Race I: 1. Teuchert (MV-Agusta); 2. Nebel (Yamaha); 3. Hafenegger (Yamaha); 4. Schulten (Honda); 5. Knobloch (Yamaha); 6. Bauer (A, Honda); 7. Meklau (A, Suzuki); 8. Wegscheider (I, Suzuki); 9. Lindström (S, Kawasaki); 10. Kellner (Suzuki).
Race II: 1. Teuchert (MV-Agusta); 2. Meklau (A, Suzuki); 3. Hafenegger (Yamaha); 4. Schulten (Honda); 5. Nebel (Yamaha); 6. Bauer (A, Honda); 7. Ulm (A, Yamaha); 8. Wegscheider (I, Suzuki); 9. Knobloch (A, Yamaha); 10. Daemen (B, Honda).

5th June - Pannoniaring - Hungary
Race I: 1. Meklau (A, Suzuki); 2. Wegscheider (I, Suzuki); 3. Nebel (Yamaha); 4. Knobloch (Yamaha); 5. Teuchert (MV-Agusta); 6. Bauer (A, Honda); 7. Ulm (A, Yamaha); 8. Waldmann (Honda); 9. Hahn (Kawasaki); 10. Schulten (Honda).
Race II: 1. Meklau (A, Suzuki); 2. Nebel (Yamaha); 3. Teuchert (MV-Agusta); 4. Hafenegger (Yamaha); 5. Lindström (S, Kawasaki); 6. Knobloch (Yamaha); 7. Bauer (A, Honda); 8. Ulm (A, Yamaha); 9. Kellner (Suzuki); 10. Waldmann (Honda).

19th June - Nürburgring
Race I: 1. Curtain (AUS, Yamaha); 2. Knobloch (A, Yamaha); 3. Nebel (Yamaha); 4. Parkes (AUS, Yamaha); 5. Van Keymeulen (B, Yamaha); 6. Schulten (Honda); 7. Meklau (A, Suzuki); 8. Ulm (A, Yamaha); 9. Hafenegger (Yamaha); 10. Wegscheider (I, Suzuki).
Race II: 1. Curtain (AUS, Yamaha); 2. Nebel (Yamaha); 3. Schulten (Honda); 4. Parkes (AUS, Yamaha); 5. Hafenegger (Yamaha); 6. Meklau (A, Suzuki); 7. Ulm (A, Yamaha); 8. Bauer (A, Honda); 9. Hahn (Kawasaki); 10. Wegscheider (I, Suzuki).

3rd July - Salzburgring - Austria
Race I: 1. Hafenegger (Yamaha); 2. Nebel (Yamaha); 3. Schulten (Honda); 4. Meklau (A, Suzuki); 5. Wegscheider (I, Suzuki); 6. Kellner (Suzuki); 7. Ulm (A, Yamaha); 8. Knobloch (A, Yamaha); 9. Waldmann (Honda); 10. Bauer (A, Honda).
Race II: 1. Nebel (Yamaha); 2. Hafenegger (Yamaha); 3. Schulten (Honda); 4. Knobloch (A, Yamaha); 5. Zaiser (A, Suzuki); 6. Daemen (B, Honda); 7. Meklau (A, Suzuki); 8. Bauer (A, Honda); 9. Hahn (Kawasaki); 10. Teuchert (MV-Agusta).

7th August - Schleiz
Race I: 1. Schulten (Honda); 2. Teuchert (MV-Agusta); 3. Wegscheider (I, Suzuki); 4. Nebel (Yamaha); 5. Waldmann (Honda); 6. Hafenegger (Yamaha); 7. Ulm (A, Yamaha); 8. Meklau (A, Suzuki); 9. Kellner (Suzuki); 10. Hahn (Kawasaki).
Race II: 1. Schulten (Honda); 2. Nebel (Yamaha); 3. Kellner (Suzuki); 4. Meklau (A, Suzuki); 5. Knobloch (A, Yamaha); 6. Bauer (A, Honda); 7. Ulm (A, Yamaha); 8. Daemen (B, Honda); 9. Hafenegger (Yamaha); 10. Ulm (A, Yamaha).

4th September - Oschersleben
Race I: 1. Schulten (Honda); 2. Nebel (Yamaha); 3. Meklau (A, Suzuki); 4. Kellner (Suzuki); 5. Ulm (A, Yamaha); 6. Knobloch (A, Yamaha); 7. Waldmann (Honda); 8. Bauer (A, Honda); 9. Wegscheider (I, Suzuki); 10. Hafenegger (Yamaha).

THE RESULTS OF THE OTHER CHAMPIONSHIPS

Race II: 1. Meklau (A, Suzuki); 2. Schulten (Honda); 3. Nebel (Yamaha); 4. Teuchert (MV-Agusta); 5. Waldmann (Honda); 6. Hafenegger (Yamaha); 7. Kellner (Suzuki); 8. Bauer (A, Honda); 9. Wegscheider (I, Suzuki); 10. Ulm (A, Yamaha).

18th September - Sachsenring
Race I: 1. Bauer (A, Honda); 2. Schulten (Honda); 3. Teuchert (MV-Agusta); 4. Nebel (Yamaha); 5. Hafenegger (Yamaha); 6. Kellner (Suzuki); 7. Meklau (A, Suzuki); 8. Knobloch (A, Suzuki); 9. Hahn (Kawasaki); 10. Lindström (S, Kawasaki).
Race II: 1. Bauer (A, Honda); 2. Meklau (A, Suzuki); 3. Nebel (Yamaha); 4. Kellner (Suzuki); 5. Wegscheider (I, Suzuki); 6. Knobloch (A, Yamaha); 7. Ulm (A, Yamaha); 8. Hahn (Kawasaki); 9. Lindström (S, Kawasaki); 10. Lammert (Suzuki).

2nd October - Hockenheim
Race I: 1. Nebel (Yamaha); 2. Bauer (A, Honda); 3. Knobloch (A, Yamaha); 4. Hafenegger (Yamaha); 5. Kellner (Suzuki); 6. Meklau (A, Suzuki); 7. Wegscheider (I, Suzuki); 8. Lindström (S, Kawasaki); 9. Hahn (Kawasaki); 10. Leuthard (CH, Yamaha).
Race II: 1. Schulten (Honda); 2. Nebel (Yamaha); 3. Hafenegger (Yamaha); 4. Teuchert (MV-Agusta); 5. Bauer (A, Honda); 6. Meklau (A, Suzuki); 7. Wegscheider (I, Suzuki); 8. Kellner (Suzuki); 9. Hahn (Kawasaki); 10. Lindström (S, Kawasaki).

FINAL CLASSIFICATION
1. Stefan Nebel — Yamaha — 300
2. Andreas Meklau (A) — Suzuki — 241
3. Michael Schulten — Honda — 224

4. P. Hafenegger (Yamaha), 193; 5. M. Bauer (A, Honda), 181; 6. J. Teuchert (MV-Agusta), 149; 7. G. Knobloch (A, Yamaha), 146; 8. M. Wegscheider (I, Suzuki), 132; 9. C. Kellner (Suzuki), 130; 10. R. Ulm (A, Yamaha), 111.

SIDE-CARS

15th May - Lausitz
1. Roscher/Hänni (D/CH, LCR-Suzuki); 2. Moser/Wäfler (A/CH, LCR-Honda); 3. J. Steinhausen/Kölsch (LCR-Suzuki); 4. Centner (LCR-Yamaha); 5. Göttlich/Höss (LCR-Suzuki); 6. Schlosser/Kolloch (CH/D, LCR-Suzuki); 7. Hainbucher/Adelsberger (A, RSR-Suzuki); 8. Schröder (CH, LCR-Suzuki); 9. Eilers/Freund (LCR-Suzuki); 10. Kohlmann/Anderle (LCR-Suzuki).

5th June - Pannoniaring - Hungary
1. J. Steinhausen/Kölsch (LCR-Suzuki); 2. Laidlow/Farrance (GB, LCR-Suzuki); 3. Moser/Wäfler (A/CH, LCR-Honda); 4. Roscher/Hänni (D/CH, LCR-Suzuki); 5. Schlosser/Kolloch (CH/D, LCR-Suzuki); 6. M. Grabmüller/B. Grabmüller (A, LCR-Yamaha); 7. Hainbucher/Adelsberger (A, RSR-Suzuki); 8. Göttlich/Höss (LCR-Suzuki); 9. Kohlmann/Anderle (LCR-Suzuki); 10. Nagel/Hildebrandt (LCR-Suzuki).

19th June - Nürburgring
1. J. Steinhausen/Kölsch (LCR-Suzuki); 2. Moser/Wäfler (A/CH, LCR-Honda); 3. Roscher/Hänni (D/CH, LCR-Suzuki); 4. Doppler/Wagner (A, LCR-Yamaha); 5. Laidlow/Farrance (GB, LCR-Suzuki); 6. Schröder/Burkard (CH, LCR-Suzuki); 7. Hainbucher/Adelsberger (A, RSR-Suzuki); 8. M. Grabmüller/B. Grabmüller (A, LCR-Yamaha); 9. Hock/Becker (Hock-Kawasaki); 10. Eilers/Freund (LCR-Suzuki).

3rd July - Salzburgring - Austria
1. J. Steinhausen/Kölsch (LCR-Suzuki); 2. Moser/Wäfler (A/CH, LCR-Honda); 3. Laidlow/Farrance (GB, LCR-Suzuki); 4. Roscher/Hänni (D/CH, LCR-Suzuki); 5. Doppler/Wagner (A, LCR-Yamaha); 6. Schlosser/Kolloch (CH/D, LCR-Suzuki); 7. Hainbucher/Adelsberger (A, RSR-Suzuki); 8. Hauzenberger/Wechselberger (A, Yamaha); 9. Schröder/Burkard (CH, LCR-Suzuki); 10. M. Grabmüller/B. Grabmüller (A, LCR-Yamaha).

7th August - Schleiz
1. Hock/Becker (Hock-Kawasaki); 2. Göttlich/Höss (LCR-Suzuki); 3. Schlosser/Kolloch (CH/D, LCR-Suzuki); 4. Eilers/Freund (LCR-Suzuki); 5. Hainbucher/Adelsberger (A, RSR-Suzuki); 6. Moser/Wäfler (A, LCR-Honda); 7. Schröder/Burkard (CH, LCR-Suzuki); 8. Zimmermann/Ziegler (LCR-Suzuki); 9. Hagel/Hildebrandt (LCR-Suzuki); 10. Kohlmann/Anderle (LCR-Suzuki).

4th September - Oschersleben
1. J. Steinhausen/Kölsch (LCR-Suzuki); 2. Moser/Wäfler (A/CH, LCR-Honda); 3. Schlosser/Kolloch (CH/D, LCR-Suzuki); 4. Hock/Becker (Hock-Kawasaki); 5. Göttlich/Höss (LCR-Suzuki); 6. Eilers/Freund (LCR-Suzuki); 7. Hainbucher/Adelsberger (A, RSR-Suzuki); 8. Zimmermann/Ziegler (LCR-Suzuki); 9. Kohlmann/Anderle (LCR-Suzuki); 10. Dagnino/Wedele (I/D, LCR-Suzuki).

18th September - Sachsenring
1. Moser/Wäfler (A/CH, LCR-Honda); 2. Roscher/Hänni (D/CH, LCR-Suzuki); 3. Schlosser/Kolloch (CH/D, LCR-Suzuki); 4. Doppler/Wagner (A, LCR-Yamaha); 5. Göttlich/Höss (LCR-Suzuki); 6. Hock/Becker (Hock-Kawasaki); 7. Hainbucher/Adelsberger (A, RSR-Suzuki); 8. Eilers/Freund (LCR-Suzuki); 9. Schröder/Burkard (CH, LCR-Suzuki); 10. Zimmermann/Ziegler (LCR-Suzuki).

2nd October - Hockenheim
1. J. Steinhausen/Kölsch (LCR-Suzuki); 2. Schlosser/Kolloch (CH/D, LCR-Suzuki); 3. Moser/Wäfler (A/CH, LCR-Honda); 4. Hock/Becker (Hock-Kawasaki); 5. Roscher/Hänni (D/CH, LCR-Suzuki); 6. Doppler/Wagner (A, LCR-Yamaha); 7. Hainbucher/Adelsberger (A, RSR-Suzuki); 8. Eilers/Freund (LCR-Suzuki); 9. Kohlmann/Anderle (LCR-Suzuki); 10. Zimmermann/Ziegler (LCR-Suzuki).

FINAL CLASSIFICATION
1. Moser/Wäfler (A/CH) — LCR-Honda — 151
2. J. Steinhausen/Kölsch — LCR-Suzuki — 141
3. Roscher/Hänni (D/CH) — LCR-Suzuki — 101

4. Schlosser/Kolloch (CH/D, LCR-Suzuki), 101; 5. Hainbucher/Adelsberger (A, RSR-Suzuki), 75; 6. Hock/Becker (Hock-Kawasaki), 68; 7. Göttlich/Höss (LCR-Suzuki), 62; 8. Eilers/Freund (LCR-Suzuki), 62; 9. Kohlmann/Anderle (LCR-Suzuki), 48; 10. Doppler/Wagner (A, LCR-Yamaha), 47.

SPAIN CHAMPIONSHIP

125
2004

14th November - Valencia
1. Gadea (Aprilia); 2. J. Miralles Junior (Aprilia); 3. Sandi (I, Aprilia); 4. Ranseder (A, KTM); 5. M. Hernandez Junior (Aprilia); 6. Faubel (Aprilia); 7. Tamburini (I, Aprilia); 8. Espargaro (Honda); 9. Bonache (Honda); 10. De Rosa (I, Aprilia).

21st November - Jerez de la Frontera
1. Corsi (I, Aprilia); 2. Hommel (I, Aprilia); 3. Ranseder (A, KTM); 4. Espargaro (Honda); 5. Sandi (I, Aprilia); 6. Danese (I, Aprilia); 7. De Rosa (I, Aprilia); 8. Tuñez (Aprilia); 9. Gadea (Aprilia); 10. Nakajo (J, Honda).

FINAL CLASSIFICATION
1. Aleix Espargaro — Honda — 88
2. Julian Miralles Jnr — Aprilia — 81
3. Manuel Hernandez Jnr — Aprilia — 77

4. Terol, 58; 5. Carchano, 56; 6. Sandi (I, Aprilia), 49; 7. Jerez (Honda), 48; 8. Danese (I, Aprilia), 44; 9. Iannone (I, Aprilia), 37; 10. Bonache (Honda), 35.

2005

8th May - Albacete
1. Saez (Aprilia); 2. Bianco (I, Aprilia); 3. Grotzkyj (I, Aprilia); 4. Tuñez (Aprilia); 5. Castelo (Honda); 6. Van den Berg (NL, Aprilia); 7. Vazquez (Honda); 8. Garrido (Honda); 9. Tutusaus (Honda); 10. B. Smith (GB, Honda).

19th June - Valencia
1. Tuñez (Aprilia); 2. Bianco (I, Aprilia); 3. Espargaro (Honda); 4. Tamburini (I, Aprilia); 5. Sommer (D, Honda); 6. Vazquez (Honda); 7. Saez (Aprilia); 8. Tutusaus (Honda); 9. Perren (ARG, Honda); 10. Baroni (I, Aprilia).

17th July - Catalunya
1. Tuñez (Aprilia); 2. Bianco (I, Aprilia); 3. Sommer (D, Honda); 4. Bonache (Honda); 4. Ramos Alvaro (Aprilia); 5. Vazquez (Honda); 6. Tutusaus (Honda); 7. P. Espargaró (Honda); 8. Smith (GB, Honda); 9. Jerez (Derbi); 10. Tamburini (I, Aprilia).

4th September - Jerez de la Frontera
1. Tuñez (Aprilia); 2. Vazquez (Honda); 3. P. Espargaro (Honda); 4. Coghlan (GB, Honda); 5. Smith (GB, Honda); 6. Bianco (I, Aprilia); 7. Tamburini (I, Aprilia); 8. Webb (GB, Honda); 9. Bonache (Aprilia); 10. Petrini (I, Aprilia).

9th October - Albacete
1. Smith (GB, Honda); 2. Bianco (I, Aprilia); 3. Vazquez (Honda); 4. Tamburini (I, Aprilia); 5. Cluzel (F, Honda); 6. Sommer (D, Honda); 7. Petrini (I, Aprilia); 8. P. Espargaró (Honda); 9. Coghlan (GB, Honda); 10. Tuñez (Aprilia).

(*) : Les deux dernières races (Valencia le 20 et Jerez de la Frontera, le 27 novembre) se sont déroulées après le bouclement rédactionnel de «L'Année Grands Prix Moto».

SUPERSPORT
2004

14th Nvoember - Valencia
1. Tizon (Yamaha); 2. Fores (Suzuki); 3. Tiberio (F, Yamaha); 4. Perez (Honda); 5. Salom (Yamaha); 6. Torres (Honda); 7. Abellan (Yamaha); 8. Ortega (Yamaha); 9. Piñera (Yamaha); 10. Steenhoudt (Yamaha).

21st November - Jerez de la Frontera
1. Cardeñas (COL, Yamaha); 2. Fores (Suzuki); 3. Piñera (Yamaha); 4. Jara (Yamaha); 5. Ortega (Suzuki); 6. Mazuecos (Yamaha); 7. Tizon (Yamaha); 8. Steenhoudt (Yamaha); 9. Perez (Honda); 10. Salom (Yamaha).

FINAL CLASSIFICATION
1. Martin Cardeñas (COL) — Yamaha — 116
2. Arturo Tizon — Yamaha — 95
3. Javier Fores — Suzuki — 89

4. Carrasco (Honda), 81; 5. Mazuecos (Yamaha), 61; 6. Jara (Yamaha), 53; 7. Salom (Yamaha), 52; 8. Lozano (Yamaha), 48; 9. Perez (Honda), 46; 10. Delgado (Yamaha), 41.

2005

8th May - Albacete
1. Tizon (Yamaha); 2. Carrasco (Yamaha); 3. Piñera (Kawasaki); 4. Torres (Yamaha); 5. Lascorz (Honda); 6. Bonastre (Yamaha); 7. Salom (Suzuki); 8. I. Martinez (Yamaha); 9. Pedro (Yamaha); 10. Aldoma (Yamaha).

19th June - Valencia
1. Carrasco (Yamaha); 2. Tizon (Yamaha); 3. Torres (Yamaha); 4. Salom (Suzuki); 5. Araujo (Honda); 6. Piñera (Kawasaki); 7. Ortega (Suzuki); 8. Barragan (Honda); 9. I. Martinez (Yamaha); 10. Rivas (Honda).

17th July - Catalunya
1. Tizon (Yamaha); 2. Salom (Suzuki); 3. Araujo (Honda); 4. Barragan (Honda); 5. Aldoma (Yamaha); 6. Hidalgo (Honda); 7. Ortega (Suzuki); 8. Gamell (Yamaha); 9. I. Martinez (Yamaha); 10. Rodriguez (Yamaha).

4th September - Jerez de la Frontera
1. Tizon (Yamaha); 2. Carrasco (Yamaha); 3. Torres (Yamaha); 4. Piñera (Kawasaki); 5. Lascorz (Honda); 6. Barragan (Honda); 7. Hidalgo (Honda); 8. Lozano (Suzuki); 9. I. Martinez (Yamaha); 10. Aguilar (Yamaha).

9th October - Albacete
1. Tizon (Yamaha); 2. Carrasco (Yamaha); 3. Torres (Yamaha); 4. Bonastre (Yamaha); 5. Lascorz (Honda); 6. Lozano (Suzuki); 7. Garrido (Yamaha); 8. Torres (Yamaha); 9. Moral (Aprilia); 10. Hidalgo (Honda).

(*) : Les deux dernières races (Valencia le 20 et Jerez de la Frontera, le 27 novembre) se sont déroulées après le bouclement rédactionnel de «L'Année Grands Prix Moto».

FORMULA EXTREME
2004

14th November - Valencia
1. Cardoso (Yamaha); 2. De Gea (Honda); 3. Tomas (Yamaha); 4. L. Oliver (Suzuki); 5. Del Amor (Yamaha); 6. Ribalta (Yamaha); 7. Sarda (Kawasaki); 8. Fernandez (Yamaha); 9. Vallcañeras (Yamaha); 10. Scassa (I, Yamaha).

21st November - Jerez de la Frontera
1. Cardoso (Yamaha); 2. Tomas (Yamaha); 3. De Gea (Honda); 4. Morales (Yamaha); 5. L. Oliver (Suzuki); 6. Ribalta (Yamaha); 7. Silva (Yamaha); 8. Sarda (Kawasaki); 9. Noyes (Honda); 10. Fernandez (Yamaha).

FINAL CLASSIFICATION
1. José Luis Cardoso — Yamaha — 166
2. Iván Silva — Yamaha — 113
3. José David De Gea — Honda — 91

4. Tomas (Yamaha), 90 ; 5. Del Amor (Yamaha), 71 ; 6. Ribalta (Yamaha), 68 ; 7. L. Oliver (Suzuki), 56 ; 8. Fernandez (Yamaha), 48 ; 9. Monge (Yamaha), 44 ; 10. Sarda (Kawasaki), 39.

2005

8th May - Albacete
1. Silva (Yamaha); 2. Monge (Yamaha); 3. Del Amor (Yamaha); 4. De Gea (Honda); 5. Morales (Suzuki); 6. Sarda (Yamaha); 7. Fernandez (Yamaha); 8. Mazuecos (Yamaha); 9. Fuertes (Suzuki); 10. Vallcañeras (Yamaha).

19th June - Valencia
1. De Gea (Honda); 2. Silva (Yamaha); 3. Del Amor (Yamaha); 4. Sarda (Yamaha); 5. Monge (Yamaha); 6. Morales (Suzuki); 7. Tomas (Honda); 8. Fernandez (Yamaha); 9. Ribalta (Yamaha); 10. Pandilla (Kawasaki).

17th July - Catalunya
1. Tomas (Honda); 2. Del Amor (Yamaha); 3. De Gea (Honda); 4. Silva (Yamaha); 5. Ribalta (Suzuki); 6. Morales (Yamaha); 7. Noyes (Yamaha); 8. Monge (Yamaha); 9. Fernandez (Suzuki); 10. Mazuecos (Yamaha).

4th September - Jerez de la Frontera
1. De Gea (Honda); 2. Monge (Yamaha); 3. Morales (Suzuki); 4. Del Amor (Yamaha); 5. Sarda (Yamaha); 6. Tomas (Honda); 7. Noyes (Yamaha); 8. J. Gomez (Suzuki); 9. Casas (Suzuki); 10. Mazuecos (Yamaha).

THE RESULTS OF THE OTHER CHAMPIONSHIPS

9th October - Albacete

1. De Gea (Honda); 2. Del Amor (Yamaha); 3. Tomas (Honda); 4. Silva (Yamaha); 5. Monge (Yamaha); 6. Fernandez (Yamaha); 7. Noyes (Yamaha); 8. D. Gomez (Kawasaki); 9. J. Gomez (Suzuki); 10. Pandilla (Kawasaki).

(*) : Les deux dernières races (Valencia le 20 et Jerez de la Frontera, le 27 novembre) se sont déroulées après le bouclement rédactionnel de «L'Année Grands Prix Moto».

FRANCE CHAMPIONSHIP

125

20th March - Le Mans

1. Gines (Honda); 2. Deschamps (Honda); 3. Dunikowski (Honda); 4. Cluzel (Honda); 5. K. Foray (Honda); 6. Lougassi (Aprilia); 7. Black (Honda); 8. Nouveau (Honda); 9. Basseville (Honda); 10. Ongaro (Honda).

27th March - Magny-Cours

1. Gines (Honda); 2. Larrive (Aprilia); 3. M. Lussiana (Honda); 4. Dunikowski (Honda); 5. Lougassi (Aprilia); 6. Deschamps (Honda); 7. Cluzel (Honda); 8. Michel (Honda); 9. Saada (Aprilia); 10. Ongaro (Honda).

24th April - Nogaro

1. Cluzel (Honda); 2. Gines (Honda); 3. M. Lussiana (Honda); 4. Dunikowski (Honda); 5. Deschamps (Honda); 6. Lemarie (Honda); 7. Michel (Honda); 8. Bonnet (Honda); 9. Chevalley (Honda); 10. Roma (Honda).

8th May - Carole

1. Larrive (Aprilia); 2. M. Lussiana (Honda); 3. Cluzel (Honda); 4. K. Foray (Honda); 5. Deschamps (Honda); 6. Violland (Aprilia); 7. Black (Honda); 8. Gines (Honda); 9. Lemarie (Honda); 10. Chevalley (Honda).

29th May - Le Vigeant

1. Gines (Honda); 2. Cluzel (Honda); 3. Black (Honda); 4. Deschamps (Honda); 5. Violland (Aprilia); 6. Bellaire (Honda); 7. Nouveau (Honda); 8. Rouvière (Honda); 9. I. Foray (Yamaha); 10. Servaes (Honda).

19th June - Lédenon

1. Gines (Honda); 2. Black (Honda); 3. Deschamps (Honda); 4. M. Lussiana (Honda); 5. K. Foray (Honda); 6. Dunikowski (Honda); 7. Chevalley (Honda); 8. Nouveau (Honda); 9. Michel (Honda); 10. Violland (Aprilia).

3rd July - Albi

1. Gines (Honda); 2. Dunikowski (Honda); 3. Cluzel (Honda); 4. Deschamps (Honda); 5. Chevalley (Honda); 6. Violland (Aprilia); 7. K. Foray (Honda); 8. Pernoud (Honda); 9. Rouvière (Honda); 10. Lemarie (Honda).

FINAL CLASSIFICATION

1. Mathieu Gines	Honda	153
2. Jules Cluzel	Honda	99
3. Yannick Deschamps	Honda	94

4. Dunikowski (Honda), 72; 5. M. Lussiana (Honda), 65; 6. G. Black (Honda), 54; 7. Larrive (Aprilia), 45; 8. K. Foray (Honda), 44; 9. Chevalley (Honda), 38; 10. Violland (Aprilia), 37.

SUPERSPORT

20th March - Le Mans

1. Muscat (Ducati); 2. Rogier (Yamaha); 3. Bouan (Yamaha); 4. Lefort (Yamaha); 5. Y. Lussiana (Yamaha); 6. Metro (Suzuki); 7. Pavoine (Honda); 8. Servol (Yamaha); 9. J. Petit (Honda); 10. Capela (Yamaha).

27th March - Magny-Cours

1. Muscat (Ducati); 2. J. Enjolras (Yamaha); 3. Y. Lussiana (Yamaha); 4. Metro (Suzuki); 5. Bouan (Yamaha); 6. Lefort (Yamaha); 7. Richier (Honda); 8. Capela (Yamaha); 9. Pavoine (Honda); 10. Sotter (Honda).

24th April - Nogaro

1. Muscat (Ducati); 2. Bouan (Yamaha); 3. Y. Lussiana (Yamaha); 4. Lefort (Yamaha); 5. Metro (Suzuki); 6. Servol (Yamaha); 7. J. Petit (Honda); 8. Sotter (Honda); 9. Lavandier (Honda); 10. Polesso (Yamaha).

8th May - Carole

1. Y. Lussiana (Yamaha); 2. Metro (Suzuki); 3. Bouan (Yamaha); 4. J. Petit (Honda); 5. Servol (Yamaha); 6. Capela (Yamaha); 7. Sotter (Honda); 8. Kieger (Yamaha); 9. Perret (Kawasaki); 10. Lavandier (Honda).

29th May - Le Vigeant

1. Muscat (Ducati); 2. Y. Lussiana (Yamaha); 3. J. Petit (Honda); 4. Nigon (Honda); 5. Metro (Suzuki); 6. Servol (Yamaha); 7. Lefort (Yamaha); 8. Sotter (Honda); 9. Pavoine (Honda); 10. Bonnière (Kawasaki).

19th June - Lédenon

1. Muscat (Ducati); 2. Bouan (Yamaha); 3. F. Millet (Honda); 4. Lefort (Yamaha); 5. Bouffier (Kawasaki); 6. Brian (Yamaha); 7. Pavoine (Honda); 8. Lavandier (Honda); 9. Metro (Suzuki); 10. S. Demaria (Honda).

3rd July - Albi

1. Muscat (Ducati); 2. J. Enjolras (Yamaha); 3. Bouan (Yamaha); 4. Y. Lussiana (Yamaha); 5. Metro (Suzuki); 6. Trolard (Honda); 7. Lefort (Yamaha); 8. Brian (Yamaha); 9. Le Bail (Yamaha); 10. Pavoine (Honda).

FINAL CLASSIFICATION

1. David Muscat	Ducati	150
2. Yann Lussiana	Yamaha	101
3. Denis Bouan	Yamaha	99

4. T. Metro (Suzuki), 83; 5. G. Lefort (Yamaha), 67; 6. F. Pavoine (Honda), 46; 7. J. Petit (Honda), 45; 8. J. Enjolras (Yamaha), 40; 9. R. Servol (Yamaha), 39; 10. Y. Sotter (Honda), 35.

SUPERPRODUCTION/STOCKSPORT

20th March - Le Mans

1. M. Lagrive (Suzuki SPP); 2. D. Checa (E, Yamaha SPP); 3. Piot (Kawasaki SPP); 4. Dietrich (Suzuki STK); 5. Moreira (Kawasaki STK); 6. O. Four (Suzuki STK); 7. Moisan (Kawasaki STK); 8. Lagain (Honda SPP); 9. S. Hernandez (Suzuki STK); 10. Fastre (Yamaha STK).

27th March - Magny-Cours

1. Piot (Kawasaki SPP); 2. M. Lagrive (Suzuki SPP); 3. D. Checa (E, Yamaha SPP); 4. Moreira (Kawasaki STK); 5. Dietrich (Suzuki STK); 6. Fastre (Yamaha STK); 7. O. Four (Suzuki STK); 8. S. Hernandez (Suzuki STK); 9. Gibet (Yamaha STK); 10. Protat (Yamaha SPP).

24th April - Nogaro

1. M. Lagrive (Suzuki SPP); 2. Piot (Kawasaki SPP); 3. Moreira (Kawasaki STK); 4. O. Four (Suzuki STK); 5. Dietrich (Suzuki STK); 6. Moisan (Kawasaki STK); 7. Gibet (Yamaha STK); 8. Tangre (Suzuki STK); 9. Gomez (Suzuki SPP); 10. F. Foray (Yamaha STK).

8th May - Carole

1. Fremy (Suzuki); 2. Piot (Kawasaki SPP); 3. O. Four (Suzuki STK); 4. Moisan (Kawasaki STK); 5. Moreira (Kawasaki STK); 6. Dietrich (Suzuki STK); 7. Michel (Suzuki SPP); 8. Tangre (Suzuki STK); 9. Fastre (Yamaha STK); 10. Guersillon (Suzuki STK).

29th May - Le Vigeant

1. M. Lagrive (Suzuki SPP) ; 2. Fremy (Suzuki) ; 3. Dietrich (Suzuki STK) ; 4. O. Four (Suzuki STK) ; 5. Gibet (Yamaha STK) ; 6. Tangre (Suzuki STK) ; 7. Lagain (Honda SPP) ; 8. Guersillon (Suzuki STK) ; 9. Stey (Honda SPP) ; 10. Molinier (Suzuki SPP).

19th June - Lédenon

1. Piot (Kawasaki SPP); 2. M. Lagrive (Suzuki SPP); 3. Moreira (Kawasaki STK); 4. Dietrich (Suzuki STK); 5. Moisan (Kawasaki STK); 6. J. Tangre (Suzuki STK); 7. Gibet (Yamaha STK); 8. Stey (Honda SPP); 9. C. Tangre (Suzuki STK); 10. F. Foray (Yamaha STK).

3rd July - Albi

Race I: 1. M. Lagrive (Suzuki SPP); 2. D. Checa (E, Yamaha SPP); 3. Da Costa (Kawasaki SPP); 4. Dietrich (Suzuki STK); 5. Costes (Yamaha SPP); 6. Moreira (Kawasaki STK); 7. Moisan (Kawasaki STK); 8. O. Four (Suzuki STK); 9. Stey (Honda SPP); 10. Sohier (Yamaha STK).

Race II: 1. D. Checa (E, Yamaha SPP); 2. M. Lagrive (Suzuki SPP); 3. Dietrich (Suzuki STK); 4. O. Four (Suzuki STK); 5. Moreira (Kawasaki STK); 6. Gibet (Yamaha STK); 7. Sohier (Yamaha STK); 8. Stey (Honda SPP); 9. F. Foray (Yamaha STK); 10. Guersillon (Suzuki STK).

FINAL CLASSIFICATION

1. Matthieu Lagrive	Suzuki	165
2. Olivier Four	Suzuki	108
3. Guillaume Dietrich	Suzuki	102

4. P. Piot (Kawasaki), 101; 5. F. Moreira (Kawasaki), 91; 6. R. Moisan (Kawasaki), 67; 7. A. Gibet (Yamaha), 62; 8. J. Tangre (Suzuki), 52; 9. L. Fremy (Suzuki), 45; 10. B. Stey (Honda), 32.

STOCKSPORT

1. Guillaume Dietrich	Suzuki	142
2. Olivier Four	Suzuki	138
3. Frédéric Moreira	Kawasaki	146

4. R. Moisan (Kawasaki), 94; 5. A. Gibet (Yamaha), 81; 6. J. Tangre (Suzuki), 71; 7. F. Foray (Yamaha), 51; 8. L. Fremy (Suzuki), 50; 9. P. Guersillon (Suzuki), 40; 10. C. Tangre (Suzuki), 37.

SIDE-CARS

20th March - Le Mans

1. Delannoy/Bidaut (Suzuki); 2. Baer/Rault (Suzuki); 3. Le Bail/Chaigneau (Yamaha); 4. Gallerne/Lelias (Windle); 5. Lacour/Lebeau (Suzuki); 6. S. Bessy/R. Bessy (Suzuki); 7. Bourchis/Scellier (Honda); 8. Marzelle/Lavidalie (Suzuki); 9. J.-C. Huet/J. Huet (Molyneux); 10. Beneteau/Lailheugue (Yamaha).

27th March - Magny-Cours

1. Delannoy/Bidaut (Suzuki); 2. Le Bail/Chaigneau (Yamaha); 3. Lacour/Lebeau (Suzuki); 4. Baer/Rault (Suzuki); 5. Bourchis/Scellier (Honda); 6. Hergott/Josse (Yamaha); 7. F. Leblond/S. Leblond (Honda); 8. Geffray/Mairot (Kawasaki); 9. Bajus/Darras (Yamaha); 10. Gallerne/LeLias (Windle).

24th April - Nogaro

1. Delannoy/Bidaut (Suzuki); 2. Laidlow/Farrance (GB, Suzuki); 3. J. Cluze/G. Cluze (LCR); 4. Le Bail/Chaigneau (Yamaha); 5. Baer/Rault (Suzuki); 6. Lacour/Lebeau (Suzuki); 7. Marzelle/Lavidalie (Suzuki); 8. Barbier/Barillet (Suzuki); 9. Bourchis/Scellier (Honda); 10. Ducouret/Gandois (Suzuki).

8th May - Carole

1. Delannoy/Bidaut (Suzuki); 2. Le Bail/Chaigneau (Yamaha); 3. S. Bessy/R. Bessy (Suzuki); 4. Lacour/Lebeau (Suzuki); 5. Gallerne/Le Lias (Windle); 6. Ducouret/Gandois (Suzuki); 7. Barbier/Barillet (Suzuki); 8. Bourchis/Scellier (Honda); 9. Marzelle/Lavidalie (Suzuki); 10. Bajus/Darars (Yamaha).

29th May - Le Vigeant

1. Delannoy/Bidaut (Suzuki); 2. Le Bail/Chaigneau (Yamaha); 3. Baer/Rault (Suzuki); 4. S. Bessy/R. Bessy (Suzuki); 5. Ducouret/Gandois (Suzuki); 6. Barbier/Barillet (Suzuki); 7. Marzelle/Lavidalie (Suzuki); 8. Bourchis/Scellier (Honda); 9. Lacour/Lebeau (Suzuki); 10. Guigue/Lavorel (Suzuki).

19th June - Lédenon

1. Delannoy/Bidaut (Suzuki); 2. Baer/Rault (Suzuki); 3. Lacour/Lebeau (Suzuki); 4. Le Bail/Chaigneau (Yamaha); 5. Ducouret/Gandois (Suzuki); 6. Marzelle/Lavidalie (Suzuki); 7. Pilault (Suzuki); 8. Guigue/Lavorel (Suzuki); 9. Bourchis/Scellier (Honda); 10. Beneteau/Lailheugue (Yamaha).

3rd July - Albi

Race I: 1. Delannoy/Bidaut (Suzuki); 2. Baer/Rault (Suzuki); 3. Le Bail/Chaigneau (Yamaha); 4. Lacour/Lebeau (Suzuki); 5. Barbier/Barillet (Suzuki); 6. Beneteau/Lailheugue (Yamaha); 7. Ducouret/Gandois (Suzuki); 8. Bourchis/Scellier (Honda); 9. F. Leblond/S. Leblond (Honda); 10. Bajus/Bijon (Yamaha).

Race II: 1. Delannoy/Bidaut (Suzuki); 2. Baer/Rault (Suzuki); 3. Lacour/Lebeau (Suzuki); 4. Barbier/Barillet (Suzuki); 5. Bourchis/Scellier (Honda); 6. Beneteau/Lailheugue (Yamaha); 7. Ducouret/Gandois (Suzuki); 8. Guigue/Lavorel (Suzuki); 9. J.-C. Huet/J. Huet (Molineux); 10. Bajus/Bijon (Yamaha).

FINAL CLASSIFICATION

1. Delannoy/Bidault	Suzuki	175
2. Le Bail/Chaigneau	Yamaha	117
3. Baer/Rault	Suzuki	98

4. Lacour/Lebeau (Suzuki), 88,5; 5. Bourchis/Scellier (Honda), 58,5; 6. Ducouret/Gandois (Suzuki), 48; 7. Marzelle/Lavidalie (Suzuki), 47; 8. Barbier/Barillet (Suzuki), 44; 9. S. Bessy/R. Bessy (Suzuki), 42; 10. Hergott/Joss (Yamaha), 35,5.

GREAT BRITAIN CHAMPIONSHIP

125

28th March - Brands Hatch Indy

1. Coghlan (Honda); 2. Guiver (Honda); 3. Clark (Honda); 4. Elkin (Honda); 5. Smith (Honda); 6. Webb (Honda); 7. Linfoot (Honda); 8. Morris (Honda); 9. Lowes (Honda); 10. Gault (Malaguti).

10th April - Thruxton

1. Elkin (Honda); 2. Coghlan (Honda); 3. Wilcox (Honda); 4. Clark (Honda); 5. Beech (Honda); 6. Lowes (Honda); 7. Morris (Honda); 8. Guiver (Honda); 9. Webb (Honda); 10. Pearson (Honda).

24th April - Mallory Park

1. Elkin (Honda); 2. Linfoot (Honda); 3. Guiver (Honda); 4. Beech (Honda); 5. Webb (Honda); 6. Westmoreland (Honda); 7. Pearson (Honda); 8. Wilcox (Honda); 9. Grant (Honda); 10. Kuhne (Honda).

2nd May - Oulton Park

1. Elkin (Honda); 2. Linfoot (Honda); 3. Jones (Honda); 4. Beech (Honda); 5. Guiver (Honda); 6. Grant (Honda); 7. A. Walker (Aprilia); 8. Clark (Honda); 9. Westmoreland (Honda); 10. Hayward (Honda).

15th May - Mondello Park

1. Guiver (Honda); 2. Linfoot (Honda); 3. Westmoreland (Honda); 4. Elkin (Honda); 5. Smith (Honda); 6. Weston (Honda); 7. Clark (Honda); 8. Beech (Honda); 9. Jones (Honda); 10. Webb (Honda).

5th June - Croft

1. Jones (Honda); 2. Linfoot (Honda); 3. Weston (Honda); 4. Westmoreland (Honda); 5. Guiver (Honda); 6. Wilcox (Honda); 7. Hayward (Honda); 8. Ford (Honda); 9. Elkin (Honda); 10. Lowes (Honda).

26th June - Knockhill

1. Coghlan (Honda); 2. Westmoreland (Honda); 3. Jones (Honda); 4. Smith (Honda); 5. Beech (Honda); 6. Clark (Honda); 7. W. Dunlop (Honda); 8. Cooper (Honda); 9. Guiver (Honda); 10. Weston (Honda).

10th July - Snetterton

1. Jones (Honda); 2. Guiver (Honda); 3. Westmoreland (Honda); 4. Elkin (Honda); 5. Clark (Honda); 6. Wilcox (Honda); 7. Pearson (Honda); 8. W. Dunlop (Honda); 9. Ford (Honda); 10. Pallett (Honda).

THE RESULTS OF THE OTHER CHAMPIONSHIPS

21st August - Silverstone
1. Westmoreland (Honda); 2. Jones (Honda); 3. Coghlan (Honda); 4. Smith (Honda); 5. Clark (Honda); 6. Guiver (Honda); 7. Elkin (Honda); 8. Linfoot (Honda); 9. Beech (Honda); 10. Wilcox (Honda).

29th August - Cadwell Park
1. Westmoreland (Honda); 2. Guiver (Honda); 3. Lowes (Honda); 4. Elkin (Honda); 5. Cooper (Honda); 6. Linfoot (Honda); 7. Walker (Aprilia); 8. Wilcox (Honda); 9. Weston (Honda); 10. Noon (Honda).

11th September - Oulton Park
1. Smith (Honda); 2. Guiver (Honda); 3. Westmoreland (Honda); 4. Coghlan (Honda); 5. Linfoot (Honda); 6. Beech (Honda); 7. Elkin (Honda); 8. A. Walker (Aprilia); 9. Cooper (Honda); 10. Pearson (Honda).

25th September - Donington Park
1. Westmoreland (Honda); 2. Elkin (Honda); 3. Beech (Honda); 4. Wilcox (Honda); 5. M. Lussiana (F, Honda); 6. Weston (Honda); 7. Clark (Honda); 8. Dunikowski (F, Honda); 9. Hayward (Honda); 10. Hipwell (Honda).

9th October - Brands Hatch GP
1. Elkin (Honda); 2. Lowes (Honda); 3. Linfoot (Honda); 4. Walker (Aprilia); 5. Noon (Honda); 6. Ford (Honda); 7. Weston (Honda); 8. Pallett (Honda); 9. Pearson (Honda); 10. N. Coates (Honda).

FINAL CLASSIFICATION
1. Christian Elkin — Honda — 197
2. Jack Westmoreland — Honda — 173
3. Rob Guiver — Honda — 168

4. D. Linfoot (Honda), 134; 5. C. Jones (Honda), 109; 6. K. Coghlan (Honda), 99; 7. A. Beech (Honda), 93; 8. B. Clark (Honda), 87; 9. M. Wilcox (Honda), 75; 10. B. Smith (Honda), 73.

SUPERSPORT

28th March - Brands Hatch Indy
1. J. Vincent (Honda); 2. Easton (Ducati); 3. Jones (Honda); 4. Camier (Honda); 5. Riba Cabana (E, Kawasaki); 6. E. Laverty (Honda); 7. Tunstall (Honda); 8. Murphy (Honda); 9. Quigley (Honda); 10. J. Robinson (Honda).

10th April - Thruxton
1. Camier (Honda); 2. Easton (Ducati); 3. J. Vincent (Honda); 4. Jones (Honda); 5. Murphy (Honda); 6. J. Robinson (Honda); 7. Crutchlow (Honda); 8. Riba Cabana (E, Kawasaki); 9. Sykes (Suzuki); 10. Andrews (Suzuki).

24th April - Mallory Park
1. Camier (Honda); 2. Sykes (Suzuki); 3. Jones (Honda); 4. Crutchlow (Honda); 5. J. Robinson (Honda); 6. J. Vincent (Honda); 7. Easton (Ducati); 8. Riba Cabana (E, Kawasaki); 9. Young (Honda); 10. E. Laverty (Honda).

2nd May - Oulton Park
1. Sykes (Suzuki); 2. Crutchlow (Honda); 3. Young (Honda); 4. Jones (Honda); 5. Murphy (Honda); 6. Quigley (Honda); 7. Shoesmith (Yamaha); 8. Seward (Kawasaki); 9. Longden (Honda); 10. Neate (Honda).

15th May - Mondello Park
1. Sykes (Suzuki); 2. Jones (Honda); 3. Riba Cabana (E, Kawasaki); 4. Crutchlow (Honda); 5. Easton (Ducati); 6. E. Laverty (Honda); 7. J. Robinson (Honda); 8. Owens (Honda); 9. Murphy (Honda); 10. Llewellyn (Honda).

5th June - Croft
1. Easton (Ducati); 2. Camier (Honda); 3. Jones (Honda); 4. Sykes (Suzuki); 5. Riba Cabana (E, Kawasaki); 6. J. Robinson (Honda); 7. Frost (Honda); 8. Owens (Honda); 9. Tunstall (Honda); 10. Murphy (Honda).

26th June - Knockhill
1. Camier (Honda); 2. Easton (Ducati); 3. Jones (Honda); 4. J. Robinson (Honda); 5. E. Laverty (Honda); 6. Riba Cabana (E, Kawasaki); 7. Frost (Honda); 8. Crutchlow (Honda); 9. Andrews (Suzuki); 10. Tunstall (Honda).

10th July - Snetterton
1. Camier (Honda); 2. Riba Cabana (E, Kawasaki); 3. Crutchlow (Honda); 4. J. Robinson (Honda); 5. Frost (Honda); 6. Tunstall (Honda); 7. Owens (Honda); 8. Llewellyn (Honda); 9. E. Laverty (Honda); 10. Jessopp (Ducati).

21st August - Silverstone
1. Riba Cabana (E, Kawasaki); 2. Jones (Honda); 3. Crutchlow (Honda); 4. Camier (Honda); 5. J. Robinson (Honda); 6. Easton (Ducati); 7. Da Costa (F, Suzuki); 8. Andrews (Suzuki); 9. Frost (Honda); 10. J. Vincent (Honda).

29th August - Cadwell Park
1. Crutchlow (Honda); 2. Andrews (Suzuki); 3. Camier (Honda); 4. Jones (Honda); 5. Riba Cabana (E, Kawasaki); 6. E. Laverty (Honda); 7. Frost (Honda); 8. J. Vincent (Honda); 9. Da Costa (F, Suzuki); 10. Neate (Honda).

11th September - Oulton Park
1. Crutchlow (Honda); 2. Camier (Honda); 3. Sykes (Suzuki); 4. Jones (Honda); 5. Riba Cabana (E, Kawasaki); 6. Easton (Ducati); 7. Robinson (Honda); 8. Llewellyn (Honda); 9. Andrews (Suzuki); 10. J. Vincent (Honda).

25th September - Donington Park
1. Riba Cabana (E, Kawasaki); 2. Vincent (Honda); 3. E. Laverty (Honda); 4. Jones (Honda); 5. Easton (Ducati); 6. Robinson (Honda); 7. Camier (Honda); 8. Andrews (Suzuki); 9. Llewellyn (Honda); 10. Dickinson (Honda).

9th October - Brands Hatch GP
1. Easton (Ducati); 2. Jones (Honda); 3. Crutchlow (Honda); 4. Sykes (Suzuki); 5. Camier (Honda); 6. E. Laverty (Honda); 7. J. Robinson (Honda); 8. Frost (Honda); 9. Andrews (Suzuki); 10. Tunstall (Honda).

FINAL CLASSIFICATION
1. Leon Camier — Honda — 202
2. Craig Jones — Honda — 189
3. Stuart Easton — Ducati — 161

4. C. Crutchlow (Honda), 161; 5. P. Riba Cabana (E, Kawasaki), 155; 6. T. Sykes (Suzuki), 119; 7. J. Robinson (Honda), 112; 8. J. Vincent (Honda), 91; 9. E. Laverty (Honda), 84; 10. S. Andrews (Suzuki), 67.

SUPERSTOCK

28th March - Brands Hatch Indy
1. Tinsley (Suzuki); 2. Mainwaring (Suzuki); 3. Fitzpatrick (Yamaha); 4. Jackson (Yamaha); 5. Coates (Suzuki); 6. Johnson (Suzuki); 7. R. Rainey (Yamaha); 8. Young (Yamaha); 9. Reilly (Kawasaki); 10. Bridewell (Kawasaki).

10th April - Thruxton
1. Coates (Suzuki); 2. Jackson (Yamaha); 3. Tinsley (Suzuki); 4. Mainwaring (Suzuki); 5. Reilly (Kawasaki); 6. Thompson (Suzuki); 7. R. Rainey (Yamaha); 8. Fitzpatrick (Yamaha); 9. Bridewell (Kawasaki); 10. Hickman (Kawasaki).

24th April - Mallory Park
1. Young (Yamaha); 2. Jackson (Yamaha); 3. Fitzpatrick (Yamaha); 4. Neill (Kawasaki); 5. Johnson (Suzuki); 6. R. Rainey (Yamaha); 7. Reilly (Kawasaki); 8. Shand (Yamaha); 9. Bridewell (Kawasaki); 10. Davis (Suzuki).

2nd May - Oulton Park
1. Young (Yamaha); 2. Jackson (Yamaha); 3. Johnson (Suzuki); 4. Crockford (Suzuki); 5. Shand (Yamaha); 6. Tinsley (Suzuki); 7. Hickman (Kawasaki); 8. R. Rainey (Yamaha); 9. Bridewell (Kawasaki); 10. Neill (Kawasaki).

15th May - Mondello Park
1. Tinsley (Suzuki); 2. Young (Yamaha); 3. Jackson (Yamaha); 4. R. Rainey (Yamaha); 5. Coates (Suzuki); 6. Coxhell (Suzuki); 7. Fitzpatrick (Yamaha); 8. Shand (Yamaha); 9. Neill (Kawasaki); 10. Seeley (Yamaha).

5th June - Croft
1. Young (Yamaha); 2. Coates (Suzuki); 3. Johnson (Suzuki); 4. Bridewell (Kawasaki); 5. Fitzpatrick (Yamaha); 6. Reilly (Kawasaki); 7. Ingram (Suzuki); 8. Rock (Yamaha); 9. Robb (Suzuki); 10. R. Rainey (Yamaha).

26th June - Knockhill
1. Young (Yamaha); 2. Shand (Yamaha); 3. Fitzpatrick (Yamaha); 4. Crockford (Suzuki); 5. Bridewell (Kawasaki); 6. Allan (Kawasaki); 7. Reilly (Kawasaki); 8. R. Rainey (Yamaha); 9. Hickman (Kawasaki); 10. L. Jackson (Yamaha).

10th July - Snetterton
1. Coates (Suzuki); 2. Bridewell (Kawasaki); 3. Zanotti (Kawasaki); 4. R. Rainey (Yamaha); 5. Young (Yamaha); 6. Johnson (Suzuki); 7. Fitzpatrick (Yamaha); 8. Shand (Yamaha); 9. Ingram (Suzuki); 10. Hutchinson (Honda).

21st August - Silverstone
1. Coates (Suzuki); 2. Bridewell (Kawasaki); 3. L. Jackson (Yamaha); 4. Fitzpatrick (Yamaha); 5. Allan (Kawasaki); 6. Johnson (Suzuki); 7. Shand (Yamaha); 8. Neill (Kawasaki); 9. R. Rainey (Yamaha); 10. Hickman (Kawasaki).

29th August - Cadwell Park
1. L. Jackson (Yamaha); 2. Coates (Suzuki); 3. Bridewell (Kawasaki); 4. Hickman (Kawasaki); 5. Fitzpatrick (Yamaha); 6. Allan (Kawasaki); 7. J. Laverty (Honda); 8. Shand (Yamaha); 9. Hutchinson (Suzuki); 10. Neill (Kawasaki).

11th September - Oulton Park
1. Shand (Yamaha); 2. L. Jackson (Yamaha); 3. Coates (Suzuki); 4. Young (Yamaha); 5. Reilly (Kawasaki); 6. Fitzpatrick (Yamaha); 7. Hutchinson (Suzuki); 8. Hickman (Kawasaki); 9. Ingram (Suzuki); 10. Thompson (Suzuki).

25th September - Donington Park
1. Hutchinson (Suzuki); 2. J. Laverty (Honda); 3. Sanders (Kawasaki); 4. L. Jackson (Yamaha); 5. Coates (Suzuki); 6. Shand (Yamaha); 7. Johnson (Suzuki); 8. Fitzpatrick (Yamaha); 9. Allan (Kawasaki); 10. Reilly (Kawasaki).

9th October - Brands Hatch GP
1. Fitzpatrick (Yamaha); 2. L. Jackson (Yamaha); 3. Hickman (Kawasaki); 4. Hutchinson (Suzuki); 5. Reilly (Kawasaki); 6. Zanotti (Kawasaki); 7. Bridewell (Kawasaki); 8. Allan (Kawasaki); 9. Cox (Yamaha); 10. Thompson (Suzuki).

FINAL CLASSIFICATION
1. Lee Jackson — Yamaha — 194
2. Paul Young — Yamaha — 166
3. Adrian Coates — Suzuki — 165

4. C. Fitzpatrick (Yamaha), 152; 5. O. Bridewell (Kawasaki), 124; 6. L. Shand (Yamaha), 110; 7. D. Johnson (Suzuki), 84; 8. R. Rainey (Yamaha), 83; 9. P. Hickman (Kawasaki), 81; 10. K. Reilly (Kawasaki), 78.

SUPERBIKE

28th March - Brands Hatch Indy
Race I: 1. Kiyonari (J, Honda); 2. Lavilla (E, Ducati); 3. Richards (Kawasaki); 4. Rutter (Honda); 5. Emmett (Yamaha); 6. K. Harris (Honda); 7. McWilliams (Honda); 8. Thomas (AUS, Kawasaki); 9. Reynolds (Suzuki); 10. Hill (Yamaha).
Race II: 1. Kiyonari (Honda); 2. Rutter (Honda); 3. Lavilla (E, Ducati); 4. L. Haslam (Ducati); 5. Emmett (Yamaha); 6. K. Harris (Honda); 7. Richards (Kawasaki); 8. S. Smart (Suzuki); 9. Reynolds (Suzuki); 10. Mason (Honda).

10th April - Thruxton
Race I: 1. Kiyonari (J, Honda); 2. Rutter (Honda); 3. Lavilla (E, Ducati); 4. Haslam (Ducati); 5. Emmett (Yamaha); 6. K. Harris (Honda); 7. S. Smart (Suzuki); 8. Thomas (AUS, Kawasaki); 9. Richards (Kawasaki); 10. Hill (Yamaha).
Race II: 1. Kiyonari (Honda); 2. Lavilla (E, Ducati); 3. Rutter (Honda); 4. Emmett (Yamaha); 5. Richards (Kawasaki); 6. Thomas (AUS, Kawasaki); 7. L. Haslam (Ducati); 8. K. Harris (Honda); 9. McWilliams (Honda); 10. Plater (Kawasaki).

24th April - Mallory Park
Race I: 1. Rutter (Honda); 2. Richards (Kawasaki); 3. L. Haslam (Ducati); 4. Emmett (Yamaha); 5. S. Smart (Suzuki); 6. Thomas (AUS, Kawasaki); 7. M. Laverty (Honda); 8. Mason (Honda); 9. Beaumont (Honda); 10. Brogan (Honda).
Race II: 1. Rutter (Honda); 2. Richards (Kawasaki); 3. Lavilla (E, Ducati); 4. Thomas (AUS, Kawasaki); 5. L. Haslam (Ducati); 6. K. Harris (Honda); 7. Mason (Honda); 8. S. Smart (Suzuki); 9. M. Laverty (Honda); 10. Emmett (Yamaha).

2nd May - Oulton Park
Race I: 1. Rutter (Honda); 2. Lavilla (E, Ducati); 3. K. Harris (Honda); 4. L. Haslam (Ducati); 5. Richards (Kawasaki); 6. Thomas (AUS, Kawasaki); 7. Mason (Honda); 8. Haydon (Suzuki); 9. S. Smart (Suzuki); 10. Clarke (Honda).
Race II: 1. L. Haslam (Ducati); 2. Rutter (Honda); 3. K. Harris (Honda); 4. Haydon (Suzuki); 5. Da Costa (F, Kawasaki); 6. Richards (Kawasaki); 7. Plater (Kawasaki); 8. Clarke (Honda); 9. Rea (Honda); 10. M. Laverty (Honda).

15th May - Mondello Park
Race I: 1. Kiyonari (J, Honda); 2. Rutter (Honda); 3. Lavilla (E, Ducati); 4. K. Harris (Honda); 5. S. Smart (Suzuki); 6. M. Laverty (Honda); 7. Emmett (Yamaha); 8. Mason (Honda); 9. McWilliams (Honda); 10. Haydon (Suzuki).
Race II: 1. Lavilla (E, Ducati); 2. L. Haslam (Ducati); 3. Kiyonari (J, Honda); 4. M. Laverty (Honda); 5. M. Rutter (Honda); 6. Richards (Kawasaki); 7. K. Harris (Honda); 8. S. Smart (Suzuki); 9. Mason (Honda); 10. McWilliams (Honda).

5th June - Croft
Race I: 1. Kiyonari (J, Honda); 2. Rutter (Honda); 3. Lavilla (E, Ducati); 4. M. Laverty (Honda); 5. Richards (Kawasaki); 6. L. Haslam (Ducati); 7. Rea (Honda); 8. Haydon (Yamaha); 9. Mason (Honda); 10. Thomas (AUS, Kawasaki).
Race II: 1. Lavilla (E, Ducati); 2. Rutter (Honda); 3. Kiyonari (J, Honda); 4. Richards (Kawasaki); 5. Mason (Honda); 6. Thomas (AUS, Kawasaki); 7. Plater (Kawasaki); 8. Clarke (Honda); 9. Brogan (Honda); 10. J. Laverty (Honda).

188 MOTORCYCLE YEARBOOK 2005

THE RESULTS OF THE OTHER CHAMPIONSHIPS

26th June - Knockhill
Race I: 1. Kiyonari (J, Honda); 2. Rutter (Honda); 3. M. Laverty (Honda); 4. Richards (Kawasaki); 5. L. Haslam (Ducati); 6. G. Lavilla (E, Ducati); 7. Reynolds (Suzuki); 8. K. Harris (Honda); 9. Mason (Honda); 10. Thomas (AUS, Kawasaki).
Race II: 1. Kiyonari (J, Honda); 2. Rutter (Honda); 3. Lavilla (E, Ducati); 4. M. Laverty (Honda); 5. L. Haslam (Ducati); 6. Reynolds (Suzuki); 7. Richards (Kawasaki); 8. Haydon (Suzuki); 9. Rea (Honda); 10. Thomas (AUS, Kawasaki).

10th July - Snetterton
Race I: 1. Kiyonari (J, Honda); 2. L. Haslam (Ducati); 3. Reynolds (Suzuki); 4. Haydon (Suzuki); 5. Rutter (Honda); 6. K. Harris (Honda); 7. Plater (Honda); 8. Mason (Honda); 9. Wilson (Kawasaki); 10. Hill (Yamaha).
Race II: 1. Lavilla (E, Ducati); 2. M. Laverty (Honda); 3. Rutter (Honda); 4. Reynolds (Suzuki); 5. Plater (Honda); 6. Wilson (Kawasaki); 7. Hill (Yamaha); 8. Mason (Honda); 9. Thomas (Kawasaki); 10. Burns (Yamaha).

21st August - Silverstone
Race I: 1. Lavilla (E, Ducati); 2. L. Haslam (Ducati); 3. Reynolds (Suzuki); 4. K. Harris (Honda); 5. Richards (Kawasaki); 6. Thomas (AUS, Kawasaki); 7. Mason (Honda); 8. Kiyonari (Honda); 9. Hill (Yamaha); 10. Haydon (Suzuki).
Race II: 1. Kiyonari (Honda); 2. Lavilla (E, Ducati); 3. L. Haslam (Ducati); 4. Rutter (Honda); 5. Richards (Kawasaki); 6. Thomas (AUS, Kawasaki); 7. Mason (Honda); 8. Haydon (Suzuki); 9. K. Harris (Honda); 10. Hill (Yamaha).

29th August - Cadwell Park
Race I: 1. Hill (Yamaha); 2. Lavilla (E, Ducati); 3. Richards (Kawasaki); 4. K. Harris (Honda); 5. Kiyonari (J, Honda); 6. L. Haslam (Ducati); 7. Haydon (Suzuki); 8. Rutter (Honda); 9. Thomas (AUS, Kawasaki); 10. Buckingham (Suzuki).
Race II: 1. L. Haslam (Ducati); 2. Lavilla (E, Ducati); 3. Kiyonari (J, Honda); 4. Hill (Yamaha); 5. K. Harris (Honda); 6. Haydon (Suzuki); 7. Thomas (AUS, Kawasaki); 8. Reynolds (Suzuki); 9. Plater (Honda); 10. Mason (Honda).

11 septembre - Oulton Park
Race I: 1. Kiyonari (J, Honda); 2. Lavilla (E, Ducati); 3. Reynolds (Suzuki); 4. Haslam (Ducati); 5. Richards (Kawasaki); 6. Haydon (Suzuki); 7. Hill (Yamaha); 8. K. Harris (Honda); 9. Mason (Honda); 10. Rutter (Honda).
Race II: 1. Kiyonari (J, Honda); 2. Lavilla (E, Ducati); 3. Reynolds (Suzuki); 4. Haslam (Ducati); 5. K. Harris (Honda); 6. Hill (Yamaha); 7. Thomas (AUS, Kawasaki); 8. Richards (Kawasaki); 9. Mason (Honda); 10. Plater (Honda).

25th September - Donington Park
Race I: 1. Lavilla (E, Ducati); 2. Kiyonari (J, Honda); 3. Haslam (Ducati); 4. Richards (Kawasaki); 5. Reynolds (Suzuki); 6. Rutter (Honda); 7. S. Smart (Kawasaki); 8. Hill (Yamaha); 9. Thomas (AUS, Kawasaki); 10. Mason (Honda).
Race II: 1. Lavilla (E, Ducati); 2. Haslam (Ducati); 3. Kiyonari (J, Honda); 4. Rutter (Honda); 5. Haydon (Suzuki); 6. Thomas (AUS, Kawasaki); 7. Mason (Honda); 8. S. Smart (Kawasaki); 9. K. Harris (Honda); 10. M. Laverty (Honda).

9th October - Brands Hatch GP
Race I: 1. Lavilla (E, Ducati); 2. L. Haslam (Ducati); 3. Haydon (Suzuki); 4. Kiyonari (J, Honda); 5. Thomas (AUS, Kawasaki); 6. Rutter (Honda); 7. Mason (Hodna); 8. Plater (Honda); 9. McWiliams (Honda); 10. Rea (Honda).
Race II: 1. L. Haslam (Ducati); 2. Lavilla (Ducati); 3. Plater (Honda); 4. Kiyonari (J, Honda); 5. Thomas (AUS, Kawasaki); 6. Richards (Kawasaki); 7. Mason (Honda); 8. Rutter (Honda); 9. Hill (Yamaha); 10. Rea (Honda).

FINAL CLASSIFICATION
1. Gregorio Lavilla (E) — Ducati — 461
2. Ryuichi Kiyonari (J) — Honda — 429
3. Michael Rutter — Honda — 371

4. L. Haslam (Ducati), 350; 5. G. Richards (Kawasaki), 241; 6. D. Thomas (AUS, Kawasaki), 198; 7. K. Harris (Honda), 195; 8. G. Mason (Honda), 174; 9. J. Reynolds (Suzuki), 139; 10. M. Laverty (Honda), 129.

ITALY CHAMPIONSHIP
125 GP

17th April - Vallelunga
1. Baroni (Aprilia); 2. Conti (Honda); 3. Grotzkyj (Aprilia); 4. Leardini (Honda); 5. Narduzzi (Aprilia); 6. S. Bradl (D, KTM); 7. Bianchi (Aprilia); 8. Palumbo (Aprilia); 9. Biliotti (Aprilia); 10. Rossi (Honda).

1st May - Monza
1. Conti (Honda); 2. Baroni (Aprilia); 3. Grotzkyj (Aprilia); 4. Palumbo (Aprilia); 5. Rossi (Honda); 6. Vivarelli (Honda); 7. Lombardi (Aprilia); 8. Donetti (Honda); 9. Vigilucci (Honda); 10. Verdini (Aprilia).

22nd May - Imola
1. Baroni (Aprilia); 2. Conti (Honda); 3. Grotzkyj (Aprilia); 4. Tamburini (Aprilia); 5. Petrini (Aprilia); 6. Palumbo (Aprilia); 7. Vivarelli (Honda); 8. Verdini (Aprilia); 9. Rossi (Honda); 10. Donetti (Honda).

3rd July - Misano
1. Tamburini (Aprilia); 2. Bianchi (Aprilia); 3. Grotzkyj (Aprilia); 4. Lombardi (Aprilia); 5. Baroni (Aprilia); 6. Fratticci (Honda); 7. Boscoscuro (Honda); 8. Filice (Honda); 9. Rossi (Honda); 10. La Marra (Aprilia).

31st July - Mugello
1. Petrini (Aprilia); 2. Cluzel (F, Honda); 3. Grotzkyj (Aprilia); 4. Danese (Aprilia); 5. Verdini (Aprilia); 6. Palumbo (Aprilia); 7. Biliotti (Aprilia); 8. Filice (Honda); 9. Fratticci (Honda); 10. Vivarelli (Honda).

25th September - Misano
1. Pellino (Malaguti); 2. Grotzkyj (Aprilia); 3. Baroni (Aprilia); 4. Conti (Aprilia); 5. Palumbo (Aprilia); 6. Leardini (Honda); 7. Filice (Honda); 8. Lombardi (Aprilia); 9. Bizzotto (Aprilia); 10. Fratticci (Honda).

FINAL CLASSIFICATION
1. Simone Grotzkyj — Aprilia — 108
2. Lorenzo Baroni — Aprilia — 99
3. Michele Conti — Honda — 78

4. Palumbo (Aprilia), 55; 5. Bianchi (Aprilia), 45; 6. Rossi (Honda), 42; 7. Lombardi (Aprilia), 39; 8. Petrini (Aprilia), 38; 9. Verdini (Aprilia), 31; 10. Fratticci (Honda), 28.

SUPERSPORT

17th April - Vallelunga
1. Antonello (Kawasaki); 2. Sanna (Honda); 3. Proietto (Honda); 4. Giugovaz (Honda); 5. Goi (Honda); 6. A. Aldrovandi (Honda); 7. Di Paolo (Suzuki); 8. Carlacci (Yamaha); 9. Maggiori (Yamaha); 10. Canepa (Kawasaki).

1st May - Monza
1. Foret (F, Honda); 2. Sanna (Honda); 3. Cruciani (Yamaha); 4. Giugovaz (Honda); 5. Goi (Yamaha); 6. Antonello (Kawasaki); 7. Mariottini (Yamaha); 8. Baiocco (Kawasaki); 9. Corti (Yamaha); 10. Canepa (Kawasaki).

22nd May - Imola
1. Sanna (Honda); 2. Cruciani (Kawasaki); 3. Antonello (Kawasaki); 4. Giugovaz (Honda); 5. Corti (Yamaha); 6. Mariottini (Honda); 7. Goi (Yamaha); 8. Boccolini (Kawasaki); 9. Baiocco (Kawasaki); 10. Canepa (Kawasaki).

3rd July - Misano
1. Parkes (AUS, Yamaha); 2. Sanna (Honda); 3. Corti (Yamaha); 4. Cruciani (Yamaha); 5. Goi (Yamaha); 6. Mariottini (Honda); 7. Proietto (Honda); 8. Giugovaz (Honda); 9. Antonello (Kawasaki); 10. A. Aldrovandi (Honda).

31st July - Mugello
1. Antonello (Kawasaki); 2. Corradi (Ducati); 3. Mariottini (Honda); 4. Cruciani (Yamaha); 5. Goi (Yamaha); 6. Corti (Yamaha); 7. Sanna (Honda); 8. C. Migliorati (Yamaha); 9. Tarizzo (Honda); 10. Carlacci (Yamaha).

25th September - Misano
1. Antonello (Kawasaki); 2. Mariottini (Honda); 3. Goi (Yamaha); 4. Canepa (Kawasaki); 5. Giugovaz (Honda); 6. Sanna (Honda); 7. Aldrovandi (Honda); 8. Carlacci (Yamaha); 9. Corti (Yamaha); 10. Cruciani (Kawasaki).

FINAL CLASSIFICATION
1. Simone Sanna — Honda — 114
2. Roberto Antonello — Kawasaki — 110
3. Stefano Cruciani — Kawasaki — 75

4. Goi (Yamaha), 73; 5. Mariottini (Honda), 67; 6. Giugovaz (Honda), 62; 7. Corti (Yamaha), 56; 8. Aldrovandi (Honda), 38; 9. Canepa (Kawasaki), 36; 10. Proietto (Yamaha), 35.

SUPERSTOCK 1000 UNDER 30

17th April - Vallelunga
1. Pellizzon (Aprilia); 2. Polita (Suzuki); 3. Tortoroglio (Kawasaki); 4. Guareschi (Kawasaki); 5. Rocamora (E, Suzuki); 6. Scassa (Yamaha); 7. Tallevi (Yamaha); 8. Saltarelli (Yamaha); 9. Cottini (Yamaha); 10. Rossi (Kawasaki).

1st May - Monza
1. Polita (Suzuki); 2. Prattichizzo (Kawasaki); 3. Roccoli (Yamaha); 4. Scassa (Yamaha); 5. Lunadei (Yamaha); 6. Martinez (Yamaha); 7. Guareschi (Yamaha); 8. Vitiello (Yamaha); 9. Melone (Suzuki); 10. Sassaro (Yamaha).

22nd May - Imola
1. Roccoli (Yamaha); 2. Polita (Suzuki); 3. Pratichizzo (Kawasaki); 4. Lunadei (Yamaha); 5. Guareschi (Kawasaki); 6. Brunelli (Yamaha); 7. Saltarelli (Yamaha); 8. Melone (Suzuki); 9. Tumminello (Yamaha); 10. Caffiero (Yamaha).

3rd July - Misano
1. Roccoli (Yamaha); 2. Prattichizzo (Kawasaki); 3. Guareschi (Yamaha); 4. Polita (Suzuki); 5. Scassa (Yamaha); 6. W. De Angelis (Yamaha); 7. Pellizzon (Aprilia); 8. Brunelli (Yamaha); 9. Saltarelli (Yamaha); 10. Magnani (Suzuki).

31st July - Mugello
1. Roccoli (Yamaha); 2. Polita (Suzuki); 3. Scassa (Yamaha); 4. Pellizzon (Aprilia); 5. Prattichizzo (Kawasaki); 6. Martinez (Yamaha); 7. Guareschi (Yamaha); 8. Sassaro (Yamaha); 9. Caffiero (Yamaha); 10. Tortoroglio (Kawasaki).

25th September - Misano
1. Polita (Suzuki); 2. Scassa (Yamaha); 3. Magnani (Yamaha); 4. Prattichizzo (Kawasaki); 5. Roccoli (Yamaha); 6. Guareschi (Kawasaki); 7. W. De Angelis (Yamaha); 8. Lunadei (Yamaha); 9. Tortoroglio (Kawasaki); 10. Sassaro (Yamaha).

FINAL CLASSIFICATION
1. Alessandro Polita — Suzuki — 123
2. Massimo Roccoli — Yamaha — 102
3. Maurizio Prattichizzo — Kawasaki — 80

4. Scassa, 71; 5. Guareschi (Kawasaki), 70; 6. Pellizzon (Aprilia), 48; 7. Lunadei (Yamaha), 38; 8. Tortoroglio (Kawasaki), 30; 9. W. De Angelis (Yamaha), 30; 10. Magnani (Suzuki), 28.

SUPERBIKE

17th April - Vallelunga
1. Borciani (Yamaha); 2. Gallina (MV-Agusta); 3. Pedercini (Ducati); 4. Brignola (Ducati); 5. Conti (Honda); 6. Antonelli (Yamaha); 7. Dionisi (Suzuki); 8. Di Giannicola (Suzuki); 9. Valia (Yamaha); 10. Conforti (Ducati).

1st May - Monza
1. Alfonsi (Yamaha); 2. Gramigni (Yamaha); 3. Pedercini (Ducati); 4. Conforti (Ducati); 5. Brignola (Ducati); 6. Borciani (Yamaha); 7. Cardoso (E, Yamaha); 8. Velini (Ducati); 9. Blora (Yamaha); 10. Valia (Yamaha).

22nd May - Imola
1. Brignola (Ducati); 2. Pini (Honda); 3. Conforti (Ducati); 4. Gallina (MV-Agusta); 5. Velini (Ducati); 6. De Noni (Yamaha); 7. Di Maso (Suzuki); 8. Brunelli (Yamaha); 9. Tomassoni (Suzuki); 10. Zannini (Yamaha).

3rd July - Misano
1. Pedercini (Ducati); 2. Vizziello (Yamaha); 3. Conforti (Ducati); 4. Brignola (Ducati); 5. Borciani (Ducati); 6. Pini (Honda); 7. Mazzali (MV-Agusta); 8. Brunelli (Yamaha); 9. Romanelli (Suzuki); 10. De Noni (Yamaha).

31st July - Mugello
1. Borciani (Ducati); 2. Gramigni (Yamaha); 3. Brignola (Ducati); 4. Alfonsi (Yamaha); 5. Pedercini (Ducati); 6. Conforti (Ducati); 7. Dionisi (Yamaha); 8. Pini (Honda); 9. Gallina (MV-Agusta); 10. Di Maso (Ducati).

25th September - Misano
1. Vizziello (Yamaha); 2. Pedercini (Ducati); 3. Gonzales-Nieto (Kawasaki); 4. Brignola (Ducati); 5. Gramigni (Yamaha); 6. Conforti (Ducati); 7. Sanchini (Kawasaki); 8. Lucchiari (Ducati); 9. Dionisi (Suzuki); 10. Mazzali (MV-Agusta).

FINAL CLASSIFICATION
1. Norino Brignola — Ducati — 94
2. Luca Pedercini — Ducati — 88
3. Marco Borciani — Ducati — 74

4. L. Conforti (Ducati), 72; 5. A. Gramigni (Yamaha), 53; 6. L. Vizziello (Yamaha), 48; 7. Gallina (MV-Agusta), 47; 8. Pini (Honda), 44; 9. Alfonsi (Yamaha), 38; 10. Dionisi (Suzuki), 29.

SWITZERLAND CHAMPIONSHIP
PROMOSPORT 600

27 March - Lédenon - France
Race I: 1. Rohner (Suzuki); 2. Sutter (Honda). 2 finishers.
Race II: 1. Rohner (Suzuki); 2. Sutter (Honda). 2 finishers.

THE RESULTS OF THE OTHER CHAMPIONSHIPS

24th April - Brno - Czech Republic

Race I: 1. Rohner (Suzuki); 2. Sutter (Honda); 3. Eigenheer (Honda); 4. Ummel (Kawasaki). 4 finishers.
Race II: 1. Sutter (Honda); 2. Rohner (Suzuki); 3. Eigenheer (Honda); 4. Ummel (Kawasaki). 4 finishers.

22nd May - Oschersleben - Germany

Race I: 1. Sutter (Honda); 2. Rohner (Suzuki); 3. Eigenheer (Honda); 4. Ummel (Kawasaki). 4 finishers.
Race II: 1. Sutter (Honda); 2. Rohner (Suzuki); 3. Ummel (Kawasaki); 4. Egenheer (Honda). 4 finishers.

17th July - Dijon - France

Race I: 1. Sutter (Honda); 2. Rohner (Suzuki); 3. Ummel (Kawasaki); 4. Eigenheer (Honda).
Race II: 1. Sutter (Honda); 2. Rohner (Suzuki); 3. Graf (Suzuki); 4. Eigenheer (Honda); 5. Ummel (Kawasaki).

4th September - Schleiz - Germany

Race annulée

23rd October - Lédenon - France

Race I: 1. Sutter (Honda); 2. Rohner (Suzuki); 3. Eigenheer (Honda). 3 finishers.
Race II: 1. Sutter (Honda); 2. Rohner (Suzuki); 3. Eigenheer (Honda). 3 finishers.

FINAL CLASSIFICATION

1. Daniel Sutter	Honda	235
2. Sven Rohner	Suzuki	215
3. Hatty Eigenheer	Honda	122

4. R. Ummel (Kawasaki), 100. 4 finishers.

SUPERSTOCK 600

27th March - Lédenon - France

Race I: 1. Polesso (F, Yamaha); 2. Grosjean (Kawasaki); 3. F. Millet (F, Honda); 4. Vuille (Kawasaki); 5. Junod (Suzuki) ; 6. Leibundgut (Honda); 7. Savary (Suzuki); 8. Rüegg (Yamaha); 9. D. Berclaz (Suzuki); 10. Häfeli (Yamaha). 11 finishers.
Race II: 1. Rüegg (Yamaha); 2. F. Millet (F, Honda); 3. Junod (Suzuki); 4. Polesso (F, Yamaha); 5. Grosjean (Kawasaki); 6. Leibundgut (Honda); 7. Savary (Suzuki); 8. Häfeli (Yamaha); 9. Vuille (Kawasaki); 10. G. Berclaz (Suzuki). 12 finishers.

24th April - Brno - Czech Republic

Race I: 1. Rüegg (Yamaha); 2. F. Millet (F, Honda); 3. Grosjean (Kawasaki); 4. Junod (Suzuki); 5. Leibundgut (Honda); 6. G. Berclaz (Suzuki); 7. Häfeli (Yamaha); 8. Moulin (F, Yamaha); 9. D. Berclaz (Suzuki); 10. Herbillon (F, Yamaha).
Race II: 1. F. Millet (F, Honda); 2. Grosjean (Kawasaki); 3. Junod (Suzuki); 4. Leibundgut (Honda); 5. Häfeli (Yamaha); 6. G. Berclaz (Suzuki); 7. Vuille (Kawasaki); 8. D. Berclaz (Suzuki); 9. Herbillon (F, Yamaha); 10. Nadalet (Kawasaki).

22nd May - Oschersleben - Germany

Race I: 1. F. Millet (F, Honda); 2. Junod (Suzuki); 3. Grosjean (Kawasaki); 4. Rüegg (Yamaha); 5. Leibundgut (Honda); 6. Savary (Suzuki); 7. Vuille (Kawasaki); 8. G. Berclaz (Suzuki); 9. Häfeli (Yamaha); 10. D. Berclaz (Suzuki).
Race II: 1. F. Millet (F, Honda); 2. Junod (Suzuki); 3. Rüegg (Yamaha); 4. Savary (Suzuki); 5. Grosjean (Kawasaki); 6. Leibundgut (Honda); 7. G. Berclaz (Suzuki); 8. Vuille (Kawasaki); 9. D. Berclaz (Suzuki); 10. Strebel (Kawasaki).

17th July - Dijon - France

Race I: 1. F. Millet (F, Honda); 2. Junod (Suzuki); 3. Rüegg (Yamaha); 4. Leibundgut (Honda); 5. Schmid (Yamaha); 6. Savary (Suzuki); 7. Grosjean (Kawasaki); 8. Vuille (Kawasaki); 9. G. Berclaz (Suzuki); 10. Nadalet (Kawasaki).
Race II: 1. F. Millet (F, Honda); 2. Rüegg (Yamaha); 3. Grosjean (Kawasaki); 4. Schmid (Yamaha); 5. Leibundgut (Honda); 6. Vuille (Coffrane); 7. G. Berclaz (Suzuki); 8. Häfeli (Yamaha); 9. Nadalet (Kawasaki). 9 finishers.

4th September - Schleiz - Germany

Race annulée

23rd October - Lédenon - France

Race I: 1. Grosjean (Kawasaki); 2. Vuille (Kawasaki); 3. F. Millet (F, Honda); 4. Junod (Suzuki); 5. Rüegg (Yamaha); 6. Savary (Suzuki); 7. Leibundgut (Honda); 8. Häfeli (Yamaha); 9. D. Berclaz (Suzuki); 10. G. Berclaz (Suzuki).
Race II: 1. F. Millet (F, Honda); 2. Rüegg (Yamaha); 3. Grosjean (Kawasaki); 4. Junod (Suzuki); 5. Vuille (Kawasaki); 6. Savary (Suzuki); 7. Leibundgut (Honda); 8. Sennhauser (Suzuki); 9. Häfeli (Yamaha); 10. G. Berclaz (Suzuki).

FINAL CLASSIFICATION

1. Franck Millet (F)	Honda	222
2. Pascal Grosjean	Kawasaki	161
3. Christian Rüegg	Yamaha	154

4. G. Junod (Suzuki), 142; 5. D. Leibundgut (Honda), 109; 6. P. Vuille (Kawasaki), 100; 7. G. Berclaz (Suzuki), 79; 8. M. Savary (Suzuki), 72; 9. C. Häfeli (Yamaha), 71; 10. D. Berclaz (Suzuki), 53. 15 finishers.

SUPERSTOCK 1000

27th March - Lédenon - France

Race I: 1. Devoyon (F, Suzuki); 2. Portmann (Kawasaki); 3. Hofmann (Kawasaki); 4. Gantner (Yamaha); 5. Künzi (Yamaha); 6. Flückiger (Kawasaki); 7. Wildisen (Suzuki); 8. Bucher (Suzuki); 9. Huldi (Yamaha); 10. Mahler (Suzuki). 13 finishers.
Race II: 1. Devoyon (F, Suzuki); 2. Bucher (Suzuki); 3. Portmann (Kawasaki); 4. Hofmann (Kawasaki); 5. Wildisen (Suzuki); 6. Flückiger (Kawasaki); 7. Künzi (Yamaha); 8. Huldi (Yamaha); 9. Gantner (Yamaha); 10. Mahler (Suzuki). 16 finishers.

24th April - Brno - Czech Republic

Race I: 1. Hofmann (Kawasaki); 2. Devoyon (F, Suzuki); 3. Künzi (Yamaha); 4. Bucher (Suzuki); 5. Flückiger (Kawasaki); 6. Portmann (Kawasaki); 7. Wildisen (Suzuki); 8. Dähler (Yamaha); 9. Huldi (Yamaha); 10. Mahler (Suzuki).
Race II: 1. Hofmann (Kawasaki); 2. Devoyon (F, Suzuki); 3. Künzi (Yamaha); 4. Flückiger (Kawasaki); 5. Wildisen (Suzuki); 6. Portmann (Kawasaki); 7. Dähler (Yamaha); 8. Mahler (Suzuki); 9. Huldi (Yamaha); 10. Lupberger (Honda).

20th-22nd May - Oschersleben - Germany

Race I: 1. Künzi (Yamaha); 2. Flückiger (Kawasaki); 3. Wildisen (Suzuki); 4. Devoyon (F, Suzuki); 5. Huldi (Yamaha); 6. Mahler (Suzuki); 7. Dähler (Yamaha); 8. Pollheide (D, Suzuki); 9. Bucher (Suzuki); 10. Beglinger (Suzuki).
Race II: 1. Devoyon (F, Suzuki); 2. Künzi (Yamaha); 3. Flückiger (Kawasaki); 4. Dähler (Yamaha); 5. Portmann (Kawasaki); 6. Huldi (Yamaha); 7. Pollheide (D, Suzuki); 8. Bucher (Suzuki); 9. Beglinger (Suzuki); 10. Lupberger (Honda).

15-17th July - Dijon - France

Race I: 1. Devoyon (F, Suzuki); 2. Flückiger (Kawasaki); 3. Wildisen (Suzuki); 4. Saiger (A, Suzuki); 5. Bucher (Suzuki); 6. Portmann (Kawasaki); 7. Mahler (Suzuki); 8. Jaeck (F, Yamaha); 9. Huldi (Yamaha); 10. Lupberger (Honda).
Race II: 1. Devoyon (F, Suzuki); 2. Bucher (Suzuki); 3. Künzi (Yamaha); 4. Wildisen (Suzuki); 5. Flückiger (Kawasaki); 6. Portmann (Kawasaki); 7. Saiger (A, Suzuki); 8. Mahler (Suzuki); 9. Huldi (Yamaha); 10. Da Silva (Yamaha).

2nd-4th September - Schleiz - Germany

Race annulée

21st-23rd October - Lédenon - France

Race I: 1. Portmann (Kawasaki); 2. Devoyon (F, Suzuki); 3. Flückiger (Kawasaki); 4. Künzi (Yamaha); 5. Dähler (Yamaha); 6. Wildisen (Suzuki); 7. Huldi (Yamaha); 8. Meier (Kawasaki); 9. Lupberger (Honda); 10. Beglinger (Suzuki).
Race II: 1. Devoyon (F, Suzuki); 2. Künzi (Yamaha); 3. Flückiger (Kawasaki); 4. Huldi (Yamaha); 5. Wildisen (Suzuki); 6. Dähler (Yamaha); 7. Meier (Kawasaki); 8. Lupberger (Honda); 9. Kramer (F, Yamaha); 10. Beglinger (Suzuki).

FINAL CLASSIFICATION

1. Jean-Louis Devoyon (F)	Suzuki	223
2. Christian Künzi	Yamaha	146
3. Thomas Flückiger	Kawasaki	143

4. R. Portmann (Kawasaki), 112; 5. M. Wildisen (Suzuki), 106; 6. P. Bucher (Suzuki), 87; 7. H. Huldi (Yamaha), 86; 8. A. Hofmann (Kawasaki), 79; 9. W. Dähler (Yamaha), 74; 10. G. Mahler (Suzuki), 55. 24 finishers.

SUPERMOTARD

PRESTIGE OPEN S1

24th April - Eschenbach

Race I: 1. Götz (KTM); 2. Möri (Yamaha); 3. Ferrari (Husqvarna); 4. Wehrli (KTM); 5. Schüpbach (Kawasaki); 6. Herger (Honda); 7. Terraneo (Honda); 8. Öhri (Yamaha); 9. Gysi (KTM); 10. Spörri (KTM).
Race II: 1. Götz (KTM); 2. Wehrli (KTM); 3. Ferrari (Husqvarna); 4. Möri (Yamaha); 5. Laimbacher (KTM); 6. Schüpbach (Kawasaki); 7. Scheidegger (Suzuki); 8. Öhri (Yamaha); 9. Herger (Honda); 10. Alpstäg (KTM).

8th May - Büron

Race I: 1. Götz (KTM); 2. Wehrli (KTM); 3. Ferrari (Husqvarna); 4. Laimbacher (KTM); 5. Alpstäg (KTM); 6. Saxer (KTM); 7. Schüpbach (Kawasaki); 8. Herger (Honda); 9. Scheidegger (Suzuki); 10. Boudier (Yamaha).
Race II: 1. Götz (KTM); 2. Ferrari (Husqvarna); 3. Alpstäg (KTM); 4. Öhri (Yamaha); 5. Möri (Yamaha); 6. Laimbacher (KTM); 7. Schüpbach (Kawasaki); 8. Herger (Honda); 9. Gysi (KTM); 10. Scheidegger (Suzuki).

26th June - St Stephan

Race I: 1. Götz (KTM); 2. Ferrari (Husqvarna); 3. Wehrli (KTM); 4. Herger (Grisoni); 5. Alpstäg (KTM); 6. Laimbacher (KTM); 7. Gysi (KTM); 8. Saxer (KTM); 9. Jappert (Husaberg); 10. Scheidegger (Suzuki).
Race II: 1. Götz (KTM); 2. Ferrari (Husqvarna); 3. Wehrli (KTM); 4. Herger (Honda); 5. Möri (Yamaha); 6. Öhri (Yamaha); 7. Alpstäg (KTM); 8. Scheidegger (Suzuki); 9. Spörri (KTM); 10. Gsell (Husqvarna).

31st July - Buchs

Race I: 1. Götz (KTM); 2. Laimbacher (KTM); 3. Wehrli (KTM); 4. Alpstäg (KTM); 5. Ferrari (Husqvarna); 6. Oehri (Yamaha); 7. Herger (Honda); 8. Gysi (KTM); 9. Möri (Yamaha); 10. Jappert (Husaberg).
Race II: 1. Wehrli (KTM); 2. Laimbacher (KTM); 3. Alpstäg (KTM); 4. Herger (Honda); 5. Ferrari (Husqvarna); 6. Terraneo (Honda); 7. Möri (Yamaha); 8. Spörri (KTM); 9. De Simone (KTM); 10. Jappert (Husaberg).

14th August - Malters

Race I: 1. Herger (Honda); 2. Jasinski (D, Husaberg); 3. Ferrari (Husqvarna); 4. Götz (KTM); 5. Laimbacher (KTM); 6. Scheidegger (Suzuki); 7. Öhri (Yamaha); 8. Schüpbach (Kawasaki); 9. Alpstäg (KTM); 10. De Simone (KTM).
Race II: 1. Götz (KTM); 2. Herger (Honda); 3. Jasinski (D, Husaberg); 4. Wehrli (KTM); 5. Ferrari (Husqvarna); 6. Öhri (Yamaha); 7. Spörri (KTM); 8. Scheidegger (Suzuki); 9. Laimbacher (KTM); 10. Schüpbach (Kawasaki).

28th August - Frauenfeld

Race I: 1. Götz (KTM); 2. Jasinski (D, Husaberg); 3. Herger (Honda); 4. Möri (Yamaha); 5. Ferrari (Husqvarna); 6. Scheidegger (Suzuki); 7. Öhri (Yamaha); 8. Alpstäg (KTM); 9. Terraneo (Honda); 10. Wehrli (KTM).
Race II: 1. Götz (KTM); 2. Jasinski (D, Husaberg); 3. Wehrli (KTM); 4. Herger (Honda); 5. Ferrari (Husqvarna); 6. Scheidegger (Suzuki); 7. Alpstäg (KTM); 8. Laimbacher (KTM); 9. Terraneo (Honda); 10. Schüpbach (Kawasaki).

25th September - Tourtemagne

Race I: 1. Götz (KTM); 2. Wehrli (KTM); 3. Scheidegger (Suzuki); 4. Möri (Yamaha); 5. Terraneo (Honda); 6. Alpstäg (KTM); 7. Öhri (Yamaha); 8. Bucher (Husaberg); 9. Kromer (Suzuki); 10. Kieliger (KTM).
Race II: 1. Götz (KTM); 2. Wehrli (KTM); 3. Scheidegger (Suzuki); 4. Möri (Yamaha); 5. Öhri (Yamaha); 6. Terraneo (Honda); 7. Kromer (Suzuki); 8. Jasinski (D, Husaberg); 9. De Simone (KTM); 10. Bucher (Husaberg).

FINAL CLASSIFICATION

1. Marcel Götz	KTM	319
2. Adrian Wehrli	KTM	236
3. Enzo Ferrari	Husqvarna	226

4. R. Herger (Honda), 213; 5. M. Alpstäg (KTM), 189; 6. R. Öhri (Yamaha), 175; 7. J. Möri (Yamaha), 173; 8. E. Scheidegger (Suzuki), 173; 9. U. Laimbacher (KTM), 170; 10. P. Terraneo (Honda), 111.

PRESTIGE 450 S2

24th April - Eschenbach

Race I: 1. D. Müller (Yamaha); 2. Zachmann (Suzuki); 3. Jasinski (D, Husaberg); 4. Rohner (KTM); 5. Wunderlin (Honda); 6. S. Scheiwiller (Yamaha); 7. Gautschi (Husqvarna); 8. Meusburger (A, Yamaha); 9. Hiemer (D, Yamaha); 10. P. Dupasquier (KTM).
Race II: 1. D. Müller (Yamaha); 2. Wunderlin (Honda); 3. Zachmann (Suzuki); 4. Jasinski (D, Husaberg); 5. Hiemer (D, Yamaha); 6. Züger (KTM); 7. Gautschi (Husqvarna); 8. P. Dupasquier (KTM); 9. Meusburger (A, Yamaha); 10. A. Marti (KTM).

8th May - Büron

Race I: 1. Wunderlin (Honda); 2. Aggeler (Yamaha); 3. Zachmann (Suzuki); 4. D. Müller (Yamaha); 5. Welink (D, KTM); 6. Gautschi (Husqvarna); 7. S. Scheiwiller (Yamaha); 8. Notari (Suzuki); 9. Waeber (Yamaha); 10. Rohner (KTM).
Race II: 1. D. Müller (Yamaha); 2. Wunderlin (Honda); 3. Jasinski (D, Husaberg); 4. Zachmann (Suzuki); 5. Welink (D, KTM); 6. Züger (KTM); 7. S. Scheiwiller (Yamaha); 8. Singele (Yamaha); 9. Gautschi (Husqvarna); 10. Tschupp (Husqvarna).

26th June - St Stephan

Race I: 1. D. Müller (Yamaha); 2. Wunderlin (Honda); 3. Züger (KTM); 4. Zachmann (Suzuki); 5. Meusburger (A, Yamaha); 6. Gautschi (Husqvarna); 7. S. Scheiwiller (Yamaha); 8. Monsch (Yamaha); 9. Singele (Yamaha); 10. Aggeler (Yamaha).
Race II: 1. D. Müller (Yamaha); 2. Wunderlin (Honda); 3. Züger (KTM); 4. Zachmann (Suzuki); 5.

THE RESULTS OF THE OTHER CHAMPIONSHIPS

Aggeler (Yamaha); 6. Meusburger (A, Yamaha); 7. Rohner (KTM); 8. S. Scheiwiller (Yamaha); 9. Von Gunten (Honda); 10. Waeber (Yamaha).

31st July - Buchs

Race I: 1. D. Müller (Yamaha); 2. Volz (D, KTM); 3. Meusburger (A, Yamaha); 4. Wunderlin (Honda); 5. Zachmann (Suzuki); 6. Züger (KTM); 7. Martin (Yamaha); 8. Rohner (KTM); 9. S. Scheiwiller (Yamaha); 10. Monsch (Yamaha).
Race II: 1. D. Müller (Yamaha); 2. Volz (D, KTM); 3. Zachmann (Suzuki); 4. Züger (KTM); 5. Wunderlin (Honda); 6. Meusburger (A, Yamaha); 7. Singele (Yamaha); 8. Martin (F, Yamaha); 9. Baruth (D, KTM); 10. Kromer (Suzuki).

14th August - Malters

Race I: 1. Wunderlin (Honda); 2. Zachmann (Suzuki); 3. Meusburger (A, Yamaha); 4. Volz (KTM); 5. Rohner (KTM); 6. S. Scheiwiller (Yamaha); 7. Gautschi (Husqvarna); 8. Monsch (Yamaha); 9. Züger (KTM); 10. D. Müller (Yamaha).
Race II: 1. D. Müller (Yamaha); 2. Wunderlin (Honda); 3. Zachmann (Suzuki); 4. Volz (D, KTM); 5. Meusburger (A, Yamaha); 6. Gautschi (Husqvarna); 7. Monsch (Yamaha); 8. Schaufelberger (Yamaha); 9. Von Gunten (Honda); 10. A. Marti (KTM).

28th August - Frauenfeld

Race I: 1. D. Müller (Yamaha); 2. Wunderlin (Honda); 3. Zachmann (Suzuki); 4. Volz (D, KTM); 5. Hiemer (Yamaha); 6. S. Scheiwiller (Yamaha); 7. Aggeler (Yamaha); 8. Baruth (D, KTM); 9. Gautschi (Husqvarna); 10. Züger (KTM).
Race II: 1. D. Müller (Yamaha); 2. Wunderlin (Honda); 3. Zachmann (Suzuki); 4. Volz (KTM); 5. Hiemer (Yamaha); 6. S. Scheiwiller (Yamaha); 7. Züger (KTM); 8. P. Dupasquier (KTM); 9. Monsch (Yamaha); 10. Singele (Yamaha).

25th September - Tourtemagne

Race I: 1. D. Müller (Yamaha); 2. Zachmann (Suzuki); 3. Ott (D, KTM); 4. P. Dupasquier (KTM); 5. Wunderlin (Honda); 6. Meusburger (A, Yamaha); 7. Volz (D, KTM); 8. Grauf (D, Honda); 9. Monsch (Yamaha); 10. Aggeler (Yamaha).
Race II: 1. D. Müller (Yamaha); 2. Zachmann (D, Suzuki); 3. Ott (D, KTM); 4. Volz (D, KTM); 5. Wunderlin (Honda); 6. P. Dupasquier (KTM); 7. Meusburger (A, Yamaha); 8. Monsch (Yamaha); 9. Aggeler (Yamaha); 10. Grauf (D, Honda).

FINAL CLASSIFICATION

1. Daniel Müller	Yamaha	329
2. Beat Wunderlin	Honda	288
3. Sigi Zachmann	Suzuki	276

4. H. Meusburger (A, Yamaha), 183; 5. S. Züger (KTM), 158; 6. M. Volz (D, KTM), 152; 7. S. Scheiwiller (Yamaha), 150; 8. B. Gautschi (Husqvarna), 133; 9. P. Singele (Yamaha), 126; 10. M. Aggeler (Yamaha), 113.

CHALLENGER

24th April - Eschenbach

Race I: 1. C. Müller (Suzuki); 2. Hofer (KTM); 3. Tschudin (KTM); 4. Bader (Kawasaki); 5. Haag (Yamaha); 6. Murer (Husaberg); 7. Schnegg (Yamaha); 8. Beeler (KTM) ; 9. Schmied (Yamaha); 10. D. Hüsler (Honda).
Race II: 1. Aregger (Yamaha); 2. K. Marti (KTM); 3. B. Hüsler (Honda); 4. C. Müller (Suzuki); 5. Schnegg (Yamaha); 6. Altherr (KTM); 7. D. Hüsler (Honda); 8. Murer (Husaberg); 9. Nyffeler (Husaberg); 10. Delacombaz (KTM).

8th May - Büron

Race I: 1. C. Müller (Suzuki); 2. Aregger (Yamaha); 3. Frommelt (KTM); 4. Moroso (Husqvarna); 5. Salina (Yamaha); 6. Schnegg (Yamaha); 7. Bader (Kawasaki); 8. Schilliger (Yamaha); 9. Murer (Husaberg); 10. Schumacher (Yamaha).
Race II: 1. Aregger (Yamaha); 2. C. Müller (Suzuki); 3. Schnegg (Yamaha); 4. Moroso (Husqvarna); 5. Frommelt (KTM); 6. Aegerter (Husqvarna); 7. Schilliger (Yamaha); 8. Murer (Husaberg); 9. Bader (Kawasaki); 10. Nyffeler (Husaberg).

26th June - St Stephan

Race I: 1. Aregger (Yamaha); 2. Schnegg (Yamaha); 3. Lugemwa (Yamaha); 4. Frommelt (KTM); 5. Tschudin (KTM); 6. C. Müller (Suzuki); 7. Bader (Kawasaki); 8. Bosshard (Yamaha); 9. K. Marti (KTM); 10. Hüsler (Honda).
Race II: 1. Frommelt (KTM); 2. Schnegg (Yamaha); 3. C. Müller (Suzuki); 4. Lugemwa (Yamaha); 5. Bader (Kawasaki); 6. Schmied (Yamaha); 7. Bolliger (KTM); 8. K. Marti (KTM); 9. Bosshard (Yamaha); 10. Tschudin (KTM).

31st July - Buchs

Race I: 1. Schnegg (Yamaha); 2. Hofer (KTM); 3. K. Marti (KTM); 4. Nyffeler (Husaberg); 5. Aregger (Yamaha); 6. C. Müller (Suzuki); 7. Schmied (Yamaha); 8. Frommelt (KTM); 9. Bader (Kawasaki); 10. Lugemwa (Yamaha).
Race II: 1. Aregger (Yamaha); 2. Schnegg (Yamaha); 3. Lugemwa (Yamaha); 4. C. Müller (Suzuki); 5. Hofer (KTM); 6. Marti (KTM); 7. Schmied (Yamaha); 8. Studer (Honda); 9. Nyffeler (Husaberg); 10. Hüsler (Honda).

14th August - Malters

Race I: 1. Aregger (Yamaha); 2. Hüsler (Honda); 3. Lugemwa (Yamaha); 4. C. Müller (Suzuki); 5. K. Marti (KTM); 6. Hüsler (Honda); 7. Murer (Husaberg); 8. Bolliger (KTM); 9. Kaufmann (Suzuki); 10. Nyffeler (Husaberg).
Race II: 1. Aregger (Yamaha); 2. Schnegg (Yamaha); 3. Hüsler (Honda); 4. K. Marti (KTM); 5. Nyffeler (Husaberg); 6. Murer (Husaberg); 7. C. Müller (Suzuki); 8. Kaufmann (Suzuki); 9. Lugemwa (Yamaha); 10. Bosshard (Yamaha).

28th August - Frauenfeld

Race I: 1. Aregger (Yamaha); 2. Frommelt (KTM); 3. C. Müller (Suzuki); 4. K. Marti (KTM); 5. Hüsler (Honda); 6. Nyffeler (Husaberg); 7. Schnegg (Yamaha); 8. Lugemwa (Yamaha); 9. Iten (KTM); 10. Schumacher (Yamaha).
Race II: 1. Aregger (Yamaha); 2. K. Marti (KTM); 3. Frommelt (KTM); 4. Schädler (Yamaha); 5. Hüsler (Honda); 6. Schumacher (Yamaha); 7. Nyffeler (Husaberg); 8. Griette (Husqvarna); 9. Schmied (Yamaha); 10. Murer (Husaberg).

25th September - Tourtemagne

Race I: 1. Aregger (Yamaha); 2. Schnegg (Yamaha); 3. Lugemwa (Yamaha); 4. Murer (Husaberg); 5. B. Hüsler (Honda); 6. Hofer (KTM); 7. C. Müller (Suzuki); 8. Wiederkehr (Husqvarna); 9. D. Hüsler (Honda); 10. Nyffeler (Husaberg).
Race II: 1. Aregger (Yamaha); 2. Schnegg (Yamaha); 3. C. Müller (Suzuki); 4. Lugemwa (Yamaha); 5. Murer (Husaberg); 6. Hofer (KTM); 7. B. Hüsler (Honda); 8. D. Hüsler (Honda); 9. Wiederkehr (Husqvarna); 10. Marti (KTM).

FINAL CLASSIFICATION

1. Joseph Aregger	Yamaha	299
2. Christoph Müller	Suzuki	246
3. Nicolas Schnegg	Yamaha	243

4. K. Marti (KTM), 188; 5. G. Murer (Husaberg), 157; 6. A. Frommelt (KTM), 156; 7. K. Lugemwa (Yamaha), 154; 8. R. Nyffeler (Husaberg), 148; 9. D. Hüsler (Honda), 127; 10. Bader (Kawasaki), 118.

ROOKIE

24th April - Eschenbach

Race I: 1. Zimmermann (Yamaha); 2. Werfeli (KTM); 3. Walker (Yamaha); 4. Höfliger (Honda); 5. Imboden (Yamaha); 6. Birrer (Husqvarna); 7. Ricklin (KTM); 8. Minoggio (Suzuki); 9. Meyer (Yamaha); 10. Burch (Yamaha).
Race II: 1. Imboden (Yamaha); 2. Kalberer (Yamaha); 3. Zimmermann (Yamaha); 4. Werfeli (KTM); 5. Walker (Yamaha); 6. Höfliger (Honda); 7. Birrer (Husqvarna); 8. Meyer (Yamaha); 9. Lanz (KTM); 10. Joos (Yamaha).

8th May - Büron

Race I: 1. Zimmermann (Yamaha); 2. Imboden (Yamaha); 3. Kalberer (Yamaha); 4. Ricklin (KTM); 5. Joos (Yamaha); 6. Calabresi (Yamaha); 7. Höfliger (Honda); 8. Walker (Yamaha); 9. Birrer (Husqvarna); 10. Minoggio (Suzuki).
Race II: 1. Kalberer (Yamaha); 2. Imboden (Yamaha); 3. Zimmermann (Yamaha); 4. Calabresi (Yamaha); 5. Höfliger (Honda); 6. Ricklin (KTM); 7. Walker (Yamaha); 8. Aeschbacher (KTM); 9. Werfeli (KTM); 10. Burch (Yamaha).

26th June - St Stephan

Race I: 1. Kalberer (Yamaha); 2. Walker (Yamaha); 3. Höfliger (Honda); 4. Imboden (Yamaha); 5. Joos (Yamaha); 6. Zimmermann (Yamaha); 7. Lanz (KTM); 8. Werfeli (KTM); 9. Birrer (Husqvarna); 10. Calabresi (Yamaha).
Race II: 1. Kalberer (Yamaha); 2. Höfliger (Honda); 3. Imboden (Yamaha); 4. Walker (Yamaha); 5. Werfeli (KTM); 6. Joos (Yamaha); 7. Zimmermann (Yamaha); 8. Calabresi (Yamaha); 9. Haag (Yamaha); 10. Burch (Yamaha).

31 juillet - Buchs

Race I: 1. Zimmermann (Yamaha); 2. Erne (Suzuki); 3. Imboden (Yamaha); 4. Meyer (Yamaha); 5. Burch (Yamaha); 6. Britschgi (Yamaha); 7. Joos (Yamaha); 8. Walker (Yamaha); 9. Höfliger (Honda); 10. Ricklin (KTM).
Race II: 1. Zimmermann (Yamaha); 2. Erne (Suzuki); 3. Höfliger (Honda); 4. Walker (Yamaha); 5. Meyer (Yamaha); 6. Lanz (KTM); 7. Burch (Yamaha); 8. Britschgi (Yamaha); 9. Joos (Yamaha); 10. Ricklin (KTM).

14th August - Malters

Race I: 1. Höfliger (Honda); 2. Imboden (Yamaha); 3. Zimmermann (Yamaha); 4. Erne (Suzuki); 5. Kalberer (Yamaha); 6. Britschgi (Yamaha); 7. Würsch (Suzuki); 8. Walker (Yamaha); 9. Birrer (Husqvarna); 10. Minoggio (Suzuki).
Race II: 1. Höfliger (Honda); 2. Kalberer (Yamaha); 3. Imboden (Yamaha); 4. Walker (Yamaha); 5. Zimmermann (Yamaha); 6. Joos (Yamaha); 7. Erne (Suzuki); 8. Birrer (Husqvarna); 9. Würsch (Suzuki); 10. Meyer (Yamaha).

28th August - Frauenfeld

Race I: 1. Kalberer (Yamaha); 2. Joos (Yamaha); 3. Zimmermann (Yamaha); 4. Höfliger (Honda); 5. Meyer (Yamaha); 6. Erne (Suzuki); 7. Walker (Yamaha); 8. Lanz (KTM); 9. Würsch (Suzuki); 10. Burch (Yamaha).
Race II: 1. Joos (Yamaha); 2. Zimmermann (Yamaha); 3. Höfliger (Honda); 4. Haag (Yamaha); 5. Erne (Suzuki); 6. Walker (Yamaha); 7. Würsch (Suzuki); 8. Birrer (Husqvarna); 9. Meyer (Yamaha); 10. Burch (Yamaha).

25th September - Tourtemagne

Race I: 1. Tellenbach (KTM); 2. Zimmermann (Yamaha); 3. Kalberer (Yamaha); 4. Meyer (Yamaha); 5. Würsch (Suzuki); 6. Burch (Yamaha); 7. Werfeli (KTM); 8. Höfliger (Honda); 9. Lanz (KTM); 10. Haag (Yamaha).
Race II: 1. Meyer (Yamaha); 2. Würsch (Suzuki); 3. Zimmermann (Yamaha); 4. Burch (Yamaha); 5. Kalberer (Yamaha); 6. Höfliger (Honda); 7. Tellenbach (KTM); 8. Lanz (KTM); 9. Haag (Yamaha); 10. Walker (Yamaha).

FINAL CLASSIFICATION

1. Mario Zimmermann	Yamaha	284
2. Pius Höfliger	Honda	254
3. Andreas Kalberer	Yamaha	231

4. C. Walker (Yamaha), 217; 5. M. Imboden (Yamaha), 186; 6. D. Meyer (Yamaha), 171; 7. M. Joos (Yamaha), 168; 8. U. Burch (Yamaha), 153; 9. B. Erne (Suzuki), 127; 10. R. Ricklin (KTM), 122.

YOUNGSTER

24th April - Eschenbach

Race I: 1. Reinhard (Honda); 2. Tellenbach (KTM); 3. Reynaud (Husqvarna); 4. Rüdisüli (KTM); 5. C. Scheiwiller (Yamaha); 6. Limacher (Yamaha); 7. Weibel (Yamaha); 8. M. Graf (KTM); 9. S. Martignoni (Husqvarna); 10. Mabillard (Husqvarna).
Race II: 1. Reinhard (Honda); 2. Tellenbach (KTM); 3. C. Scheiwiller (Yamaha); 4. Rüdisüli (KTM); 5. Reynaud (Husqvarna); 6. Limacher (Yamaha); 7. Joos (Yamaha); 8. Weibel (Yamaha); 9. S. Martignoni (Husqvarna); 10. Brägger (Yamaha).

8th May - Büron

Race I: 1. Reinhard (Honda); 2. C. Scheiwiller (Yamaha); 3. Waldburger (Yamaha); 4. Tellenbach (KTM); 5. Limacher (Yamaha); 6. Rüdisüli (KTM); 7. Reynaud (Husqvarna); 8. Kaenel (KTM); 9. Brägger (Yamaha); 10. S. Martignoni (Husqvarna).
Race II: 1. Reinhard (Honda); 2. S. Martignoni (Husqvarna); 3. Rüdisüli (KTM); 4. Reynaud (Husqvarna); 5. Waldburger (Yamaha); 6. Tellenbach (KTM); 7. Mabillard (Husqvarna); 8. Zenone (Husqvarna); 9. Bürgi (Husqvarna); 10. Frei (Yamaha).

26th June - St Stephan

Race I: 1. Reinhard (Honda); 2. Tellenbach (KTM); 3. Rüdisüli (KTM); 4. Limacher (Yamaha); 5. M. Graf (KTM); 6. Reynaud (Husqvarna); 7. J. Martignoni (Husqvarna); 8. Costa (Sachs); 9. Frei (Yamaha); 10. Berger (Yamaha).
Race II: 1. Reinhard (Honda); 2. Tellenbach (KTM); 3. Reynaud (Husqvarna); 4. M. Graf (KTM); 5. C. Scheiwiller (Yamaha); 6. Rüdisüli (KTM); 7. Zenone (Husqvarna); 8. Frei (Yamaha); 9. Waldburger (Yamaha); 10. Berger (Yamaha).

31st July - Buchs

Race I: 1. Tellenbach (KTM); 2. C. Scheiwiller (Yamaha); 3. Reynaud (Husqvarna); 4. Zenone (Husqvarna); 5. Reinhard (Honda); 6. Rüdisüli (KTM); 7. Walder (KTM); 8. Fischer (Yamaha); 9. Limacher (Yamaha); 10. Bürgi (Husqvarna).
Race II: 1. Tellenbach (KTM); 2. Reinhard (Honda); 3. C. Scheiwiller (Yamaha); 4. Joos (Yamaha); 5. Reynaud (Husqvarna); 6. Zenone (Husqvarna); 7. Walder (KTM); 8. Känel (KTM); 9. Limacher (Yamaha); 10. Waldburger (Yamaha).

14th August - Malters

Race I: 1. Reinhard (Honda); 2. Tellenbach (KTM); 3. Limacher (Yamaha); 4. Rüdisüli (KTM); 5. S. Martignoni (Husqvarna); 6. Känel (KTM); 7. Joos (Yamaha); 8. R. Graf (KTM); 9. Waldburger (Yamaha); 10. Weibel (Yamaha).
Race II: 1. Tellenbach (KTM); 2. Reinhard (Honda); 3. Limacher (Yamaha); 4. M. Graf (KTM); 5. Walder (KTM); 6. Weibel (Yamaha); 7. R. Graf (KTM); 8. Waldburger (Yamaha); 9. Känel (KTM); 10. J. Martignoni (Husqvarna).

28th August - Frauenfeld

Race I: 1. Reinhard (Honda); 2. Tellenbach (KTM); 3. Reynaud (Husqvarna); 4. M. Graf (KTM); 5. Limacher (Yamaha); 6. Weibel (Yamaha); 7. R. Graf (KTM); 8. Fischer (Yamaha); 9. Waldburger (Yamaha); 10. S. Martignoni (Husqvarna).

THE RESULTS OF THE OTHER CHAMPIONSHIPS

Race II: 1. Reinhard (Honda); 2. Tellenbach (KTM); 3. Limacher (Yamaha); 4. Joos (Yamaha); 5. S. Martignoni (Husqvarna); 6. M. Graf (KTM); 7. Waldburger (Yamaha); 8. Weibel (Yamaha); 9. J. Martignoni (Husqvarna); 10. Walder (KTM).

25th September - Tourtemagne
Race I: 1. Reinhard (Honda); 2. Weibel (Yamaha); 3. Reynaud (Husqvarna); 4. Martignoni (Husqvarna); 5. Zenone (Husqvarna); 6. Costa (Sachs); 7. Fischer (Yamaha); 8. Joos (Yamaha); 9. Känel (KTM); 10. Limacher (Yamaha).
Race II: 1. Reinhard (Honda); 2. Weibel (Yamaha); 3. Reynaud (Husqvarna); 4. Martignoni (Husqvarna); 5. Fischer (Yamaha); 6. Limacher (Yamaha); 7. Zenone (Husqvarna); 8. Joos (Yamaha); 9. C. Scheiwiller (Yamaha); 10. Känel (KTM).

FINAL CLASSIFICATION
1. Kevin Reinhard — Honda — 332
2. Patrick Tellenbach — KTM — 262
3. Patrik Limacher — Yamaha — 201

4. L. Reynaud (Husqvarna), 197; 5. F. Rüdisüli (KTM), 182; 6. S. Martignoni (Husqvarna), 160; 7. C. Scheiwiller (Yamaha), 148; 8. M. Weibel (Yamaha), 140; 9. M. Waldburger (Yamaha), 137; 10. R. Joos (Yamaha), 134.

PROMO

24th April - Eschenbach
Race I: 1. E. Lüthi (Yamaha); 2. U. Müller (Yamaha); 3. Hehli (Honda); 4. P. Geissbühler (Yamaha); 5. B. Geissbühler (KTM); 6. Blondin (Honda); 7. Orlandini (Husaberg); 8. A. Gautschi (Husqvarna); 9. Schmid (Suzuki); 10. Britschgi (Honda).
Race II: 1. E. Lüthi (Yamaha); 2. U. Müller (Yamaha); 3. Hehli (Honda); 4. Blondin (Honda); 5. A. Gautschi (Husqvarna); 6. P. Geissbühler (Yamaha); 7. B. Geissbühler (KTM); 8. Herrmann (Honda); 9. Bucheli (KTM); 10. Orlandini (Husaberg).

8th May - Büron
Race I: 1. Nutt (KTM); 2. U. Müller (Yamaha); 3. Hehli (Honda); 4. Albert (Kawasaki); 5. Spichtig (Honda); 6. Bucheli (KTM); 7. Walther (Honda); 8. Kaeslin (KTM); 9. Mathieu (Husaberg); 10. Blondin (Honda).
Race II: 1. Nutt (KTM); 2. U. Müller (Yamaha); 3. Hehli (Honda); 4. Albert (Kawasaki); 5. Spichtig (Honda); 6. E. Lüthi (Yamaha); 7. Bucheli (KTM); 8. Walther (Honda); 9. Minoggio (Suzuki); 10. Calouri (KTM).

26th June - St Stephan
Race I: 1. Schranz (Husaberg); 2. Albert (Kawasaki); 3. E. Lüthi (Yamaha); 4. P. Geissbühler (Yamaha); 5. B. Geissbühler (KTM); 6. Bucheli (KTM); 7. Mathieu (Husaberg); 8. Marschner (KTM); 9. Spichtig (Honda); 10. Walther (Honda).
Race II: 1. E. Lüthi (Yamaha); 2. Schranz (Husaberg); 3. Bucheli (KTM); 4. Albert (Kawasaki); 5. Blondin (Honda); 6. Käslin (KTM); 7. Tschanz (TM); 8. Hehli (Honda); 9. B. Geissbühler (KTM); 10. Walker (KTM).

31st July - Buchs
Race I: 1. U. Müller (Yamaha); 2. Blondin (Honda); 3. Schmid (Suzuki); 4. Meyer (Suzuki); 5. Mathieu (Husaberg); 6. Käslin (KTM); 7. Bucheli (KTM); 8. Zberg (KTM); 9. Gautschi (Husqvarna); 10. Albert (Kawasaki).
Race II: 1. Walther (Honda); 2. Meyer (Suzuki); 3. Bucheli (KTM); 4. U. Müller (Yamaha); 5. B. Geissbühler (KTM); 6. Albert (Kawasaki); 7. Blondin (Honda); 8. Mathieu (Husaberg); 9. Gautschi (Husqvarna); 10. Gerber (Husaberg).

14th August - Malters
Race I: 1. E. Lüthi (Yamaha); 2. U. Müller (Yamaha); 3. Mathieu (Husaberg); 4. Walther (Honda); 5. Gerber (Husaberg); 6. Albert (Kawasaki); 7. Walker (KTM); 8. Heierli (Honda); 9. Graber (Yamaha); 10. Bichsel (Yamaha).
Race II: 1. E. Lüthi (Yamaha); 2. Gautschi (Husqvarna); 3. Spichtig (Honda); 4. Walther (Honda); 5. U. Müller (Yamaha); 6. Bucheli (KTM); 7. Gerber (Husaberg); 8. Walker (KTM); 9. Debrunner (Husaberg); 10. Hehli (Honda).

28th August - Frauenfeld
Race I: 1. Herzog (KTM); 2. Mathieu (Husaberg); 3. Albert (Kawasaki); 4. U. Müller (Yamaha); 5. Hehli (Honda); 6. Frauchiger (KTM); 7. Graber (A, Yamaha); 8. Walther (Honda); 9. Bucheli (KTM); 10. Gerber (Husaberg).
Race II: 1. Herzog (KTM); 2. Mathieu (Husaberg); 3. U. Müller (Yamaha); 4. Graber (Yamaha); 5. Albert (Kawasaki); 6. Frauchiger (KTM); 7. Alig (Husaberg); 8. E. Lüthi (Yamaha); 9. Gerber (Husaberg); 10. Nutt (KTM).

25th September - Tourtemagne
Race I: 1. S. Gysi (KTM); 2. Gerber (Husaberg); 3. Mathieu (Husaberg); 4. E. Lüthi (Yamaha); 5. B. Geissbühler (KTM); 6. Zberg (KTM); 7. Meyer (Suzuki); 8. Walther (Honda); 9. Frauchiger (KTM); 10. Gautschi (Husqvarna).
Race II: 1. S. Gysi (KTM); 2. Gerber (Husaberg); 3. Mathieu (Husaberg); 4. E. Lüthi (Yamaha); 5. B. Geissbühler (KTM); 6. Zberg (KTM); 7. Bucheli (KTM); 8. Albert (Kawasaki); 9. Walther (Honda); 10. Meyer (Suzuki).

FINAL CLASSIFICATION
1. Urs Müller — Yamaha — 222
2. Ernest Lüthi — Yamaha — 209
3. Guillaume Bucheli — KTM — 185

4. L. Albert (Kawasaki), 177; 5. P. Mathieu (Husaberg), 155; 6. A. Hehli (Honda), 154; 7. D. Walther (Honda), 145; 8. B. Gerber (Husaberg), 123; 9. J. Blondin (Honda), 118; 10. A. Gautschi (Husqvarna), 115.

WOMEN

24th April - Eschenbach
Race I: 1. Bucher (Yamaha); 2. Andexlinger (KTM); 3. Berglas (Husaberg); 4. Salhi (KTM). 4 finishers.
Race II: 1. Bucher (Yamaha); 2. Berglas (Husaberg); 3. Andexlinger (KTM); 4. Salhi (KTM). 4 finishers.

8th May - Büron
Race I: 1. Andexlinger (KTM); 2. Bucher (Yamaha); 3. Sandoz (Husqvarna); 4. Berglas (Husaberg); 5. Bomonti (Husqvarna); 6. Steingruber (Yamaha); 7. Pexa (A, Husaberg). 7 finisheres.
Race II: 1. Andexlinger (KTM); 2. Bucher (Yamaha); 3. Sandoz (Husqvarna); 4. Berglas (Husaberg); 5. Pexa (A, Husaberg); 6. Bomonti (Husqvarna); 7. Steingruber (Yamaha). 7 finishers.

26th June - St Stephan
Race I: 1. Andexlinger (KTM); 2. Bucher (Yamaha); 3. Berglas (Husaberg); 4. Bomonti (Husqvarna). 4 finisheres.
Race II: 1. Andexlinger (KTM); 2. Bucher (Yamaha); 3. Sandoz (Husqvarna); 4. Berglas (Husaberg); 5. Bomonti (Husqvarna). 5 finishers.

31st July - Buchs
Race I: 1. Sandoz (Husqvarna); 2. Andexlinger (KTM); 3. Bucher (Yamaha); 4. Köpfli (Husqvarna); 5. Berglas (Husaberg); 6. Nagele (KTM); 7. Bomonti (Husqvarna).7 finishers.
Race II: 1. Sandoz (Husqvarna); 2. Andexlinger (KTM); 3. Bucher (Yamaha); 4. Nagele (KTM); 5. Berglas (Husaberg); 6. Köpfli (Husqvarna). 6 finishers.

14th August - Malters
Race I: 1. Andexlinger (KTM); 2. Bucher (Yamaha); 3. Nagele (KTM); 4. Sandoz (Husqvarna); 5. Köpfli (Husqvarna); 6. Berglas (Husaberg).
Race II: 1. Andexlinger (KTM); 2. Bucher (Yamaha); 3. Sandoz (Husqvarna); 4. Berglas (Husaberg); 5. Nagele (KTM); 6. Köpfli (Husqvarna). 9 finishers.

28th August - Frauenfeld
Race I: 1. Andexlinger (KTM); 2. Andexlinger (KTM); 3. Bucher (Yamaha); 4. Berglas (Husaberg); 5. Nagele (KTM); 6. Salhi (KTM); 7. Düsel (Gas-Gas); 8. Schmid (Suzuki); 9. Steingruber (Yamaha). 9 finisheres.
Race II: 1. Andexlinger (KTM); 2. Bucher (Yamaha); 3. Nagele (KTM); 4. Salhi (KTM); 5. Steingruber (Yamaha); 6. Sandoz (Husqvarna); 7. Düsel (Gas-Gas); 8. Schmid (Suzuki); 9. Berglas (Husaberg). 9 finishers.

25th September - Tourtemagne
Race I: 1. Andexlinger (KTM); 2. Bucher (Yamaha); 3. Sandoz (Husqvarna); 4. Berglas (Husaberg); 5. Steingruber (Yamaha); 6. Nagele (KTM).
Race II: 1. Andexlinger (KTM); 2. Bucher (Yamaha); 3. Andexlinger (KTM); 4. Berglas (Husaberg); 5. Nagele (KTM); 6. Steingruber (Yamaha).

FINAL CLASSIFICATION
1. Vera Andexlinger — KTM — 328
2. Nadia Bucher — Yamaha — 308
3. Irène Berglas — Husaberg — 247

4. M. Sandoz (Husqvarna), 233; 5. A. Bomonti (Husqvarna), 79; 6. E. Salhi (KTM), 69; 7. B. Düsel (Gas-Gas), 28.